Christian Thought
A Historical Introduction

The story of Christian thought is essential to understanding Christian faith today and the last two millennia of world history. This fresh and lively introduction explores the central ideas, persons, events, and movements that gave rise to Christian thought, from early beginnings to its present forms. By highlighting the important but often neglected role of women and the influence of non-Christian ideas and movements, this book provides a broader context for understanding the history of Christian ideas and their role in shaping our world. *Christian Thought*:

- provides an overview of the context of Christianity's origin, including discussion of the influence of Hebrews, Greeks, and Romans;
- explores the major events and figures of the history of Christian thought, while drawing attention to significant voices which have often been suppressed;
- analyses the impact on Christian thought of widely discussed events such as The Great Schism, the Scientific Revolution, and modernism;
- surveys contemporary trends such as fundamentalism, feminism, and postmodernism.

This fully revised and updated second edition features a new chapter on liberal theology and reflects recent scholarship in the field. Complete with figures, timelines and maps, this is an ideal resource for anyone wanting to learn more about the development of Christian thought and its influence over the centuries. Further teaching and learning resources are available on the companion website at www.routledge.com/meister.

Chad Meister is Professor of Philosophy and Theology at Bethel College in Indiana, USA. He is the co-editor of *The Routledge Companion to Modern Christian Thought* (2016) and co-author of *Contemporary Philosophical Theology* (2016).

J.B. Stump is Senior Editor at BioLogos and Visiting Scholar at the University of Notre Dame, USA. He is co-editor of the *Blackwell Companion to Science and Christianity* (2012) and author of *Science and Christianity: An Introduction to the Issues* (2016).

Christian Thought

A Historical Introduction

Second edition

Chad Meister and J. B. Stump

Routledge
Taylor & Francis Group

NEW YORK AND LONDON

Second edition published 2017
by Routledge
711 Third Avenue, New York, NY 10017

and by Routledge
2 Park Square, Milton Park, Abingdon, Oxon, OX14 4RN

Routledge is an imprint of the Taylor & Francis Group, an informa business

© 2017 Taylor & Francis

First edition published 2010 by Routledge

Library of Congress Cataloging in Publication Data
Names: Meister, Chad V., 1965- author. | Stump, J. B., author.
Title: Christian thought : a historical introduction / by Chad Meister and J.B. Stump.
Description: 2 [edition]. | New York : Routledge, 2016. | Includes bibliographical references and index.
Identifiers: LCCN 2016017613 (print) | LCCN 2016034327 (ebook) | ISBN 9781138910607 (alk. paper) | ISBN 9781138910614 (alk. paper) | ISBN 9781315693354
Subjects: LCSH: Church history. | Theology--History.
Classification: LCC BR145.3 .M45 2016 (print) | LCC BR145.3 (ebook) | DDC 230.09--dc23
LC record available at https://lccn.loc.gov/2016017613

ISBN: 978-1-138-91060-7 (hbk)
ISBN: 978-1-138-91061-4 (pbk)
ISBN: 978-1-315-69335-4 (ebk)

Typeset in Charter
by HWA Text and Data Management, London
Printed in Canada

Contents

Illustrations

Figures

Timelines

Maps

Preface to the Second Edition

We are pleased that this book is being published in a second edition. The feedback we received from students and others who used the first edition was encouraging and also pointed to some areas that could use improvement. For this edition we have added a new chapter on liberal theology of the nineteenth and twentieth centuries, and have expanded and updated what are now chapters 28 and 29. As we display throughout the book, theology is not a stagnant discipline; it has continued to evolve even since our first edition came out. Exciting discussions have developed in areas like comparative theology, environmental theology, and astrotheology. We've included some discussion of these in the new sections. We've also gone through the entire text and corrected errors and modified language as we now deem appropriate.

We have worked with some new staff at Routledge on this edition, and are grateful to Eve Mayer, Laura Briskman, and the team for their help and support on this project. Routledge has developed a terrific companion website for the book, which includes PowerPoint slides, glossary, flash cards, further readings, links to useful web resources, and test questions and answers. It can be accessed at routledge.com/textbooks.

Acknowledgments

The standard advice is to caution good friends from working together on a project like this. We've discovered that such advice has some merit. Inevitably there are differences of opinion that need to be navigated and even conflicts that need to be resolved in order to move on with the project and with your relationship. Yet for us, we feel that both the book and our friendship are stronger for having done this together. Of course we also benefited from the help and encouragement of lots of other people.

Our home institution, Bethel College (Indiana), deserves acknowledgement in several areas. Support was provided for this project through a grant from the Lilly Foundation to Bethel. The resources accessible to us through the library are second to none for a school like ours, and Mark Root could always find for us those resources less readily available. Bethel also provides us with classes and students, on whom much of the material in this book was tried out.

We thank two anonymous reviewers who gave many helpful comments and saved us from some errors. Our colleagues Timothy Erdel and David Cramer read portions of the manuscript and offered insightful feedback with large doses of encouragement. Nancy Stump read most of the manuscript and helped us see things through the eyes of a non-specialist in the field. Special thanks to Micah Richey for the elegant timelines and maps. We are also grateful to Lesley Riddle and Amy Grant at Routledge who have been unfailing in their support.

Most importantly, we thank our wives and sons: Tammi Meister and Christine Stump; Justin and Joshua Meister; and Casey, Trevor, and Connor Stump. They were all involved at various levels (from reading and commenting on early drafts, to looking up references, to listening to funny stories). As our personal and professional lives are intricately entangled, we can't imagine our work without them.

Finally, we acknowledge our extended families and their heritage – the many Meisters, Stumps, Ummels, and Huffmans – who form that great cloud of witnesses through whom we became acquainted with the Christian tradition. It is to them that this book is dedicated.

*I*ntroduction

About 1,500 years ago a Christian monk calculated that Jesus Christ was born 753 years after the founding of Rome. In Latin he called that year *anno domini* – the year of our Lord – and made it year number one. Almost ever since, the birth of Jesus has served as the focal point for most of those who chronicle world history, measuring time in years AD and BC.[1] It doesn't matter that the monk was probably off by a few years on Jesus's birth. Nor is it very significant that in our present pluralistic day, scholars have begun describing the same numbered years as belonging to the Common Era (CE) and Before the Common Era (BCE) in an effort to disassociate dates with a religious figure. The point remains that virtually the whole world reckons its history with reference to the appearance of Jesus Christ. As the calendar testifies, he is surely one of the most influential and important figures in the history of the world. But even though his name will come up regularly, this book is not really about the person known as Jesus of Nazareth.

According to the title, we're giving a historical introduction to Christian thought. A book with such a title could legitimately cover what Christians think and have thought about anything and everything – politics, sport, space exploration, and so on. Christians do think about such things, so presumably those thoughts belong under the general heading of Christian thought. But this book makes no attempt to discuss all of what could be lumped into that broad and diverse category. Our more modest (though still audaciously large) aim for this volume is to survey the history of that part of Christian thought that is often called "theology."

Theology comes from the two Greek words *theos* (god) and *logos* (word or rational account). So theology is that discipline which purports to give a rational and systematic account of ideas that relate to a divine being or beings. We might think of these theological accounts as theories which are not wholly unlike scientific theories. Essentially, theories are attempts to give explanations of data. They are carefully reasoned answers to the question, "What must we suppose to be true (about the world or about God) in order to account for the data available to us?" Where science differs from theology is that scientific data generally derives from controlled experiments while theological data may come from holy books believed to be of divine origin, from the religious experience of saints and other religious practitioners, and from religious traditions.[2] Christian theology, then, has the added dimension of thinking about God and providing explanations in light of the tradition that traces its origin and inspiration to Jesus Christ.

Interestingly, like many of the other great teachers of world history, Jesus did not write any books (so far as we know). Our access to his teachings and ideas, then, comes through the communities which preserved them orally and then eventually wrote them down. It is the members of these communities who were called Christians, for they understood Jesus to be the *Christ* – the Greek term for "messiah" or "anointed one." So it is their thought, their theology that we are after in this book.

The history of Christian thought, then, is not a chronicle of attempts to recover and interpret the words of Jesus. There is a sense in which it is important for Christian thinkers to know what Jesus himself taught, and we discuss this in Chapter 2. But even among those faith communities which treat the Bible as authoritative in this regard (which is the majority of Christians throughout history), questions will continually arise about the correct interpretation and application of his teachings. Furthermore, in the accounts we have of Jesus's teachings, there are many topics which are only hinted at (such as the Trinity) or not addressed at all (such as worship styles). So Christians are forced to reason out the implications of what was passed down to them, and they weigh these truths against their own experience. Each successive generation of Christians lays its thought around and incorporates that of the previous generations like so many rings in the trunk of a tree. Some "rings" in this tree of Christian thought will be larger and so represent more fertile times of growth and development. At other times there have been branches that went off in different directions from the main trunk. Here in the third millennium after Christ, the tree is massive indeed. And those who attempt to think about the central themes of Christian theology today without drawing on this history might be compared to hollow trunks. By working through this book, we hope that readers will come to understand and appreciate the development and growth of Christian thought.

OUR APPROACH

From the massive pool of people, ideas, and movements in the history of Christian thought, we have highlighted some to tell a story. Undoubtedly, other stories could be culled from the same pool by emphasizing things differently. Of course there are certain high points or landmarks that need to be covered in any adequate survey of the material. But beyond these there is room for details which show the story in a certain light. Criticisms can rightly be leveled that in the interest of the story, we have simplified and even imposed structure on what is more complicated and multi-faceted. In a one-volume treatment of this enormous subject, there is no doubt that subtlety of analysis is sometimes sacrificed. We have had to make difficult decisions on what to include and what not to include – and even how to include what we have. But we've been guided in these decisions by several principles which, we believe, distinguish this work from others.

First, we have endeavored to draw attention to forgotten or suppressed voices where appropriate. For example, we have a chapter dedicated to the desert fathers *and mothers* – the latter being women who were influential in the fourth and fifth centuries but who are often ignored in works on Christian history. And we have highlighted other women throughout the volume who have been major players in the development of Christian thought. We have also included non-Christian voices which were influential in Christian thought historically, most notably Muslims and Jews. In addition, we have discussed some of the minority movements of recent times, such as Christian feminists, liberation and black theologians, Pentecostals, and others.

Next, as a book on Christian *thought*, this is neither a work of church history nor even the history of Christianity in which primary attention is paid to the development of institutions, rituals, and practice. But neither have we presented a history of Christian thought that is isolated from its human contexts. It is often acknowledged that theory informs practice, but we also try to show those instances where practice has been influential on the development of theory. So while we are emphasizing key theological and intellectual themes that have been instrumental in the development of Christian thought, we also weave into the story accounts of real people, real events, and real places which help to explain the ideas.

Finally, we have attempted to be as even-handed as we can be in a work of this nature. History is not a purely objective discipline, and when the history in question is related to religion, biases can be even more pronounced. We have tried to keep matters of historical faith distinct from matters of historical fact, and we have worked hard at presenting contentious issues in a manner that, if not agreed upon by all, will at least be recognized as fair by those from a variety of perspectives.

It is worth mentioning in this regard that there is a long history of believing that theologians themselves must exhibit the kinds of lives worthy of their subject matter. According to this line of thinking, theology is not just solving conceptual puzzles and analyzing complex ideas. It cannot be separated from the religious life it grows out of; in order to understand its deep truths, one must be a committed participant. Gregory of Nazianzus (330–390 CE) claimed that:

> Discussion of theology is not for everyone, I tell you, not for everyone – it is no such inexpensive and effortless pursuit. Nor, I would add, is it for every occasion, or every audience; neither are all its aspects open to inquiry. It must be reserved for certain occasions, for certain audiences, and certain limits must be observed. It is not for all [people], but only for those who have been tested and have found a sound footing in study, and, more importantly, have undergone, or at the very least are undergoing, purification of body and soul. For one who is not pure to lay hold of pure things is dangerous, just as it is for weak eyes to look at the sun's brightness.[3]

Perhaps there is something to be said for Gregory's position. An argument can be made that theology itself should take place within and for a community of committed believers. Nonetheless, in studying the history of theology we need not agree with all of the ideas that have been promulgated in the name of Christianity in order to benefit from working through them. Even those completely outside of the Christian faith will find it useful for understanding Western culture which has been so permeated with Christian ideas. Because Christian thought has shaped our culture and provided many of the categories through which we think and live, whether you're a member of a Christian community or not, we hope you will find what is chronicled here important and enlightening.

MAJOR DIVISIONS OF THE TEXT

Most histories of Christian thought begin in the second century. It is true that in specialized academic settings, the first century belongs more to the discipline of biblical studies than to historical theology. But we have found that a brief overview of the historical context in which Christianity arose helps to situate the ensuing discussions. Furthermore, although there are historical difficulties involved in discussing the thought of Jesus and Paul, chapters treating these iconic figures remind us that Christianity began not with a set of ideas, but with certain people. In Part I, then, we include chapters on these subjects as well as a chapter on the latter years of the first century during which Christianity increasingly separated from Judaism.

The Patristic Period is the next major division of the book (Part II). Here you'll find the substantial issues of Christology, the Trinity, and the definitive formation of the New Testament canon. These were not isolated debates, and we've chosen to give chapters by topic rather than strictly chronologically. That means that we'll tell slightly different stories through the same centuries (sometimes even including some of the same people) depending on the topic. In this part we also include chapters on persecutions, desert fathers and mothers, and some of the sects or off-shoots from the main line of Christian thought. The towering figure of Augustine gets his own chapter as a bridge into the medieval period.

Sometimes the theology of the Medieval period is presented as a dry and arcane reflection of the Dark Ages. In reality, this thousand-year stretch of time is creative and diverse in its Christian thought. Besides the prominent episode of Eastern Christianity splitting off from the West and the monumental works of Thomas Aquinas, Anselm, and others, we try to show in Part III some of the diversity of the period by including chapters on the monastic movements, Islamic and Jewish engagement, and women thinkers.

Martin Luther and John Calvin have become household names for the Protestant Reformation. But beyond their Lutheran and Reformed traditions, Reformation occurred in significant ways in other Christian traditions as well. The Anabaptists, English reforms, and the Counter-Reformation of the Catholics lend their voices to the chorus of reform that sang out during the sixteenth and seventeenth centuries. These are described in Part IV.

The last major division of the book concerns the Modern period. We've organized these chapters according to the various responses of Christian thought to the challenge that modern scientific and philosophical developments posed for traditional theology. Some tried to accommodate these developments, some ignored them, and some attempted to chart a different course altogether for theology. By Chapter 28, our accounts of major movements in that recent period are briefer and somewhat more suggestive as we wait for their lasting influence to become more clear.

We conclude the book, then, with a chapter which is even more speculative – one about contemporary and emerging Christian theological movements and where they may be headed. Christian theology is far from stagnant, and many new and creative ideas have been introduced in recent times. Indeed, it seems that the face of Christianity will look significantly different in the coming decades.

FEATURES OF THE TEXT

You'll notice that each chapter begins with a set of questions to be explored. These are numbered and correspond to the numbered divisions within each chapter and then to the summary points at the end of each chapter. Our intention is not to suggest that complex material can be easily distilled into bullet points, but to give "handles" for readers to keep a grasp on the large amount of names, movements, and ideas presented.

Each chapter also includes boxes set apart from the main text which provide further explanations of key terms and ideas, or substantial excerpts from primary sources. There are, in addition, icons, paintings, and pictures to assist in getting a sense of the cultural milieu of the time, what the people involved looked like, and what the artistic genres of the different periods were like. There are timelines in each chapter to help place the people, events, and ideas in their proper historical order, and there are also maps sprinkled throughout the book to place events in their proper locales. As there may be many terms that are unfamiliar to readers, we have included an extensive glossary of key terms at the back of the book. Finally, at the end of each chapter there is an annotated bibliography of further reading. These are not comprehensive lists of all the relevant scholarly research on the subject matter, but rather helpful books which we believe to be good next steps for those who want to dive deeper into the topics covered. We've tried to provide details of accessible editions of some primary sources along with reliable and balanced secondary sources that should be manageable after reading the survey accounts we offer.

We hope that by working through this book you not only get a concrete sense of the central themes in the history of Christian thought, but that you are also encouraged to explore many of these ideas and issues in greater detail. What we offer here is more than a trivial pursuit of names, dates, and movements. The people discussed were wrestling with some of the most fundamental questions of life: What is the nature of God? Who was Jesus Christ, and what is his significance in world history? What is the good life? How does one find salvation? We continue to ask these questions today, and by reading and reflecting on what many of the leading Christian thinkers of the past had to say, we engage in an ongoing dialogue with some of the greatest minds of world history.

Part 1

Incubations and origins

The ancient period 500BCE–70CE

1

The pre-history of
Christian thought

QUESTIONS TO BE ADDRESSED IN THIS CHAPTER

1   What ideas came from Hebrew/Jewish history to influence Christian thought?
2   How did the Greeks shape the intellectual climate within which Christian thought developed?
3   What was the Roman contribution to the early development of Christian thought?
4   What was the relationship between the governing authorities in Jerusalem, Judea, and the Roman Empire?

Christian thought began in the third or fourth decade of the first century of what is now known as the Common Era (CE). This is when Jesus of Nazareth – later known as Jesus Christ – began his career of public teaching. But before beginning the story of Christian thought, some attention to its context will be prudent. Even if Jesus was "God come to earth in human form" as most Christians believe, he came at a specific time and to a specific place in world history. His thought – and perhaps even more so, the thought of his followers – was conditioned by a definite context that included geographical, political, cultural, and intellectual factors. Having at least a cursory overview of this context will prove helpful in trying to understand the thought that sprang from it. The three civilizations which had converged at the time of Christ in a stretch of land along the eastern shore of the Mediterranean Sea are most relevant in this respect: the Hebrews, the Greeks, and the Romans.

How far back do we need to go in order to understand the context? We stand now at some 2,000 years after the time of Christ; it is for more than symmetry's sake that we'll start just as far on the other side of the timeline.

1 HEBREWS

According to Hebrew tradition, sometime around the dawn of the second millennium before Christ – a milestone which, of course, would have meant nothing at the time – a family group set out from Ur for the land of Canaan. We don't know why Terah, the patriarch of the group, decided to do this. Ur was probably the largest city in the world at that time, and was situated in the fertile crescent of ancient civilization. And Terah couldn't have known much about Canaan except that it was peopled with barbarian nomadic tribes. At any rate, after traveling close to 1,000 kilometers northwest up the Euphrates, Terah, his son Abram, and his grandson Lot (who was Abram's nephew) settled at Haran in what is now Turkey. There Terah died, and the prospering family was left in Abram's charge.

They must have stayed in Haran for a while, because when the voice of Yahweh (their God) came to Abram, it told him to leave what had become his country and his people and go to a new land. This time we understand the motivation for uprooting, because Yahweh promised:

> I will make you into a great nation and I will bless you;
> I will make your name great, and you will be a blessing.
> I will bless those who bless you,
> And whoever curses you I will curse;
> And all peoples on earth will be blessed through you.

> (Genesis 12:2–3)

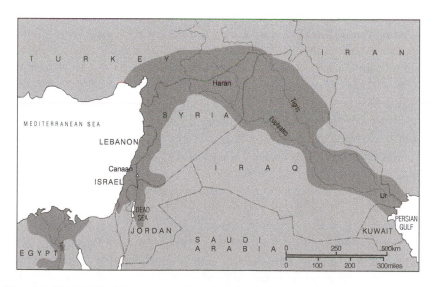

Map 1.1 The Fertile Crescent and modern boundaries

YAHWEH

The transliterated name for the one God of the Hebrew people. Sometimes this is rendered in English as "Jehovah," and usually translated in the Old Testament scriptures as "THE LORD".

So with this promise in mind, Abram left Haran and eventually settled in Canaan, some 650 kilometers southwest toward the Mediterranean.

Once there, Yahweh spoke to him again, spelling out the details of the covenant. Abram's name was changed to Abraham, meaning "father of many." It must have been awkward to tell the neighbors his new name, since Abraham and his wife Sarah were childless and beyond the age of being able to do anything about that. But Abraham believed Yahweh. More tangibly at the moment, he was also given the land of Canaan as an everlasting possession to his people. For Abraham's part of the bargain, he had to acknowledge Yahweh as the one and only God and to circumcise all male descendants as the mark of their fidelity.[1]

So were born the Hebrew people and the Israelitic tradition from which Judaism later developed.[2] The next parts of the story are known to most people educated in the Western tradition: the promised heir Isaac was born to Abraham and Sarah in very old age and nearly sacrificed on an altar by Abraham; Isaac fathered the twins Esau and Jacob; Jacob's son Joseph was sold into slavery by his brothers, but then rose to prominence in the court of Egypt where he brought the whole family to live during a time of famine; later Egyptians would enslave the growing Hebrew population until they were led out of their bondage in a mass exodus by Moses; they crossed the Red Sea, received the Ten Commandments, and wandered in the desert for forty years; Joshua led the charge across the Jordan River back into Canaan and fought the battle of Jericho, where the walls came tumbling down, and the Hebrews took possession of their promised land once more. Eventually, the Hebrew nation was ruled by a series of kings, beginning with Saul, then more famously David and his son Solomon.

Of course the details of many of these events are sketchy and accessible to us only through the lenses of the Hebrews themselves and their oral traditions, which were eventually written down. Quibbling over the historicity of these won't concern us here, though, since the distinctively

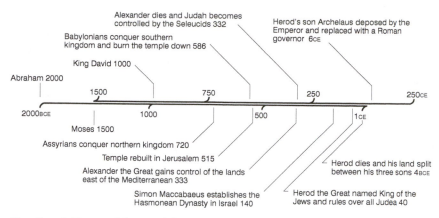

Timeline 1 The pre-history of Christian thought

Hebrew ideas that are important elements of the context of Christian thought emerge from this story whether it happened precisely as recounted or not. Among these distinctively Hebrew ideas are the following:

- **Monotheism**: There is one God, Yahweh. Other nations worship other "gods," but these are false gods. Perhaps these others have some limited power, but Yahweh is the only supreme being, the creator of all that is, and the only one who should be worshiped.
- **Election**: Yahweh singled out the Hebrew people through Abraham to have a special covenant relationship with him. They were to be blessed and would prosper in the land that was given to them. Eventually, all people of the earth would be allowed to participate in the permanent kingdom that God would establish through the Hebrew people.
- **Righteousness**: Yahweh seems to be unique among the gods of all known ancient civilizations in that the righteousness he demanded went beyond an ethic of justice. In the stories of other gods, they merely wanted to be respected and treated well, but Yahweh intended for his people to be holy and just, to be humble, to be compassionate – moral demands that were defined by his character and the law he gave them and that were expected to be obeyed.

At the height of the Hebrew civilization under King Solomon, the law was obeyed and the people prospered. A magnificent temple was built where Yahweh was worshiped. But in the ensuing generations, the people did not always follow the ways of their ancestors. Prophets tried to call them back to the way of righteousness, predicting that Yahweh would withdraw his hand of blessing from them if they didn't turn from their evil ways. The lure of present earthly power, though, was more tempting than some utopian ideal passed down in bedtime stories. Rivals vied for control of the kingdom, and it was split into two parts: the northern kingdom of Israel and the southern kingdom of Judah.

The kings of Israel led the people further away from Yahweh and his expectations for them. So, as the prophets predicted, Yahweh removed himself from their land. Around 720BCE, the Assyrians conquered this northern kingdom and exiled most of its inhabitants. Their land was resettled by several ethnic groups who intermarried with the remaining Hebrew peasants, and these people became known as the Samaritans.

The southern Kingdom of Judah with its capital city of Jerusalem lasted longer. But some of the Judahite kings also turned from following Yahweh, and Judah was conquered by King Nebuchadnezzar of Babylon in 586BCE. Most devastatingly, he plundered the treasures of the temple and burned the temple to the ground. The Judean elites were also carried off to Babylon as slaves and kept in exile there for two generations until the Babylonians were conquered by King Cyrus of the Persians. While making it clear that the land was under his dominion (there would be no king in Judah), King Cyrus encouraged the Hebrew people to return to their homeland in 538BCE.

Rebuilding the temple in Jerusalem was tremendously important for Jewish religious life.[3] This was completed in 515BCE, and the period of Jewish history known as Second Temple Judaism began. Priests continued to occupy themselves with the rituals associated with the temple, but in the absence of a monarchy, a new class of religious leaders known as Pharisees came to prominence in Jewish culture. Pharisees, who figure prominently in the Gospels, emphasized study of the Torah and believed that Jewish identity was to be preserved by strict adherence to the law.

The Old Testament book of Nehemiah recounts the story of rebuilding the wall around Jerusalem. This took place around 445BCE during the time that Artaxerxes I was king of the Persian Empire. Judah, as a province of that empire, was markedly insignificant in global terms. It extended no more than 20 miles in any direction from Jerusalem, and would not have appeared much different from the numerous other temple-states

TORAH

The Jewish law as contained in the first five books of the Old Testament: Genesis, Exodus, Leviticus, Numbers, Deuteronomy.

PHARISEES

A sect which developed out of the scribes and sages during the Second Temple period of Judaism. Pharisees emphasized strict adherence to the Law even while Jewish culture was being assimilated by the Alexandrian and then Roman Empires.

in the empire.[4] There was another culture, however, which successfully resisted assimilation by these same Persians and stood out as few have in the history of the world. The Greeks of the fifth century CE were enjoying their golden age.

2 GREEKS

It is difficult to avoid superlatives when describing the people and accomplishments of ancient Greece. Historian Michael Grant calls it, "the most wonderful civilization in the world's history," and claims that, "never in the history of the world has there been such a multiplication of varied talents and achievements within so limited a period."[5] Athens, in just the fifth century, boasted some of the world's most impressive and important figures not only of their time, but of all time. They founded and developed disciplines that were the wellspring of Western civilization: drama (Aeschylus, Sophocles, Euripides, and Aristophanes), poetry (Pindar); history (Herodotus, Thucydides); sculpture and architecture (Phidias, Polyclitus); philosophy (Parmenides, Socrates, Plato); medicine (Hippocrates); politics (Pericles); military strategy (Themistocles). As a comparison, it would be as though Shakespeare, Dante, DaVinci, Michelangelo, Eiffel, Picasso, Descartes, Kant, Jefferson,

Napoleon, and Einstein were all living at the same time in a city of about 100,000 people.

This is not the place for a full discussion of the history and influence of Greek thought, but we must mention some of the ideas originating in ancient Greece which proved to be very influential for Christian thought as it was developing during the first centuries:

- Rationality: The Greeks emphasized reason and rationality much more than the Jewish people did. Greek thinkers found themselves in a world that needed to be figured out – why things were the way they were, and how they could be understood.
- The real existence of an intelligible world: Contrasted with the world that is immediately apparent to the senses, there is a realm that is only to be comprehended by reason. Plato, for example, illustrated this with ideal "objects" like mathematical constructs and, most famously, the Forms from which the visible world is but a copy.
- Immortality and the soul: By the time of Plato, many Greeks understood the soul to be trapped in the body. It is the soul which is eternal and survives the death of the body by its very nature. This becomes increasingly important in later Christian thinking in contrast to the Jewish view of a bodily resurrection in which eternal life is a supernatural event enjoyed by a reawakened body and soul as a unified existence.

Of course, none of these ideas would have affected Christian thought had the land of Judah remained a small, out-of-the-way province of Persia. Jews and Greeks were almost completely isolated at this time. But that would change in the next century when the Greek way of life was spread throughout the Middle East and beyond by the exploits of their famous king, Alexander the Great.

The insignificant kingdom of Judah didn't even merit mentioning when Plutarch recorded the victories of Alexander the Great. But around 333BCE Alexander stormed from Turkey down to Egypt and wrested control of all the land in his path (including Judah) away from the Persians. The Greek influence on Jewish thought is seen most clearly in Alexandria – the city Alexander named after himself in Egypt around 331BCE. Over the next couple of centuries it became an important enclave for Jews who had been scattered from their homeland. These Jews maintained

PHILO OF ALEXANDRIA (C. 25BCE–50CE)

Philo exemplifies best the syncretism of Judaism and Greek thought that was occurring in Alexandria. Not much is known about his life, but he left some thirty books, most of which are allegorical interpretations of the Hebrew Bible.

Philo and other Jews in Alexandria probably didn't read Hebrew very well, and so their theology was shaped by Greek terminology. The more Greek their understanding of God became, the more detached and transcendent this God was from the material world of physical existence. The Jews still needed some mechanism for God's interaction with the world, some intermediary that could relate both to God and to humans. For Philo, this intermediary was found in the Greek word *logos*, which translates to English as "reason" or "word." The Word was given a kind of independent existence by Philo, and we can readily see how this concept would be appropriated by Christians in explaining the dual nature (human and divine) of Christ:

> And the Father who created the universe has given to his archangelic and most ancient Word [logos] a pre-eminent gift, to stand on the confines of both, and separated that which had been created from the Creator. And this same Word is continually a suppliant to the immortal God on behalf of the mortal race, which is exposed to affliction and misery; and is also the ambassador, sent by the Ruler of all, to the subject race. And the Word rejoices in the gift, and, exulting in it, announces it and boasts of it, saying, "And I stood in the midst, between the Lord and You" (Numbers 16:48) neither being uncreate [sic.] as God, nor yet created as you, but being in the midst between these two extremities, like a hostage, as it were, to both parties.
>
> ("On Who is Heir of Divine Things"[6])

what religious traditions they could, but inevitably their ideas came to be shaped more and more by the dominant culture around them. These ideas, in turn, were influential for early Christians.

When Alexander died in 323BCE, his kingdom was divided among his generals. The region between Egypt and Mesopotamia, including the insignificant land of Judah, became part of the Seleucid Empire. The seventh Seleucid ruler, Antiochus Epiphanes (*c.* 215–164BCE), actively imposed Greek culture into the lands he controlled, including the establishment of a Greek gymnasium (educational center for both mind and body) in Jerusalem. Many of the Jewish people accepted this, even going so far as to disguise their circumcisions so as not to stand out in the customary nude exercises of the gymnasium. But when Antiochus dedicated an altar to Zeus in the Jewish temple in 167, some Jews had had enough. The Maccabean Revolt ensued. A woefully understaffed and under-equipped army, led by Judas "Maccabeus" (the Hammer) of the Hasmonean family, stormed Jerusalem fueled with holy zeal. They took the temple back and rededicated it to their God with an eight-day festival – the occasion celebrated in Hanukkah today. Judas's brother Simon helped to shed the overlordship of the Seleucids and established what is known as the Hasmonean Dynasty, which ruled a relatively independent Judah until the next superpower entered the scene and Latinized the name to Judea.

3 ROMANS

While the Hasmoneans were governing in Judea, the Roman Republic was growing in extent and power in the lands formerly controlled by Alexander. Pompey was a very successful Roman military general with a reputation for quelling disturbances in the lands all around the Mediterranean which Rome was acquiring. In 64BCE he and his troops were on the eastern end of the Mediterranean settling a dispute when they heard news of a conflict in Jerusalem. There the peace was being disturbed by a quarrel between two brothers, Hyrcanus and Aristobulus, over which of them should become the next Hasmonean ruler of Judea. Pompey investigated and took the side of Hyrcanus. They routed the supporters of Aristobulus who had barricaded themselves in the temple. When Pompey's army had broken into their stronghold, the general himself brashly entered the Holy of Holies in the temple and was truly surprised to find no statues of their God on the altar (though all sorts of stories were concocted about what he found[7]). He inflicted no further damage to Judaism beyond the sacrilege of a non-Jew entering the temple, and he installed Hyrcanus as high priest and local ruler. And so Judea became a province of Rome.

About this same time, the Roman Republic was giving way to the Roman Empire: public rule, with its checks and balances between the senate, the magistrates, and various legislative bodies of citizens could not keep control of the expanding populace and its power-hungry personalities. In the grab for power, Pompey lost out to Julius Caesar who assumed the dictatorship of the empire in 49BCE.

The Roman Empire probably contributed less directly to the content of early Christian thought than did Judaism and Greek philosophy. Indeed, there is much in Roman thought that mitigates against Christianity; for example, the Epicureans' pursuit of bodily pleasure, and the Stoics' belief that virtue consists in apathetic acceptance of one's fate. And there is little in the Roman system of values that comports well with the main Christian themes of love, compassion, sin, and forgiveness.

One of the ideas pervading Roman thought, however, did influence Christian thinking: natural law. Building on Aristotle, the Stoics (the dominant school of thought in the first century) believed that all rational people, regardless of cultural differences, could discern the pervading reason in the universe and live according to its dictates. This was no personal embodiment of reason as Christians would take the Greek *logos* to be, but it is certainly a forerunner of the Apostle Paul's claim that all people are without excuse for their actions because God has made himself known through his creation. It is no coincidence that the claim was in Paul's letter to the Romans (Romans 1:19–20), and that Paul himself was a Roman citizen and familiar with Roman thinkers. Later Christian thinkers like Augustine and Aquinas were important proponents of natural law theory.

Some concept of natural law seems to be a necessary condition for empire builders. The Romans (no less than America and its allies today) were sure that there were universal values to which all people and cultures should subscribe. And while there were some who professed not to accept the superpower's way, the Romans were convinced that such people would be better off in the long run if they went along with Roman values. So the goal of the empire at the time of Christ was not merely conquest and military might; they believed they could govern best and wanted to see peace throughout the land – understanding that peace often required the sword to enforce.

Probably more influential than their theories were their practices. The Romans provided the kind of infrastructure without which Christian thought could not have spread and flourished as it did in the first few centuries after the time of Christ. They were practical people. They acknowledged that the Greeks had more subtle intellects, but they also noted that intellect alone didn't seem to translate into stable Greek societies. Drama festivals may be nice, but in order to flourish, cities needed aqueducts for proper sanitation, and empires needed proper roads for the transportation of goods and communication. To put it simply, Romans didn't care as much about what people thought as about what they could do. Getting things done was necessary to create and sustain a successful empire. And it was the form of that empire itself that would come to influence Christianity so significantly within a couple of hundred years.

This pragmatic attitude also pervaded Greco-Roman religion around the time of Christ. The gods were useful for what they could do for the Romans in everyday life: making crops plentiful, protecting mothers in childbirth, prospering the empire, and so on. Among the Romans, there was not much close to the sophistication in theology that the Christians would develop within just a few centuries. Like Greece before them (from whom they incorporated much into their system of gods), their emphasis was on mythology rather than theology. And by the time of Christ the Romans were adding the cult of emperor worship to their religious practices. This reinforced the mythological nature of their religion by suggesting that all the gods were originally heroes of times long gone who had been deified after their deaths.[8]

Mythology also reinforced a dependence on visual images of the gods – especially in the form of statues. These were physical representations which conveyed the gods' natures to the people; also, the presence of one of these statues evoked the god's authority. Statues of emperors were erected all around the empire so that people outside Rome would know who the emperor was and could pay respect to him. It worked the same way for statues of other gods. These were ubiquitous and promoted a climate of religiosity.

When visiting Athens in the middle of the first century, the Apostle Paul was deeply distressed to see the city full of these statues, which he called

Each city, O Lælius, has its own peculiar religion; we have ours. While Jerusalem was flourishing, and while the Jews were in a peaceful state, still the religious ceremonies and observances of that people were very much at variance with the splendour of this empire, and the dignity of our name, and the institutions of our ancestors. And they are the more odious to us now, because that nation has shown by arms what were its feelings towards our supremacy. How dear it was to the immortal gods is proved by its having been defeated, by its revenues having been farmed out to our contractors, by its being reduced to a state of subjection.

(Cicero, "On Behalf of Flaccus"[9])

"idols" (Acts 17:16). Because the Christians would at this time continue the Jewish prohibition against making images of their God, pagans sometimes charged that they were godless (remember Pompey's shock at finding the Holy of Holies "empty"). In response to Paul's preaching about Jesus in Athens, the Stoic and Epicurean philosophers accused him of trying to introduce foreign gods. There was nothing too remarkable about importing gods in and of itself; religion in the Roman Empire had absorbed hundreds of gods from peoples they conquered. But when these captives tried to impose their gods on others and replace the official state gods, Rome generally didn't respond too kindly.

In the century before Christ, the Roman orator Cicero had, in a court case, spoken against the Jewish people of Rome for failing to allow their religion to be subsumed and incorporated into the empire. This was the central concern of religion in the Roman Empire: that it uphold the integrity of the empire and its governing structures. These governing structures, and their relationship to the ongoing organization of Jewish life under their Roman overlords, are important for understanding the threat that Jesus and his religion posed. We attempt to clarify this in the next section.

4 THE JEWISH PEOPLE AS ROMAN SUBJECTS

Written in the style of ancient historical documents, the Gospel of Luke parades forth a number of names of public authorities and their positions:

> In those days a decree went out from Emperor Augustus that all the world should be registered. This was the first registration and was taken while Quirinius was governor of Syria.
>
> (Luke 2:1–2)

> In the fifteenth year of the reign of Emperor Tiberius, when Pontius Pilate was governor of Judea, and Herod was ruler of Galilee, and his brother Philip ruler of the region of Ituraea and Trachonitis … during the high priesthood of Annas and Caiaphas, the word of God came to John son of Zechariah in the wilderness.
>
> (Luke 3:1–2)

Caesar Augustus was the Roman Emperor from 27BCE until he died in 14CE. Emperors didn't have much involvement in the actual governing of lands that were some distance from the capital. Rather, there were several layers of rulers between him and the people. In the case of Judea, when General Pompey asserted Roman authority there, the land was placed under the jurisdiction of the Governor of Syria. Quirinius served in this position at the time of Jesus's birth, and he appears to have been responsible for organizing a census throughout the land which caused Mary and Joseph to travel to Bethlehem.

King Herod "the Great" was a Jew who worked himself into the political machinery of Rome. In 40BCE when the last of the Hasmonean rulers was overthrown, Herod got himself named "King of the Jews" by the senate in Rome because the Judaeans had supported Julius Caesar during the Roman civil wars. Herod was technically the face of the Roman government in Judea, so was not well-liked by his fellow Jews. But he ruled effectively (though in the manner of an efficient and brutal tyrant) and increased Judea's prominence as well as the fortunes of the Jewish people. The second temple was reconstructed around 10BCE under his supervision (and so is sometimes called Herod's temple). At this time, the Romans largely left Judea alone, because Herod was doing what was expected of him: paying the requisite tribute of tax to Rome, keeping the peace among inhabitants, and making sure the borders stayed secure.

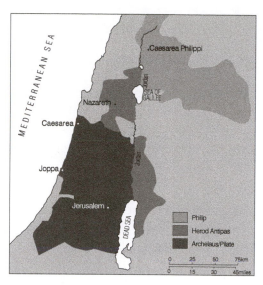

Map 1.2 Territories of Herod's sons

When Herod the Great died in 4BCE, Caesar Augustus divided all of Judea between Herod's three sons as follows:

Philip: the outlying areas Luke calls Ituraea and Trachonitis
Antipas (who also took the name Herod): the area to the north called Galilee
Archelaus: Samaria and Jerusalem, which came to be called Judea.[10]

Philip and Antipas proved to be capable rulers, and they were still in power under the next Roman emperor, Tiberius.[11] Archelaus, however, was not able to keep the peace the way Rome expected, so in 6CE Augustus deposed him and appointed a Roman governor to that area. The governor (who was Pontius Pilate at the time of Jesus's death) lived in the seaside town of Caesarea. He came to Jerusalem with additional Roman troops only during the times of major festivals as the possibility of upheaval was greater then. The day-to-day governance of towns and villages was left to appointed local rulers. In Jerusalem, this was carried out by the high priest and his advisors.

Before the Hasmonean Dynasty, the office of high priest was inherited. The Hasmonean rulers were not part of this line, but changed the rules and made themselves the high priests in Jerusalem. During King Herod

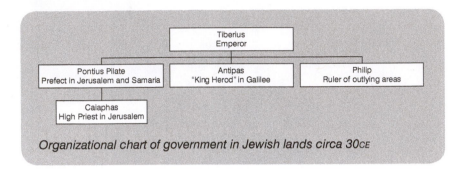

Organizational chart of government in Jewish lands circa 30CE

the Great's rule, he instituted the practice of appointing the high priest in Jerusalem, and this was continued by the Roman governor. Luke mentions Annas and Caiaphas both as high priest. The Roman governor deposed Annas in 15CE, but according to Jewish law the position was given for life. So Annas probably continued to exercise some of the authority of the position even when his son-in-law Caiaphas was appointed by the Romans to officially occupy it.

To recap: Jerusalem, as a city in Judea, was governed by the high priest, who was appointed by the Roman governor of Judea and Samaria; just to the north in Galilee, the ruler equivalent to the governor was a Jewish "tetrarch" or "king" – Antipas (who was called Herod, after his father); and the outlying areas to the north and east of Galilee were ruled by Philip (who rebuilt Caesarea Philippi). These three answered to Tiberius, the Roman emperor.

This was the political situation in Judea at the time of Jesus. Apart from festival times, there was not much of a Roman presence in Jerusalem and the smaller towns around Judea and Galilee. The Jews were free to practice their religion so long as they didn't stir up trouble. Trouble usually came in the form of revolutionaries who bucked against Roman rule.

In the case of Jesus, his ideas would cause significant tensions among the various rulers in the political system. But his aim was not to stir up people against their Roman overlords. His ideas were passed down to us in Greek – the *lingua franca* of the time – and so subsequent generations of Christian thinkers would develop their thought in the categories afforded by the Greek philosophical tradition. But ultimately, the ideas incited a different sort of revolution among a small band of Jews. They came to reinterpret how God was acting in world history through the Jewish people to bring a final kingdom into existence that would last for all time.

SUMMARY OF MAIN POINTS

1   Yahweh's election of the Hebrew people, through whom he would bless all nations, formed a central guiding idea for early Christian thought.
2   The Greeks' emphasis on rationality affected the intellectual climate within which Christian doctrines were worked out.
3   The Romans imposed order and pragmatism on the territories and people they conquered.
4   The high priest in Jerusalem reported to the governor of Judea, who reported to the emperor.

FOR FURTHER READING

Elias Bickerman, *The Jews in the Greek Age* (Cambridge, MA: Harvard University Press, 1990). A more scholarly but still vivid account of the Jewish people from the conquest of Palestine to the Maccabean Revolt.

Thomas Cahill, *The Gifts of the Jews* (New York: Anchor Books, 1998). A popular historian chronicles the story of the Hebrew People from Abraham to the Babylonian captivity in an engaging style.

Everett Ferguson, *Backgrounds of Early Christianity*, 3rd edition (Grand Rapids, MI: Eerdmans, 2003). A thematically structured comprehensive resource text of the world of the first Christians.

Robert M. Grant, *Gods and the One God* (Philadelphia, PA: Westminster Press, 1986). A look at the religious context of the rise of Christianity in Greco-Roman culture.

1 and 2 Maccabees. Historical books in the apocrypha detailing the story of the Maccabean Revolt.

The Works of Philo (Peabody, MA: Hendrickson Publishers, 1993). A good edition of the writings of the important Jew from Alexandria.

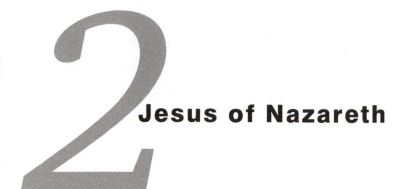

2 Jesus of Nazareth

QUESTIONS TO BE ADDRESSED IN THIS CHAPTER

1   What can we know about Jesus of Nazareth?
2   Who was Jesus?
3   What did Jesus teach?
4   How did Jesus understand himself?

At the beginning of his career as an itinerant teacher, Jesus went to the synagogue in his hometown of Nazareth. He stood before the people and read from the scroll of Isaiah as follows:

> The Spirit of the Lord is upon me,
> Because he has anointed me to bring good news to the poor.
> He has sent me to proclaim release to the captives
> And recovery of sight to the blind,
> To let the oppressed go free,
> To proclaim the year of the Lord's favor.
>   (Luke 4:18–19, quoting from Isaiah 61:1–2)

Then in one of the most dramatic moments in all of literature, Jesus rolled up the scroll, handed it back to the attendant, and took the seat of the teacher in the synagogue. There was not a sound as all eyes were fixed upon him, waiting to hear what he would say next. Would he expound on the words of Isaiah, or connect them to other sayings of the

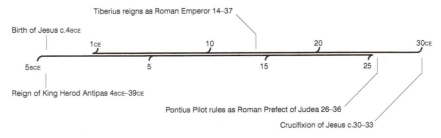

Timeline 2 Jesus of Nazareth

prophets? No. He simply said, "Today, this scripture has been fulfilled in your hearing" (Luke 4:21).

Why this is so dramatic and momentous is lost on modern readers who are unfamiliar with the context. Jews believed that their God, Yahweh, spoke through the voice of the prophet to tell them what *he* was going to do in the world. His actions would bring about the end of the age and usher in the glorious kingdom of heaven. But then the Gospel of Luke records Jesus saying that the prophesy was now fulfilled because *he himself* was the one who would be doing what Yahweh was going to do. It seems that Jesus thought there was something unique and remarkable about himself. Or did he?

There is no doubt that Jesus was a revolutionary figure. Ostensibly, he is the reason there is 2,000 years' worth of Christian thought to be chronicled. But there are legitimate questions to be asked about how much the Christ that has been the object of Christian worship throughout these centuries corresponds to the actual historical figure of Jesus of Nazareth. What can we really know about him? What has been added to (or taken

Figure 2.1 Christ Pantocrator

away from) what he taught by later traditions and Jesus movements? Did he really believe himself to be the Son of God and the Messiah?

Any discussion of the thought of the historical Jesus is fraught with difficulties. To begin with, traditional Christians believe that Jesus is still alive.[1] If Jesus was resurrected from the dead and continues to communicate with the faithful, then his thought is an open and potentially evolving subject. Of course the resurrection (and the supernatural in general) is a significant point of contention between different interpretations of Christianity. But even aside from the issue of whether Jesus himself continues to teach people today, there is a legitimate question to be asked about whether it is the actual Jesus of history or later believers' understandings of Christ which are more important for Christian faith.

There are those who argue that even contrasting the Jesus of history and the Christ of faith is misleading. According to them, by separating these two, we give undue precedence to the historians and discount the role of the Church. For example, if historians can't produce irrefutable proof that the historical figure of Christ believed himself to be the son of God, then what should Christians' response be? Those who oppose the distinction claim it is not the historian's job to tell Christians what they should believe; history is rarely capable of providing irrefutable proof

JESUS OF HISTORY VS. CHRIST OF FAITH

There is no doubt that there was a person named Jesus (or Yeshua in his native tongue of Aramaic) from the city of Nazareth in the early first century of the Common Era. It is this figure who is designated the Jesus of History by those who endeavor to learn as much as they can about him through rigorous historical methodology. Many of these same researchers claim that this historical figure was transformed into a fictional character by his early followers when they attributed to him all sorts of sayings and supernatural actions that never happened. The researchers find it helpful to refer to this fictional character as the Christ of Faith, whom they believe is the figure worshiped by Christians.

anyway. Rather, it is the mission of the church to bear witness to the reality of the risen Christ and to deepen her understanding of him. This tradition is the legitimate source of faith.[2]

It is not our task in this volume to judge whether the beliefs of later Christians are legitimate or illegitimate; nor is it to determine whether such beliefs are consistent with the teachings of the historical Jesus. Our task is to understand the beliefs of Christians throughout the ages, to make sense of them within their contexts. For this task, it doesn't matter at all what the historical Jesus did or said or thought (and even less what we can prove that he did or said or thought). Chapters 3 through 28 of this book are a chronicle of what others thought about him – or at least what they thought about the idealized version of Jesus that was available to them in the Christian tradition in which they found themselves. But this present chapter is an attempt to look at Jesus himself as the first Christian thinker, as the founder of Christian thought. So here it is important that we try to sort out what can be known about him and his thought during the time that he walked the earth.

1 SEARCHING FOR THE JESUS OF HISTORY

The central difficulty in getting at the thought of Jesus of Nazareth is that he himself doesn't appear to have written anything (unless we count the words he wrote in the dirt at the scene of the adulteress about to be stoned in John 8:6; but we don't even know what those words were, and the passage itself is disputed as spurious!). So our access to what Jesus believed and taught is entirely mediated by the writings of others. And scholars today disagree sharply in their interpretations and assessments of the first century writings about Jesus that have survived.

The first couple of decades after the crucifixion of Jesus (c. 30–33ce) are shrouded in literary silence about him. Undoubtedly there was a vibrant oral tradition of the teachings of Jesus that were recounted among his followers. And we might reasonably conclude that many of these had been written in a document which may have circulated among churches. But no such document has been found today or is even unequivocally referred to by the extant texts. So the earliest written accounts of Jesus are the gospels that found their way into the New Testament. By even the most conservative estimates, these were not constructed in the forms we've received them until at least the 60s ce, and other scholars date them decades later. Church tradition has assigned the authorship that is ascribed to the gospels today, but scholars also debate the roles that the historical figures of Matthew, Mark, Luke, and John had in writing the texts that now bear their names. And while these gospels do conform to the ancient pattern of biography, they are not the sort of histories that we expect today with dates and chronology carefully tended to.[3] Furthermore, the gospels were written in Greek, the *lingua franca* of the day, while Jesus would have spoken Aramaic, a Semitic language akin to Hebrew. Finally, the extant writings about Jesus from the first century are almost entirely by people who were sympathetic to the cause of Jesus and who had particular theological points to make. These authors were people from the "inside" of the Jesus movement rather than objective observers.

All of these issues contribute to the difficulty of ascertaining what the historical Jesus of Nazareth actually said and did. If in the case of more recent figures for whom immense amounts of primary sources exist – like Queen Victoria or Abraham Lincoln – there are very different interpretations offered by their biographers, how much more should we expect a range of interpretations for the life of Jesus? One's preconceived notions will affect the outcome much more when there is comparatively little raw data to constrain interpretations. So, we get one kind of Jesus if we are convinced that there is no supernatural – as Thomas Jefferson believed and so cut out all of the miracle passages from his Bible. But Jesus looks very different if the evidence is assembled and assessed by one who antecedently believes him to be divine. This point was made in 1906 when Albert Schweitzer wrote his *The Quest of the Historical Jesus*. His central claim was that the understandings of Jesus which had been

GOSPEL

From the old English word godspell which meant "good news"; in the New Testament, the good news refers to the story of Jesus Christ's life, death, resurrection, and teachings. Gospel also refers to the semi-biographical accounts of Jesus's life, four of which are collected in the New Testament as the Gospels of Matthew, Mark, Luke, and John.

constructed during the Enlightenment were more reflections of their authors than biographies of a historical figure. This began a movement of more serious attempts to ascertain what could be known about the life of Jesus.

More recently, there has been another wave of New Testament scholars trying to uncover the historical Jesus. The "Jesus Seminar," as it is called, has received considerable press in the mainstream media. Beginning in 1985, they met twice a year to discuss and debate the authenticity of various sayings attributed to Jesus in the gospels. Each member would cast a vote on particular sayings with various colored beads, which represented his or her confidence that those words were really spoken by the historical person of Jesus. In 1993, the Jesus Seminar published its own translation of the four gospels of the New Testament along with the Gospel of Thomas in a book called *The Five Gospels*.[4] Instead of Jesus's words being printed in red as has been customary in some modern editions of the New Testament, *The Five Gospels* prints the words attributed to Jesus in one of four colors according to the voting of the seminar:

red: Jesus undoubtedly said this or something very like it.
pink: Jesus probably said something like this.
gray: Jesus did not say this, but the ideas contained in it are close to his own.
black: Jesus did not say this; it represents the perspective or content of a later or different tradition.[5]

The result is a rainbow of script throughout the gospels. For example, the Jesus Seminar concluded that it is very likely that Jesus said, "Love your enemies" as recorded in Matthew 5:44, and that he told the parable of the Good Samaritan (Luke 10); so these passages are colored red. The Prodigal Son story (Luke 15), though, only achieved pink text. They explain, "Almost 50 percent of the Fellows voted red; a few black votes pulled the average into the pink category."[6] Jesus's statement of the Golden Rule, "You are to love your neighbor as yourself" (Mark 12:31, Matthew 22:39) fared even worse, meriting only gray. And Jesus's claim, "I am the way, the truth, and the life ..." at John 14:6 is judged to be wholly inauthentic and colored black.

In the introduction to *The Five Gospels*, the authors liken themselves to Galileo and others of the scientific revolution who freed the culture

THE LORD'S PRAYER ACCORDING TO THE COLORS USED BY THE JESUS SEMINAR

Our Father (red) in the heavens, (black)

your name be revered. (pink)

Impose your imperial rule, (pink)

enact your will on earth as you have in heaven. (black)

Provide us with the bread we need for the day. (pink)

Forgive our debts (pink)

to the extent that we have forgiven those in debt to us. (pink)

And please don't subject us to test after test, (gray)

but rescue us from the evil one. (black)

from dogmatic acceptance of the authority of the Church. They see themselves as freeing the real person of Jesus from the fundamentalist interpretations of Scripture that have held sway for too long especially in American culture.

According to the Jesus Seminar, "Eighty-two percent of the words ascribed to Jesus in the gospels were not actually spoken by him."[7] How do they come up with this? They have developed an extensive set of "rules of evidence" according to which the various sayings of Jesus are weighed. However, some argue that these rules themselves are not reasoned conclusions based on the evidence, but the presuppositions they bring to the evidence. For example, one of the rules is, "Sayings and narratives that reflect knowledge of events that took place after Jesus's death are the creation of the evangelists or the oral tradition before them."[8] As an example they reference the saying attributed to Jesus in Mark 13:9 in which the disciples are warned that they will be beaten and hauled before various authorities. Jesus couldn't have really said this, they reason, because those beatings didn't start happening until after Jesus had died, so he couldn't have known about them. They conclude, then, that the writer of Mark put those words into the mouth of his fictionalized Jesus. This presumes that there could not have been anything supernatural about Jesus.

Luke Timothy Johnson, an eminent New Testament scholar, has written a book called *The Real Jesus* which is critical of the Jesus Seminar.[9] He thoroughly documents that the Jesus Seminar does not speak for the guild of New Testament studies, and that the real innovation in their project has been the degree to which they have become media savvy in getting their message out. He argues that they display a naïve understanding of what history itself is as they create fantastic hypotheses based on very limited evidence, trying to force answers out of texts that were designed for very different purposes.[10]

Other leading scholars also disagree with the conclusions of the Jesus Seminar.[1] These scholars are not fundamentalists who claim that the New Testament books were dictated word for word by God to their human scribes. They understand the scholarly issues involved but judge that the gospels are generally reliable in their portrayal of Jesus and his words. In further agreement with this assessment, eminent religion scholar Keith Ward says, "It is reasonable to take [the gospels] as generally reliable records of a person who had a unique unity with God, and who understood his life as realizing a Messianic vocation. And that, I suggest, is all that Christian faith requires of our knowledge of the historical Jesus."[12]

We can't pretend there are no interpretive difficulties with the New Testament texts. These difficulties should not be dismissed from discussion. And undoubtedly we cannot expect perfect objectivity in the recounting of history. But when we lay aside prejudice as much as possible and apply credible historical methodology, it is plausible to believe that the central strains of the Christian message and the person of Jesus are made accessible to us by the first century witness.[13]

2 WHO WAS JESUS?

Even if we cannot verify the authenticity of all the sayings attributed to Jesus, there are well-established facts about his life which are agreed upon by historians of all persuasions.[14] Jesus was born into a Jewish family and lived most of his early life in Nazareth – a village of fewer than 2,000 people in the hills about ten miles southwest of the Sea of Galilee. As an adult (probably in his late twenties) he was attracted to the teaching of an apocalyptic prophet known to us as John the Baptist, who was Jesus's cousin according to the Gospel of Luke. Jesus himself received baptism from John, which signified that he had accepted John's teaching and oriented his life to John's message that the long-awaited kingdom of God was at hand.

Jesus began teaching about the kingdom of God in the villages and countryside in the area around the Sea of Galilee, and he started attracting his own disciples. Over a period of one to three years, his followers grew in number and boldness, and he went up to Jerusalem where he caused quite a stir. There was an incident of some sort at the temple, and undoubtedly his teaching caused the Jewish establishment much unease. After a Passover meal with his closest disciples, he was arrested by the Jewish authorities and interrogated by the high priest

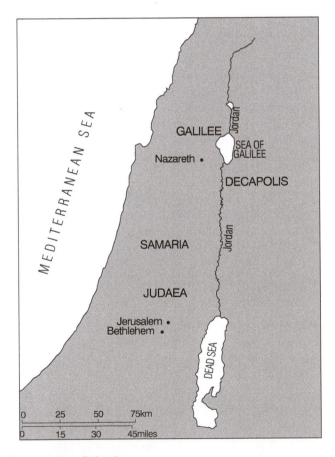

Map 2.1 First century Palestine

Caiaphas. Jesus was put to death under the authority of Pontius Pilate, the Roman prefect in the region.

The specific dating of Jesus's death cannot be verified. From extra-biblical sources, we know that Pontius Pilate was the prefect in Judea during the years 26–36 (as we count them now) and that Caiaphas was the high priest from 18–36. By taking clues from the gospels, then, it is reasonable to assign the crucifixion somewhere between 29 and 33.

Of course it is a central part of the Christian story that Jesus was resurrected after his death and appeared again to his disciples. Setting aside the perspective of faith and using only historical methodology, it is very difficult to defend the claim that nothing remarkable happened in the days after Jesus's death. Many of Jesus's disciples believed that he appeared to them – not as a ghost or merely in a dream, but as a resurrected messiah who was living proof that the kingdom of God had begun to be established on earth. Indeed, apart from such a belief, it is difficult to give a reasonable account of the earliest Christians' refusal to disband and of their willingness to endure the martyrdom that awaited almost all of them. New Testament scholar, E. P. Sanders says, "That Jesus's followers (and later Paul) had resurrection experiences is, in my judgment, a fact. What the reality was that gave rise to the experiences I do not know."[15]

Explaining the resurrection experiences will remain a matter of speculation for scholars and lies beyond the scope of this discussion. It is his teaching that interests us here. What was it that attracted so many, and got him into such trouble with the Jewish leaders?

3 WHAT DID JESUS TEACH?

The majority of scholars accept that the main themes of Jesus's teaching in the New Testament (with the possible exception of the Gospel of John) are traceable back to the historical person of Jesus. The teachings recorded in Matthew 5–7 known as the Sermon on the Mount contain much of the core of his message. Another version of the same message is recorded in Luke Chapter 6 and sometimes called the Sermon on the Plain. As an itinerant preacher in the small towns in the region of the Sea of Galilee, he would have undoubtedly repeated similar messages in a variety of contexts.

Sometimes the Sermon on the Mount is upheld as an admirable ethical ideal even by those who make no profession of Christianity. It is here that we find such well-known sayings as:

- Blessed are the peacemakers, for they will be called children of God (5:9);
- If someone strikes you on the right cheek, turn to him the other also (5:39);
- Love your enemies and pray for those who persecute you (5:44);
- Do not judge or you too will be judged (7:1); and
- Do to others as you would have them do to you (7:12).

But while these are sensible and ethical adages, to treat them only as such radically misses the point of Jesus's teaching.

The central theme of Jesus's teaching is one that builds upon John the Baptist's preaching: the reign and rule of God is about to be established, and indeed it has already been inaugurated. This was the hope of the Jewish people for centuries, and by the time of Jesus there were essentially three different ways of expecting that coming kingdom: first, groups like the Essenes (who wrote the Dead Sea Scrolls) separated themselves from culture and waited for the kingdom to come; second, others like King Herod worked themselves into the political structure of the Romans, and hoped that God might work things out so that the kingdom of this world would become the kingdom of God; or third, there were the Zealots who believed that they needed to take matters into their own hands and forcibly bring about the rule of God by running the Romans out of their land.

N.T. Wright and others argue persuasively that the Sermon on the Mount is Jesus's attempt to provide an alternative way of seeing the kingdom of God come and be enacted on earth.[16] In this sense, the sermon could have been a political speech among his closest followers in the hills where Jews went to plot revolutions. Essentially Jesus was, "calling his hearers, quite simply, to a new way of being Israel, a new way of being God's people for the world."[17] In contemporary campaigning parlance he might have said, "The methods of the status quo aren't working; we need real change. Follow me and we can make this happen."

Relative to contemporary Christian teaching, Jesus had remarkably little to say about how to get to heaven when you die. The good news that

Jesus brought was that the kingdom of God was becoming available to all who would choose to live according to the rule of God. The poor in spirit, those who mourn, the meek, and the merciful were the last you'd expect to come out on top in some sort of social order. But now even these were blessed according to Jesus because in spite of their condition, the good life in the kingdom was equally available to them as to everyone else. Or perhaps these outcasts even had an advantage because the others who had it good now would be tempted to hold on to their fleeting, temporary goods.

The citizens of the new kingdom could be the light of the world (Matthew 5:14), but not in the way the Jews had expected. It was not by following the Jewish law more and more closely that they would show the world the true light of God. Rather, it was by going beyond the law, beyond the outward appearances, to a transformation of the inner life that the kingdom would be manifested in people's lives. You've heard it

BEATITUDES

Blessed are the poor in spirit: for theirs is the kingdom of heaven.

Blessed are they that mourn: for they shall be comforted.

Blessed are the meek: for they shall inherit the earth.

Blessed are they which do hunger and thirst after righteousness: for they shall be filled.

Blessed are the merciful: for they shall obtain mercy.

Blessed are the pure in heart: for they shall see God.

Blessed are the peacemakers: for they shall be called the children of God.

Blessed are they which are persecuted for righteousness' sake: for theirs is the kingdom of heaven.

Blessed are ye, when men shall revile you, and persecute you, and shall say all manner of evil against you falsely, for my sake. Rejoice, and be exceeding glad: for great is your reward in heaven: for so persecuted they the prophets which were before you.

(Matthew 5:3–12, King James Version)

said in the law, Jesus claimed, that you shall not murder; but refraining from the outward act of murdering is not enough. The root evil is the inward anger that you have toward people (Matthew 5:21–26). Similarly, it is easy to think you're in a right sexual relationship with others if you don't commit the outward act of adultery. But those who live under the rule of God will recognize that lusting after someone in their hearts has already crossed the line into a wrong and destructive mode of sexuality that makes people into objects (Matthew 5:27–30).

Jesus consistently takes the focus off the easily identifiable outward indicators and emphasizes the attitudes with which these actions are done: when you give alms to the poor, do it secretly; when you pray, don't do it for show; when you fast, don't even let others know that you're doing it.

Instead of perpetuating a cycle of violence and revenge with their enemies, Jesus invites people to try a different approach: bless those who curse you, pray for those who persecute you, show love and kindness to your enemies. Those are the rules under which the kingdom of God operates according to Jesus. They are counter-intuitive, but this was how the world would be changed. This was how God's chosen people would bring the peaceful reign of God to all the earth.

The Sermon on the Mount and the Sermon on the Plain end with a very overt reference to the superiority of this way of living compared to the traditional Jewish way and its emphasis on the temple (and its concomitant sacrificial system). Jesus says, "Whoever hears these words of mine and puts them into practice is like a wise man who built his house on the rock" (Matthew 7:24, Luke 6:48). Jesus's Jewish listeners would have understood that the "house on the rock" was a reference to the temple in Jerusalem – which was built on a huge rock. Jesus was saying that obeying his teachings, which have fulfilled and gone beyond the traditional law, was the superior way to be the people of God in the new kingdom.

But again, Jesus's teaching was not just a good moral message about how to make the world a better place. It was very consciously a response to the eschatological hope of the Jewish people. They hoped that God would act decisively in history and establish his rule permanently, vindicating his people and giving them salvation from their Roman oppressors and salvation to the kingdom of God. Jesus claimed that he himself was God's decisive act. But what gave Jesus the authority to proclaim this? What did he understand his role to be in all this?

4 HOW DID JESUS UNDERSTAND HIMSELF?

Jesus is commonly referred to as Jesus Christ, as though "Christ" were his surname. But Christ is not a person or family. It is a title that is applied to a person – much like "the Buddha" is a designation applied to a person because of his role, not because that is his name, as in "Gautama Buddha." The English word Christ comes from *christos* in the Greek, which means "messiah" and more literally translates as "anointed one." As early as the writings of the Apostle Paul in the middle of the first century, the name and title were concatenated to Jesus Christ, by which we understand Paul to mean that he believed that Jesus of Nazareth was in fact the long-awaited messiah.

It is clear that all four of the New Testament gospel writers also regarded Jesus as the messiah, but scholars do not agree whether Jesus believed that about himself. Of course much of this question hinges on what we mean by "messiah." It doesn't seem to be a title that Jesus was particularly eager to embrace. He knew that he was not going to be the sort of messiah that the Jews were looking for. John the Baptist appeared to be confused by what Jesus was doing. Even though John had deflected messianic attributions away from himself to Jesus, he later sent two of his own followers to Jesus to ask whether he was really the one they were waiting for, or whether there was another coming to be the messiah. After the crucifixion, Cleopas tells a stranger (who turns out to be the resurrected Jesus in disguise) about the recent events concerning Jesus of Nazareth and said, "we had hoped that he was the one to redeem Israel" (Luke 24:21). Clearly, Jesus wasn't fitting the expected messianic mold.

The Jewish people had been longing for one who would reestablish the political prominence of Israel, and there were more than a few messianic claimants who attempted to do just that.[18] But Jesus didn't even to try to be that sort of messiah. And since there is no record of an unambiguous public proclamation of the sort of messiah that he was, many scholars question his understanding of himself as a messiah.[19]

It is defensible, though, that Jesus understood himself to have a unique relationship with God. Of course the Christian understanding now is that he was and is the Son of God. But the historical Jesus doesn't seem ready to own that title either (at least in Matthew and Luke). All three of the earlier gospels record the scene when Jesus was being interrogated before his crucifixion. In Matthew, the high priest commands, "Tell us if you are the Messiah, the Son of God." Jesus answers evasively, "You have said so" (26:64). In Luke, it is the whole council of chief priests and scribes who ask, "Are you, then, the Son of God?" Here again, Jesus is said to answer, "You say that I am" (22:70). It is only Mark's Jesus who answers unambiguously. There the high priest asks, "Are you the Messiah, the Son of the Blessed One?" And Jesus answers, "I am" (14:62). In attempting to judge what was actually said, it seems reasonable to conclude that Jesus probably said something evasive along the lines that Matthew and Luke report, while Mark adds an interpretive gloss to Jesus's words.

The Gospel of John gives clear statements about Jesus's understanding of his sonship, but most scholars attribute these to later understandings of who Jesus was, rather than his own statements (again, this does not mean they are wrong – just that Jesus probably didn't say them himself). However we interpret these passages, Jesus certainly didn't go around announcing that he was the second member of the Trinity. It would take a couple of hundred years for the Church to work up to an explicit understanding of him as such.

The title Jesus seemed to favor for himself was "Son of Man." It is found in the gospels fifty-one times, and it would be a difficult case to make that this was completely the invention of later understandings of Jesus. Also, the title was never really worked into the theology of later Christians, so it probably wouldn't have been the case that these writers gave it the prominence it has in the gospels unless it had really been used by Jesus.[20]

In using the title "Son of Man," Jesus was intentionally linking himself and his mission to the apocalyptic scene in the Old Testament book of Daniel. There the Son of Man represents one who stands for the nation of Israel in distinction to the beasts that are the other nations. This individual represents the true Israel and ushers in the kingdom of God.

If this is what is meant by "messiah," then Jesus did embrace the concept. Clearly, he understands himself as one anointed by God to speak and act on God's behalf, and even to forgive sins. Given the significant ambiguity that surrounded the title of messiah, though, Sanders prefers to say that Jesus understood himself to be God's viceroy.[21] He was God's agent in the present world and would continue to be so in the world to come.

SON OF MAN

In my vision at night I looked, and there before me was one like a son of man, coming with the clouds of heaven. He approached the Ancient of Days and was led into his presence. He was given authority, glory and sovereign power; all peoples, nations and men of every language worshiped him. His dominion is an everlasting dominion that will not pass away, and his kingdom is one that will never be destroyed.

(Daniel 7:13–14)

CONCLUSION

There is a lot we don't know about the historical figure of Jesus of Nazareth. We can say with confidence, though, that he believed himself to be on a mission from God. Jesus was loath to call himself the messiah or the Son of God. These were loaded terms that would stir up a lot of trouble. And perhaps the fact that he didn't try very hard to dissuade other people from attributing these titles to him is what led to the trouble which culminated in his crucifixion. But he always seemed to redirect people's expectations of him. If he was messiah, he wasn't going to be their kind of messiah; if he was King of the Jews, he wasn't the sort of king that sat in a palace and counted his money. His kingdom was not of this world and his subjects were all those who would willingly align themselves with the causes and mission he believed God had given him:

> to preach good news to the poor;
> to proclaim that the captives could be released,
> the blind healed,
> and the oppressed freed;
> and to announce the year of the Lord's favor had come.

Later generations of those who would call themselves Christians – which was originally applied as a derogatory term to followers of Christ – would commit themselves to Christ's mission and to sorting out what all of this meant. It is the thought of that great cloud of witnesses which forms the subject of the rest of this book.

SUMMARY OF MAIN POINTS

1   Although the primary texts about Jesus contain significant interpretive difficulties, it is reasonable to accept that we can learn about the historical Jesus from them.
2   Jesus of Nazareth was a Jewish itinerant teacher from the region of Galilee who was put to death by the Romans (at the instigation of the Jewish rulers); his followers believed that he resurrected from the dead.
3   Jesus taught that there was a new way of seeing the kingdom of God come to earth.
4   Jesus believed himself to be specially anointed by God to speak and act on his behalf and to rule in the new kingdom.

FOR FURTHER READING

John Dominic Crossan, *Jesus: A Revolutionary Biography* (San Francisco, CA: HarperSanFrancisco, 1994). One of the superstars of the historical Jesus movement. This is a popularized version of his more scholarly 1991 book, *The Historical Jesus: The Life of a Mediterranean Jewish Peasant*.

Craig A. Evans, *Jesus* (Grand Rapids, MI: Baker, 1992). An annotated bibliography of more than 500 sources of historical Jesus research, produced by the Institute for Biblical Research Bibliographies.

Robert W. Funk, Roy W. Hoover, and the Jesus Seminar, trans. and eds, *The Five Gospels* (New York: Macmillan Publishing Company, 1993). The multi-colored Jesus Seminar translation of the four New Testament gospels and the Gospel of Thomas.

Luke Timothy Johnson, *The Real Jesus* (San Francisco, CA: HarperSanFrancisco, 1996). A Roman Catholic scholar takes the Jesus Seminar to task both in their conclusions as well as their methodology.

E.P. Sanders, *The Historical Figure of Jesus* (New York: Penguin, 1993). A very accessible yet substantial and fair-minded treatment by one of the leading scholars of Judaism and Christianity in the Greco-Roman world.

N.T. Wright, *The Challenge of the Jesus: Rediscovering Who Jesus Was and Is* (Downer's Grove, IL: Intervarsity Press, 1999). A thorough introduction to the critical issues in Jesus studies by one of the world's leading New Testament scholars.

3 The Apostle Paul

His thought and context

QUESTIONS TO BE ADDRESSED IN THIS CHAPTER

1   Who was Paul?
2   What influence did Paul's former commitment to Judaism have on his Christian thought?
3   How does Paul understand the end times and Christ's resurrection?
4   What is salvation?
5   What is expected of Christians?

According to the biblical book of the Acts of the Apostles, Jesus appeared to his disciples following his resurrection and taught them for forty days (Acts 1:3). Then he ascended into heaven, instructing them to wait in Jerusalem for the Holy Spirit to come. Once this happened, they were to bear witness to what they had learned from him throughout the whole world. Ten days after the ascension they were still waiting in Jerusalem when one of the annual Jewish festivals called Pentecost was going on. Pentecost, literally "fifty days" (after Passover), occurs in late May or early June when the first fruits of the harvest are gathered. It also came to be remembered as the day when the Ten Commandments were given to Moses on Mount Sinai, thus ranking it in importance among Jewish holy days second only to Passover.

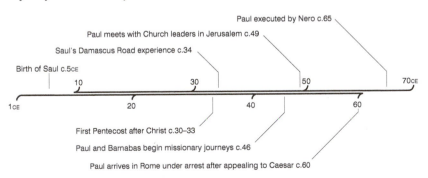

Paul executed by Nero c.65

Paul meets with Church leaders in Jerusalem c.49

Saul's Damascus Road experience c.34

Birth of Saul c.5CE

10   30   50   70CE

1CE   20   40   60

First Pentecost after Christ c.30–33

Paul and Barnabas begin missionary journeys c.46

Paul arrives in Rome under arrest after appealing to Caesar c.60

Timeline 3 The Apostle Paul: his thought and context

But Pentecost has come to have significance for Christians too. It was on that day when many were in Jerusalem for the festival – fifty days after the first Easter Sunday – that the Holy Spirit was poured out onto the believers in Christ as promised. The Apostle Peter addressed the crowds to explain what had happened by quoting from the Old Testament book of Joel: "In the last days it will be, God declares, that I will pour out my Spirit on all flesh ..." (Acts 2:17). With these words Peter announced to all that they were living in the last days, that something of eschatological importance had happened. Namely, the long-awaited messiah had come and had ushered in a new age of salvation as evinced by the resurrection of Jesus and now by this outpouring of the Holy Spirit. The Kingdom of the Heavens had begun to be revealed on earth. Peter gave another speech (recorded in Acts 3) in which he claimed that Jesus would return to earth to bring this process to completion as promised by God long ago.

So because of this Pentecost experience (and the Resurrection event), these Christians almost 2000 years ago believed themselves to be living in the last days. But they were expecting something else to happen that would bring the last days to their climactic conclusion. Things weren't quite over just yet. And while it appears that they initially expected the conclusion to happen within a generation, they didn't waver in their belief that it would happen. They understood that they ought to fill that "in-between" time with preaching the good news that God had fulfilled the first part of his covenant. It's not so clear, though, that those first Christians knew precisely how they were to understand these recent events fitting in with the long-held expectations of how the end times would unfold. One commentator calls the thinking of the earliest post-Pentecost Christians coherent but largely unorganized.[1] It would not take long, though, for there to arrive on the scene one who would bring some order to Christian thought.

ESCHATON

From the Greek word for "last"; the last days before the end of the world in its present phase. *Eschatology* is the study of or doctrines pertaining to the last days.

1 SAUL/PAUL AND CHRISTIANITY

When time indicators in the Acts of the Apostles and in Paul's letters are applied to extra-biblical records of rulers, we can reasonably estimate that the Pharisee known as Saul of Tarsus had a dramatic experience not much more than a year after that first Christian Pentecost.[2] Saul was traveling the road north from Jerusalem to Damascus, the capital of Syria, with permission from the Jewish high priest to bring back any Christians from the synagogues there as prisoners on account of their heresy. But the Acts of the Apostles records that his trip was interrupted by a brilliant flash of light which rendered Saul blind for three days. Apparently his companions didn't see what Saul did. But the text indicates that they heard the sound that ultimately led Saul to radically change his attitude toward this sect of Jews who claimed that the messiah had come. According to Paul, as he was known by his new Christian community, the risen Christ himself appeared in that blinding light on the Damascus Road, identifying himself as "Jesus, whom you are persecuting" (Acts 9:5). Paul was led to one of the Christians in Damascus who baptized him into the Christian faith. Then, instead of persecuting the Christians, Paul spent the rest of his life traveling far and wide proclaiming the good news of the risen Christ. As he did this, he also developed a theology which was an outgrowth of his previous life as a Pharisee and his encounter on the way to Damascus.

Figure 3.1 Apostle Paul. Andrei Rublev/Public domain/Wikimedia Commons

Most of what we know about Paul's thought comes from the historical book of Acts and from the epistles, or letters, attributed to him that found their way into the collection of authoritative texts Christians later adopted as their New Testament. He maintained correspondence with the groups of Christian believers in the cities he visited, such as Corinth and Galatia, and in cities he hoped to visit, such as Rome. Other letters, called the Pastoral Epistles, were written to individuals like Timothy and Titus. Scholars don't all agree on whether Paul actually wrote the Pastoral Epistles himself or whether they were penned after his death by others who identified with the School of Paul. In addition to these authorship issues, there are interpretive difficulties getting at the systematic thought of Paul because his letters are only parts of larger conversations and instructions that Paul had given to these audiences. When visiting a church, he would often stay for months at a time, instructing the believers in person. So most of the letters we have are "occasional" letters, that is to say, follow-ups or clarifications of points rather than systematic expositions. Because of this ambiguity there are different interpretations of Paul's theology which can be plausibly argued.

Since the Protestant Reformation of the sixteenth century, the standard interpretation of Paul has him reacting against the Pharisees and Judaizing Christians. These groups were supposedly treating justification before God and salvation to eternal life as something that could be earned by adherence to the law. On this interpretation, Paul's conversion turned him from his allegiance to the system of works righteousness

WRITINGS ATTRIBUTED TO PAUL IN THE NEW TESTAMENT

Undisputed	*Questioned*	*More strongly disputed*
Romans	Ephesians	1 and 2 Timothy
1 and 2 Corinthians	Colossians	Titus
Galatians	2 Thessalonians	
Philippians		
1 Thessalonians		
Philemon		

PHARISEES AND JUDAIZERS

Pharisees were a sect of Judaism which emphasized strict adherence to the law. The "Judaizing Christians" believed that even Gentiles who converted to Christianity should be forced to follow the Jewish law.

espoused by Jews, to embracing a new gospel that was centered on the grace of God and justification by faith. Furthermore, Paul was seen by the reformers to have embraced Greek forms of thought as he took this message away from the Jews who had rejected Jesus as messiah, and brought it to Gentile audiences.

In recent decades, however, there has been an important new perspective on Paul that began with the work of E.P. Sanders in his 1977 landmark work, *Paul and Palestinian Judaism*.[3] From it we've been forced to reevaluate the continuing import that Paul's Jewish background had on his thinking after his conversion experience. This new interpretation has significant implications for how we understand Paul's doctrines of justification and salvation, his eschatology and emphasis on the resurrection, and his instructions about spiritual life and practice.

2 THE PHARISAICAL CONTEXT OF PAUL'S THOUGHT

From what we know of Paul's early life, he was certainly not isolated from the wider culture in an ultra-conservative Jewish setting. Paul was from Tarsus, which was an important commercial city on the southern coast of modern-day Turkey. There were land and sea trade routes passing through Tarsus, giving it a cosmopolitan feel. Although we can't be certain, Paul was probably born not too long after Jesus was. His parents were Jews, but significantly, his father was also a Roman citizen. His household would probably have spoken the Jewish tongue of Aramaic as well as Greek, the common language of the culture. At some point, it appears that his family relocated to Jerusalem, where Paul was taught by the prominent Pharisee Gamaliel (Acts 22:3), but Gamaliel appears to have been moderate in his religious views (see Acts 5:34–40). And Paul's education almost certainly included formal training outside the typical Jewish course of study (for example, he quotes pagan authors several times in his letters and often uses Hellenic rhetorical style). It is reasonable to expect that these influences would have softened his Jewishness. But somewhere along the line he aligned himself with a militant, extremist Jewish sect.

By the end of the first century, there were at least two very distinct sects of Jewish Pharisees – moderate and lenient ones known as Hillelites, and strict, hard-liners known as Shammaites. In the middle 30s, at the time of Paul's Damascus Road conversion, the parties were not yet segregated into exclusive factions, but the impulse for each was clearly discernable. When Peter and the other apostles were brought before the ruling body of Pharisees for violating the order not to preach in Jesus's name, Paul's former teacher Gamaliel exhibited the relaxed demeanor of the Hillelites: he urged the Pharisees to leave them alone, because if what they were preaching was human invention, it would fail; if it was from God, they wouldn't be able to stop them anyway (Acts 5:34–39). Pre-conversion Saul did not share this "live and let live" attitude toward Christians.

Our first introduction to Saul in the book of Acts (7:58–8:1) portrays him as an accomplice to the stoning death of Stephen – one of the early believers in Christ and the first recorded Christian martyr. Paul recounted later in his letter to the Galatians, "You have heard, no doubt, of my earlier life in Judaism. I was violently persecuting the church of God and

HILLEL AND SHAMMAI

These were two of the greatest rabbis of the Second Temple period of Judaism, and each developed devoted followings during the first century. Hillel generally took a more open and lenient interpretation of the Jewish law, while Shammai pushed for strict adherence. Hillel was the president of the Sanhedrin, or chief ruling council of the Jews, in Jerusalem until his death around 10CE, and then Shammai took over. Each of their schools exercised significant influence on Judaism over the first few centuries of the Common Era.

was trying to destroy it. I advanced in Judaism beyond many among my people of the same age, for I was far more zealous for the traditions of my ancestors" (1:13–14). Those who were zealous for their traditions were the Shammaite Pharisees. It would not be wholly inaccurate to compare them with religious radicals of our own day. They were concerned not just about the personal piety of individual Jews, but also about the impious behavior of communities of Jews. It was this communal failing which allowed the pagan rulers of the land to retain power and to keep the Jews from their God-given right to the land and to a theocratic kingdom. Sure, the Gamaliels of Hillelism would be content so long as the Roman oppressors allowed them to study Torah in relative peace, but the "zeal" of the Shammaites – which included violence when necessary – would not subside until the apocalyptic climax when their God would restore all things for his chosen people. N.T. Wright sums up the situation:

> The extreme right wing of the Shammaites merged into the general viewpoint which we might think of as 'zeal' – zeal for a holy revolution in which the pagans would be defeated once and for all, and in which as well, renegade Jews would either be brought into line or be destroyed along with the pagans.[4]

It was not just the Christians who were singled out for persecution at the hands of the Shammaites. They thought that all those who refused to follow the Jewish law were hindering the process of the coming kingdom of God. It is true, as Saul and the Shammaites believed, that all nations and peoples of the earth would have God's blessing extended to them eventually: God had told Abraham, "in you all the families of the earth shall be blessed" (Genesis 12:3). But not yet; that was to happen at the end of times once God had acted in the world to honor the covenant he had made with the Jews. This is crucial for understanding Paul.

The dominant critical interpretation of Paul that has held sway for most of the last five centuries since the Protestant Reformation is that Paul was an innovator and the real founder of the Christian religion. Central to this position is the claim that in the thought of Paul there is little continuity with the teachings of Jesus himself. It must be admitted that there is a startling lack of references to specific teachings or sayings of Jesus in the letters of Paul, and a few of the places where he seems to mention specifically a teaching of Jesus, it is in the context of Paul providing a different nuance to that message.[5] Paul, so the story goes, replaced the practical message of Jesus the Jewish prophet – love for enemies, care for the poor, and non-judgmentalism – with a Hellenized, theoretical religion of justification, vicarious atonement, and the propitiation of sins.[6] But the insights of the new perspective on Paul have shown how Paul's thought is continuous with the message of Jesus and continues in the Judaic framework.

Pre-conversion Saul persecuted Christians because he thought they were foolishly perpetuating belief in a failed messiah. There had been many people who had come claiming to be the one who would lead the Jews back to a glorious position within the culture, but none of these had delivered on their promises (Gamaliel specifically addresses two such instances in Acts 5:33–39 about Theudas and Judas the Galilean). This Jesus of Nazareth, in Saul's estimation, was no different. Jesus had come preaching about the kingdom of God, but instead of leading the Jews in triumphant revolt against their Roman oppressors, he was put to death by them. As far as Saul was concerned, the case was closed on Jesus's claim to be messiah. There were no dead messiahs. But then there came the Damascus Road encounter.

3 CHRIST'S RESURRECTION AND ESCHATOLOGY

In Paul's retelling of the event, this was no mystical vision or psychological experience of Christ on the way to Damascus. It was Jesus himself, the risen Christ who was appearing to Paul in the same way that he had appeared to others of the apostles right after the resurrection (see his description in 1 Corinthians 15:3–8). Paul was confronted directly with what he and the other Christians took to be the reality of the resurrection of Jesus. Undoubtedly the significance of this revelation took some time to sink in, for it was not exactly as expected. But the Pharisees (unlike another Jewish sect called the Sadducees) did expect a resurrection. In the last days, God was going to resurrect his people, thereby vindicating them and allowing them to share in the glorious age to come in the kingdom of God. The theologically mature Paul would see the resurrection of Christ as the "first fruits" of that more general resurrection (1 Corinthians 15:21) and as the mark that Christ (and his messiahship) had been vindicated by God (Romans 1:4).

Saul, as part of the Shammaite movement, had been fighting to purify the Jews in order to hasten the day in which God would act decisively in history and fulfill his covenant with the Jewish people. The Jews would be redeemed, vindicated, and freed from their oppressors. Saul believed they were still living in exile because there had been no messiah, no resurrection, no extension of the blessing to the Gentiles. But then with the appearance of the risen Christ, these things did happen – or at least they started happening. The last days had begun, but they were not happening quite as expected.

This interpretation of Paul's thought does not represent an overthrowing or abandoning of the essentially Jewish framework in which he operated. Church historian Ivor Davidson describes the situation:

> What Paul became convinced of was that Jesus was alive and that God had done for Jesus what Paul expected he would do for Israel. Paul had thought that God would vindicate Israel and bring about her deliverance; now he believed that God had vindicated Jesus and in him had acted definitively to transform the condition of Israel. Instead of Jesus being, as Paul had imagined, a failed Messiah who had deluded a group of Jews who were lax in their observance of the law and lukewarm in their attitude to the temple, the resurrection showed that he was indeed who his disciples said he was: the true Messiah, the one through whose actions the last times had already been ushered in.[7]

This meant for Paul that nothing less than that which he had been fighting for had in fact happened. He understood that he and his contemporaries were living in the last days, but there was something else to come. "Already, but not yet" would become the eschatological description of their situation.[8]

Another indicator for Paul that the last days had arrived was that he was instructed to take the good news to the Gentiles. The blessing of God upon Abraham and the Jewish people was being opened to all nations. In fact, in Christ such distinctions were no longer relevant. Paul claimed,

> there is no longer Jew or Greek, there is no longer slave or free, there is no longer male and female; for all of you are one in Christ Jesus. And if you belong to Christ, then you are Abraham's offspring, heirs according to the promise.
>
> (Galatians 3:28–29)

It is not easy to construct one coherent model of the last times out of all the passages in the New Testament attributed to Paul. Again, these letters were not written as systematic expositions of topics, but rather addressed specific issues to his audiences. If we take the great resurrection chapter (1 Corinthians 15) as the central framework, the "already not yet" eschatology seems to play out this way: Christ, as the first fruits of the resurrection, ushered in the new age during which he is the ruler over all; but evidently there are still some ("his enemies") who do not acknowledge his Lordship. When he returns, all the people who are "in Christ" will be resurrected to rule with him until such a time as all his enemies are put under his feet. Then this kingdom will be turned over to God the father, so that "God may be all in all." It is at that point that the last days will see their consummation. The eschatological passages in 1 and 2 Thessalonians add some other details about the timing: it seems that Paul believes that Christ's return could be at any moment – it will come like a "thief in the night" (1 Thessalonians 5:2), but also must be preceded by the man of lawlessness, a.k.a., the antichrist (2 Thessalonians 2:3–12). On a straightforward reading, he seemed to believe that the second coming of Christ would occur very soon, perhaps during the lifetime of his readers. It is reasonable to think, however, that just as the initial coming of the messiah was somewhat different than expected (though still falling within the general parameters of the plan of redemption), so too the second coming might differ as well. The central point that Paul was making is that those who are in Christ will share in the resurrection and the glorious age to come.

4 JUSTIFICATION AND SALVATION

Who, then, are those who are "in Christ"? This is the question of salvation, but it might be asked a couple of different ways. We might ask, "How does one enter into a saving relationship with God?" or we could ask, "What is the mark of those who have been saved?" Of course these are related questions, but there is a difference of emphasis that is important. The typical way of reading Paul since the time of Luther in the sixteenth century has been that he offered his doctrine of justification by faith as an answer to the former question. How is one saved? By being justified by faith. That is to say, because of Christ's death on the cross, sinners are justified or declared to be innocent before God the judge when they repent and profess their faith in Christ; their sins won't be held against them and they'll be permitted to enter heaven when they die. Paul's theory on this interpretation is seen in contrast to the works righteousness that Saul the Pharisee had espoused and fought for prior to his conversion. Supposedly Saul and the Pharisees held that they could justify themselves before God by doing the right things (that is, by following the law).

However, the emphasis on justification by faith is more the reaction of Luther to medieval Catholicism than it is the reaction of Paul to the Pharisees.[9] We might conjecture that Paul would have responded the same way as Luther did to medieval Catholicism, but that is not what he was responding to. Paul's concern was more the other question we noted above: What is the mark of those who have been saved? Or we might frame the question as, How do we know who has been saved? And justification is Paul's answer to this question. "Justification," as the term was understood in first century Judaism, is not so much about individuals and how to obtain proper standing with God as it is a doctrine about what had happened between God and a certain group of people – the heirs of the Abrahamic covenant. God had promised to vindicate them as a people, and then through them to take the blessing of the covenant to all people. Justification is the mark that you are one of those people. Christ's resurrection from the dead was the mark that he had been vindicated and therefore justified by God. Those who follow Christ receive the Holy Spirit as the sign that they are included in that justification. It is these people who are vindicated, no longer held in bondage, and free to enter into and participate in the kingdom of God which has been inaugurated (though not yet fully enacted).

The question still remains, how do you become of one those people? When we ask how Paul taught that people come into a right relationship with the living God, it is not answered in terms of forensic justification. Rather,

> The message about Jesus and his cross and resurrection ... is announced to them; through this means, God works by his Spirit upon their hearts; as a result, they come to believe the message; they join the Christian community through baptism, and begin to share in its common life and its common way of life. That is how people come into relationship with the living God.[10]

Paul's gospel was not some formula about how to become a Christian; it was simply the amazing good news that Jesus Christ, through his death and resurrection, had been revealed as Lord of the universe. Paul had been given the task of bringing that news to the Gentiles (see Ephesians 3:8) so that they might understand that they too could align themselves with Christ the King.

This is not works righteousness because God had authored the plan of salvation. It was enacted at his initiative – not as a result of any good works that people might perform. And the plan was the satisfaction of the Abrahamic covenant which itself was made by God in his grace. That is not to say, however, that Paul thought nothing more was expected of God's people in response to this work of grace.

5 TRAINING TO BE GODLY

Paul told the Corinthians, "If anyone is in Christ, there is a new creation: everything old has passed away; see, everything has become new!" (2 Cor. 5:17). There is something qualitatively different about those who have chosen to align themselves with Jesus Christ. But just as Christ's resurrection inaugurated the end times without yet bringing about the consummation of all times, so too the change in a person at conversion is just the beginning of the transformation that is to occur. Jesus said to his disciples, "Be perfect, therefore, as your heavenly Father is perfect" (Matthew 5:48); the same Greek root used for "perfect" in that passage (*telos*) is used by Paul in his famous chapter on love:

> For we know only in part, and we prophesy only in part, but when the complete (*telos*) comes, the partial will come to an end … For now we see in a mirror dimly, but then we will see face to face. Now I know only in part; then I will know fully, even as I have been fully known.
>
> (1 Cor. 13:9–12)

Something has already happened, but not all that is going to happen. Already, but not yet.

So what is expected of people in this in-between time? Paul often answered this question using athletic metaphors: "Train yourself in godliness" he instructs Timothy (1 Tim. 4:7). The Greek verb translated as "train" is *gumnazo*, from which we get our word "gymnasium." Paul

Late in life sitting in a prison cell, Paul wrote to the church in Philippi:

> I want to know Christ and the power of his resurrection and the fellowship of sharing in his sufferings, becoming like him in his death, and so, somehow to attain to the resurrection from the dead. Not that I have already obtained all this, or have already been made perfect [here is *telos* in a verb form], but I press on to take hold of that for which Christ Jesus took hold of me. Brothers, I do not consider myself yet to have taken hold of it. But one thing I do: Forgetting what is behind and straining toward the goal to win the prize for which God has called me heavenward in Christ Jesus.
>
> (Philippians 3:10–14, New International Version)

is very consciously referring to the kind of training that athletes of the time participated in. Even more explicitly in 1 Corinthians he says, "Do you not know that in a race all the runners run, but only one gets the prize? Run in such a way as to get the prize. Everyone who competes in the games goes into strict training. They do it to get a crown that will not last; but we do it to get a crown that will last forever" (9:24–25, NIV). We do *it*? We do what? We go into strict training. Paul seems to have meant this quite literally, but the meaning of his words is often lost on modern readers. What is the strict training for Christians?

Paul lived in a time when it was commonplace for practitioners of all religions and ethical systems to be engaged in physical activities for the purpose of spiritual benefits. In the ancient Greek traditions this was usually understood to be an attempt to free the soul from the prison of the body. And this sort of attitude toward the body carried over into Gnostic Christian beliefs during the first few centuries after Christ. But it is a mistake to read Paul's "training" passages as anti-body in the Greek sense as some have done. The continuation of the 1 Corinthians 9 passage which reads, "I beat my body and make it my slave" in the NIV translation can be understood in the broader context of Paul's teaching to mean, "I discipline my body so that I am master over it." For even though Paul may sometime use "flesh" as a metaphor for sinful nature, most of the time it is used to designate "finite humanity" – an aspect of which is the "meat" out of which we are physically composed. And in this sense, the flesh could be trained to sustain good habits or bad habits. The reality of the situation is that in the fallen world, all people's flesh becomes accustomed to gratifying itself. So when the new creation comes about through the conversion process, it is still inhabiting or constituted by the flesh which had been trained in bad habits. Thus there is the conflict between the flesh and spirit that Paul describes so insightfully in the passages beginning at Romans 7:14 and Galatians 5:16.[11]

Paul's instructions, then, were for Christians to train their bodies in ways that will come to sustain positive habits. He doesn't spell this out explicitly, but he didn't have to because his readers were able to read between the lines when he used such language. Undoubtedly he had instructed the Christians he was with to use fasting and other forms of periodic abstinence, prayer, times of solitude and silence, and other disciplines in order to train themselves to be godly. In many of his letters there are passages in which he refers to the way they were taught to train themselves (e.g. Eph 4:22, Phil. 4:9, Col. 2:7, 2 Tim. 3:10). And even congregations he had not personally visited were referred to the "form of teaching to which you were entrusted" (Rom. 6:17), which would have conveyed the training message.

In emphasizing the training or work that Paul expected of the converts to Christianity, we have to be careful not to imply that he was somehow advocating a system of personal holiness that was earned by the things that a person could do. It was only the initiative of God through Christ which made it possible to escape the bondage of sin in people's lives. But Paul emphasized throughout all of his letters the responsibility that individuals had for doing the sorts of things that mature believers ought to be doing such that God would continue to work his grace in their lives. These two emphases are conjoined in his passage, "work out your own salvation with fear and trembling; for it is God who is at work in you" (Phil. 2:12–13).

Finally, it should be noted that Paul's concern for people to advance in becoming like Christ was not to get them holy enough to make it into heaven when they died. If that was the only concern, then God could certainly just zap them into such a state upon death. Instead, Paul is interested in bringing the kingdom of heaven to earth in accordance with the line from the Lord's Prayer, "thy kingdom come, thy will be done, on earth as it is in heaven." Recall the Jewish framework of thought that Saul the Pharisee was fighting for: a community that was purified and ready to inhabit the kingdom of God and to accept God's perfect rule. There is something like this going on in Paul's Christian theology when he argues that the Christians are to build up the body of Christ "until all of us come to the unity of the faith and of the knowledge of the Son of God, to maturity [*telos* again], to the measure of the full stature of Christ" (Eph. 4:13). He's not concerned with the Greek problem of humankind in which people's souls need to be freed from the tomb of their bodies; nor is he any longer conceiving the Jewish apocalyptic scenario that the righteous need to be freed from the oppression of the wicked. Rather, the plight of people is that they are not "in Christ" and need to be.[12] Only in this way would the struggle against the power structures of this world prove effective in seeing the kingdom of God spread while they were still waiting for the perfect enactment of that kingdom at the return of Christ.

CONCLUSION

Christian thought in the work of Paul is really an extension of his earlier Jewish thought. There is the new, and at some level unexpected, revelation of Jesus as the messiah. But this is not really a departure from the Jewish understanding of the way that God was dealing with people. Rather, Paul saw Jesus to be the fulfillment of the expectations from long ago that God had kept his part of the covenant he made with Abraham. The thinking of Christians in the generations to succeed Paul, however, did not remain so tightly linked to that Jewish frame of reference. This shift of Christian thought away from its Judaic moorings is the subject of the next chapter.

SUMMARY OF MAIN POINTS

1   Paul was a Jew from Tarsus who accepted Christianity after persecuting Christians as part of a hard-line sect within Judaism.
2   Paul's Christian thought retained an essentially Jewish character, but he accepted that Jesus was the long-awaited messiah who ushered in the end times.
3   Christ's resurrection was the definitive sign that he had been justified by God and that the last days had begun and would culminate with Christ's return.
4   All people – not just Jews – were able to share in the blessing inaugurated with Abraham and be resurrected to eternal life in the kingdom of God.
5   Christians in this life are to be conformed more and more to the likeness of Christ as they participate in spiritual training.

FOR FURTHER READING

Paul Barnett, *Paul: Missionary of Jesus* (Grand Rapids, MI: Eerdmans (2008). An accessible defense of Paul's continuity with the message of Jesus.

Jouette M. Bassler, *Navigating Paul: An Introduction to Key Theological Concepts* (Louisville, KY: Westminster John Knox Press, 2007). Detailed description of some central theological words and phrases in Paul's letters.

Wayne Meeks and John Fitzgerald, eds, *The Writings of St. Paul*, 2nd edition, (New York: W.W. Norton & Company, 2006). Contains annotated text of all of Paul's writings as well as a wealth of commentary from both ancient and modern writers.

E.P. Sanders, *Paul* (Oxford: Oxford University Press 1991). A brief introduction to the massive work that Sanders did on Paul and the development of the "new perspective."

N.T. Wright, *What Saint Paul Really Said* (Grand Rapids, MI: Eerdmans (1997)). An excellent short overview of the thought of Paul from the perspective of his historical Jewishness.

4

The break from Judaism

QUESTIONS TO BE ADDRESSED IN THIS CHAPTER

1   What did the first generation of Jewish Christians think should be done with Gentile converts?
2   What was the importance of the Council of Jerusalem?
3   How did New Testament writings after Paul describe salvation in regard to non-Jews?
4   What effect did the destruction of the temple have on Christian thought?

Jewish Christian believers did not easily accept Paul's claim that the blessing of God had been opened up to non-Jews with the coming of Christ. Even those Jewish Christians who acknowledged that God intended to save Gentiles through Christ struggled to know how to interact with Gentiles in ways that weren't offensive. Ultimately Christianity would go its own way and cease to be a sect of Judaism. But before that would happen there was a transition period when the first generation of Christians wrestled with the Jewishness of their allegiance to the Lordship of Christ.

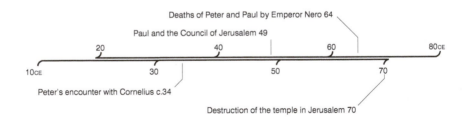

Timeline 4 The break from Judaism

1 WHAT TO DO WITH GENTILES

Immediately after the account of Paul's conversion and commissioning to the Gentiles, the Acts of the Apostles relates a fascinating story about the Apostle Peter – one of Jesus's closest companions. In the story, the author emphasizes again that the Gentiles had become eligible for participating in the salvation that God had provided for his people. Peter had been traveling around to smaller towns in the vicinity of Jerusalem, telling people the good news about Jesus and his resurrection. In the seaside town of Joppa, where he had reportedly raised a woman from the dead, he had a vision in which animals considered unclean by Jews were lowered in a sheet from heaven with instructions for him to eat. Being a law-observing Jew, he refused; but a voice from heaven reprimanded him, "Don't call anything impure that God has made clean" (Acts 10:15). While Peter was still puzzling over what this meant, he was approached by messengers from a God-fearing Gentile named Cornelius who lived about 40 miles up the coast in the town of Caesarea. Cornelius had a vision too. In it he was instructed to send for Peter in order that he might hear the good news.

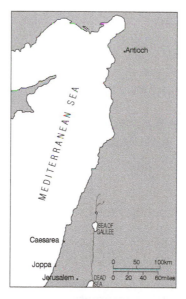

Map 4.1 Eastern Mediterranean region: first century CE

Not only were certain foods unacceptable for Jews to eat, they were not allowed to associate with "unclean" people – that is, people who did not follow the Jewish law. But then Peter understood that the point of his own vision was to prepare him for taking the good news to the house of this "unclean" Gentile. So, as the text indicates, he broke the Jewish law, went to Cornelius' house, and shared the story of Christ with the entire household. The Holy Spirit came to them just as it had to the Jews at Pentecost. This convinced Peter that these Gentiles could be baptized into the name of Christ. He reported the amazing event back to the Jewish believers in Jerusalem, and after their initial shock at his associating with Gentiles, they praised God saying, "So then, God has granted even the Gentiles repentance unto life" (Acts 11:18).

There seemed to be, then, general acceptance by the Jewish Christians that the message of Christ could go out to Gentiles. But what was expected of these Gentile believers? Should they convert to Judaism and follow the law? If not, how were the relations between Jewish Christians (who were following the law) and Gentile Christians to be negotiated? These were important questions, and their answers carried very significant practical implications for the early church.

In his letter to the Galatians, Paul said that he sought out the blessing of the apostles in Jerusalem for his mission to the Gentiles. These "pillars of the church," as Paul called them, were Peter, James (the brother of Jesus), and John. Paul said he was given their blessing to preach to the Gentiles, and was asked by them only to remember the poor in his mission (Gal. 2:9–10). This was a victory for Paul against the "Judaizers" – those who were putting pressure on male Gentile converts to Christianity to be circumcised like the Jews. There may have been some concern among the Judaizers that Gentile Christians would soon outnumber Jewish Christians. Forcing them to undergo circumcision would be a way to make conversion less attractive to Gentiles.[1]

Christianity was very attractive to a kind of Gentile referred to as "God-fearing." These God-fearing Greeks were often on the fringe of synagogue congregations, listening to the reading of the word and hearing the messianic hope that Jews had. They believed in the one God and may have even participated in worship. But generally they were unwilling to go through the ritual conversion required to become Jewish. Then they heard that the messiah had come and opened up the way for them too to be incorporated into the people of God. As

Paul had said, the distinction between Jew and Greek was eliminated in Christ.

But culture runs deep. For most Jewish Christians who had all their lives treated certain kinds of meat as unclean, sitting at the same table with Gentiles who ate it freely was more than they could stomach. In his encounter with Cornelius, Peter had crossed a line. Not only had he accepted Gentiles into the faith without requiring them to conform to the law, but also he himself seemed to regard his own observance of the law as optional by entering Cornelius' house.

It appears, however, that Peter later gave in to the pressure of those who maintained that continued observance of the law was necessary. Paul writes in Galatians 2 that he opposed Peter to his face in the city of Antioch because Peter had stopped eating with Gentile believers out of fear of what the Jewish Christians would think of him. It is clear at this point in the development of Christian thought that no general consensus had yet developed regarding the status of Gentile Christians in relation to Jewish law. In another letter, Paul himself would promote a kind of situational observance of customs according to the offense they might cause to others. He urged abstaining from practices contrary to the law if they would cause offense.[2] But in Antioch – one of Paul's significant home bases during his missionary journeys – the greater danger was the offense of clinging to an understanding of the Gospel that would impede its progress to the ends of the earth.

2 THE COUNCIL OF JERUSALEM

Sometime around the late 40s, Paul and his missionary partner Barnabas were staying in Antioch. They had been having a good deal of success in persuading Gentiles to convert to Christianity. Indeed, it was there that the followers of Christ were first called Christians – an appellation that probably would not have taken hold in a Jewish congregation. While they were still there, some other traveling Christian teachers came to town who were advocating circumcision for all male Gentile converts. This caused such sharp disagreement with Paul that the Antioch church commissioned him and Barnabas to go again to Jerusalem to discuss the issue with the apostles and elders there, and hopefully come to some resolution of the issue. The meeting that ensued has come to be known as the Council of Jerusalem.[3]

In Acts Chapter 15, the Council of Jerusalem is described as a public open forum among the Christians in Jerusalem, and it was presided over by James the brother of Jesus. The Judaizers comprised a vocal faction and argued that Christianity must be practiced by all from within the confines of the Jewish law. If their viewpoint had prevailed, it would have significantly altered the understanding of Christ's resurrection as the first fruits of the fulfillment of the covenant; but this is not the way things went. After much debate, Peter made a speech that sounds like repentance from the table manners attributed to him in Galatians 2. He claimed that through Christ there had come to be no distinction made between Jews and Gentiles in the eyes of God. So it would be silly to saddle Gentiles with requirements of the law that had proved to be unbearable for Jews and were not the means of salvation anyway.

Figure 4.1 Council of Jerusalem © Cologne Cathedral

Then Paul and Barnabas related the wonderful things that God had done through them among the Gentiles as evidence that God had indeed opened the blessing to them.

James, then, is portrayed as having the authority to make a ruling on the discussion that had occurred. In his speech he interpreted the prophet Amos as speaking of the time when the Gentiles would be admitted into the family of God. This appears to set things up in such a way that Gentiles would not be expected to conform to the law in order to share in the blessing. But then he gave a decision that sounds more like a compromise:

> Therefore I have reached the decision that we should not trouble those Gentiles who are turning to God, but we should write to them to abstain only from things polluted by idols and from fornication and from whatever has been strangled and from blood.
>
> (Acts 15:19–20)

A letter was drafted to this effect, and with the consent of the whole church in Jerusalem, a couple of the members of the Council along with Paul and Barnabas carried it back to Antioch. When the believers there heard the decision, it is reported that they were filled with joy. Undoubtedly circumcision was the big issue on their minds, and after escaping that, a few dietary restrictions and the prohibition against fornication seemed only small inconveniences. But why were these Jewish restrictions still included as "essential" observances for Gentile Christians?

The subsequent relations of Jewish and Gentile Christians would seem to suggest that there were two distinct things going on in this ruling. The first and foremost issue was whether the law was to be imposed on Gentile believers, and circumcision was the sign of this. So not requiring converts to be circumcised meant that they were not to be subject to the law as Peter urged in his speech. But whether or not there was an obligation to follow the law, there was still a significant cultural issue for Jews and Gentiles. These other "essentials" were aimed at having them get along with each other in mixed company, and even then the dietary regulations were highly circumstantial. After this episode we don't hear about the table rules any more, and in later letters Paul urges respect for others while maintaining freedom from certain Jewish requirements.[4]

The main take-away from the Council of Jerusalem, then, was that the rules of the covenant had changed. In Genesis 17, God's part of the covenant was to make Abraham the father of many nations and give the land of Canaan to him and his descendents; as for Abraham and his descendents, their part of the bargain was for all males to be set apart through circumcision as the symbol of their entrance into the covenant. But according to the Council of Jerusalem, that was no longer necessary. Peter and Paul's understanding of the covenant prevailed for Christianity: entrance into the covenant relationship with God was available to all who would acknowledge Christ as Lord and be baptized into his name. In a sense, then, Paul's very Jewish understanding of the gospel message undermined those who attempted to keep Christianity within the confines of Judaism.

3 LATER NEW TESTAMENT WRITERS

Not much is known about Christian thought for most of the next decade and a half after the Council of Jerusalem. Besides Paul's letters, few of the New Testament documents were written before the late 60s by the estimation of even the most conservative scholars. And these were tense days for Christians, as they faced persecution both from Jews who did not accept the messiahship of Jesus and from the Romans. The fourth century church historian Eusebius maintains that Peter and Paul were both martyred under Emperor Nero in Rome.[5] It is reasonable to date their deaths around 64.

A case can be made that Peter wrote the letters attributed to him just before his death. Of the two books in the New Testament bearing the name of Peter, the stronger case can be made for 1 Peter being authentic in its authorship. Some critical scholars claim it to be pseudonymous and written toward the end of the first century. But the events described in the letter fit well with the reign of Nero in the 60s and the references to the Christian church are consistent with what we know about it during that time. And in the second century, the Petrine authorship of 1 Peter was asserted by several of the church fathers.

The general theme of the letter is that Christians could have victory over the suffering they found themselves encountering. It is not entirely clear to whom Peter was speaking in his letter. The introductory paragraph says it is to the "exiles of the Dispersion" which leads us to believe his primary readers are Jews who had become Christians and who were living outside Israel. But much of the letter gives the impression that there are Gentiles being addressed as well. Determining who the audience was for 1 Peter is an important textual problem, but whether it was Jewish Christians or Gentile Christians, there are similar points to be made about the new rules of Christianity with respect to Judaism before the time of Christ. Consider the following passage:

> You know that you were ransomed from the futile ways inherited from your ancestors … with the precious blood of Christ. … Through him you have come to trust in God.
>
> (1 Peter 1:18–21)

If the "ancestors" he is talking about are the pagan Gentiles before the time of Christ, then the point is that the Gentiles now are able to participate in the kingdom of God because of the sacrifice of Christ. If the "ancestors" in this passage refers to Jews before the time of Christ, then the point is that the Jewish system was futile (which fits with his speech at the Council of Jerusalem) and had to be replaced with the new program under Christ. Either way, Peter affirms that the coming of Christ changed the old rules, and the way has been opened to all who will believe (2:6).

The Epistle to the Hebrews is unique among New Testament writings in that tradition does not ascribe a particular author to the letter. It is also uncertain whether it was written before or after the cataclysmic events in 70 to be discussed shortly. It is clear, though, that the audience is predominantly a Jewish one and that the central message is that there is now a new covenant which supersedes the covenant made between God and Israel which was only temporary. The writer argues from passages in the Old Testament that a time was coming when the sacrificial system of the Jews would no longer be needed. This would be a time when there would be a more permanent kingdom of rest which would no longer be at war with those around it. The only way this could happen, though, would be if the long-awaited messiah would be both priest and king – only a priest could deal with the sacrificial issue and only a king could rule. The problem with this happening, according to Jewish minds, was that priests had to come from the ancestral line of Levi, and kings had to come from the line of David (who was from the tribe of Judah). The writer of Hebrews notes, however, that priests from Levi would be just more of the same sort of priests who perpetuate the temporary system of sacrifices. There was another priest, however, who predated the entire Levitical line of priests, and had the authority based not on ancestry but on the call of God to the office. This was the sort of priest called for in the messianic prophesies from Psalm 110. And it is just this sort of priest that Jesus the Messiah had become. He was from the line of David, and so qualified for the role of King according to ancestry; his resurrection validated that the call of God was upon him to be the new priest; and his sacrifice on the cross put an end to all sacrifices for sin. There is a new covenant, then, that can be embraced by all people, and this is what the Old Testament had been pointing to all along. With the death and resurrection of Christ, the terms of the new covenant were enacted.

To readers today, the book of Revelation is one of the strangest in the Christian Bible. It is filled with apocalyptic imagery along with numbers and symbols that have been interpreted to represent all manner of things. Early church tradition attributes the book to John – the same John who supposedly wrote the Gospel of John; but this authorship has been debated for centuries. The book was probably written sometime in the 90s under the reign of Emperor Domitian.

Without getting bogged down in the details of the text, we can give a description of the main episodes of the book in broad strokes. It opens with a vision of Jesus Christ which very intentionally links him to the Son of Man spoken of in the Old Testament book of Daniel (7:13–14). He would be worshiped by people of all nations and his dominion would never end. Then after some messages that this Christ had for various Churches, the vision continues by showing a scroll that no one had been able to open. This scroll represents God's salvation plan and so the author weeps bitterly that it cannot be opened and enacted. But then he is told that someone has appeared who can accomplish the task. The Lion of the tribe of Judah, the great king from the line of David, has conquered death and so is worthy to open the scroll. In response, all sorts of creatures worship him:

> You are worthy to take the scroll and to open its seals, for you were slaughtered and by your blood you ransomed for God saints from every tribe and language and people and nation; you have made

HEBREWS 8

Now the main point in what we are saying is this: we have such a high priest, one who is seated at the right hand of the throne of the Majesty in the heavens, a minister in the sanctuary and the true tent that the Lord, and not any mortal, has set up. For every high priest is appointed to offer gifts and sacrifices; hence it is necessary for this priest also to have something to offer. Now if he were on earth, he would not be a priest at all, since there are priests who offer gifts according to the law. They offer worship in a sanctuary that is a sketch and shadow of the heavenly one; for Moses, when he was about to erect the tent, was warned, "See that you make everything according to the pattern that was shown you on the mountain." But Jesus has now obtained a more excellent ministry, and to that degree he is the mediator of a better covenant, which has been enacted through better promises. For if that first covenant had been faultless, there would have been no need to look for a second one.

God finds fault with them when he says: "The days are surely coming, says the Lord, when I will establish a new covenant with the house of Israel and with the house of Judah; not like the covenant that I made with their ancestors, on the day when I took them by the hand to lead them out of the land of Egypt; for they did not continue in my covenant, and so I had no concern for them, says the Lord. This is the covenant that I will make with the house of Israel after those days, says the Lord: I will put my laws in their minds, and write them on their hearts, and I will be their God, and they shall be my people. And they shall not teach one another or say to each other, 'Know the Lord,' for they shall all know me, from the least of them to the greatest. For I will be merciful towards their iniquities, and I will remember their sins no more." In speaking of "a new covenant," he has made the first one obsolete. And what is obsolete and growing old will soon disappear.

them to be a kingdom and priests serving our God, and they will reign on earth.

(Rev. 5:9–10)

John too understood that the salvation brought by Christ was for all people, not just for the Jews. And the kingdom to be established was not some far off heaven on a cloud, but a kingdom on earth where the ransomed would reign with Christ.

There are a lot of battles depicted through the middle chapters of the book which probably have some connection to the difficulties Christians had been having, and would have in increasing measure, with the Roman Empire (also known as the new Babylon). Then at the end of the book, a more detailed description is given of the coming kingdom, which again stands in stark contrast to the popular understanding of heaven according to later Christians (who were influenced by non-Jewish conceptions). Here was a heaven that came to earth, as in the Lord's Prayer, "Thy kingdom come on earth as it is in heaven":

Now the dwelling of God is with men, and he will live with them. They will be his people, and God himself will be with them and be their God. He will wipe every tear from their eyes. There will be no more death or mourning or crying or pain, for the old order of things has passed away.

(21:3–4)

We get some description, then, of streets of gold and pearly gates, but again, this is conceived as a real place into which the current order of things will be transformed. It is the "New Jerusalem" where the kingdom and rule of God is completely and permanently established. Despite this Jewish imagery, however, there is an unexpected revelation: "I saw no temple in the city, for its temple is the Lord God the Almighty and the Lamb" (21:22). No temple in the kingdom? It is hard to imagine Christianity persisting as a sect of Judaism without the temple. By the time Revelation was written, though, Christianity had gotten along fine without the temple for a couple of decades. For that matter, Judaism had too, because the temple had been destroyed. But as we'll see next, that event set Judaism and Christianity on very different paths.

EPISTLE OF BARNABAS

A late first century or early second century writing known as the Epistle of Barnabas was written against those who wanted to see Christianity continue in its Jewish traditions. The letter is cited by early church fathers, but was not included in the final collection that made up the New Testament. It gives another glimpse of Christian thought from the time period. This gives the author's opinion of the importance of the temple:

> I will also speak with you concerning the Temple, and show how the wretched men erred by putting their hope on the building, and not on the God who made them, and is the true house of God. For they consecrated him in the Temple almost like the heathen. But learn how the Lord speaks, in bringing it to naught, "Who has measured the heaven with a span, or the earth with his outstretched hand? Have not I?" saith the Lord. "Heaven is my throne, and the earth is my footstool, what house will ye build for me, or what is the place of my rest?" You know that their hope was vain.[6]

4 THE DESTRUCTION OF THE TEMPLE

Throughout the middle 60s the Romans had been clamping down on Jews who seemed not to give proper allegiance to the empire. Governors who had no sympathy for Judaism were sent to the region. They taxed the Jews excessively and watched impassively as rioters destroyed Jewish property and lives. By 66, the more radical Jewish groups, perhaps not unlike the one pre-conversion Saul belonged to, had enough and started to revolt. This prompted Emperor Vespasian and his son Titus to lay siege to Jerusalem. The temple was destroyed in 70. There is a fragment of text preserved by the fifth-century writer Sulpicius Severus – perhaps from a lost part of Tacitus's *Histories* – that recounts their motivation for destroying the temple. According to it, Titus (his father's military commander in the region) thought that,

> The temple should most certainly be demolished, in order that the Jewish and Christian religions might be the more completely wiped out; for although these religions were mutually hostile, they nevertheless shared the same origin; the Christians were an offshoot of the Jews, and if the root were destroyed the stock would quickly perish.[7]

Of course this action destroyed neither Judaism nor Christianity, but it had a tremendous influence on both, and most significantly for this account, on the relationship between the two.

Titus noted that Jews and Christians were already hostile toward each other. The destruction of the temple heightened that hostility. Later Christian writers would interpret the Roman aggression against the Jews in overtly anti-Jewish tones and as a vindication of Christianity over Judaism. Hippolytus, a Christian writer of the second and third centuries, gives his answer to why the temple was destroyed:

> Was it on account of that ancient fabrication of the calf? Was it on account of the idolatry of the people? Was it for the blood of the prophets? Was it for the adultery and fornication of Israel? By no means ... for in all these transgressions they always found pardon open to them, and benignity; but it was because they killed the Son of their Benefactor, for He is coeternal with the Father.[8]

Eusebius too interpreted the fall of Jerusalem as punishment from God against the Jews for "their crime against the Christ of God."[9]

For their part, Jews who had not recognized Jesus as messiah had lost the central tangible symbol of their faith. It was not the first time the temple had been destroyed, so there was some reason to hold faith that it would be restored again. But when that did not happen immediately, Judaism had to reconcile itself to life without this pillar of their existence. The destruction of the temple began the period for Jews called Rabbinic Judaism. Without the temple, priests also lost their role as intermediaries for the people with God. Instead, the Pharisees who had not participated in the Jewish revolt were given permission by the Romans to set up a rabbinical school. From this developed the tradition of commentary on the Jewish law (Talmud) which would become central to Judaism and so replace the geographical focus on the temple.[10] The dissemination of Rabbinic Judaism would take some time; it is an oversimplification to say that after the destruction of the temple all that was left was Rabbinic Judaism and Gentile Christianity. In time though, these became the two principal and separate heirs of Second Temple Judaism when that period ended in 70.

Immediately after the destruction of the temple, there was continued interchange between Jews, Jewish Christians, and Gentile Christians. The local synagogues, however, began adopting rules that precluded Gentile Christians, and then even Jewish Christians, from participation in worship. Such preclusion led Christians to take their message to groups that were further removed from Judaism than just the "God-fearing Greeks." Thus the background context or worldview of more and more Christians was that of the Roman Empire and the Greek ideas which permeated that dominant culture. The questions that were asked and the message that was framed came increasingly to take the shape of the belief system of the Roman Empire.

The Greek influence would push Christians to grapple more deeply with understanding the human and divine natures of Jesus. Furthermore, because the expected return of Christ to complete the establishment of his kingdom had not yet occurred, Christian ideas of eschatology shifted away from the Jewish ideas of Paul. Gentile Christians began to import notions of immortality that were more akin to the popular mystery cults than they were to the Jewish notion of eternal life in the kingdom.[11] And Christianity was broken free from the organization of temple and synagogue.

What would the liturgical celebration of the risen Christ look like in Christian worship? Since most of the apostles had died, how was their authority to be replaced? What would be the guide and guarantor of sound doctrine on these and other issues? Christian thinking was poised to move into a significant period of defining itself apart from Judaism. As we'll see in the next part, this happened through the development of creeds and its own canon of Scripture, as well as an organizational structure that would flourish in and come to define the culture around it.

SUMMARY OF MAIN POINTS

1   In the early years, there was no consensus about the need for Gentile conformity to the Jewish law.
2   According to the Council of Jerusalem, circumcision – and so adherence to the Jewish law – was not necessary for Gentile converts, but respect for cultural differences was expected.
3   Later New Testament writers affirmed universal significance of Christ's message.
4   The destruction of the temple escalated the emerging divergence of Christianity from Judaism.

FOR FURTHER READING

All of the books of the New Testament are relevant for understanding the development of Christian thought during the first few generations.

F.F. Bruce, *New Testament History* (New York: Doubleday, 1971). Gives a thorough and accessible account (with lots of references) of the Roman and Jewish context of the birth and first two generations of Christianity.
James Dunn, *The Parting of the Ways between Christianity and Judaism and their Significance for the Character of Christianity* (London: SCM Press, 1991). An extended study of the central issue of this chapter.
Josephus, *The Jewish War* (many published editions). The standard first century account of the war with the Romans and the siege of Jerusalem by this Jewish historian.
Oskar Skarsaune, *In the Shadow of the Temple: Jewish Influences on Early Christianity* (Downers Grove, IL: Intervarsity Press, 2002). This Norwegian scholar challenges much of the conventional wisdom of the enmity between Jews and Christians.

Part 2

Definition and resistance

The Patristic period 70–500

5

Persecution of Christians

QUESTIONS TO BE ADDRESSED IN THIS CHAPTER

1   Why were Christians persecuted in the early centuries after Christ?
2   How did Christians understand martyrdom?
3   How did the doctrine of the Church develop in response to the problem of apostasy?
4   What happened to the apocalyptic tendencies of the early Christians?

Because the separation of Christianity from Judaism became more apparent after the destruction of the temple in 70CE, the way was opened for the Roman Empire to treat Christians differently from how it treated Jews. Jews enjoyed comparative toleration from the empire for their religious beliefs, having the status of *religio licita*, or approved religion (as opposed to the "illicit" religions). Of course there was some persecution of Jews under the Roman Empire – for instance, all Jews were expelled from the city of Rome by Emperor Claudius in 49CE – and many of them were enslaved or killed by Roman officials. But such persecution was usually the result of revolts by certain Jewish factions. On the whole, the mainstream of Judaism had reconciled itself fairly well to Roman rule and was therefore tolerated by the Romans as a religion.

There are various reasons suggested for this.[1] One is that the sheer number of Jews in the empire – certainly a couple of million by then – made it dangerous to systematically persecute them. But also, their numbers were not dramatically rising and posing much of a threat to the political stability of the empire. Furthermore, the Jews were willing to incorporate into their daily temple rituals sacrifices for the Caesars and the Roman nation. And this is really what lies at the heart of Roman tolerance of Judaism and its persecution of Christianity: the Romans understood religion to be a contract with the gods – the gods would protect the Roman Empire from ruin so long as they were honored and sacrificed to in the proper ways. Christians would not sacrifice to Caesar, and for this they were considered disloyal and a political threat to the empire.

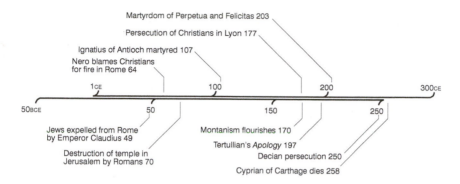

Timeline 5 Persecution of Christians

1 PERSECUTION OF CHRISTIANS

From what we can reconstruct through historical documents, the persecution of Christians was not an attempt to systematically eliminate all Christians from society. It was not the sort of genocide or ethnic (or better, religious) cleansing in which Roman soldiers dragged all the Christians out of their homes and marched them off to the amphitheater to be eaten by wild animals. There certainly were Christians who perished in this way, but there were many more who did not, and they were able to lead public lives as Christians. It is true that there was a consistent Imperial policy that Christians could be punished merely for holding to their religious scruples which forbade sacrificing to Caesar, but until the mid-third century those persecutions came about abruptly, more like mob violence, when the citizenry became especially angry with these traitors. This could be occasioned by about anything. The African church father Tertullian wrote his *Apology*, or defense, of Christianity to the Roman rulers around 197ce. In it he protests that,

> They think the Christians the cause of every public disaster, of every affliction with which the people are visited. If the Tiber rises as high as the city walls, if the Nile does not send its waters up over the fields, if the heavens give no rain, if there is an earthquake, if there is famine or pestilence, straightway the cry is, "Away with the Christians to the lion."[2]

TERTULLIAN

Tertullian (*c.* 155–230) lived in Carthage on the northern coast of Africa. He was an important defender of Christian faith and representative of the Latin speaking theologians of the western Roman Empire. Although he broke away from the Church to join a more rigorously ascetic sect, the Montanists, he remained very influential for Christian thinkers through the ages.

If natural disasters could justify persecution of Christians, what should be done to them in times of calm? When Pliny the Younger, the governor of Bithynia (in modern-day north central Turkey), asked Emperor Trajan what to do with the Christians around 115CE, Trajan answered that he need not seek them out nor go to arrest them on the evidence of anonymous informants. But if Christians were brought to him and would refuse to make the sacrifices to the official Roman gods, then they should be punished by death.[3]

Pliny referred to the Christians' "stubbornness and inflexible obstinacy" and their "depraved and enormous superstition;" he thought them to be afflicted with some sort of "madness." Such accusations seem to have at their root the fact that Christians would not go along with the sacrifices necessary for the good of the empire, and so were traitors of the empire. But there were other charges too. Ten years before Pliny's letter, the great historian Tacitus chronicled Nero's persecution of Christians for the great fire of 64CE in Rome (which Nero almost certainly instigated himself). In it he introduced Christians to his readers as "that class hated for their abominations." The word on the street was that they were atheists, cannibals, incestuous, and dangerously anti-family.

NERO AND THE CHRISTIANS

But all human efforts, all the lavish gifts of the emperor, and the propitiations of the gods, did not banish the sinister belief that the conflagration was the result of an order. Consequently, to get rid of the report, Nero fastened the guilt and inflicted the most exquisite tortures on a class hated for their abominations, called Christians by the populace. Christus, from whom the name had its origin, suffered the extreme penalty during the reign of Tiberius at the hands of one of our procurators, Pontius Pilatus, and a most mischievous superstition, thus checked for the moment, again broke out not only in Judaea, the first source of the evil, but even in Rome, where all things hideous and shameful from every part of the world find their centre and become popular. Accordingly, an arrest was first made of all who pleaded guilty; then, upon their information, an immense multitude was convicted, not so much of the crime of firing the city, as of hatred against mankind. Mockery of every sort was added to their deaths. Covered with the skins of beasts, they were torn by dogs and perished, or were nailed to crosses, or were doomed to the flames and burnt, to serve as a nightly illumination, when daylight had expired. Nero offered his gardens for the spectacle, and was exhibiting a show in the circus, while he mingled with the people in the dress of a charioteer or stood aloft on a car. Hence, even for criminals who deserved extreme and exemplary punishment, there arose a feeling of compassion; for it was not, as it seemed, for the public good, but to glut one man's cruelty, that they were being destroyed.

(Tacitus, *Annals*, XV.44)

The reality was that Christians could be reasonably charged with these "abominations" in relation to the accepted cultural norms of the day. The Romans had a list of officially approved gods, and the Christians would not acknowledge any of them; this made them atheists in the eyes of Romans, and thus they were considered to be a direct threat to the unity of the state. Christians were thought to be cannibals because it was rumored that they dined on the "body and blood" of their savior in secret ceremonies. And they engaged in something called "love feasts" (which, in the minds of the Romans could only be orgiastic) while calling each other "brother" and "sister." It doesn't take too much imagination to understand how such things could be misunderstood and misconstrued within a culture that was predisposed to hate and mistrust them.

Christians also undermined the rights accorded to a father and husband in Roman culture. Roman sons were prized far above daughters, and fathers had absolute authority over the lives of his children – born or unborn. The frequent practice of infanticide of girls led to a male to female ratio of 131 to 100 in the city of Rome, and even higher elsewhere.[4] In a letter dating from around 1BCE, a husband displays the casual attitude toward infanticide that was common at the time:

> Know that I am still in Alexandria. And do not worry if they all come back and I remain in Alexandria. I ask and beg you to take good care of our baby son, and as soon as I receive payment I shall send it up to you. If you are delivered of a child [before I come home], if it is a boy keep it, if a girl discard it. You have sent me word, "Don't forget me." How can I forget you? I beg you not to worry.[5]

Furthermore, husbands in Roman society were free to divorce their wives for any reason whatsoever – unwanted wives were merely sent away and consigned to a beggar's existence. Within marriage, fidelity was expected of women, but not of men. Husbands had sex with prostitutes and slaves without any moral condemnation at all.

The pervasiveness and acceptance of these practices in the Roman world (and before it, the Greek) seems almost inconceivable to us today. So too, then, was the effrontery of Christians who opposed and condemned these practices which were the norms and important elements of family life in the Roman context. Yet just such a challenge to the culture was found in the *Didache* – one of the earliest manuals of Christian practice.[6]

Furthermore, in contrast to their Roman counterparts, Christian husbands were taught to practice fidelity within their marriages and were expected not to divorce their wives.[7] This further opposed the rights of Roman fathers and "undermined" their concept of family.

Assuming there to be something inherently wrong with treating one's wife with callous disrespect and with leaving newborn children to die of exposure because of their gender, it is easy to see that the Romans would be threatened by Christians on moral grounds. These Christians acted as a kind of pang to the conscience. In Tertullian's *Apology* it is claimed that Christians' virtuousness stood in such stark relief to the Romans' vice that the Romans' shame manifested itself as hatred toward Christians:

> But it is mainly the deeds of a love so noble that lead many to put a brand upon us. *See*, they say, *how they love one another*, for themselves are animated by mutual hatred; how they are ready even to die for one another, for they themselves will sooner put to death. And they are wroth with us, too, because we call each other brethren; for no other reason, as I think, than because among themselves names of consanguinity are assumed in mere pretence of affection. But we are your brethren as well, by the law of our common mother nature, though you are hardly men, because brothers so unkind.[8]

Christians stood out in Roman culture and were hated because of their beliefs, practices, and values. Not only did they love each other, but they were even instructed to love their enemies. And in those days it was not difficult for them to identify their enemies.

2 MARTYRDOM

Tertullian's *Apology* may have sounded rather contentious and even scathing to its intended audience – though there is no evidence that the Roman rulers to whom it was addressed ever responded to or even read the work. The more general attitude of the Christians to their persecutors, however, did not display bitterness or malevolence. The accounts we have of Christians being persecuted are set in an apocalyptic framework, and they see their struggle as being against Satan – not merely their Roman persecutors. The command to love their enemies cannot sufficiently explain Christians' attitudes toward suffering; instead we must look also at their conception of martyrdom.

The attitude taken toward martyrdom by the Christians of the first few centuries was a conscious continuation of the attitudes of Jesus and Paul. Jesus said that he would acknowledge before God those who acknowledge him before men, but disown those who disowned him before men (Matthew 10:32–33). This teaching was manifestly before the minds of those who were being asked to sacrifice to other gods or face torture and death. It would be an act of disowning Christ to toss the incense before the foreign gods. And by acknowledging that only Christ is Lord before the Roman executor, they were guaranteeing their place in glory with Christ for eternity. As the Apostle Paul said, "We are heirs – heirs of God and co-heirs with Christ, if indeed we share in his sufferings in order that we may also share in his glory" (Romans 8:17). After the Church had endured a couple of centuries of persecution, Origen would call martyrdom the "cup of salvation" and see it as the most perfect gift that a person could give back to God for all that was done for him or her.[9]

With this desire to share in the glory of Christ, Ignatius of Antioch was martyred sometime early in the second century. According to tradition, he was appointed Bishop of Antioch by the Apostle Peter himself and was a disciple of the Apostle John. At any rate, he was one of the group that has come to be known as the "apostolic fathers" on account of his proximity to the first followers of Jesus. Ignatius was arrested in Antioch during the reign of Emperor Trajan and condemned to die in the Colosseum at Rome. While guards were escorting him to Rome, delegates from five of the area churches came to see him and provided him with provisions for his journey and a sincere farewell into the grace of God. Later on the journey Ignatius wrote letters to these congregations, as well as to the congregation in Rome whom he would be meeting soon, and another to Polycarp, the Bishop of Smyrna. These seven letters have been preserved and provide considerable insight into the thought of the early Christians.

Understandably, letters from someone on his way to be devoured by wild beasts in the amphitheater are concerned with death and suffering. In his letter to the Roman congregation, Ignatius pleads with them not to interfere with the martyrdom that is to be his, because he sees in martyrdom the chance to attain to true life and the imitation of Christ. Here too we see an inversion of accepted values. To Ignatius, it is *death* to continue living and *life* to die:

THE APOSTOLIC FATHERS

The apostolic fathers do not refer to people as much as to writings or collections of writings. The title has been used because their authors – some of whom are unknown to us now – were presumed to have had personal contact with the original apostles of Christ. Generally accepted today as constituting the apostolic fathers are the following:

- The Epistles of Clement of Rome
- The *Didache*
- The Epistles of Ignatius of Antioch
- The *Epistle of Polycarp*
- Writings of Papias of Hierapolis
- The *Epistle of Barnabas*
- The *Shepherd of Hermias*
- The *Epistle to Diognetus*

The pangs of a new birth are upon me. Bear with me, brethren. Do not hinder me from living; do not desire my death ... Suffer me to receive the pure light. When I am come thither, then shall I be a man. Permit me to be an imitator of the passion of my God.[10]

Here, then, seems to be the central meaning and insight into martyrdom for these believers: the imitation of and identification with Christ. Irenaeus, who was the second Bishop of Lyons, would characterize people like Ignatius as "those who strive to follow the footprints of the Lord's Passion."[11] Martyrdom was not something that was to be stoically accepted if one happened to be in the wrong place at the wrong time; rather it was to be sought after and treasured.

Irenaeus was the second Bishop of Lyons because the first bishop there, Ponthinus, was martyred during a significant outbreak of persecution and killing around 177CE during the reign of Emperor Marcus Aurelius. A report of this was written by one of the Christians who did survive, and was sent to the churches in Asia. Most of that letter was preserved in the important *Ecclesiastical History* written by Eusebius in the fourth century. Ponthinus was over 90 years old, but the governor had him dragged about, beaten, and then thrown back into his prison cell where he died two days later.

The story of Blandina, a Christian slave woman who suffered during the Lyons persecution, is particularly noteworthy. It is recorded that she received all manner of beatings that left her body "broken and open" and should have extinguished her life. But she kept gaining in vigor and kept confessing, "I am a Christian woman and nothing wicked happens among us."[12] Then she was hanged on a stake to be devoured by wild animals in the midst of a gladiatorial contest (in which several other Christians were martyred), but the animals would not touch her. She became in her imitation of Christ a great source of strength to the others who were perishing:

> She seemed to be hanging in the shape of a cross, and by her continuous prayer gave great zeal to the combatants, while they looked on during the contest, and with their outward eyes saw in the form of their sister him who was crucified for them, to persuade those who believe on him that all who suffer for the glory of Christ have for ever fellowship with the living God.[13]

After more tortures, then, she was put into a net and thrown to a bull to be mauled until she was completely senseless, and she finally died. The non-Christians themselves marveled that she suffered so much and so long.

The account of the martyrdom of Perpetua and Felicitas, an African Christian and her slave girl, is also worth mentioning. Their deaths occurred in 203 in Carthage under the reign of Emperor Septimus Severus, who seemed to be trying to dissuade converts to Christianity by persecuting the catechumens (those undergoing training in the faith) like these two women. Perpetua kept a diary while she was in prison awaiting her execution. This is the oldest surviving Christian writing known to have been penned by a female, and it records her resoluteness in facing death even against the angry entreaties of her father to renounce her faith and live. She was flogged, torn apart by wild animals, and then beheaded. Felicitas was pregnant and had a difficult childbirth while in prison. One of the guards wondered that if she had difficulty with that, how would she handle being thrown to the beasts? Felicitas answered, "Now I suffer what I suffer: but then Another will be in me who will suffer for me, because I too am to suffer for him."[14]

Martyrs such as these were granted to be part of a special class of Christians who powerfully imitated and identified with Christ. Of course

Figure 5.1 Perpetua and Felicitas © Br. Robert Lentz/Trinity Stores

one did not need to be a martyr in order to achieve heaven, but Cyprian, a church father of the third century, would claim that the honors and rewards were more easily attained through martyrdom.[15]

3 APOSTASY AND THE CHURCH

In many of the accounts we have of martyrs who stood firm in their commitment to Christ and suffered the ultimate punishment, it is also mentioned that there were Christians who did not remain true to their faith. The "confessors" (those who did remain true) wrestled with what to do with these "lapsed Christians," especially when the latter wanted to return to fellowship with the Church. This crisis reached its peak after the most systematic and comprehensive persecution the empire had seen during the reign of Emperor Decius in 250 and 251. Decius was installed as emperor in November of 249 after battling and defeating Emperor Philip. Decius pledged to restore Rome to its traditional values, and in January of 250, issued an edict that required everyone in the empire to sacrifice to Jupiter and the other Roman gods for the good of the empire. To enforce this edict, each city formed a commission to issue a certificate called a *libellus* to those who performed the sacrifice. People who were found without the *libellus* and who would not immediately perform the sacrifice were sentenced to death.

It is not clear that Decius was specifically targeting Christians as much as all those who were "disloyal" to the empire; still, he undoubtedly understood that Christians would not find his edict easy to comply with. And it appears that he was correct. Large numbers of Christians, who had enjoyed about fifty years of relative peace in the empire, caved in and performed the commanded rituals – which even included eating meat that was sacrificed to the gods. Euctemon, the Bishop of Smyrna in Asia Minor, is said to have led his entire congregation to the pagan temple to comply with the order! Other Christians obtained a *libellus* without making the sacrifice from corrupt commissioners who could be bribed. These Christians came to be called *libellatici* in distinction to the *sacrificati* who actually made the sacrifices. The reign of Decius – and also this policy – ended in June of 251 when he was killed in battle.

In 252 a terrible plague broke out which accelerated the problem of what to do about the lapsed Christians. The reality of the plague brought to the lapsed Christians an understanding that this time the potential deaths they were facing could not be escaped by uttering a few "harmless" words – words which happened to repudiate their faith. So they were confronted with what might happen to them when they died, and their "faith" returned. But would the Church accept them? This was a new and important question. The basis for inclusion in the Church to this point had been belief in the teachings and baptism. Now, these lapsed Christians came back to the Church professing the creed and having been baptized (or they were willing to be rebaptized if required to do so). But not all would agree that they should merely be readmitted. A new criterion for acceptance within the Church was needed. All that is missing here for a good controversy are a couple of strong personalities. Enter Cyprian of Carthage and Novatian of Rome.

Fabian, the Bishop of Rome, was martyred under the Decian persecution in 250. Before his death he identified two men as his potential successors: Cornelius and Novatian. Novatian was probably the more gifted leader of the two, but Cornelius won the election because he had adopted a liberal policy of forgiveness for the lapsed (and there were many of them). This greatly upset the hard-line Novatian, and it didn't take long for many of Novatian's supporters (which included a good number of confessors) to recognize him as Bishop of Rome. Novatian accepted this position and sought support for his rule from the very influential Cyprian.

Cyprian of Carthage was born in the early third century and did not convert to Christianity until he was well over 40 years old. But he quickly became popular with the Christians in the important city of Carthage, and he was elected bishop just before the Decian persecution. Rather than leading his flock into apostasy or facing martyrdom, he fled to the desert where he hid and communicated with the Christians via letters.

Cyprian had a good deal of influence over the Church in the West and wanted to lead people correctly with regard to the controversy in Rome. He investigated the claims of Novatian and while sympathizing with the more rigorist approach to the lapsed, he decided that because Cornelius had been properly elected, the latter should be recognized as bishop. This angered Novatian who appointed a new bishop in Carthage, and many of the hardliners there accepted the rival to Cyprian. Thus there emerged two parallel churches in Rome and Carthage. Cyprian called a synod of bishops to try to resolve this schism and wrote his important work, "On the Unity of the Church."

In this work we find articulated and defended the position which would come to hold sway, namely that the principle of acceptance or unity is to be found in the Church itself – not in belief or creed that could be debated back and forth. Furthermore, the Church is held together by the bishops who have been officially appointed to the episcopate. What this means is that anyone who rebels against the bishop is rebelling against the Church and the Christian faith. Cyprian said, "He can no longer have God for his father, who has not the Church for his mother."[16] Therefore, if the officially appointed bishop accepted you into the Church, you were in; if he did not, you had no hope of salvation.

Many of the congregations who had initially followed Novatian did return to the "orthodox" catholic church (though references to Novatian congregations are found as late as the seventh century). Cyprian's influence led also to wide acceptance of a middle way with regard to the lapsed. He taught (and urged other bishops to accept) that the *libellatici* could be readmitted to the Church if they did penance. The more seriously apostate *sacrificati* could only be readmitted to fellowship with the Church on their deathbeds after doing penance all their lives – or by proving themselves faithful during another wave of persecution. Those who held office in the Church but lapsed during the persecution could be admitted back into the church, but could no longer hold office. And finally Cyprian taught that those heretics who broke away from the Church through schism (that is, leaving over a dispute and starting their own church) ought to be excommunicated.

In response to the problem of apostasy, Cyprian is to be credited with raising the power and authority of the Church to the point where it could be asserted, "there is no salvation outside of the Church."[17]

4 ESCHATOLOGY

The formation of this doctrine of the Church was a decisive moment in the history of Christian thought. It provided greater impetus for the institutionalization of the Church. But it was not the only contributing factor. Another force involved the changing views on eschatology (theory of the last days). Indeed it might be claimed that all of Christian thought in the first few generations had at its basis the apocalyptic vision of a soon returning messiah.[18] Certainly the persecution that the Christians faced was easy to interpret through apocalyptic lenses, especially early in its existence. But as the years went on and the Parousia continued to be delayed, the Church needed an organizational structure to survive from generation to generation. But there were some who resisted attempts at institutional organization.

In the middle of the second century a movement known as Montanism had resisted an elaborate formal organization of the Church based on its

PAROUSIA

From the Greek *parousía*, being present; the Second Coming of Jesus Christ.

apocalyptic understanding of the faith. Its founder, Montanus, believed that the return of Christ was at hand, and rather than adapting the structure of the Church in order to become a more stable and permanent institution, he taught that what was needed was a stricter moral code and a tightening of the Church's expectations in order to prepare Christians for the Holy Spirit. Tertullian himself became enamored with this rigorist sect later in life, and most of what we know of the Montanists comes through him and the records of Eusebius.

Montanus taught that he and two prophetesses, Priscilla and Maximilla, were the conduits of the final revelation of God to people. After them, there would be no more. These were the last days, and the culmination of all human history would be happening shortly. The New Jerusalem would be installed in the Phrygian countryside of Asia Minor, and Christians were encouraged to seek martyrdom. In this vein, Tertullian records that all the Christians of one province presented themselves to the Roman official demanding to be executed for their faith. The Roman official responded that if they wanted to kill themselves they could go jump off the cliffs![19]

The Montanists were but one group of early Christians whose thought was organized explicitly around the expectation of the imminent return of Christ. When this did not come about, the hopes of many within the Church for the quick end of all things began to fade, and there was more willingness to adopt formal organizational structures.[20]

Although there continued to be apocalyptic predictions all throughout the history of the Church up to the present day, the focus of mainstream eschatology shifted away from the present reality of the end of all things, to the future hope of glory. There remained, however, the belief that the kingdom of God had already broken into the order of things in the present life with the first coming of Christ. It was not enacted in its full form, but the kingdom was present in those who had submitted to the will of God. This "already, but not yet" approach to eschatology has persisted in Christian thought with remarkable consistency.

It seemed the Church would have to survive on earth indefinitely without the second coming of Christ. And survive it did, but the events that were to occur in the political arena of the empire would give the Church a very different shape.

SUMMARY OF MAIN POINTS

1   Christians' beliefs, practices, and values stood at odds with Roman culture; this created significant tension and led to persecution.
2   Martyrdom was believed by many to be the perfect imitation of Christ.
3   Membership in the Church – not belief or faith – determined one's eligibility for salvation.
4   The "already, not yet" eschatological attitude developed in response to the delayed Parousia.

FOR FURTHER READING

Brian Daley, *The Hope of the Early Church: A Handbook of Patristic Eschatology* (Peabody, MA: Hendrickson Publishers, 2003). A catalog of the eschatological positions of all the major figures in the early Church.

Ivor J. Davidson, *The Birth of the Church* (Grand Rapids, MI: Baker Books, 2004). The first volume of a new history of the Church covering the years 30–312.

Bart Ehrman, *The Apostolic Fathers I and II* (Cambridge, MA: Harvard University Press, 2003). A dual-language edition of all the texts of the apostolic fathers.

W.H.C. Frend, *Martyrdom and Persecution in the Early Church* (New York: New York University Press, 1967). A comprehensive account of the major persecutions of Christians in Roman times.

6
Spirituality and asceticism
The desert fathers and mothers

QUESTIONS TO BE ADDRESSED IN THIS CHAPTER

1 Why did Christian men and women move to the desert in the fourth and fifth centuries?
2 What did these ascetics take to be the role of the body in spiritual formation?
3 What was the Eastern emphasis on theosis and how was this achieved?
4 How did ascetic practices influence Christian thought?
5 What happened to the desert fathers and mothers?

1 MOVING TO THE DESERT

In the year 312, on 28 October, Constantine found himself in a decisive battle against Maxentius, a rival to the imperial throne. Constantine's father, Constantius, had been one of the four rulers of Rome (known as the Tetrarchy) which was established in 293 in order to rule the affairs of the expansive empire more efficiently. When Constantius died in 306, his troops declared Constantine to be his replacement. Another of the four rulers, Galerius, saw things differently and named Severus to the open post. And Maxentius, the son of a previous Tetrarch, Maximian, thought he himself should not have been passed over.

There were attempts to resolve this uneasy state of affairs diplomatically, but ultimately military conflict ensued. Constantine brought his army to Rome. Maxentius chose to engage Constantine in front of the Milvian Bridge before he could cross the Tiber River and enter Rome. But Maxentius incurred heavy losses in the battle and turned to retreat across the bridge and into the city. The bridge collapsed and Maxentius was found among the drowned.

Some years later Emperor Constantine related the story to the church historian Eusebius, who chronicled it in his panegyric, *Life of Constantine*. Constantine claimed that at about noon on that day at the bridge, a vision appeared to him: "A cross of light in the heavens, above the sun, and

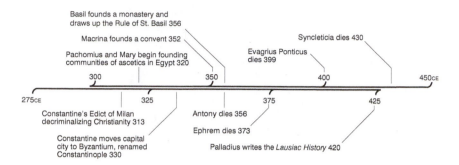

Timeline 6 Spirituality and asceticism

bearing the inscription, Conquer by this, *In hoc signo vinces*."[1] The phrase became the battle cry, and Constantine had the Chi Rho symbol – ☧ the first two letters of "Christ" in Greek – displayed on standards, shields, and helmets. He won the day and the imperial throne.

The following year, Constantine issued the Edict of Milan, which decriminalized Christianity throughout the empire and returned the confiscated property of Christians. It was not yet the "official" religion of the empire (that didn't happen until the end of the fourth century under Theodosius I), but the fortunes of the fledgling new religion appeared to be changing. Not all Christians thought the changes were for the better.

It is true that Christians could now assemble publicly without fear of persecution. They could build churches and enter into civic life. In short, the way was opened for the Church to become an institution within the Roman Empire. But while this might have been a boon to the respectability of Christians in the eyes of the world around them, and was even thought by some to be a step toward the establishment of the kingdom of God on earth, many saw the Romanization of Christianity as an inhibitor to the real purpose of Christ, namely, to make people holy. So, many of this latter group quit society and removed themselves to the desert to seek out those who had adopted solitary lifestyles there. Whom did they find in the desert? What were the beliefs that drove them there? What kinds of beliefs were formed as a result of living and worshiping in such an environment?

Figure 6.1 St. Antony. Giovanni di Nicola da Pisa/Public domain/Wikimedia Commons.

2 ASCETICISM AND THE BODY

Among the earliest and certainly the most famous of the desert dwellers was Antony (*c.* 251–356). He is reputed by Athanasius, his biographer, to have lived to the age of 105 – most of which was spent in solitude in the Egyptian desert. At about the age of 20 he was drawn to the ascetic life upon hearing a sermon on the text, "If you wish to be perfect, go sell all your possessions, and give the money to the poor" (Matthew 19:21). Antony obeyed the directive and sought mentoring from the spiritual men of his village – Heraclea – and by others in the surrounding area. Not long after this he went into the desert and secluded himself in a fort about fifty miles west of Alexandria. There he lived for twenty years in almost complete solitude, engaging in spiritual disciplines like all night prayer vigils, fasting, and sleeping on the ground.

There is a popular misunderstanding that these disciplines were undertaken by ascetics as means of punishing or mortifying their bodies – as though that were the goal. Of course we can find examples of ridiculous extremes that were taken by some (these are the stories that tend to be repeated), and there is no doubt that something akin to athletic competition and the drive to outdo each other was present to some degree. But most of the ascetics pursued their lifestyles for the same reason that set Antony on his path: the goal of spiritual perfection. The disciplines were seen as means to that end and pursued only as intermediate steps toward purity of heart. Abba Moses (330–405, also known as Moses the Black), a well-known desert father, said, "Solitude, watches in the night, manual labour, nakedness, reading and the other disciplines – we know that their purpose is to free the heart from injury by bodily passions and to keep it free; they are to be the rungs of a ladder up which it may climb to perfect charity."[2]

ABBA MOSES ON THE GOAL OF LIFE

The ultimate goal of our way of life is, as I said, the kingdom of God, or kingdom of heaven. The immediate aim is purity of heart. For without purity of heart none can enter into that kingdom. We should fix our gaze on this target, and walk towards it in as straight a line as possible. If our thoughts wander away from it even a little, we should bring back our gaze towards it, and use it as a kind of test, which at once brings all our efforts back onto the one path … It is for this end – to keep our hearts continually pure – that we do and endure everything, that we spurn parents and home and position and wealth and comfort and every earthly pleasure. If we do not keep this mark continually before the eyes, all our travail will be futile waste that wins nothing, and will stir up in us a chaos of ideas instead of singlemindedness.

(Abba Moses in Cassian's *Conferences*, §1.6)

Antony and the other *abbas* and *ammas* (the Aramaic words for "fathers" and "mothers," as the denizens of the desert were often called) of the desert understood their physical bodies to be part and parcel of the spiritual quest. Their bodies brought with them desires, passions, and habits that had to be overcome on the way to purity of heart. But also, once trained properly, the body could become the carrier of positive habits which would sustain the soul. So the purpose of asceticism was not to punish the body, nor was it to make oneself holy or to curry favor with God by means of works. Rather, their disciplines were very intentionally aimed at restoring human nature to what it ought to be. These physical activities were designed to remove the obstacles that their corrupted human nature had placed in the way so that the Holy Spirit would penetrate to their core being.[3]

In this vein, J. Heinrich Arnold, something of a twentieth century version of a desert monk, said, "Christian discipleship is not a question of our own doing, it is a matter of making room for God so that he can live in us."[4] Those who went to the desert did so with the intention of making room in their lives so that God might truly live in them, that their spirits might truly be awakened.

One of our chief sources of material about the desert fathers and mothers comes from Evagrius Ponticus (345–399), an eyewitness to their activities. In 330 Constantine moved the capital of the empire from Rome to the city of Byzantium and renamed it Constantinople – modern day Istanbul. As a result, the city grew in size and stature, and with this came the pressures and temptations of a big city. The ubiquitous greed, lust, gluttony, and sloth finally became too much for Evagrius to bear. So this highly educated churchman left the city and went to a monastery in Jerusalem, and then to the Egyptian desert to join a community of monks. He spent at least fourteen years there pursuing a holy life and writing down much of what he saw and learned. He was able to bring his theologically astute mind to bear on the experiences he had as an ascetic and more clearly form a theology of the desert.

Evagrius too believed that there are impediments to the holy life, and that these manifest themselves in the form of passions or evil thoughts which disturb the soul. We have no control over whether the thoughts arise in us, but we do have control over whether they are allowed to linger in us and arouse passions. It is passionlessness, or *apatheia,* which is the goal of the disciple so that one can achieve a kind of purity of heart

THE EIGHT EVIL PASSIONS OF EVAGRIUS

First is that of gluttony;

And with it, sexual immorality;

Third, love of money;

Fourth, sadness;

Fifth, anger;

Sixth acedia (listlessness, boredom);

Seventh, vainglory;

Eighth, pride.

Whether these thoughts are able to disturb the soul or not is not up to us; but whether they linger or not, and whether they arouse passions or not; that is up to us.

(Evagrius, *Praktikos*, §6)

which is free of all earthly desires. This freedom from desires is achieved by spiritual disciplines like reading, vigils (depriving oneself of sleep), prayer, fasting, work, solitude, singing Psalms, patient endurance, and showing mercy.[5] Here again we see the connection between the physical and the spiritual. Evagrius understood the body to be the training ground for the spirit: when the spirit can demonstrate its mastery over the normal bodily desires, it is strong enough to withstand the temptations that would inhibit the spiritual growth. The body is not to be despised in this. Evagrius says,

> Our holy teacher, who was very experienced in the ascetical life said, "The monk ought always to be ready as if he were to die tomorrow, but at the same time he should use his body as if he were going to live with it for many years to come. The first approach cuts back the thoughts of listlessness and makes the monk more zealous, while the second preserves the body and keeps its self-control balanced.[6]

One of the disciples of Evagrius was Palladius (born *c.* 364). After spending many years in various desert locations he wrote the *Lausiac*

History (c. 420), a kind of encyclopedia of holy people he met during travels through the desert – not only in Egypt, but also in Syria, Palestine, and Asia Minor. One of the more striking features in reading through the work is the number of women that are included. Many of the contemporary surveys of Christian thought or Church history that include any treatment of the desert movement barely mention that women participated in the movement. From Palladius's work, however, we can estimate that there were more women than men who took to the desert either as solitary hermits or (more often) to live in ascetic communities. Their contribution to desert spirituality and to the theology which developed in response to desert experiences has been under-appreciated for much of the history of the church. Recently there has been scholarship revealing the influence of women, but their story has yet to be woven into the grander narrative of the history of Christian thought in proper proportion.

Amma Syncletica was born sometime not too long before 350 and lived to around 430. She was a kind of female counterpart to Antony in the reverence given to her and the degree to which she was upheld as an example. A *Life* was written (by someone claiming to be Athanasius – imitating the author of Antony's *Life*) commemorating Syncletica in the fifth century and preserved by the church. As with many of the women who moved to the desert, she was born into a relatively well-to-do family. But when her two brothers and parents died, she sold all that the family possessed and moved outside Alexandria with her blind sister to the family tomb and began her life as an ascetic. Contrary to her desires, a great many women started coming to her for instruction and training about the spiritual life.

Asceticism for Syncletica was the means of being shaped into what God would have people become – a process that was not easy or quick. She instructed those who would come to the ascetic life,

> In the beginning there are a great many battles and a good deal of suffering for those who are advancing towards God and, afterwards, ineffable joy. It is like those who wish to light a fire. At first they are choked with smoke and cry, until they obtain what they seek.[7]

Desert ascetics understood a significant part of their battles to be with demons – demons who would plant impure thoughts, who might bring feelings of inferiority or pride, and who might even be the cause of

Figure 6.2 Desert mothers © The HTM

physical pain. But most of all, the demons stood as an obstacle between the ascetic and union with God. For this is what was desired above all. Syncletica noted that as one advanced in spiritual maturity, the battles became ever stronger, "Those who are great athletes must contend against stronger enemies."[8]

Many of these battles were solitary affairs, but this was not the only mode of desert habitation. Sometime around 320, a former pagan soldier who had become a Christian and lived for several years as an isolated desert monk, felt a calling to bring these isolated monks together to live in community. Pachomius is now revered as the father of cenobitic, or communal, monasticism. He founded a monastery on an island in the Nile River where several hundred men came to live under a common rule and the authority of a superior. Their lives were spent in work, private meditation, and common meals and worship. Pachomius's sister Mary

> It is dangerous for someone not 'formed' by experience of the ascetic life to try to teach; it is as if someone whose house is unsound were to receive guests and cause them injury by the collapse of the building. ... For the mere articulation of words is like the inscriptions painted in perishable colours which a very short period of time has destroyed with blasts of wind and splashes of rain. Teaching that is based on ascetic experience, on the other hand, not even all eternity could destroy. By chiseling away the rough edges of the soul, the spoken word bestows on the faithful Christ's everlasting image done in stone.
>
> (*The Life of Blessed Syncletica*, v. 79.50)

became the head of a women's monastery which was located right across the river. By the generation after his death (*c.* 348), there were thousands of monasteries for women and men all over Egypt populated by those who were seeking an alternative to the city life in which the Christian faith was being transformed into a public institution. The monks were seeking something more from Christianity, something less superficial. They were seeking to become like God.

3 THEOSIS AND THE CAPPADOCIANS

Divinization, or *theosis,* was a major theme of the desert. Athanasius's famous quote about Christ, "He was made man that we might be made God,"[9] is typical and reflective of this desert culture. The doctrine of *theosis* – becoming divine – is more pronounced in the Christianity and desert ascetics of the East than the West. In the eastern part of the empire there was more of an emphasis put on the contribution that people make to their on-going spiritual development; being a Christian was seen as a process, rather than a state that one entered into. The theologians of the East took the words of 2 Peter 1:4–5 as a framework for their understanding of the Christian life, "Thus he has given us, through these things, his precious and very great promises, so that through them you may escape from the corruption that is in the world because of lust, and may become participants of the divine nature. For this very reason, you must make every effort. ..." This passage provided a statement of the current state of affairs, of the possibility for the future, and some indication of the method for attaining that future. First, there is corruption in the world due to lust; second, they may escape this corruption and become participants in the nature of the divine; and finally, there is effort required of them to achieve these things.

Some of the best exemplars of the theology of the East during the fourth and fifth centuries are found in the Cappadocian fathers and their sister, Macrina. The region of Cappadocia was in Asia Minor in what now is eastern Turkey, and is perhaps most famous for its underground cities which can still be seen today – huge multi-story labyrinths cut into the earth and used as protection against invaders.

Macrina (c. 324–380) was the eldest of ten children from a family of local landed aristocracy, already Christian for two generations. Two of her brothers became known to church history as Gregory of Nyssa and Basil of Caesarea. These two, together with a close family friend, Gregory of Nazianzen, are now known as the Cappadocian fathers. They were prolific and influential writers during the latter part of the fourth century. Very little is generally reported about how influential the life and thought of Macrina was to them.

Macrina was said (by her brother!) to be the most beautiful maiden in the land and was pledged to be married to a young suitor who had impressed her father, but before the wedding he unexpectedly died. Macrina would not take another as her husband. Instead she founded a convent on her family's estate in 352 where she lived out her days with other family members and dependants, pursuing a life of holiness and instructing others in the ascetic way. She had a great influence on her brother Basil, who stayed with her for a time, convincing him of the futility of worldly pursuits. Most of what we know about her comes from her brother Gregory, who obviously held her in very high esteem and wrote a *Life* of her which was preserved and revered by the church.

Gregory also wrote a dialogue called, "On the Soul and the Resurrection," which purports to record the last conversation he had with his sister Macrina while she was on her deathbed. There is little doubt that the dialogue contains much that is not part of that historical conversation, but it is remarkable nonetheless that Gregory assigns to Macrina the role of the wise teacher: it is the female who instructs the male.

Following the themes of *apatheia* and *theosis*, Macrina asserted that the soul becomes godlike when it has separated from all emotions.[10] We should be careful to note that despite language seemingly to the contrary at times, none of these Christians were claiming that they could become gods or that they become a part of God – they were not pantheists. But in the sense in which the Old Testament claimed that humans were created in the image of God, the process of theosis was a reclaiming of that image that had been marred through sin. It is reclaiming the true human nature and thus sharing in the life of God.

Gregory wrote a letter to a friend in which he explored the question, "What is meant by the term 'Christian'?" This letter was probably written close to the time Christianity became the official religion of the empire (and even before that official action it was becoming politically advantageous to be a Christian). Gregory was concerned to show, however, that it is not merely a name – that to truly be a Christian meant something more than aligning oneself with a group of people. To be a Christian meant to imitate God, to make one's life, as far as possible, free of evil and purified in thought and deed from all vileness. "This is truly the imitation of the divine and the perfection connected with the God of heaven."[11] Furthermore, this kind of imitation is possible for us, Gregory reasoned, because the first humans were created in the image of God. Christianity, therefore, is about reclaiming that image.

4 ASCETIC PRACTICE INFLUENCING THEOLOGY

There was not just a one-directional influence for the desert fathers and mothers from their beliefs to their practices; the reverse was also true. Especially in the East, the ascetic practices of the desert came to shape and influence the theology of that region. This is clearly seen in the thought of Ephrem (*c.* 308–373), who is regarded as one of the most important theologians of the Eastern Church. He came from the town of Nisibis and then settled in Edessa in modern-day Turkey, where he lived the remaining ten years of his life as something of a hermit.

Ephrem wrote in Syriac (a later development of Aramaic) and in poetry – both more conducive of reinforcing the mystery of the divine than analyzing it. More than 400 of his hymns have been preserved, though many more than that are known to have been written by him. His poetry frequently posits a link between the material and spiritual worlds. Here again we see that at the bottom of asceticism there is no despising the flesh.[12] The impulse to do so is worn away by years of training the flesh. The ascetics come to see that the flesh is the vehicle through which theosis comes, and so are thankful for it. Ephrem applied this insight also to the person of Jesus Christ. Salvation came because the Word became flesh. We ought to be grateful, then, for Christ's flesh. In the thirty-first hymn in the collection on Faith, Ephrem thanks God for the various body parts of Christ and for using such language – the language of flesh – so that he can speak to us in ways we can identify with. Ephrem continues:

> By means of what belongs to us did He draw close to us:
> He clothed himself in language,
> So that He might clothe us in his mode of life.
> He asked for our form and put this on,
> And then, as a father with his children,
> He spoke with our childish state.[13]

Another influence from ascetic practices to theology comes from meditation. Through the contemplation that is part of the ascetic's life, one comes to an awareness of the ineffability of God. Such transcendence, then, becomes the foundation of what is called the apophatic, or negative, approach to theology. According to apophatic theologians we can only say what God isn't, rather than what he is. This approach, again, is more pronounced in the East where the mystery of faith was emphasized. The mystery of God was to be experienced rather than analyzed, and reflection on this experience resulted in awareness of what God is not.

Apophatic theology would come to fruition in the later theologians of the East, but it was obviously developing in the thinkers we've been

APOPHATIC

From the Greek *apophanai*, to deny: pertaining to knowledge that can be obtained only by denial or negation.

EPHREM'S APOPHATIC APPROACH TO THEOLOGY

The difference between these two approaches, Hellenic and Semitic, can be well illustrated if one visualizes a circle with a point in the center, where the point represents the object of theological enquiry; the philosophical tradition of theology will seek to define, to set *horoi*, "boundaries" or "definitions," to this central point, whereas St. Ephrem's Semitic approach through his poetry will provide a series of paradoxical statements situated as it were at opposite points on the circumference of the circle: the central point is left undefined, but something of its nature can be inferred by joining up the various opposite points around the circumference. St. Ephrem is always very insistent that, since the center point representing the aspect of God's being under discussion stands outside creation, it thus lies beyond the ability of the created intellect to comprehend – and any claim to be able to do so is blasphemous. In all this St. Ephrem is obviously very much in harmony with the apophatic tradition of later Greek theology.

(Sebastian Brock in the introduction to Ephrem,
Hymns on Paradise, 40–41)

considering here. For example, Gregory had Macrina say in his dialogue, "We learn much about many things when we say that something does not exist."[14] And Basil writes in a letter,

The question is asked whether we know what we worship. Of course we want to say that we do, but we don't know the essence of God. We know some of his attributes because of his acts or operations: he is just, merciful, awful, etc. But from these we cannot know the essence of God: "His operations come down to us, but His essence remains beyond our reach."[15]

God's nature cannot be understood through human investigation or rational inquiry; however, he has made himself available to us through the Incarnation.[16] Apophatic theologians would claim that the purpose of God's revelation to us is not to give us knowledge but salvation.

5 WHAT BECAME OF THE DESERT FATHERS AND MOTHERS?

The ascetic life played a significant role in the thought of the most important of the Cappadocian thinkers, Basil of Caesarea. Here again we see the influence of Macrina. His sister persuaded him not to pursue a life of public recognition and fame. Instead, Basil made a tour of the great monastic sites in Egypt, Syria, and Mesopotamia, and when he returned he stayed with his sister in the retreat she had established. A few years later he entered back into public life, but instead of a post in government, he became the Bishop of Caesarea in Cappadocia.

Basil's significant contribution to Christian thought with respect to the ascetic movements was to bring many of these rogue ascetics into larger conformity with the Church. There was little organization of those who took to the desert, and even when they began living in communities there was little connection to the Church – and sometimes even outright opposition. Recall that one of the motivations of those who went to the desert was to escape the creeping institutionalism and enculturation that attended the political freedom of the Church in the fourth century. Basil, however, was the consummate diplomat and organizer. He succeeded in bringing the monks of his bishopric under the authority of the Church while still maintaining for them a rule of life that set them apart. He developed a system of rules by which the monks should live. These rules concerned things like prayer, obedience to one's superior, work, and care for the poor. Subsequent generations revised the lists, but Basil's inspiration is evident as the basis of the Rule of Benedict which would have such a lasting impact on the Church (see Chapter 12).

While Basil reined in the ascetics and so effected change among them, this assimilation also brought the spirit of ascetic practices more into the mainstream life of the Church.[17] He was able to curb some of the extremism found in ascetic communities, but then in speaking to the lay people of the cities, he urged more attention to denial of self in order to attain to union with God. In the end, monasticism retained a flavor of the resistance to the world as exemplified by the desert fathers and mothers; but it was also civilized and tamed so as to be respectable within the confines of the established and institutionalized Church.

The Church was also concerned to rein in and protect the fundamental beliefs and teachings of Christianity in order to defend them against those who thought it was false and dangerous, and to clarify and unify the beliefs of various factions that were springing up within Christianity. In the next chapter we retrace much of the same time period and tell the story again from the perspective of the apologists.

SUMMARY OF MAIN POINTS

1   Christian men and women moved to the desert in order to pursue perfection of their spirits apart from the increasingly institutionalized Church.
2   The flesh was not despised, but taken to be the means through which spiritual advancement could be achieved.
3   Theosis, or divinization, was the process of reclaiming original human nature which was created in God's image.
4   Ascetic practices led to the development of apophatic theology and to the greater awareness of and appreciation for spiritual disciplines in the Church.
5   Through the efforts of Basil, ascetic communities became organized and even institutionalized into monasteries and convents.

FOR FURTHER READING

Owen Chadwick, ed., *Western Asceticism* (Philadelphia, PA: Westminster Press, 1958). Contains *Sayings of the Fathers,* Cassian's *Conferences,* and other original sources.

David G.R. Keller, *Oasis of Wisdom* (Collegeville, MN: Liturgical Press, 2005). A recent treatment of the desert fathers and mothers.

Robert T. Meyer, ed., *Palladius: The Lausiac History* (Westminster, MD: Newman Press, 1965). Another classic source for sayings from the desert fathers and mothers.

Margaret Miles, *Fullness of Life: Historical Foundations for a New Asceticism* (Philadelphia, PA: Westminster Press, 1981). An interpretation of the causes and meanings of asceticism in the ancient world.

Laura Swan, *The Forgotten Desert Mothers: Sayings, Lives, and Stories of Early Christian Women* (New York: Paulist Press, 2001). A treatment of many of the important women of the early centuries of Christianity who have been largely ignored by historians.

7

The Christian apologists

Interacting with Gnosticism and other "heresies"

QUESTIONS TO BE ADDRESSED IN THIS CHAPTER

1   What is apologetics and why did it emerge in early Christianity?
2   How did the notions of orthodoxy and heresy develop in the second century?
3   What is Gnosticism and how does it differ from orthodox Christianity?
4   How did the emphases of Jesus's humanity and divinity lead to polar heresies?
5   How did the persecution of Christians and early offshoots of Christianity lead to the systematic development of theology?

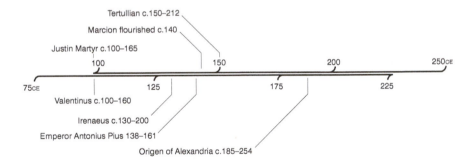

Timeline 7 The Christian apologists

In response to the persecution of Christians and the development of factions within Christianity, "apologists" emerged in the second century. Apologists, from the Greek word for defense in a court of law, attempted to defend what they took to be the true faith. Offering a defense of the faith was not new to Christianity. Even in the earliest writings of the New Testament, there are clear indications that the first disciples of Jesus (such as Peter) and later church leaders (including the Apostle Paul) spent much time "defending," "contending," and "persuading" others to believe that Christianity was the true and right view of God and salvation (e.g. 1 Peter 3:15; Acts 17:2–4; 19:8; 2 Corinthians 10:5; Philippians

1:7, 27; Jude 3). In response to the conditions of the mid-second century, however, apologetics took on new fervor.

1 THE EARLY CHRISTIAN APOLOGISTS

One of the most prominent of these early Christian apologists was Justin Martyr (c. 100–c. 165). (His surname was not "Martyr"; rather, as you might guess, he was himself martyred for his Christian faith). Justin had been raised as a pagan – a person who held to one of the various Greco-Roman polytheistic religions. He was schooled in Greek philosophy, primarily Stoicism and Platonism, and considered himself a Platonist well into his twenties. However, the steadfastness of the Christian martyrs as well as the claims of Christianity impressed him, as can be seen from his own later writings:

> For I myself, too, when I was delighting in the doctrines of Plato, and heard the Christians slandered, and saw them fearless of death, and of all other things which are counted fearful, perceived that it was impossible that they could be living in wickedness and pleasure.[1]

He eventually came to view the Christian faith as the completion of pagan philosophy. At the age of thirty he converted to Christianity, and he went on to establish a training school in Rome for Christians.

In line with the biblical mandate to "always be ready to make your defense" for Christian belief (1 Peter 3:15), the thrust of Justin's work involved just that – providing an intellectual defense of Christianity. He utilized his Hellenistic philosophical training in service to his Christian *apologia*, and several of his many works, which are widely taken to be some of the most original and intellectually sophisticated of the time, still exist today. In his *First Apology* – a defense of the Christian faith addressed to the Emperor Antonius Pius (138–161) – he began his

APOLOGETICS

From the Greek *apologia* = defense: the branch of theology that deals with the defense of the Christian faith.

argument by emphasizing the point that real lovers of truth and wisdom who carefully investigate the evidences in his book would find his claims to be true and reasonable:

> Reason directs those who are truly pious and philosophical to honour and love only what is true, declining to follow traditional opinions, if these be worthless. For not only does sound reason direct us to refuse the guidance of those who did or taught anything wrong, but it is incumbent on the lover of truth, by all means, and if death be threatened, even before his own life, to choose to do and say what is right. Do you, then, since ye are called pious and philosophers, guardians of justice and lovers of learning, give good heed, and hearken to my address; and if ye are indeed such, it will be manifested. For we have come, not to flatter you by this writing, nor please you by our address, but to beg that you pass judgment, after an accurate and searching investigation, not flattered by prejudice or by a desire of pleasing superstitious men, nor induced by irrational impulse of evil rumours which have long been prevalent, to give a decision which will prove to be against yourselves.[2]

Besides the pagans' attacks on Christianity, there were also criticisms by the Jews. In his book *Dialogue with Trypho*, Justin responded to the Jews by utilizing Old Testament prophesies of the coming messiah in an attempt to establish Jesus as the one foretold by the prophets, and he used the resurrection of Jesus as vindication of his messiahship. Justin's various defenses led to political opposition and his own persecution. He offered his final defense of the faith before the prefect Rusticus around 165 just before he and six of his companions were tortured and executed by beheading.[3]

Another apologist worthy of mention is a Greek philosopher who lived in Athens – a man named Athenagoras (*c.* second century). The amount of information available from the annals of history on Athenagoras is limited. Nonetheless, we do know several very important details of his life and apologetic work. First, like the Apostle Paul, he was originally set against Christianity. Ironically, it was through reading the Christian Scriptures in an attempt to refute them that he became a believer. He was perhaps the most eloquent of the early Greek apologists, and two of his masterful writings are still preserved: *On the Resurrection of the Dead* and *A Plea for the Christians* (sometimes referred to as the *Apology*), both

Figure 7.1 Icon of Justin Martyr. Russia, XIX century. Church of the Resurrection Slovusheye by Uspensky Vrazhek/Public domain / Wikimedia Commons.

dated to the late second century. In the first work, he responded to various charges brought against Christians, including the surprising allegation of atheism. As mentioned in Chapter 5, Christians were considered atheists because they did not believe in or worship the pagan deities. Athenagoras retorted that Christians are not atheists; in fact, he maintained, they are the true theists, for they believe in the one true God – the triune God of Father, Son, and Holy Spirit.

In his work on the resurrection of the dead, he set forth an argument that a resurrection of the body is not impossible. To the contrary, if God could create the first human beings from nothing, he could certainly raise their bodies from the dead. Furthermore, he argued, bodily resurrection is in accord with reason, the natural order, and the Scriptures.

CHRISTIAN APOLOGISTS AND HERESIOLOGISTS OF THE SECOND CENTURY

There were a number of orthodox Christians in the second century who took up the task of defending the faith against the pagans and those considered to be heretics. Among them were:

- Justin Martyr (*c.*100–*c.*165; Caesarea)
- Irenaeus (*c.*130–*c.*200; Lyons)
- Tertullian (*c.*150–*c.*212; Carthage)
- Athenagoras (second century)
- Hermias (second century)
- Aristides (second century; Athens)
- Theophilus (second century; Antioch)
- Melito (second century; Sardis)

2 ORTHODOXY AND HERESY

Some of the early Christian apologists are also referred to as "heresiologists." A heresiologist is one who writes an account (logos) of heresies, combining refutation with schemes of classification or origin. But what is heresy? It has come to mean false doctrine, though it is sometimes alleged that the "heretics" were simply those who were on the losing side of the controversies of vying "Christianities" in the first few centuries. No doubt there is some truth to this claim, but it is not as though the winners and losers of these debates were chosen arbitrarily or even by political force. The early historical record identifies a group of Christians in the second century who were concerned to maintain the faith as it was handed down. They defended a widespread version of Christian faith that appeared to be already quite ancient – going all the way back to the apostles themselves. As a case in point, consider the works of the Christian apologist Irenaeus, Bishop of Lyons (*c.* 130–*c.* 200).

Irenaeus was primarily concerned with "heretical" groups known to us as the Gnostics. As we will see below, the Gnostics believed many things

ORTHODOXY

From the Greek words *orthos* = right and *doxa* = belief: right belief; the theological views and normative claims of the church fathers, mothers, apologists, and heresiologists which prevailed.

HERESY

From the Greek word *haireomai* = to choose: that belief, or those beliefs, which one chooses contrary to orthodoxy.

which were contrary to Irenaeus' understanding of the Christian faith. His general strategy for responding to important questions which arose concerning the faith is spelled out in his book *Against Heresies* (see text in box).

Several important themes emerge from these paragraphs. First, Irenaeus is making the point that if some sort of controversy arises (and they were legion), Christians are not left merely to pick one of the subjective opinions of divergent "Christianities." They had both the writings of the apostles and the historic tradition of the churches which had been passed down in conformity with the Christian Scriptures (we will examine these developments of the Scriptures in Chapter 10). Other groups, however, such as the Gnostics, also claimed that *their* teachings came from the apostles. But the Gnostics maintained that their knowledge came from a secret tradition, rather than from that which was passed down openly through the churches.

Second, Irenaeus notes that even the "barbarian" (non-Greek speaking) Christians carefully preserved the "ancient tradition." It seems that there was a historic tradition of beliefs on which he based his own theological positions and from which he confronted those opposed to them.

Third, he mentions that there was an established "doctrine" of God and of Jesus Christ and his truth. Thus, the gist of his apologetic is to

IRENAEUS'S APOLOGETIC

Suppose there arise a dispute relative to some important question among us, should we not have recourse to the most ancient Churches with which the apostles held constant intercourse, and learn from them what is certain and clear in regard to the present question? For how should it be if the apostles themselves had not left us writings? Would it not be necessary, [in that case,] to follow the course of the tradition which they handed down to those to whom they did commit the Churches?

To which course many nations of those barbarians who believe in Christ do assent, having salvation written in their hearts by the Spirit, without paper or ink, and carefully preserving the ancient tradition. … Thus, by means of the ancient tradition of the apostles, they do not suffer their mind to conceive anything of the [doctrines suggested by the] portentous language of these [false] teachers, among whom neither Church nor doctrine has ever been established. …

Since, therefore, the tradition from the apostles does thus exist in the Church, and is permanent among us, let us revert to the Scriptural proof furnished by those apostles who did also write the Gospel, in which they recorded the doctrine regarding God, pointing out that our Lord Jesus Christ is the truth, and that no lie is in Him.

(*Against Heresies*, Book III, Chapters 4, 5)

demonstrate the succession of the apostles' teaching from its origin in Christ right down through the churches to the present day; this is where right doctrine (i.e. orthodoxy) is found. Orthodoxy, then, as understood by Irenaeus and the other apologists, is that set of *right beliefs* which had been taught by the apostles, written in the Scriptures, and openly passed down through the churches. Heresy, on the other hand, is any set of *recent beliefs* which do not conform to the ancient teaching of the apostles, or to the Scriptures, or to traditions held in the Church.

3 GNOSTICISM

Who were these Gnostics Irenaeus was concerned to refute? There has been much debate in recent times about the Gnostics; some scholars even go so far as to claim that the term "Gnosticism" refers to a construct, whether ancient or modern, which does not reflect any actually existing historic religion.[4] The general consensus, though, is that there were in fact a number of religious groups in the second and third centuries who held certain beliefs that can be beneficially categorized under the rubric of "Gnosticism."

The word "Gnostic" comes from the Greek word *gnosis* (knowledge), and it seems clear from the historical record that one general characteristic of all Gnostic adherents is the notion that salvation is achieved through acquiring secret knowledge. There are current and lively debates about whether Gnosticism emerged within the Christian tradition or from other older traditions (including Judaism and Asian religions). Nevertheless, what is fairly evident is that, during the second and third centuries, Gnostic beliefs were an influential alternative to Christianity.

Up until the late twentieth century, not much was known about Gnostic beliefs except what was gleaned from the writings of the early Christian apologists. These writings often included quotations from Gnostic sources, but it was not known for sure whether the apologists were accurately reflecting Gnostic views or were instead taking them out of context and twisting them for their own theological advantage. Much of this changed, however, with one of the most important archaeological discoveries of modern times.

In the fall of 1945, some Egyptian peasants were transporting fertilizer for their crops in saddlebags carried by their camels. They had stopped near a cliff called Jabal al-Tarif, located in the Nag Hammadi region of Upper Egypt, and were digging in the ground, presumably for more fertilizer. One of them – Mohammed Ali (not to be confused with the late American heavyweight boxer) – heard an unexpected clanging sound as his mattock swung into the dirt. He discovered a sealed jar that, at first, he was afraid to crack open lest he unleash an evil jinn (or genie). However, after reflecting on the possibility that it might contain gold, he decided to break it open. To his surprise, it contained neither a genie nor gold, but rather a collection of thirteen leather-bound books. He wrapped the books in his tunic, hopped onto his camel, and headed home.

At this point in the story, things turn rather bizarre, and the subsequent events confirm the adage that "truth is stranger than fiction" as blood feuds, vengeance, and finally murder are all inextricably linked. Suffice it to say that Mohammed Ali realized these books may be worth a good amount of money, and he gave one of them to a local Coptic (Egyptian Christian) priest for safe-keeping until the feuding ceased. The priest's brother-in-law – a traveling teacher of English and history – realized its potential value and took it to Cairo to sell it. It was confiscated by the authorities from the Department of Antiquities, but it was later allowed to be sold to the Coptic Museum. The director of the museum eventually tracked down the remaining twelve books and acquired them for the museum. Unfortunately, a number of pages were missing as Mrs. Ali had used them for kindling, not realizing their incredible worth.[5]

These thirteen books are now referred to as the "Nag Hammadi Library," and they consist primarily of forty-six different Gnostic treatises, or short books, most of which were previously unknown. They are written in the form of gospels, acts, letters, and even apocalypses (i.e. the writing style of the book of Revelation in the Bible). Other Gnostic works have also been uncovered in various archaeological digs, and all of this material has been copied and published and is now accessible to the general public. While there are significant differences in the beliefs of the various Gnostic groups, and while it is not easy to give a precise characterization of their diverse views, we can glean from their writings and the responses to their teachings by the heresiologists a number of general themes. Four of their fundamental beliefs can be summarized as follows:

1   **Cosmology** – the cosmos is divided into two components – the physical or material world (which is inherently flawed and evil) and the spiritual world (which is inherently good).
2   **Theology** – the true God is a transcendent being who is beyond all things and individuals. This God did not create the material world but did create other divine beings. In between the true God and human beings there exist Aeons – divine beings – and perhaps the most significant of these beings is Sophia. Over time, another divine but flawed being emanated from Sophia. This divine being – the Demiurge – created the physical cosmos in his own flawed image and imprisoned Sophia in the souls of certain human beings as divine sparks.

3   **Anthropology** – human beings are physical (material body and animal soul) and spiritual, and at least some humans contain within them the divine spark (i.e. the Goddess Sophia). The Gnostics themselves are those human beings who have within them this divine aspect.

4   **Soteriology** – salvation is the liberation of the human/divine spirit from its union with the material world. This liberation is attained through acquiring knowledge (*gnosis*) of the human condition: where we came from, who we truly are, and where we are headed. Furthermore, for many Gnostics, a cosmic savior is needed to reveal these mysteries to us, and this great revealer is the Aeon (eternal being) called Christ.

One of the most important Gnostic Christian figures was Valentinus (*c.* 100–*c.* 160). Educated in Alexandria, he was a powerful and persuasive communicator and gained a large following during the time he lived and taught in Rome (roughly 130s). The apologist Tertullian noted that Valentinus aspired to be bishop of Rome but was denied the position. According to Tertullian, it was at this point that Valentinus rejected orthodoxy:

> Valentinus had expected to become a bishop, because he was an able man both in genius and eloquence. Being indignant, however, that another obtained the dignity by reason of a claim which confessorship had given him, he broke with the church of the true faith. Just like those (restless) spirits which, when roused by ambition, are usually inflamed with the desire of revenge, he applied himself with all his might to exterminate the truth; and finding the clue of a certain old opinion, he marked out a path for himself with the subtlety of a serpent.[6]

Whether this was in fact the case or merely a rhetorical device used against Valentinus' Gnostic views, and precisely when he developed his Gnostic views, are matters of speculation and debate. One thing is clear: Valentinus was an influential Gnostic leader and teacher, and the heresiologists Tertullian and Irenaeus spent no little time attempting to refute his views. It seems that he was originally allied with the orthodox believers in Rome, but then developed his Gnostic views for which he was

> As in the case of the ignorance of a person, when he comes to have knowledge, his ignorance vanishes of itself, as the darkness vanishes when the light appears, so also the deficiency vanishes in the perfection. ... It is within Unity that each one will attain himself; within knowledge he will purify himself.
>
> (*The Gospel of Truth*, probably written by Valentinus)

excommunicated. According to Irenaeus, he wrote a book entitled *The Gospel of Truth*. Many scholars now believe that the work discovered at Nag Hammadi with the same title – an esoteric but highly sophisticated Gnostic writing – is in fact the very same book and was most likely written by Valentinus.

It is sometimes alleged that Gnosticism gave greater prominence to women than did the orthodox Church. It is true that in Gnostic teaching, there were both male and female deities, and that human women sometimes played important roles as well. For example, in the Gnostic writing called the *Gospel of Mary*, Mary Magdalene has a unique relationship with Jesus, and he gives her special revelation which he did not reveal to the *other* apostles. However, while Mary is elevated in this work, other Gnostic writings seem to denigrate the feminine. The *Gospel of Thomas*, for example, calls for women to *become* male: "Simon Peter said to them [the disciples]: 'Let Mary leave us, for women are not worthy of Life.' Jesus said, 'I myself shall lead her, in order to make her male, so that she too may become a living spirit, resembling you males. For every woman who will make herself male will enter the Kingdom of Heaven.' "[7]

4 CONFLICTING HERESIES: THE MARCIONITES AND EBIONITES

Besides Valentinus, another person toward whom Irenaeus and other Christian apologists focused their theological and rhetorical energies was Marcion (flourished *c.* 140). According to church tradition, Marcion's father was a bishop in the ancient town of Sinope (modern Turkey), and through either a moral failure or a theological dispute, Marcion was excommunicated from his church. He then went to Rome and began to work out his own theological system, developing quite a following in the process. He later presented his views to the Bishop of Rome, but they didn't take kindly to his views and also excommunicated him. He then returned to Asia Minor and developed an ecclesiastical structure similar to the church of Rome, appointing himself as the bishop.

According to Marcion's teaching, Paul was the only authentic apostle of Jesus. Paul's writings, especially the letter to the Galatians, were interpreted by Marcion to be describing a dichotomy between faith and the works of the Law. This dichotomy was so significant to Marcion's way of thinking that he came to believe two separate Gods must have been behind them: the God of the Jews who created this world and established the Jewish Law, and the God of Jesus who extended grace to overcome the requirements of the Law. On his view, Jesus was not in any way related to the just, vindictive God of the Old Testament. Jesus was sent by a different God – his loving Father. And when he came to earth to save the world, he took on the appearance of a human being, though he was not actually human, but an apparition. Marcion's non-orthodox theological ideas were based on the canon he compiled, which consisted of Luke's Gospel (minus several portions of the text) plus ten of Paul's epistles (all those in our present New Testament except 1 and 2 Timothy and Titus). Interestingly, his canon was perhaps the first canon of Scripture to be assembled in the Christian era.

The Ebionites held views contrary to Marcion and his followers.[8] Unfortunately, the only information we have about the Ebionites comes from the writings of the apologists, including Irenaeus and Tertullian. None of their own writings remains. We don't even know who founded the group, although Tertullian claims that it was a man named Ebion.[9] Fortunately, we do have enough information to know their basic beliefs, and several of them stand in stark contrast to both the Marcionites and the orthodox believers. First, it is clear that they were a group of Jewish-Christians who held tenaciously to the Jewish customs and laws, including circumcision. They rejected the teachings of Paul and, like the Marcionites, they used only one gospel. However, the gospel to which they adhered was not Luke but Matthew (as it is the most Jewish of the four Gospels).

Unlike the Marcionites and the orthodox believers, the Ebionites maintained that Jesus was not divine, but human. He was the most righteous man on earth, and God adopted him to be his own son because

Marcionites		Ebionites
• Believed in two Gods: 1) The just God of the Old Testament, and 2) the loving and forgiving God of Jesus • Held to a docetic view of Jesus; he was divine but only seemed human; he was not the Jewish Messiah, but rather was a spirit sent by his benevolent Father • Rejected the Jewish Law and held to a doctrine of divine grace • Utilized one Gospel (basically the Gospel of Luke minus the first two chapters) and ten epistles of Paul	Polar Heresies	• Believed in one God—the Jewish/Christian God • Held to an adoptionist view of Jesus; he was human, not divine; he was a righteous man whom God chose to die for the sins of the world • Maintained that a person had to convert to Judaism before becoming a Christian (Ebionite) • Utilized one Gospel (Matthew); they also followed the observance of the Jewish Law, and they considered Paul to be an apostate

Figure 7.2 Polar Heresies of the Marcionites and the Ebionites

of his steadfast observance of the Law. As the Son of God, he was given the significant role of messiah – the one who would die for the sins of the world.[10]

One Christian apologist who opposed the teachings of the Marcionites, Ebionites and Gnostics was Origen of Alexandria (*c.* 185–254). Perhaps the most astute Christian scholar of the apologists, Origen was trained in philosophy (possibly studying with Ammonius Saccas, the founder of Neo-Platonism) and the biblical languages. He began to publish his writings around 220 and, on some estimates, by the end of his life he had over 6,000 publications. His vast apologetic included defending the unity and agreement of the Old and New Testaments, the goodness of the one true God, and the eternal generation of the Son of God (the *logos*, in Greek). More than any other apologist, his monumental theological work helped to build a foundation by which the ecumenical church councils would eventually be established.

5 THE FIRST SYSTEMATIC THEOLOGIANS

The second century reflected a flurry of activity by Christian apologists and heresiologists as they attempted to defend the faith against external charges of its being a false, and even dangerous, religion and against internal theological heresies. They began the important task of clarifying fundamental Christian beliefs, such as the nature of God and of Christ, the meaning of salvation, the significance of Jesus's incarnation and resurrection, and the role of the Old Testament in Christian Scripture. In the process, they inadvertently became the first systematic theologians and created an unprecedented systematization of the faith.

In the next chapter, we will see how the theological foundation set by these apologists, along with the developing institutionalization of the Church, provided yet another type of response to heresy and to a formalization of orthodoxy.

SUMMARY OF MAIN POINTS

1   Christian apologists, or defenders of the faith, emerged in the second century in order to defend Christianity against both outsiders (pagans) and insiders (Gnostics and other "heretical" groups).

2   The apologists and heresiologists defended what they took to be the traditional apostolic doctrines, which were "orthodox," and opposed contrary doctrines, or "heresies," which they argued had no basis in what Jesus and the apostles taught.

3   One "heresy" (or, rather, group of heresies) which emerged in the second century was Gnosticism, and its worldview included a divided cosmos, multiple gods, and the requirement of secret knowledge about the self for salvation.

4   Some heretical groups affirmed the deity of Jesus to the exclusion of his humanity; others affirmed his humanity to the exclusion of his deity; the Christian apologists maintained that Jesus was both God and man.

5   In an attempt to carefully articulate the "orthodox" doctrines in their defense of the faith, the apologists began an unprecedented systematization of theology.

FOR FURTHER READING

L.W. Barnard, *Justin Martyr: His Life and Thought* (Cambridge: Cambridge University Press, 1967). A contemporary classic on Justin.

Bart D. Ehrman, *Lost Christianities: The Battles for Scripture and the Faiths We Never Knew* (Oxford: Oxford University Press, 2003). An insightful and readable study on various "Christian" (heretical) groups and their texts in the second and third centuries.

Robert Grant, *Greek Apologists of the Second Century* (Philadelphia, PA: The Westminster Press, 1988). A concise and informative treatment of the Christian apologists of the second century.

James M. Robinson, ed., *The Nag Hammadi Library*, 3rd revised edition (San Francisco, CA: HarperSanFrancisco, 1988). A one-volume English edition of the complete collection of Gnostic works discovered at Nag Hammadi in 1945.

Kurt Rudolph, *Gnosis: The Nature and History of Gnosticism*, R. McL. Wilson, trans. (San Francisco, CA: Harper & Rowe, 1987). An excellent and quite readable introduction to Gnosticism.

8

The early Church councils

Christological controversy and definition

QUESTIONS TO BE ADDRESSED IN THIS CHAPTER

1   What led to the Council of Nicea?
2   What was Nicea's central contribution to Christian thought?
3   How did Chalcedon maintain balance between the opposite extremes?
4   What were the effects of the theological controversy on Christian worship?

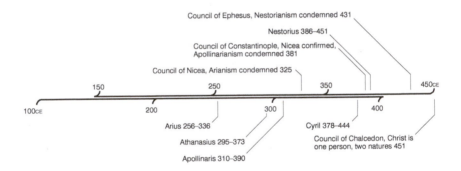

Timeline 8 The early Church councils

In the previous chapter we met some of the individuals who responded to ideas that were deemed to be outside the parameters of orthodoxy. As the Church institutionalized, there was also a collective response to heresy. Councils of bishops were assembled to hear, debate, and render judgments on controversial topics. These came to play an important role in defining Christian thinking in the fourth and fifth centuries. And given the increased prominence of the Church within the political arena, there were more factors at work than just the ideas of a few churchmen.

In this episode of the history of Christian thought, once again Emperor Constantine has an important role to play. This time he is the catalyst of a new wave of thinking about a (if not *the*) central topic of concern to Christians: the person of Jesus Christ. The year after Constantine's victory at the Milvian Bridge, the tetrarchy of rulers had been reduced to just two: Constantine in the West and Licinius in the East. The situation was not stable, and by 316 the two were openly warring with each other. Constantine did not hide the fact that he wished to unite all the Roman lands under himself, and in 324 he defeated Licinius and became the sole ruler of the empire.

With the political situation in relative stability, Constantine turned to the emerging institution of the Church. He found that there was considerable disagreement and in-fighting there – both between Eastern and Western rivals (who were separated not only by geography, but also language), and between factions within the geographical regions. Constantine perceived that ecclesiastical unity was essential to the political unity he had fought so hard for, so he tried to get the Christians to agree. When his entreaties for them to reconcile with each other were unsuccessful, Constantine decided to turn to a more dramatic solution. Taking his cue from the Council in Jerusalem recorded in Acts 15 (discussed in Chapter 4), Constantine decided to assemble the bishops from across the empire in order to sort out their differences face to face.

Constantine chose a neutral and accessible location: Nicea, in the west of what is now Turkey. He invited all 1,800 bishops in the empire to come to Nicea at his expense – travel, lodging, and food were all to be provided from the coffers of the empire. Different accounts of the Council record different numbers of bishops attending, but it must have been around 300 altogether. The official count was made difficult because each bishop was allowed to bring attending priests, presbyters, and deacons. The celebrated church historian Eusebius, who was in attendance at the Council, records, "the number of bishops exceeded two hundred and fifty, while that of the presbyters and deacons in their train, and the crowd of acolytes and other attendants was altogether beyond computation."[1] Furthermore, the Council lasted for two months, and undoubtedly the count was affected by comings and goings.

At any rate, the Council of Nicea was convened by Emperor Constantine himself on 20 May 325. He charged the attendees with coming to agreement among themselves regarding the nature of Jesus Christ. Although Constantine is portrayed by Eusebius as an astute theologian in his own right, it does not appear as though Constantine had much of an opinion about what that solution should look like, but merely that there be agreement. And agreement there was. In the end, all but two of the bishops voted to accept the proposed solution. In order to understand that solution, we must first understand the theological crisis that precipitated the calling of the Council.

1 THE ARIAN CRISIS

We find the starting point for the Christological crisis in the Egyptian city of Alexandria. Around 318 a presbyter of the church there named Arius (c. 256–336) came into conflict with his bishop, Alexander, over the nature of Christ. Arius, a Christian thinker influenced by Origen and Platonist teachings, has come to be one of the most prominent heretics in the history of the Church, but it must be emphasized that he was not attempting to undermine Christian teaching. Rather he was trying to be clear about the implications of certain presuppositions about God and Christ that were accepted and seemed innocuous. These presuppositions were that God is one and that God is transcendent (that is, beyond the conception of human existence). No one who understood the Jewish roots of their faith could object to the first, and especially in the East there was little quarrel with the second. But from these, Arius claimed, the Son of God must be a creature with a beginning – or to use his infamous phrase, "there was when he was not." To claim otherwise commits us to holding to more than one eternal being. Furthermore, speaking of the Son as begotten from or generated out of the Father is a stain against the Father's transcendence, for it subjects him to change. Therefore, according to Arius, the Son must have been created out of nothing. Furthermore, Arius took seriously the biblical language which suggests that the Son was in some sense less than the Father (for example, Proverbs 8:22 and John 14:28), though also God.

Arius was quick to add that, although a creature, the Son is a creature like no other. All other creatures were created through him, and he remained perfect and sinless throughout his entire life. But still, Christ was something less than divine – a demigod, perhaps. Some Arians would accept the Son as divine in an adopted sense, and admit that Christ's Sonship could become ours through the grace of God as we imitated his perfect example. But God he was not; only God was God.

Bishop Alexander was deeply troubled by this low and earthy view of Christ, for he was concerned to emphasize his true deity. An adopted divinity was not good enough for Alexander. He called together more than 100 bishops from around Egypt and succeeded in getting Arius condemned and thrown out of the church. Arius did not concede defeat, however, and was able to win the support of the powerful bishop Eusebius of Nicomedia (not to be confused with the great church historian, Eusebius the Bishop of Caesarea – although he too supported Arius for a time). Eusebius took Arius under his protection, and so caused a schism within the Church – the controversy which led Emperor Constantine to call the Council of Nicea.

LETTER OF ARIUS TO EUSEBIUS, BISHOP OF NICOMEDIA

But we say and believe, and have taught, and do teach, that the Son is not unbegotten, nor in any way part of the unbegotten; and that He does not derive His subsistence from any matter; but that by His own will and counsel He has subsisted before time, and before ages, as perfect God, only begotten and unchangeable, and that before He was begotten, or created, or purposed, or established, He was not. For He was not unbegotten. We are persecuted, because we say that the Son has a beginning, but that God is without beginning. This is the cause of our persecution, and likewise, because we say that He is of the non-existent this we say, because He is neither part of God, nor of any essential being. For this are we persecuted.

(Theodoret, *Ecclesiastical History*, Book I, Chapter IV)

2 THE COUNCIL OF NICEA

There is no official record of the proceedings of the Council, but many of the two months' worth of discussions can be reconstructed from various individuals' accounts that have been preserved. It seems that Alexander rather easily won the argument early on in the meetings. When Eusebius of Nicomedia asserted on behalf of Arius that there must be some subordination of the Son to the Father, his rival Bishop Alexander was able to convince the majority of the bishops that such a notion was heretical: Christ was certainly divine and begotten – not created – by the Father.[2]

A group of the bishops was commissioned to draft a formal creed for adoption by the Council. Eusebius of Caesarea (the church historian) claims that Emperor Constantine himself read the text and was happy with it so long as one more word could be added: homo-ousios.[3] This is the Greek word translated as "consubstantial" or "of one substance," and it purported to describe the relationship between the Father and Son – apparently ruling out Arianism. But in the interest of getting as much agreement as possible, Constantine avoided clearly specifying the meaning of the word. So, almost all agreed to use homo-ousios, but just what it meant was the subject of considerable and on-going debate. Justo González, a contemporary historian of Christian thought, notes that there were at least five different interpretations of what the wording in the Creed meant, and the Council didn't really do much to settle the problems.[4]

There is a very real sense in which the Arian controversy uncovered some metaphysical difficulties which had accrued with acceptance of the Hellenistic conception of God as a pure and changeless Being. Yahweh, the God of the Old Testament, was no stranger to change. He had passions, changed his mind, and entered into human affairs. The concept of a god that admits of no change whatsoever has very little grounding in either the Hebrew Scriptures or the New Testament. Still it became an important strand of Christian thought and has continued to exercise influence to the present day. And although Arius's understanding and explication of this notion of God led to turmoil in the Church, the conceptual work that ensued was some of the most creative, important, and fruitful that has occurred in the history of Christian thought.

While the Arians themselves seemed to be defeated at Nicea, the impulse to emphasize the humanity of Christ would continue to manifest itself in other thinkers for another generation. The Arian heresy would finally be conclusively and explicitly condemned at the Council of Constantinople called by Emperor Theodosius in 381. There the Nicene Creed was confirmed, and several canons were adopted which gave clarifications of duties and listed people and heresies to be condemned.

THE NICENE CREED AS FORMALIZED IN 381

We believe in one God, the Father All Governing, creator of heaven and earth, of all things visible and invisible.

And in one Lord Jesus Christ, the only-begotten Son of God, begotten from the Father before all time, Light from Light, true God from true God, begotten not created, of the same essence [*homo-ousion*] as the Father, through Whom all things came into being, Who for us men and because of our salvation came down from heaven, and was incarnate by the Holy Spirit and the Virgin Mary and became human. He was crucified for us under Pontius Pilate, and suffered and was buried, and rose on the third day, according to the Scriptures, and ascended to heaven, and sits on the right hand of the Father, and will come again with glory to judge the living and the dead. His Kingdom shall have no end.

And in the Holy Spirit, the Lord and life-giver, Who proceeds from the Father, Who is worshiped and glorified together with the Father and Son, Who spoke through the prophets; and in one, holy, catholic, and apostolic Church. We confess one baptism for the remission of sins. We look forward to the resurrection of the dead and the life of the world to come. Amen.

3 THE APOLLINARIAN AND NESTORIAN HERESIES AND THE COUNCIL OF CHALCEDON

After Nicea, the orthodox were concerned to maintain that Jesus was really divine and that he was really human. Asserting this is one thing, but it is quite another to explain how these two natures could be kept together in the one person of Jesus. Attempts to do so led to two opposite tendencies which, their critics claimed, degenerated into clearly unacceptable (and therefore, heretical) positions. The debate also had a geographical dimension, in that the two important cities of Alexandria and Antioch became centers for the rival sides.

One tendency was to emphasize the unity of God and man in the person of Jesus Christ. The advocates of this position were typically from the school of thought associated with Alexandria. They were not happy with the kind of proposal Tertullian had made in the third century whereby the complete human – both body and mind – came to be inhabited by the divine logos or mind, resulting in two distinct minds. How, they wondered, could this result in one single person? It seemed to them that such an arrangement amounts to God merely indwelling a person like he had done with the prophets. In that sense, God did not really "become" a human being but only came alongside a human being. Furthermore, according to the Alexandrians, this two-minds view of the Incarnation implies that the individual identified as Jesus of Nazareth would have had to constantly juggle and flip-flop between his human mind and his divine mind. Such psychological disunity needed to be avoided according to the Alexandrian understanding of Christ.

Athanasius (295–373) succeeded Alexander as the Bishop of Alexandria. He became one of the most influential of the church fathers in the fourth century. In order to avoid saddling Christ with two minds, Athanasius at first seemed to hold to a view in which the person of Jesus Christ was a unity of human flesh and divine mind. He also asserted that this unity was fully human and fully divine.[5] But the accepted psychology of the day dictated that a complete human being needed both human flesh and a human mind (or soul), and this composite of Athanasius did not have a human mind.

Athanasius later abandoned the view, but it was taken up by his friend Apollinaris of Laodicea (c. 310–390). He thought that having the divine mind replace the human mind in the person of Jesus was the best way to understand the unity of God becoming a human being. Such an arrangement was certainly not just an "indwelling" or "possession" of

INCARNATION

From the medieval Latin *incarnare*, to make flesh: the event in which the Son of God became a human being.

Figure 8.1 St. Athanasius the Great. Michael Damaskenos/Public domain / Wikimedia Commons.

a human being. But this Apollinarianism was ultimately condemned at Constantinople in 381 because it made Christ something less than fully human – he didn't have a human mind; how could he be fully human? The Alexandrian impulse to show the unity of God and man seemed to result in some sort of blended Christ which is neither completely human nor divine.

Reacting against the Alexandrian model is what might be called the Antiochene position. Those with allegiance to the school of Antioch were concerned to keep the human and divine natures separate in the person of Jesus Christ to avoid the hybrid of the Alexandrians. Furthermore, they felt that they must guard against attributing the very human parts of Jesus's experience (e.g. hungering, suffering, dying) to God. Nestorius (*c.* 386–451), the Patriarch of Constantinople from 428–431, had been trained in Antioch and inherited the view that the human and divine natures were "conjoined" in Christ, but not unified. Nestorius was a charismatic speaker and so became the chief spokesperson for this conjunction view, but he was not as gifted at arguing the subtleties of the Antiochene position against his opponents.

Nestorius's great rival was Cyril (378–444), the bishop of Alexandria at the time, who caricatured the Antiochene position so that it entailed that Jesus Christ was two distinct persons. Nestorius convinced Emperor Theodosius II to call another council in the hopes of resolving the conflict. This council was called at Ephesus in 431, but turned out to be something of a farce. Cyril and his supporters arrived first, and after waiting fifteen days went ahead and started the meetings without either the contingent from Antioch or the envoy from Rome representing Pope Celestine. All present readily agreed to condemn the Nestorian position. The Antiochenes arrived a few days later and declared the decision to be invalid, accusing the Alexandrians themselves of heresy. When the pope's envoy arrived two weeks after this, much debate ensued, but in the end the original decisions championed by Cyril were upheld and Nestorianism was condemned. The formula accepted by the church from the Council at Ephesus included the claim that Jesus Christ was "perfect God and perfect man, consisting of a rational soul and a body."

Of course the decision at the Council of Ephesus only served to heighten the tension between rival factions. But this tension between the extremes of Apollinarianism and Nestorianism drove the church to more sophisticated thinking and to some measure of unity regarding Christology at Chalcedon in 451.

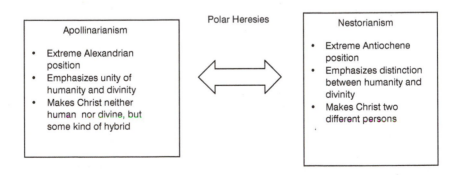

Figure 8.2 Polar heresies of Apollinarianism and Nestorianism

After the Council of Ephesus, Cyril appeared to soften somewhat his earlier, uncompromising Alexandrian position. He signed a document known as the Formulary of Reunion (or Symbol of Union) in 433 which described Christ as a union of two natures. This ended the discord between Cyril, the most outspoken proponent of the Alexandrian camp, and John of Antioch, who represented a less-extreme Antiochene position now that Nestorius had been condemned. It seemed that the mainstream of Christian thought was working its way toward a balanced view of the relation of Christ's humanity to his divinity. But John died in 441 and Cyril in 444, and there was another period of intense Christological debate (accompanied by a significant dose of politics).

Eutyches, a churchman in Constantinople, took up the mantel of Cyril's earlier extreme monophysitism, and sought to root out all suggestions of a divided Christ. It is not entirely clear that Eutyches was fairly treated by his contemporaries or later historians. Probably he lacked the skill of a careful thinker and was therefore unable to defend himself against the apparent implications of his thought – which put him back in league with the Apollinarians and a view of Christ that couldn't quite be reconciled to his humanity. So, Eutyches was excommunicated in 448 by Flavian, the Archbishop of Constantinople.

The tide turned briefly for Eutyches in 449 in what is known as the Robber Synod. Eutyches found a sympathetic ear in Dioscorus, Cyril's successor in Alexandria. Dioscorus did not accept the deposing of Eutyches by Flavian, seeing the act as a marginalization of the Alexandrian perspective. Dioscorus maneuvered politically to preside at a synod called by Emperor Theodosius to settle the dispute. Flavian wrote to Pope Leo in Rome for support, but Leo declined to attend and instead sent representatives along with a letter he had written. This letter, Leo's Tome (as it is now designated), declared the pope's support for Flavian and the view of Christ as a union of two natures in one person.

MONOPHYSITISM

From the Greek *monos* = only, alone and *physis* = nature: the belief that Christ had only one nature instead of two.

Things did not go well for Flavian at the synod: Pope Leo's letter was never read, Flavian was given no chance to speak, and Dioscorus had Flavian deposed and beaten. When news of this reached Rome, Leo was outraged and called the synod a den of robbers – hence the appellation "Robber Synod." Leo attempted to convince Emperor Theodosius to reconsider the legitimacy of the synod, but Theodosius would have none of that. It appeared that the stalemate would continue, but then in 450 Theodosius fell off his horse and died from the injuries. Marcian, a general in the army, married Theodosius's sister Pulcheria, and he determined to bring theological peace to the empire, calling the Council of Chalcedon which began on the 8th of October, 451.

More than 500 bishops attended the Council of Chalcedon with the goal of establishing a unified belief throughout the empire. Many did not want to create a new creed, but merely to reaffirm the Nicene Creed. The councils of 325, 381, and 431 were all confirmed; the "Robber Synod" of 449 was overturned. Some of the letters of Cyril were accepted as authoritative and doctrine defining, as was Pope Leo's Tome. Still, the representatives of the emperor pushed to have a new formulation of Christological doctrine that everyone would sign. This resulted in the Definition of Chalcedon as follows:

> In agreement, therefore, with the holy fathers, we all unanimously teach that we should confess that our Lord Jesus Christ is one and the same Son, the same perfect in Godhead and the same perfect in manhood, truly God and truly man, the same of a rational soul and body, consubstantial with the Father in Godhead, and the same

PRINCIPAL PLAYERS LEADING TO CHALCEDON

Alexandrians	*Antiochenes*
Apollinarius	Nestorius
Cyril	John of Antioch
Eutyches	Flavian
Discorus	

consubstantial with us in manhood, like us in all things except sin; begotten from the Father before the ages as regards His Godhead, and in the last days, the same, because of us and because of our salvation begotten from the Virgin Mary, the *Theotokos*,[6] as regards His manhood; one and the same Christ, Son, Lord, only-begotten, made known in two natures without confusion, without change, without division, without separation, the difference of the natures being by no means removed because of the union, but the property of each nature being preserved and coalescing in one *prosopon* and one *hupostasis*[7] – not parted or divined into two *prosopa*, but one and the same Son, only-begotten, divine Word, the Lord Jesus Christ, as the prophets of old and Jesus Christ Himself have taught us about Him and the creed of our fathers has handed down.[8]

Much of the wording of the Definition comes from previous documents, but the original and lasting contribution of Chalcedon comes from its affirmation of Christ's unity and his duality. He is one person (*prosopon* or *hupostasis*) not two; he has two natures – even after the Incarnation – not one. The insights of Alexandria and Antioch are held in balance.

It is sometimes claimed that those loyal to Antioch got the better deal in the Chalcedonian settlement: the monophysites of Alexandria were defeated. But these were the extreme Alexandrians whose position closely resembled the already heretical Apollinarians. The extremists on the side from Antioch (the Nestorians) had been clearly ruled out of bounds as well. So, if the Antiochene school of Christiology emerged victorious, it only did so by being tempered with the insights of Alexandria along the way.[9]

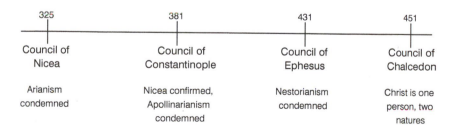

Figure 8.3 The four major ecumenical councils dealing with Christology

4 CHRISTOLOGY IN PRACTICE

The matter of Christology was not merely some abstract discussion happening only among the elite theologians of the Church. The Cappadocian father, Gregory of Nyssa, wrote that debates on the nature of Christ were happening at every turn in common society in Constantinople:

> Every place in the city is full of them: the alleys, the crossroads, the forums, the squares. Garment sellers, money changers, food vendors – they are all at it. If you ask for change, they philosophize about generate and ingenerate natures. If you inquire about the price of bread, the answer is that the father is greater and the Son inferior. If you speak about whether the bath is ready, they express the opinion that the Son was made out of nothing.[10]

Gregory himself, however, was less than optimistic about whether an explanation of the Incarnation could be grasped by human minds. He compared it to understanding the union of body and soul in a human being: there is no doubt that there are two different things, but how they are joined remains a mystery. In the same way we do not doubt that the person of Jesus of Nazareth was fully human and fully divine, but the union of these two remains beyond our comprehension.[11] Thankfully for the richness of Christian thought that was to come, others kept trying.

It is interesting and significant to note that both the Alexandrians and the Antiochenes worshiped Jesus Christ. Though their metaphysical theories about the object of their worship were different, there was unity in their practice. The Apollinarians might be criticized for worshiping something other than God because their view of Christ seemed to be neither human nor divine. But Apollinarius countered that their view allowed them "a single worship of the Logos and of the flesh which he assumed."[12] Furthermore, they anathematized those who separated the worship of the Logos from the worship of the man. Nestorius, however, would not let this anathema apply to him. He saw no trouble in distinguishing the natures of Christ while uniting the worship of him.[13] So while there was still significant disagreement in theory, there was an important unity of practice among those calling themselves Christians. That unity of practice is what held together the disputing factions and drove them to keep trying to resolve their theoretical differences.

A further instance of practice influencing theology might be found in the continued inclusion of the term *Theotokos* [God-bearer] in the Chalcedonian formulation. The term had been accepted at the Council of Constantinople, but with considerable disagreement. Nestorius advocated the term *Christotokos* [Christ-bearer] for Mary, so as to signify that she had only been responsible for bearing the human nature of Christ – not the divine. But this view was condemned along with Nestorius at Constantinople. So the position of Mary as *Theotokos* seemed to be accepted and assimilated into Christian worship in the decades after the Council of Constantinople. Thus, by the time of Chalcedon, the liturgical practice of acknowledging Mary as the God-bearer allowed for the term to be incorporated into the Definition of Chalcedon without much resistance.[14]

The Christological controversies were a subset of, and overlapped, the Trinitarian controversies of the same time period. We turn from investigating two natures and one person in Jesus Christ to three persons with a single nature in the Godhead.

SUMMARY OF MAIN POINTS

1 Arius took commonly held presuppositions about God to what he understood to be their logical conclusions, resulting in a theological crisis.

2 Nicea defined the relationship of the Son to the Father as "homo-ousios."

3 The polar extremes of Apollinarius and Nestorius regarding the nature of Christ created the tension in which the Definition of Chalcedon was held.

4 Despite the politics and division, this period was remarkable for its unity in practice: Jesus Christ, the God-man, was the object of worship.

FOR FURTHER READING

Edward R. Hardy, ed., *Christology of the Later Fathers* (Philadelphia, PA: Westminster Press, 1964). Includes primary source material from Athanasius and important letters from Arius, Cyril, and the Tome of Leo.

J.N.D. Kelly, *Early Christian Doctrines* (San Francisco, CA: HarperSanFrancisco, 1978). A standard reference on the development of doctrine, with a substantial section on Christology.

Donald Macleod, *The Person of Christ* (Downers Grove, IL: Intervarsity Press, 1998). A contemporary treatment of Christology rooted in the historical debates.

9 Trinitarian debate

QUESTIONS TO BE ADDRESSED IN THIS CHAPTER

1 What is the doctrine of the Trinity?
2 Why did Christians develop the doctrine?
3 What were the early attempts at explaining the Trinity, and why did they fail?
4 What was the result of the accepted Trinitarian definition?

Prior to the decree of Theodosius in 391 which made Christianity the official religion of the Roman Empire, the state religion was decidedly polytheistic. We saw briefly in Chapter 5 that religion for the Romans was a kind of contract between the deities and the citizens, in which gods would protect and bless the empire so long as they were respected and appeased in the proper ways by the citizenry. But the necessity for appeasement extended beyond political matters; the Roman world was filled with gods for just about every occasion.

There was the chief god, Jupiter (the equivalent of the Greeks' Zeus); and there were other well-known deities like Mars, the god of war, Neptune, the god of the sea, and Venus, the goddess of love. There were also gods who needed to be appeased regarding such important areas of life as agriculture (Ceres), health (Salus), and fertility (Faunus); and beyond these there were gods ruling over even very mundane matters like banquets (Edesia) and doorways (Janus).

Observance of religious practices varied greatly too. Some religious ceremonies took the form of what we recognize as pagan rituals: a class of priests called the Salii came around to farms each spring in full ceremonial dress and performed dances and chants to make the corn grow; and on the first day of the Roman New Year, the 14th of March (the month named for the god Mars), a man was dressed up in skins and paraded through Rome to be beaten with sticks and driven out of the city – symbolic of the old year passing away. But other seemingly normal practices were also imbued with religious significance, such as the period right before the harvest which was dedicated to cleaning out the barns and receptacles to be used during the harvest. Such routines

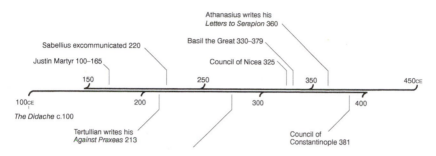

Timeline 9 Trinitarian debate

were maintained not just for pragmatic reasons, but expressly in order to satisfy the gods who governed the harvest that proper care was being taken for the bounty about to be brought in from the fields.[1]

As might be expected with such a diversity of practices and deities, there was little centralized control of religion (and even less of theology). It is true that there was an official roster of gods (called the pantheon), but this was not a static list. When Rome conquered surrounding territories, their captives' gods and religious practices could quite easily be incorporated into the system of rituals and sacrifices. All told, there were hundreds of different gods in ancient Roman religion.

Christians inherited one God from Judaism – Yahweh who was recognized as the Father by Christians. Then with their recognition of Jesus as divine, were Christians being influenced by their Greco-Roman surroundings into accepting polytheism? And besides the Father and the Son, what about the third member of the Trinity, the Holy Spirit? Christians may not count hundreds of gods, but once they add another to one, aren't they into polytheistic territory? The Christian Trinity certainly seems to be a departure from the ardent monotheism of their religious forefathers, the Jews. Or is it?

1 WHAT IS THE TRINITY?

The development of the doctrine of the Trinity must be counted among the most important and distinctive features of Christian thought. It is at the same time one of the easiest of doctrines to state, and the most difficult to explain. The doctrine of the Trinity can be stated quite succinctly in the following statements:

Identity Statements	Distinction Statements
The Father is God	The Father is not the Son
The Son is God	The Son is not the Holy Spirit
The Holy Spirit is God	The Holy Spirit is not the Father

Unity Statement
There is only one God

The Identity Statements assert the sameness of the three members of the Trinity – they are all equally God. The Distinction Statements claim there to be distinctions between these members; they are not merely different names for the same thing (like Samuel Clemens and Mark Twain). But then the surprising and tricky Unity Statement is that there is only one God. These are the commitments of Christians who hold to the doctrine of the Trinity.

It has often been represented graphically as something like this:

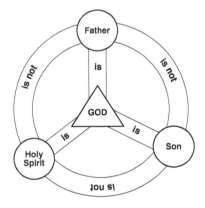

Figure 9.1 Trinity diagram

The diagram illustrates the relationships between different persons well, but it still does nothing to explain how such relationships could exist. How could there be three things that are different and distinct from each other, and yet they also remain one thing instead of three? It took very sophisticated and subtle reasoning on the parts of some of the best minds in the Christian tradition to give an explanation of this that would be accepted by the majority. But why, in the first place, was this necessary? Why were Christians so committed to these seemingly paradoxical claims?

2 THE REASON FOR THE TRINITY

At one level we can answer this question by appealing to the culture of monotheism Christians imbibed from their Jewish ancestry. It simply was not an option for them to recognize more than one god.[2] So if this was such an axiomatic commitment, the question becomes why the Son and the Spirit were taken to be God as well. Wouldn't it have been easier to maintain the divinity of God the Father and go the route of Arius or others in taking the Son and Spirit to be creatures? Yes, it would have been easier conceptually; but practically speaking, there was too much driving the Christians to accept the divinity of these others as well.

There may be some intellectual issues arising from their understanding of their faith which drove them to their Trinitarian position. For example, some would claim that Christ had to be divine in order to be the sinless sacrifice for all; others would argue that the Holy Spirit's role in creation and sanctification show the Spirit also to be divine. But these reasons and others like them were not the real driving force behind the Christians' commitments to the deity of the Son and Spirit. That force is ultimately to be found in Christians' experience of the persons of the Trinity in the practice of their religion. In this case, then, it was the practical which gave rise to the theoretical.

The New Testament documents testify to the fact that the early Christians believed Jesus to be more than just a great teacher who gave witness to God; they took him to be the revelation of God himself. The Gospel of John begins, "In the beginning was the Word, and the Word was with God, and the Word was God ... . And the Word became flesh and lived among us ..." (John 1:1, 14). The book of 1 John ends with these words: "We know that the Son of God has come and has given us understanding so that we may know him who is true; and we are in him who is true, in his Son Jesus Christ. He is the true God and eternal life" (1 John 5:20).[3] It was the experience of Jesus as God – not the verbal attestations or theorizing – which compelled the first disciples to recognize him as divine in their creeds. Consider the response attributed to Thomas in the Gospel of John when he is confronted personally with the resurrected Jesus: "My Lord and my God!" (John 20:28).

Then with the experience of Pentecost recorded in Acts 2, the Holy Spirit became the palpable presence of God in the lives of the believers. Peter explicitly identifies the spiritual power that came upon the Christians as the Spirit of God (Acts 2:17). It was the experience of the Holy Spirit in the hearts and minds of people that testified to them that they had new life in the one God (cf. Rom 8:16, 1 John 4:13).

Most contemporary expositions of the doctrine of the Trinity discuss the concept as though it was an intellectual puzzle to be figured out. Certainly understanding the Trinity was a puzzle, but we must acknowledge that the puzzle only arose because of the profound experience Christians attributed to the active work of the three members of the Trinity in their lives and among their religious communities. "If the disciples had not had that fundamental experience, we would not be talking about the Trinity today."[4]

So even though the concept of the Trinity is not explicitly mentioned anywhere in the Bible, the New Testament scriptures serve as the foundation for understanding why the concept developed. The experiences of those who were with Jesus and who were "filled with the Holy Spirit" came to be translated into liturgical language. At least three different authors of New Testament books use explicitly Trinitarian phrases. Matthew has Jesus say the familiar baptismal formula during his parting speech to the disciples: "Go therefore and make disciples of all nations, baptizing them in the name of the Father and of the Son and of the Holy Spirit" (Matthew 28:19); Peter opens his first letter by addressing people who, "have been chosen and destined by God the Father and sanctified by the Spirit to be obedient to Jesus Christ" (1 Peter 1:2); and the Apostle Paul concludes his second letter to the Corinthians with the benediction: "The grace of the Lord Jesus Christ, the love of God, and the communion of the Holy Spirit be with all of you" (2 Cor. 13:13). The Trinitarian impulse was present from the first generation of believers.

Furthermore, the apostolic tradition, while again not explicit in its exposition of the Trinity, is pregnant with Trinitarianism. Following the language of the Great Commission quoted above from Matthew, the manual on Christian practice written around the turn of the second century, *The Didache*, uses the three-fold formula in its instructions about baptism:

Now about baptism: this is how to baptize. Give public instruction on all these points, and then "baptize" in running water, "in the name of the Father and of the Son and of the Holy Spirit." If you do not have running water, baptize in some other. If you cannot in cold, then in warm. If you have neither, then pour water on the head three times "in the name of the Father, Son, and Holy Spirit."[5]

When arguing that Jesus was the messiah for whom Jews had been waiting, Justin Martyr (100–165), the great apologist of the second century, was not always consistent in his description of the deity of the Son. Sometimes he called Jesus an angel, other times he referred to him as another God besides the creator.[6] This kind of confusion was common in the writers of the second century. The problem was that concepts had not yet sufficiently developed to provide anything like an explanation of a three-in-one Trinity. They could only grope toward an explanation of what they believed they had experienced. If it had been the theory which drove practice in this instance, then it is difficult to see how the Trinitarian language would have survived, for there was no clear understanding at all of how it could be. Yet even Justin's thought was guided by the established worship practices. He said that we worship and adore the True God, the Father of righteousness, and the Son (who came forth from Him), and the prophetic Spirit.[7]

This sort of vague acknowledgement of the Trinity persisted without much attempt at explanation through the second century. Even the Nicene Creed of 325, which attempts to clarify the relationship between Father and Son, is alarmingly bereft of explanation concerning the relationship of the Holy Spirit to these other two. But the consistency of practice of the Christian communities ensured that such an explanation would have to come. Basil the Great (330–379) testified to the powerful shaping force that tradition and practice had on Christian thought: "We are bound to be baptized in the terms we have received, and to profess belief in the terms in which we are baptized."[8]

3 EXPLANATION OF THE TRINITY – EARLY ATTEMPTS

If theology took its cue from the actual practice of Christian communities, care was needed in translating the liturgical or even mystical language into the rational propositions of theology. In the poetic expressions of worship and liturgical settings, it is less problematic to attribute paradoxical claims to God; for example, the Invisible was made visible, the impassive One suffered, or the Immortal died. But how do we explain such claims? Even the creeds themselves were more about detailing *what* was to be believed than about explaining that belief.[9] Theological explanation, however, calls for more precise and understandable description. This is not easy to come by. Some of the earliest attempts at describing the relations between the three members of the Trinity sought to preserve those paradoxes and have therefore been called, "effort[s] to provide a theology for the language of devotion."[10]

As in the Christological debates, Christian thinkers were pulled in two seemingly opposite directions in trying to understand their object. Understanding the positions is complicated by the labels most often attributed to them, which have very different meanings in normal English than they do in the technical discussion of theology.

On the one hand there were the Monarchists – so called because of the literal meaning of *mono-arche*, which is "one principle." Trinitarian Monarchists were concerned to preserve the oneness of God as inherited from their Jewish roots. On the other hand there were the Economists. "Economy" comes from the Greek word *oikonomia*, which was the management of a household. Paul uses the word in Ephesians 3:9 to speak of the divine plan that God was revealing (in his management of the world). In this sense, the Trinitarian Economists emphasized the

MONARCHISTS VS. ECONOMISTS

Monarchy comes from the Greek word *monarchia*, meaning one principle or rule. The Monarchists were concerned to preserve the unity of God, and some went so far as to treat Father, Son, and Holy Spirit merely as modes – not distinct persons – of the one God.

Economy comes from the Greek word *oikonomia*, which generally means the administration or plan of a household. In the Trinitarian context, the Economists understood God's plan to be unfolding in the revelation of the threeness of God in Father, Son, and Holy Spirit.

threeness of Father, Son, and Spirit which was part of the divine plan that had only been revealed in the New Testament era.

The temptation of the Monarchists was to end up giving ground on the full divinity, or at least on the equality, of the Son and Spirit with the Father. This would play out in a couple of different ways: the Son and Spirit could be lesser "gods" than the Father, or the distinctions between the Father, Son, and Spirit could be almost completely eliminated. Some in this first group are called Adoptionists because they took the sonship and deity of Jesus to be an adopted designation that occurred only at Jesus's baptism; previous to that adoption, Jesus was not divine. In the third century, Paul of Samosata (200–275), the Bishop of Antioch, would develop a more nuanced version of monarchism that was less adoptionistic but still marginalizing to the Son. He held that only the Father was truly God, but that God's wisdom and power dwelt in the Son, who did not exist before his human birth. Because the Greek word for "power" is *dynamis*, the position has come to be known as "dynamic monarchism." It was ultimately condemned for being no more than a variant of Arianism (discussed in Chapter 8).

The other variety of monarchism that developed was what is now called "modal monarchism." Most of what we know about any of the proponents of modal monarchism comes from their opponents, so the reconstruction of their beliefs is fraught with difficulties. Noetus and Praxeas (both of the early third century) are the two names most often associated with the early modalists. They seemed concerned to hold to monotheism so strongly that the distinctions between Father, Son, and Spirit came to be merely different manifestations, or modes, of the one God. On such a model, the full divinity of Christ and the Spirit was upheld; but this was achieved at the expense of an almost complete identification of the supposedly distinct members. In their minds, any attempt to separate out Christ from the Father or the Spirit from either of these resulted in polytheism and must be avoided. So God is one, but might be manifested in various ways.

Here is the sense in which Modalistic theology captures some of the intent of the paradoxical claims made during the liturgy. The one God had seemingly contradictory properties: God as Father was eternal and immutable, but as Son was begotten and changed; God as Father and Spirit was invisible, but this self-same God as Son was visible on earth. And again, these are not somehow separate but related entities. We recognize that one person can be a mother, a daughter, and a sister and as such can be described in different ways; yet she is just one person. If the sister dies, so does the mother and daughter! And it is here that modal monarchism ran afoul of orthodoxy. If Christ suffered and died, and Christ was identical with the Father, then there is no escaping the conclusion that the Father suffered and died. This position is called patripassianism after the Latin words for "father" and "suffering" and involved all kinds of theological difficulties.

Tertullian (whom we met in Chapter 5) wrote a treatise called *Against Praxeas* around 213. According to him, Praxeas claimed that, "The Father Himself came down into the Virgin, was Himself born of her, Himself suffered, indeed was Himself Jesus Christ."[11] Tertullian asserted that this confuses the plan of salvation and Scripture (for God so loved the world that he sent his only Son), and it contradicts the impassiveness and immutability of God.

Another of the Modalists was Sabellius. Not much is known about him, and though Sabellianism came to stand for modalism in general, it seems that his was a more sophisticated version of modal monarchism – though again we are beholden to his critics for conveying what he actually believed and taught. Sabellius used several different approaches for attempting to uphold the oneness of God at the expense of real distinctions between the members of the Trinity. He called God the "Son-Father" to signify that these were truly one entity (it is not clear what he made of the Spirit on this model). But then he also employed an analogy with the sun, trying to show that there are different aspects or manifestations of the one thing: just as the sun radiates both light and heat, the Father "radiates" the Son and the Spirit. It also seems that he was concerned to avoid patripassianism, and so spoke of the different modes of the godhead being manifested only one at a time so that God-as-

PATRIPASSIANISM

From the Latin for "Father" and "suffer." An idea stemming from modalistic views of the Trinity that the suffering of Christ on the cross was equally experienced by the Father, because Father and Son are not two separate beings, but only different modes of the one God.

Father did not suffer and die – but only God-as-Son. However, he always held firm to the monarchists' conviction that making real distinctions between Father, Son, and Spirit was giving up on monotheism. Sabellius was excommunicated in 220 by Pope Callistus.

Apart from refuting heretical explanations of the Trinity, Tertullian also attempted a positive characterization of the three-in-one deity that Christians were worshiping. In fact, it seems that Tertullian was the first to use the word *trinitas* in Latin from which we get the word Trinity. He said,

> While the mystery of the [*oikonomia*] is still guarded, which distributes the Unity into a Trinity, placing in their order the three Persons – the Father, the Son, and the Holy Ghost: three, however, not in condition, but in degree; not in substance, but in form; not in power, but in aspect; yet of one substance, and of one condition, and of one power, inasmuch as He is one God, from whom these degrees and forms and aspects are reckoned, under the name of the Father, and of the Son, and of the Holy Ghost. How they are susceptible of number without division, will be shown as our treatise proceeds.[12]

Though writing in Latin, Tertullian inserted the Greek word *oikonomia* (literally, "household management," here with the sense "internal workings") into the passage, and he is the chief representative of the Economists. So while Tertullian insisted that God has existed from eternity past as a unity, he has more recently revealed himself in the divine "economy" as existing in three distinct persons. He took great care to stress that this does not create three separate gods, drawing on analogies that really only show part-whole relationships: the river and its source are distinct but not separate; so too the root and the shoot of a plant. Tertullian also uses the analogy of the sun and the sunlight that is radiated from it; but contrary to Sabellius, he thinks it shows how Father and Son are distinct entities, rather than different manifestations. At any rate, Tertullian argued that God exists as one substance (*substantia*) and three persons (*persona*). While not yet an explanation of how a Trinity could exist, this was a stride toward providing an analysis of the concept.

A problem enters, though, because of the different languages that were being used. Tertullian's Latin did not always translate very well to the Greek speaking people in the East. At this time, it was common to translate the Latin *substantia* into Greek as *hypostasis*; but the Greeks used *hypostasis* to refer to individual people. So this became terribly confusing for Greeks who read Tertullian as going to great lengths to show that Father, Son, and Holy Spirit are three distinct persons, but also understood him to be claiming that God is one person. Further progress in explaining the doctrine of the Trinity, then, required that Christian thinkers would pay more careful attention to their terminology.

4 TERMINOLOGICAL CLARIFICATION

The Trinitarian debate was going on around the same time period as the debate over Christology, and many of the terminological issues in the former were the same as those discussed in Chapter 8. We cover some of that same historical territory again here, because there is another element to be added to the story: the Holy Spirit.

Prior to the fourth century, there was not a lot of attention or import given in theological treatises to the nature of the Holy Spirit or its relation to the other members of the godhead (we've mentioned the sparse attention given to the Holy Spirit in the Nicene Creed of 325). Interestingly, there is evidence that some in the early centuries, and especially those in the East, considered the Holy Spirit to be female.[13] But by the time Christian thinkers devoted considerable theological resources to trying to understand the Spirit, the climate in the Roman Empire was decidedly androcentric and would not have accommodated such an idea.

The great twentieth-century historian of theology, Jaroslav Pelikan, claimed that there was a "lack of clarity" in the words and thought of the first generations of Christian thinkers about the Holy Spirit, and this contributed to the hesitancy of the early church fathers in addressing the Holy Spirit.[14] It was in the latter half of the fourth century when this began to change. Athanasius, who figured so prominently in the Christological controversies (see Chapter 8), also played an important role in clarifying the nature and role of the Holy Spirit. Around 360, probably while Athanasius was in exile from his bishopric at Alexandria, a bishop named Serapion from up the Nile delta in Thmuis inquired about the Holy Spirit, wondering whether the Spirit might not be just an exalted creature. Athanasius responded in what is known as his "Four Letters to Serapion," using various arguments to defend the deity of the Holy Spirit. Most significantly, the term *homo-ousios* looms large again just as it did for Christology. According to Athanasius, the relationship of Son to Spirit is such that the two must be of the same essence or nature.

OUSIA

The Greek word for "being" and sometimes translated as nature or essence; for example, different animals share the same ousia in that they are all animals.

HYPOSTASIS

The Greek word which came to be used for an individual substance; for example, one particular animal is a different hypostasis from another particular animal.

SUBSTANTIA

The Latin word for substance which was originally translated into Greek as *hypostasis*; once the meaning of *hypostasis* was more clearly defined, *substantia* translated better to *ousia*.

When back in Alexandria in 362, Athanasius called a council of bishops in order to deal with the question of *hypostases*. They affirmed the Nicean tradition of claiming the Son and Father to be *homo-ousios* (of the same substance) and applied this to the Spirit as well. But some thought that using this word committed them to just one *hypostasis* for the Trinity as well, for the terms were used interchangeably in some contexts; and again, the Latin *substantia* was generally translated into Greek as *hypostasis*. But then the earlier difficulty with the Modalists convinced Athanasius to accept some greater differentiation between the members of the Trinity. In the end, after much discussion and compromise, the council agreed that within the context of affirming Nicea and acknowledging the divinity of the Holy Spirit, it would be acceptable to treat the three individual members of the Trinity as having their own *hypostasis* so long as there was an additional emphasis to be made on the unity of these three as having a single nature (*ousia*). But this did not settle the matter; the terms continued to be used interchangeably and confusion reigned. It fell to the Cappadocians (introduced in Chapter 6) to dispel the foggy terminology with more precise definitions.

Their task was still the same: to acknowledge the oneness of the Trinity without blurring the distinctions, and to acknowledge the three-ness without obliterating the unity. Basil wanted to use the term *hypostasis* to denote the three persons. He wrote a letter to his brother, Gregory of Nyssa, concerning the difference between the two words: "That which is spoken of in a special and peculiar manner is indicated by the name of the hypostasis."[15] Drawing heavily on Greek philosophy, he argued that even among three men we recognize a common element: there is something about them that is the same since they are all men. But there is also something different between the three, because they are three separate individuals, three *hypostases*. By affirming that the members of the Trinity are three hypostases, the separateness is ensured and the threat of Sabellianism dispelled.

But then, of course, the opposite threat would raise its head: if there are three hypostases, how could it be the case that there is only one God? For Peter, James, and John have a nature (*ousia*) in common, yet we would not call them a Trinity – they are three separate beings of the same species. It was argued, however, that the unity of the three persons of the Trinity is what binds them together. Let's try to bring some further clarity to this point with an analogy from the classification of living things.

We might think of the "nature" of one individual being (a *hypostasis*) as being a composite of many natures. For example, we might say that the class of animals can be subdivided into mammals and birds. If we pick one particular mammal (which would be one *hypostasis*) and one particular bird (another *hypostasis*), these would share the nature of being animals, but they would also have other "natures" which distinguish them from each other. Even among mammals, we could pick one individual man and one individual horse; these two *hypostases* have more in common than a man and a bird (in addition to both being animals, both are mammals), but they too have other natures that can be distinguished. And finally, even among *hypostases* which are all men – Peter, James, and John – although they have even more in common than the man and the bird, or the man and the horse, they are still separate men. We might think, though, that if we keep moving up the hierarchical tree of genera and species, there could be a point at which the separate *hypostases* have so much in common that there is nothing left to distinguish individual *hypostases* other than the fact that there are three. This would be the point at which the Trinity exists, in perfect unity.

We might speak of the unity of three people, but this is only a manner of speaking.[16] The unity of the Father, Son, and Holy Spirit is real; they act in perfect unity and are unchanging. It is their simplicity and indivisibility which distinguishes them from the composite human beings and thus guarantees their oneness.[17]

It must be admitted that not everything has been cleared up about the Trinity. Basil himself admitted that what is common and what is distinct in the members of the Trinity is, "in a certain sense, ineffable and inconceivable."[18] What really occurred by the fixing of terminology is that certain parameters or boundaries were set within which theological speculation must remain for the orthodox. The important Council of Constantinople in 381 probably expanded on the creed formulated at Nicea in 325 with respect to the Trinity. The Holy Spirit was declared to be the "Lord and the life-giver, who proceeds from the Father; who with the Father and the Son is together worshiped and together glorified."[19] While no formal creed exists from that council, the year after its meeting, a group of bishops wrote a letter summarizing their findings. It explicitly states that the true faith holds Father, Son, and Holy Spirit to be equally divine and of one nature (*ousia*) while existing in three persons (*hypostases*).[20]

So the God-man, Jesus Christ, was declared to be one person with two natures; the Trinity, then, was declared to be three persons with one nature. Thus the formulae have remained for the orthodox. We may still wonder in what sense we are to understand that this one God has three persons. Perhaps the words of St. Augustine, to whom we turn in Chapter 11, summarize it best: we say "persons" not because it completely explains things, but in order not to remain completely silent on the matter.[21]

SUMMARY OF MAIN POINTS

1   The Father, Son, and Spirit are all God; they are not identical with each other; and there is only one God.
2   The first Christians' religious experience drove them to maintain the deity of Son and Spirit in addition to that of the Father.
3   Monarchists and Economists each went too far in emphasizing the oneness or the three-ness of the Trinity.
4   Postulating three persons and one nature did not completely explain the Trinity, but it did set parameters within which orthodox Christian thought should remain.

FOR FURTHER READING

Gregory of Nyssa, "On Not Three Gods." An early work by one of the Cappadocians exploring the ideas that led to the Trinitarian formulation.

J.N.D. Kelly, *Early Christian Doctrines* (San Francisco: HarperSanFrancisco, 1978). A standard reference on the development of doctrine, with a substantial section on the Trinity.

Roger E. Olson and Christopher A. Hall, *The Trinity* (Grand Rapids, MI: Eerdmans, 2002). An introductory survey to the historical development of the doctrine of the Trinity.

Tertullian, *Against Praxeas*. Tertullian's seminal work combating the monarchist view of Praxeas. Available in many collections and online.

Thomas Torrance, *The Trinitarian Faith: The Evangelical Theology of the Ancient Catholic Church* (Edinburgh: T&T Clark, 1988). A more rigorous treatment of the development of the doctrine of the Trinity.

10

Formation of the New Testament canon

QUESTIONS TO BE ADDRESSED IN THIS CHAPTER

1 What is the New Testament canon?
2 What drove Christians to establish a new canon?
3 How was the New Testament canon formed?
4 Why were certain books considered but then rejected from the canon?
5 Is the New Testament canon closed?

Soon after the founding of Islam, Muslims started referring to Jews and Christians as "people of the book." This phrase was used to signify that those groups had received revelation from God which had been written down and preserved in a holy book. In this sense, Muslims see themselves as standing in the same tradition as their monotheistic forebears, because they too have a sacred text – the Qur'an. But there are striking differences between the Qur'an and the Christian Bible with respect to their modes of composition. According to Islamic tradition, during the years 610–632CE, Muhammed received a series of special revelatory messages. He memorized these messages and recited them to his companions, who wrote them down word for word and compiled them into the Qur'an ("recitation" is the literal meaning of the Arabic word for Qur'an). Thus the Qur'an is believed to be the verbatim word of God delivered through the Prophet Muhammed.[1]

By contrast the Christians' holy book, the Bible, is more accurately described as a set of books, sixty-six in all, from Genesis to Revelation.[2] It consists of two "testaments" or "covenants": the Old Testament and the New Testament. The Old Testament is the book of the Jews, and beginning with the creation story it describes the acts of God in history, primarily through the people of Israel. Parts of the Old Testament could be compared to the Qur'an in that some of its books were written by prophets who claimed to be delivering the very word of the Lord to Israel. The New Testament, however, is a collection of books written about Jesus and the early believers and letters written by apostles giving instruction to groups of believers. These writings are understood by most Christians to be

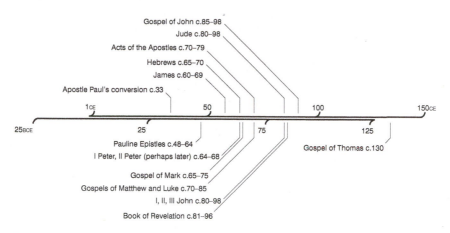

Timeline 10 Formation of the New Testament

inspired by God and are even called the Word of God, but with one possible exception none of them claims to be a transcript of God's spoken word.[3]

If God did not dictate the New Testament to Christians, and if it did not fall out of the sky directly into church pews, where did it come from? When and how was it assembled? Who was responsible for deciding which books to include and which to exclude? And why is it not still being added to today? These important issues regarding *the* book of Christian thought, faith, and practice are the subject of this chapter.

1 THE NEW TESTAMENT CANON

The word "canon" comes from the ancient Greek word *kanon* or "measuring rod"[4] and simply means a collection of texts or works considered to be authoritative and used as the basis of faith and practice. Even before its final formulation, the writings of the New Testament were fundamental to the spiritual and communal life of Christian believers. For them, they are more than important historical writings, such as the works of Homer or Hesiod or Herodotus; they are "sacred texts" and the word of God.

But again, the writings of the New Testament are not just records of conversations God supposedly had with someone, who then thought it important to inform the rest of the people. The New Testament is a set of twenty-seven different books by at least ten different authors. There are within it several distinct genres which can be delineated into the following four-fold division:

Gospels: The first four books of the New Testament are called Gospels. They each give a narrative of the life and teachings of Jesus, describing him as both divine and human – savior and servant – and as proclaiming the gospel ("good news") of the kingdom of God. Their traditional titles and authors are: Matthew, Mark, Luke, and John.

History: The Acts of the Apostles picks up where the Gospel of Luke leaves off – the resurrection of Jesus. It describes significant theological and historical events after Jesus's resurrection through the lives of the Apostles Peter and Paul. It is the historical nexus between the gospel accounts and the period of the Epistles.

Epistles: The largest number of writings in the New Testament is in the form of Epistles, or letters. There are twenty-one of these letters, written by various church leaders – the majority coming from the Apostle Paul.[5] They deal chiefly with practical and theological problems in response to issues raised in the early Christian congregations. The letters are named after either their addressees or their traditional authors. The complete list of canonical epistles is: Romans, 1 Corinthians, 2 Corinthians, Galatians, Ephesians, Philippians, Colossians, 1 Thessalonians, 2 Thessalonians, 1 Timothy, 2 Timothy, Titus, Philemon, Hebrews, James, 1 Peter, 2 Peter, 1 John, 2 John, 3 John, and Jude.

Apocalypse: The book of Revelation is the last book in the New Testament, and it is an apocalyptic writing ("apocalypse" means a revelation or disclosure). It consists of seven letters to seven churches followed by a series of visions given to the writer about forthcoming events. In symbolic prose, it depicts a cosmic battle between the warring forces of good and evil, culminating in the final binding of Satan and the ultimate triumph of Christ – the Lamb of God.

This is the authoritative list of books included in the New Testament today, and it has remained the same for well over 1,500 years. But in the first few centuries of the Christian era, there was not always agreement on which books should form their definitive canon. And in the very earliest Christian times, it is not clear that there was an intention to form a new canon. But the need for one soon developed.

2 THE NECESSITY OF A NEW TESTAMENT CANON

From the earliest times, Christians had a canon. In the first century the Jewish Scriptures, or "Old Testament" as it would later be called by Christians, fit this description of canon and was understood by both Jews and Christians – including Jesus himself – to be the authoritative Scripture. But in the decades after Jesus, his disciples and followers preserved and orally passed along many of his important sayings. Over a period of time, these sayings and stories of Jesus's life, death, and resurrection were written down in the gospels and were read in churches as sacred scripture (as sacred as the Old Testament writings). Other church leaders and apostolic authorities also wrote materials about Jesus and the Christian faith, and some of these materials were also treated with authority and accepted by Christians as guiding their faith and practice. But not all who claimed to be Christians accepted the same writings as authoritative. It was necessary, therefore, for Christians to develop a new canon, or New Testament, in conjunction with the old canon.

As we saw in Chapter 7, there were a number of budding sects in the first few centuries of the Christian era which were claiming to teach "true" Christianity. Their adherents were also writing books to support their own religious views. From the Marcionites to the Ebionites to the Gnostics and others as well, there were many contradictory belief systems all claiming to follow the teachings of Jesus. This raised obvious difficulties: who had the real teachings of Jesus? Who had the "truth?" A sacred canon was necessary to help clarify who was right and who was wrong.

Furthermore, the "heretic" Marcion (c. 85–160; discussed in Chapter 7) had provided a canon of his own, and this expedited the process for the orthodox believers to codify the Scriptures which they were affirming and using in the churches.[6] Marcion, remember, had rejected the Old Testament (and the Old Testament God as well) and regarded Paul as the only faithful apostle of Jesus. Marcion's "Bible" reflected his own theological views and consisted only of the Gospel of Luke (although he expunged those passages within Luke which were inconsistent with his own teachings) and ten books from Paul.[7] The church father Tertullian disagreed with Marcion's canon and responded by defending most of the New Testament books that we have today as being canonical (he included all but 2 Peter, James, 2 John, and 3 John).

IRENAEUS' COLLECTION OF CANONICAL BOOKS, c.180

Irenaeus' collection of authoritative scriptural writings included all of the books of the present-day New Testament with the exception of Philemon, 2 Peter, 3 John, and Jude.

Not only did some Christian sects exclude New Testament books, others included books beyond what eventually were included in the definitive canon. There were Gnostic scriptures written in the second and third centuries which were accepted as authoritative in the Gnostic communities. They had their own Gospels, Acts, Epistles, and Apocalypses which were used to promote their developing beliefs about Jesus. The existence and use of all these different "scriptures" made it necessary for the orthodox to nail down what they took to be the "authentic" writings. As noted in Chapter 7, church father Irenaeus was a virulent apologist combating the heretical (primarily Gnostic) teachings. As early as 180CE he had a defined collection of New Testament writings, approximately twenty-three of them, which he regarded as authoritative as the Old Testament.

There were other related concerns that made it necessary to have a codified canon of Scripture. For example, each Sunday when Christian believers met for worship, the Scriptures were read in the churches.[8] Which of the new books should be included in this practice? In the book of 1 Timothy there is a clear reference to Jesus's words quoted in the book of Luke as being "Scripture."[9] Which of the many writings claiming to include the words of Jesus should be taken as Scripture? Furthermore, churches needed guidance on how practical and moral issues should be handled. Some of the letters of Paul deal specifically with such issues. Does their coming from an apostle make them Scripture? These were real concerns which played an important role in the formation of a canon.

There were also political concerns that were instrumental in the formation of the canon. As noted in Chapter 5, Christians were persecuted in the first few centuries of the Christian era. This persecution involved an attempt by the Roman authorities to eliminate the sacred writings of the followers of Jesus. Church historian Eusebius describes one such event which occurred in 303:

It was in the nineteenth year of the reign of Diocletian, and the month of the Dystrus, or March, as the Romans would call it, in which, as the festival of the Saviour's passion was coming on, an imperial letter was everywhere promulgated, ordering the razing of the churches to the ground and the destruction by fire of the Scripture, and proclaiming that those who held high positions would lose all civil rights, while those in households, if they persisted in their profession of Christianity, would be deprived of their liberty.[10]

It was imperative for Christians to know which books were sacred and thus worth saving, for sometimes it would cost them their very lives!

Once the persecution ended under the Edict of Milan, authorized by Emperor Constantine in 313, another factor worked to the favor of the solidification of a unified canon. Constantine commissioned Eusebius to arrange for fifty copies of the Bible (both the Old and the New Testament) to be produced at the emperor's expense.[11] This would prove to be a significant event, for here we have an emperor ordering the publication of the Christian canon! Unfortunately, Eusebius does not tell us which books were included. Nevertheless, it is widely thought that these Bibles had significant influence on future canonical lists, and likely contained the same twenty-seven books in the New Testament we have today.

Finally, evangelism and missionary activity were also important factors in developing a canon. As missionaries in the first few centuries spread the Christian message to other lands and people groups, there was the need to translate the writings into the indigenous languages. This was time-consuming, difficult work. It was crucial to know which books were Scripture and thus worth the time and energy of translation.

3 THE FORMATION OF THE NEW TESTAMENT CANON

The process by which the New Testament canon was formed was long and complex. It was not, as some have supposed, the outcome of a single meeting or council held on a given day in early Christian history. Rather, it was a gradual process that took several centuries to complete. Unfortunately, there is no detailed description of canonization in the chronicles of the ancient Church. Modern scholars agree, however, that the processes can be more or less pieced together through a careful study of the writings of the church fathers and other sources.

It may come as a surprise that the complete list of the twenty-seven books of the New Testament first appeared in a letter written by Athanasius in 367, roughly three centuries after the books had been penned! This was followed up in 382, under the authority of Pope Damasus in Rome, by a synod in which the list of Athanasius was adopted. Pope Gelasius ratified the same list in the fifth century, and then the Second Trullan Council in 692 put closure to the issue of the New Testament canon in the East with its decision to accept the twenty-seven books. Such ratifications should not be seen as implying that the New Testament books were understood to be less than Scripture prior to these official councils. On the contrary, by the middle of the second century, every book of the New Testament had been referenced as authoritative (as a part of "Scripture") by some church father.[12]

Not every one of the early fathers in the second and third centuries was in complete agreement about which books should be a part of the canon, yet most of the New Testament writings were being read as Scripture in most of the churches by the third century. By the fourth

CRITERIA USED FOR DETERMINING NEW TESTAMENT CANONICITY

A – Apostolic authority: the book was connected to an apostle in some significant way

E – Extending back to the apostles: the book was old, extending back to the time of the apostles themselves

I – Inspired by God: the book was understood by the churches as being inspired by the Holy Spirit

O – Orthodox teaching: the book contained orthodox teaching and was spiritually edifying

U – Universal usage: the book was widely accepted among the catholic churches as canonical.

century the Church universal was basically in agreement that all and only the twenty-seven books should be included in the canon.

So how did the early Church decide which books should be included and which excluded? There were several criteria that can be gleaned from the ancient sources which were utilized in making this important determination. The following acrostic of English vowels helps specify the central criteria used for accepting or rejecting a book as canonical.

Apostolic authority. As with many of the world's great teachers, Jesus of Nazareth left nothing in writing. The New Testament documents his words, but they were written by others. In order for a book to be considered canonical, one fundamental criterion was that it was written by an apostle (or by a close associate of an apostle) who would have first-hand knowledge of Jesus and his teachings. An apostle, in this context, consisted of one of the twelve disciples sent out by Jesus to preach the Gospel (including Peter, James, and John) as well as Paul of Tarsus.

Many of the books of the New Testament include the author's name within them. Others, however, like the letter to the Hebrews and the Gospels and Acts do not have the author's name anywhere in the text. While some of the earliest church leaders and congregations probably personally knew the authors of some of these books, after a generation or two they were sometimes forgotten or the alleged author became questioned. One reason for authorial suspicion was that a number of books in the ancient world were forgeries, claiming to be written by someone who did not in fact write them. In such cases it was the task of church leaders to assess the true apostolic authority of the books. A well-known example of a book that is probably a forgery and which was considered for canonicity but eventually rejected was a book called the Epistle of Barnabas – allegedly written by Paul's companion Barnabas and denouncing Judaism as a false religion.

Another book which was questioned, but finally accepted as canonical, was the book of 2 Peter. 1 Peter was accepted as canonical primarily because it was believed to have been written by the Apostle Peter. But since it was written in a style quite different from that of 2 Peter, it was argued that the latter must have been a forgery (even though it claimed to be written by "Simon Peter, a servant and apostle of Jesus Christ" (2 Peter 1:1)). Eventually 2 Peter was admitted into the canon because the church fathers were persuaded that the Apostle Peter was in fact its true author. The stylistic differences between the books could perhaps be explained if one of the letters had been dictated by Peter in his native Aramaic to an amanuensis (that is, a copyist) who then wrote down the message in Greek.

Extending back to the apostles. Related to the first criterion of apostolic connection and authority is the idea that the book had to extend back to the time of the apostles – very close to the time of Jesus himself. If the book was written too late, even if there was some attempt to connect it to apostolic authority (perhaps by claiming that the teachings were orally transmitted from an apostle to a close confidant who then passed it on, etc.), it was rejected as a canonical work. The central reason for this criterion is that there were many works being written in the second and third centuries claiming to represent the authentic teachings of Jesus (Gnostic writings are a case in point), and many of these works were novel, if not contradictory, to orthodox teachings. The orthodox leaders were set on keeping to the original teachings of the apostles and believed that the earlier books were more trustworthy witnesses than later ones. Thus they rejected the later works, taking them to be unfit for canonical inclusion.

One example of a book that some early churches included in their worship services but which was rejected as canonical by the church fathers was the Shepherd of Hermes. The reason for rejection: its late authorship. The Muratorian Canon – a writing dating back to the second century – mentions the Shepherd of Hermes and notes that it should not be read as Scripture because it was composed "very recently, in our own times."[14]

THE MURATORIAN CANON

The Muratorian Canon (c. 170) is perhaps the earliest example of an extant canon ("extant" meaning one which still exists today). Also referred to as the "Muratorian Fragment," this important work is from the eighth century, although its contents date back to the late second century. It is a list of New Testament books which the church of Rome recognized as authoritative, and includes all of the books in the New Testament we have today except Hebrews, James, and 1 and 2 Peter,[13] as well as brief commentary on them.

Inspired by God. In the early centuries of Christianity the idea of divine inspiration was not limited to canonical works. For example, in a letter to the church in Corinth, Clement of Rome (fl. *c.* 96CE) tells the church, "You will give us joy and gladness if you are obedient to the things which we have written through the Holy Spirit."[15] Similar claims were made in reference to the writings of Ignatius of Antioch, Eusebius, Jerome, and others – authors whose writings were not included in the New Testament canon. They believed their writings were inspired by God. So inspiration was not a *sufficient* condition for determining canonicity. The early Christians believed that many people were "inspired" by God to speak or write this or that. But inspiration was a *necessary* condition. For a writing to be canonical, it had to be divinely inspired.

From the very beginning of the Christian era it was believed that the sacred Scriptures were inspired of God. This is reflected in the New Testament writings themselves. For example, 2 Timothy 3:16 says that "all Scripture is inspired by God." These divinely inspired words were not merely the writings of human beings, but somehow also the very words of God. Thus Paul says to the Thessalonian church: "We also constantly give thanks to God for this, that when you received the word of God that you heard from us, you accepted it not as a human word, but as what it truly is, God's word" (I Thess. 2:13).

Orthodox teaching. Perhaps the most important criterion for assessing whether a book was to be included in the canon was its theology. If a book contained unorthodox teachings, it was firmly rejected from consideration for the canon. As the author of the Muratorian Canon put it, "it is not fitting that gall be mixed with honey."[16] Early phrases such as "the ecclesiastical canon" and "the canon of the church" were used to refer to the body of orthodox doctrine affirmed by the churches.[17] Writings which were inconsistent with these teachings would be ruled out of bounds for canonical consideration.[18]

Universal usage. Another test for whether a book would be accepted as canonical was its widespread usage and acceptance by the established Christian churches. The book needed to be "catholic" (the Greek word for "universal") in order to be accepted. A book that had been widely used for a long period of time was in a better position to be accepted than one which only a few churches used, or one which was used more recently. In noting this criterion, Augustine (354–430) makes the following point:

Now, in regard to the canonical Scriptures, he must follow the judgment of the greater number of catholic churches; and among these, of course, a high place must be given to such as have been thought worthy to be the seat of an apostle and to receive epistles. Accordingly, among the canonical Scriptures he will judge according to the following standard: to prefer those that are received by all the catholic churches to those which some do not receive. Among those, again, which are not received by all, he will prefer such as have the sanction of the greater number and those of greater authority, to such as are held by the smaller number and those of less authority.[19]

How "universal" was universal enough? This was not always easy to discern. Thus, some books which were not as widely used as others became disputed, including the books of 2 Peter and Jude. Since it was determined that these two books were written by apostles, however, they were eventually added to the canon despite their less than full universality.[20]

4 CANONICAL DISPUTES

Once the canon was established, the disputes about which books should be in and which should be out did not immediately disappear. Actually, as we will see below, the disputes have continued down to our own day in some quarters. But in antiquity the debates often raged, especially regarding certain books. The following is a helpful classification regarding the disputes which erupted even after the canonization process had, for all intents and purposes, provided the twenty-seven books of the New Testament canon.

- **Homologoumena**: books which were widely accepted by the church fathers and orthodox churches as being canonical. The books which were universally accepted by the churches as being canonical – the *undisputed* books which appeared on most of the ancient canonical lists – consist of approximately seventeen of the twenty-seven books. They include all the books in our current New Testament from Matthew through Titus.
- **Pseudopigrapha**: books which were clearly rejected by the church fathers and orthodox churches as being canonical. There was a large

number of books written in the first and second centuries which were rejected from the start as being unfit for canonical consideration. There are various reasons why these books were rejected as "false writings," including their being written under a false name.[21] As far as the orthodox fathers and leaders were concerned, there was simply no place in the New Testament for questionable books – whether having to do with questionable theology or authorship.

- **Antilegomena**: books which were disputed by the orthodox churches as being canonical. There were some books which were challenged or disputed but yet remained on the canonical lists. These include the last ten books of the present-day New Testament: Philemon through Revelation. Consider the Book of Revelation. While it was one of the earliest books to be included in canonical lists of the apostolic fathers, it was also questioned more than perhaps any other canonical writing. Its teaching on the millennium – a thousand year reign of Jesus Christ on the earth – was the primary bone of contention. For a number of the orthodox leaders, it seemed too far-fetched to be inspired by God. However, despite its long history of suspicion, Athanasius defended its inclusion in the canon, and it was finally added to the important canonical list at the Synod of Carthage in 397. Even if they had been challenged in some of the churches and by some of the fathers, all of the antilegomena were eventually included in the New Testament canon once they were understood to be orthodox, inspired, and connected to an apostle.

- **Apocrypha**: books which were accepted by some of the early orthodox churches, but which were finally rejected as canonical. Finally, there were some books which were part of the religious literature quoted by the church fathers and even included in some of the early canonical lists, but which over the course of time were ultimately rejected as canonical for a variety of reasons. These books are sometimes referred to as Christian "apocryphal" books (not to be confused with the "Apocrypha" – Jewish texts which were included in Greek versions of the Old Testament but ultimately excluded by rabbis as being an authoritative part of the Hebrew canon[22]), and they include but are not limited to the following: Didache, Shepherd of Hermes, The Acts of Paul and Thecla, and The Seven Epistles of Ignatius.[23]

5 THE CLOSING OF THE CANON

A question is often raised about whether the Bible is an open or closed canon. Is it possible for the Church today to add or remove books from the canon? There are past and recent proposals to amend it, most especially the New Testament.[24] One book which has been proposed for canonical inclusion is the Gospel of Thomas.

The Gospel of Thomas was discovered at Nag Hammadi in 1945 and contains 114 sayings attributed to Jesus. Some of these sayings are close or identical to his sayings in the New Testament Gospels; others are very different, some even Gnostic in nature. Should this book be included among the New Testament writings? Several scholars have suggested so. However, a number of concerns have been raised against this proposal, including its questionable authorship and more importantly its non-orthodox (read "heretical") teachings. Other books which have been considered by various Christian groups for inclusion in the canon are: The Gospel of Philip, the Epistle of Peter to Philip, and the Apocryphon of John. Even the very recent writing by Martin Luther King, Jr. entitled "Letter from a Birmingham Jail" has been proposed for inclusion to the New Testament.[25] Additionally, some treat other writings on a par with the canon, such as the Book of Mormon.

Nevertheless, the likelihood of actually changing the canon, which has been closed for so many centuries, is very small. Indeed we seem to be past the time when a single body could make such a decision. Leading New Testament scholar Bruce Metzger offers what is perhaps a strong consensus statement among Christians on the topic:

> Suggestions that the canon might be enlarged by the inclusion of other "inspirational" literature, ancient or modern, arise from a failure to recognize what the New Testament actually is. It is not an anthology of inspirational literature; it is a collection of writings that bear witness to what God has wrought through the life and work, the death and resurrection of Jesus Christ, and through the founding of his Church by his Spirit.[26]

This is how the Christian tradition has understood the New Testament canon. It is a book (or collection of books) which was penned by inspired individuals over a number of decades and which, bearing witness to the works and instruction of God, provides the very foundation of Christian thought, faith, and practice. Given the historic Christian understanding of its divine inspiration, authority, and completed form, it is probably a safe bet to say that it will continue to be a closed canon for a very long time.

SUMMARY OF MAIN POINTS

1   The New Testament canon is that collection of twenty-seven books which Christians have historically taken to be the authoritative and inspired words of God and which are understood to be the norm for Christian thought, faith, and practice.

2   The following factors led from oral tradition to sacred canon: theological concerns of differentiating truth from error, practical concerns such as what to read in church services, political concerns involving persecution and book burning, and missionary concerns of Bible translation and communication.

3   In determining canonicity, the following criteria were utilized: apostolic authority; being ancient, extending back to the time period of the apostles; divine inspiration; orthodoxy; universal acceptance by orthodox churches.

4   Some books were considered but finally rejected from the canon for several reasons, primarily their being either pseudonymous or heretical.

5   While some have suggested adding or removing books from the biblical canon, it is most likely forever closed to such considerations.

FOR FURTHER READING

F.F. Bruce, *The Canon of Scripture* (Downers Grove, IL: InterVarsity Press, 1988). A prominent evangelical scholar describes the processes involved in the development of the Old and New Testaments.

Bart Ehrman, *Lost Scriptures: Books that Did Not Make It into the New Testament* (Oxford: Oxford University Press, 2003). A very helpful collection of early writings which did not make it into the canon.

Burton L. Mack, *Who Wrote the New Testament? The Making of the Christian Myth* (San Francisco, CA: HarperSanFrancisco, 1995). A controversial book which challenges traditional Christian understanding of the emergence of the New Testament and the Christian faith.

Lee Martin McDonald and James A. Sanders, eds., *The Canon Debate* (Peabody, MA: Hendrickson, 2002). A collection of important essays dealing with historical and methodological issues regarding the canon.

Bruce M. Metzger, *The Canon of the New Testament* (Oxford: Clarendon Press, 1987). A clear and authoritative description of the processes involved in the development of the New Testament canon.

Bruce M. Metzger and Bart D. Ehrman, *The Text of the New Testament: Its Transmission, Corruption, and Restoration*, 4th edition (Oxford: Oxford University Press, 2005). A contemporary classic of New Testament textual criticism.

11

Augustine

Philosopher, theologian, and church father

QUESTIONS TO BE ADDRESSED IN THIS CHAPTER

1   Why did Augustine become a Manichee and a Skeptic?
2   In what ways did Greek thinkers inspire Augustine's thought about the Christian faith?
3   How did Augustine's reaction to the Donatist controversy affect the way Christians thought about the nature of the Church and the sacraments?
4   What was Pelagianism, and how did Augustine's response to it influence Christian understandings of sin, grace, and predestination?

Aurelius Augustine (354–430), also known as "Augustine of Hippo," "St. Augustine," or simply "Augustine," is without doubt the most influential Western Christian theologian since the Apostle Paul. He has extensively impacted not only Christian thought but the whole history of Western ideas, including such notions as freedom of the will, original sin, the nature of God and the Church, and the meaning and function of the sacraments.

It could be argued that Augustine is the last thinker of the ancient, classical period or that he is the first thinker of the Middle Ages. He lived during the remarkable days of the disintegration of the Western Roman Empire. The city and empire which had become so intertwined with Christianity were being overrun with foreign invaders. Rome's fall to the Visigoths in 410 was the occasion for Augustine to write his magnificent *City of God*. It was not merely a political kingdom that would last forever, he argued, but the spiritual kingdom of God. His own city in north Africa, Hippo, was invaded and burned by Vandals as Augustine lay dying. Others of Augustine's influential and lasting ideas were linked to events in his life, and thus it will be helpful in understanding his thought to begin with a brief biography.

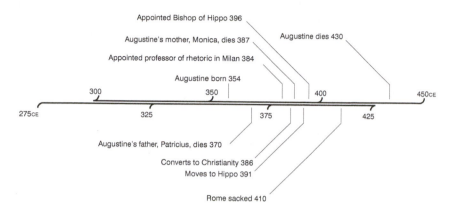

Timeline 11 Augustine

1 THE EARLY AUGUSTINE: PHILOSOPHER AND SKEPTIC

A good place to embark on Augustine's story is with his autobiographical masterpiece, the *Confessions*. In this work, he chronicles his own intellectual and spiritual journey and provides a portrayal of his parents, especially his mother, Monica (331–387). Monica was a devout Christian, a woman of faith who prayed regularly for her son and longed to see him enter the Christian faith. Patricius (d. *c.* 370), Augustine's father, was a pagan, which in Augustine's day meant something quite different from what it oftentimes means today. Paganism in antiquity was the belief in and worship of many gods, in particular the gods of one's own culture,

AUGUSTINE'S *CONFESSIONS*

The *Confessions* is a spiritual and intellectual autobiography. It is, as the title indicates, a confession – a chronicle of Augustine's life emphasizing his conversion to Christian faith. Written in Latin, it is one person's journey from divine alienation to friendship with God. It is a unique autobiographical work from the ancient world and a masterpiece of world literature.

through sacrifice, participation in religious festivals, and so on. Unlike Monica, then, who believed in and worshiped only the Christian God, Patricius paid homage to the various traditional gods of the cities of the Roman Empire.

Augustine was born in 354 and reared in Tagaste, a town in North Africa (now Souk Ahras in Algeria). He was a precocious child, and both his parents and his teachers recognized his gifted intellect early on. His mother and father were in agreement that their son would pursue an academic career, and they spared no expense to set him on this course. He received the best education of his day. At the age of seventeen he moved to the metropolis of Carthage (on the coast of present-day Tunisia) to study rhetoric, the art of persuasion. During his time of study in Carthage, a port city known for its licentiousness, Augustine developed a relationship with a woman who bore him a son, his only son (so far as we know), Adeodatus. He left this concubine (as Augustine considered her) without hope of marriage and chose instead a pursuit of wisdom and truth – a quest inspired by his reading of a work now lost to antiquity, Cicero's *Hortensius*. Through reading the pages of this book he was led to philosophy – the love of wisdom – for in reading them, he says,

> the only thing that pleased me in Cicero's book was his advice not simply to admire one or another of the schools of philosophy, but to love wisdom itself, whatever it might be, and to search for it, hold it, and embrace it firmly.[1]

This love of wisdom would lead him, eventually, to the Christian faith. But there was a long and arduous intellectual and spiritual path he would journey down before finding solace in the faith his mother had been so assiduously sharing with him for over two decades.

After reading *Hortensius*, Augustine turned to the Bible to find answers to his questions. In comparison to the arresting prose of Greek and Roman authors, however, the Bible appeared less than impressive to him. Not only was the writing style unimposing, but the Bible seemed to lack the kind of sophisticated answers to the philosophical and theological questions demanded by one with Augustine's intellect and distinguished education. One of the questions he couldn't seem to get answered had to do with evil. Where did it come from? Why does it exist? The Christians maintained that God is the creator of all things and that God is good. But

Figure 11.1 Augustine. Vittore Carpaccio/The Yorck Project: 10.000 Meister-werke der Malerei/Public domain / Wikimedia Commons

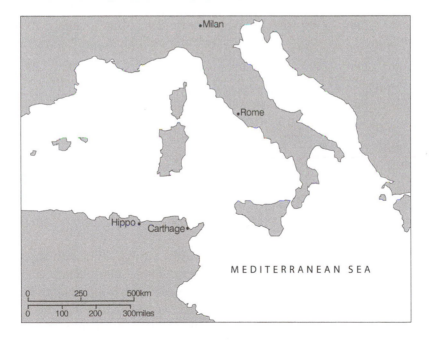

Map 11.1 North Africa and Italy at the time of Augustine

MANI

Mani (*c.* 215–276CE) was a Mesopotamian prophet and the founder of Manichaeism. He was raised in a religious sect with Gnostic features and at an early age (legend has it at the age of twelve) he received a revelation in which he was to withdraw from this sect and begin a new religion. This new religion quickly spread, eventually reaching India, China, and Central Asia. Mani was prolific, writing many books and letters, but only fragments remain today. The central tenets of Manichaeism include the following:

- Human spirits on earth are fallen and connected to evil.
- Prophets, including Zoroaster and Jesus, were given by God to reveal the principle of good to human beings.
- Mani is the last of the great prophets and the one who offers the full and final revelation for humankind.
- One of the central truths is that world conflict is due to the two opposed principles of good and evil, represented by light (God rules the kingdom of light) and darkness (Satan rules the kingdom of darkness).
- Human beings are expected to live in such a way that the light within them will bring them back to God, and this living includes ascetic purity.

if this is so, then how did evil ever arise in God's creation? At the age of nineteen, Augustine found an answer not in Christianity, but in another religious sect, Manichaeism.

The Manichaean sect emphasized reason, rational explanation, and a life focused on ascetic practices. Augustine was himself a Manichee for nine years, between the ages of nineteen and twenty-eight. What drew him to the sect was its emphasis on reason, and perhaps its most appealing facet to him was its apparent ability to rationally solve the problem of evil that had so vexed him. The Manichaean solution was

PYRRHO

Early Skepticism was founded by Pyrrho (361–270 BCE) and was also referred to as *Pyrrhonism*. As it developed through the centuries, it took on a number of variations and viewpoints, including the one Augustine was attracted to, called the New Academics. A central theme among all the Skeptics was that there seems to be equal force among opposing arguments and so dogmatism about any claim to truth should be rejected. Skepticism continued to exert influence in academic circles well beyond Augustine's time.

that there is not one eternal principle, God (or the good), from which everything emerged, but two such principles, one evil and the other good.

This solution satisfied Augustine for a time, but ultimately the Manichean system began unraveling in his mind. Augustine initially thought that the philosophical defects of their arguments were due to the intellectual inadequacies of the local Manichean teachers he encountered. But after listening firsthand to one of its leading authorities, Faustus of Milevis, while impressed with his rhetorical savvy, Augustine was thoroughly unconvinced by his responses to the thorny philosophical problems he was struggling with. In one sense his hopes had been dashed, as there no longer seemed to be the possibility of absolute knowledge of anything significant, not even by the best thinkers of the day. Shortly after this encounter he gave up his faith in Manicheism, moved to Rome, and became a philosophical Skeptic.

2 THE LATER AUGUSTINE: CHRISTIAN THEOLOGIAN AND CHURCH FATHER

Through reading the works of the Neoplatonists, Augustine eventually abandoned Skepticism when he came to believe that human reason can attain knowledge – even certain knowledge – about some fundamental truths. For example, one can be certain about the principle of contradiction: that something cannot both be and not be at the same time. While this principle does not provide comprehensive knowledge, it does offer a kind of certainty which Skepticism denied, such as that Christianity and Manicheism cannot both be true. They contradict one another, so if one is true the other must be false. Furthermore, Augustine realized that the Skeptics must acknowledge that their doubt is itself a form of certainty, for a person who doubts, at least in the way these Skeptics did (they were confident there was no knowledge), is certain about one thing: that she doubts![2]

In working through the Neoplatonic writings, Augustine also found solutions to some of the intellectual challenges that bedeviled him as a Manichean. Perhaps the most significant insight was a solution to the problem of evil which he undoubtedly gleaned from the writings of Plotinus.[3] Contrary to Plato, who believed that evil was due to ignorance, and contrary to the Manichaeans, who believed that evil was due to the principle of darkness permeating the body, Augustine came to understand evil as a privation – a lack of the good – brought about by free will.[4]

> Therefore, whatever is, is good; and evil, the origin of which I was trying to find, is not a substance, because if it were a substance, it would be good. … And when I asked myself what wickedness was, I saw that it was not a substance but perversion of the will when it turns aside from you, O God, who are the supreme substance. …[5]

So while God created the world, and all creation was good, God did not create evil, for evil is not a substance, or *thing*, to be created. It was,

THE NEOPLATONISTS

The Neoplatonists were groups of philosophers influenced by the works of Plotinus (205–270CE) who drew inspiration from Plato. Plotinus developed Plato's thought, and argued for "the One" – the transcendent One who is beyond being and is perfect, immutable, and wholly transcendent. Significant Neoplatonists after Plotinus include Porphyry (*c.* 232–*c.* 304), Proclus (*c.* 409–*c.* 487), and Simplicius (sixth century).

and is, essentially, the result of a misdirected will, a will which is turned away from God, or the good, and toward something less.

In 384, Augustine was appointed professor of rhetoric in Milan. While there, he encountered the city's bishop, Ambrose, an eloquent orator and brilliant theologian. The simple and perhaps simplistic Christian faith of Monica began to seem richer and more sophisticated as Augustine listened to the bishop's expositions on the Bible and Christian doctrine. His allegorical interpretation of parts of the Old Testament, for example, shed new light on the old stories and made much better sense to Augustine than his former literal understanding of them. Through this allegorical reading of Scripture, Augustine also saw a way to reconcile the biblical teaching with Platonist spirituality. For the first time, the Christian faith began to make sense to him. While there were still many unanswered questions, and while doubt still plagued him occasionally, Augustine's skeptical shackles began to loosen. He once again allowed religious faith to take root and in 386, at age 32, Augustine became a convert to Christianity.

Augustine's conversion occurred in his garden through what we might today call a *religious experience*. He describes it this way:

> I was ... weeping all the while with the most bitter sorrow in my heart, when all at once I heard the singing voice of a child in a nearby house. Whether it was the voice of a boy or girl I cannot say, but again and again it repeated the refrain, "Take it and read, take it and read." At this I looked up, thinking hard whether there was any kind of game in which children used to chant words like these, but I could not remember ever hearing them before. I stemmed my flood of tears and stood up, telling myself that this could only be a divine command to open my book of Scripture and read the first page on which my eyes should fall.[6]

As it turned out, his eyes fell on Romans 13:13–14: "Not in reveling and drunkenness, not in lust and wantonness, not in quarrels and rivalries. Rather, arm yourselves with the Lord Jesus Christ; spend no more thought on nature and nature's appetites." Augustine took these words to be coming straight to him from God. "For in an instant," he says, "as I came to the end of the sentence, it was as though the light of confidence flooded my heart and all the darkness and doubt was dispelled."[7] Augustine finally and fully entered into the Christian faith. Shortly after this time, he and his son were baptized by Bishop Ambrose.

For the next several years he spent his time in Tagaste in a monastic community with his son and several close friends, focusing primarily on study, meditation, and dialogue about the Christian faith. In 391 he visited the city of Hippo (modern Annaba, Algeria), with the hopes of convincing another friend to join his small band of believers. While there, the Bishop of Hippo, Valerius, ordained him as a priest. Augustine then stayed in Hippo and formed a community similar to the one in Tagaste. Four years later, upon Valerius' death, Augustine was himself made Bishop of Hippo.

During his illustrious career as bishop (a post he held from 396 until his death in 430), Augustine spent his days in regimented monastic routine, dealing with official church business and devotional endeavors in the mornings – including prayers, meditations, and meetings with the laity – and writing in the afternoons. He was a prolific author and often combined his practical duties as bishop with his theoretical musings as philosopher and author. A number of his books, for example, dealt with the teachings of the Manichees and other "heretical" groups with which those in his congregations were interacting. Besides Manicheanism, there were other controversial issues which erupted during Augustine's leadership in Hippo, and a number of his responses to them had considerable influence on the development of Christian thought. Two stand out as especially significant: the Donatist controversy and Pelagianism.

3 THE CHURCH AND THE SACRAMENTS

In the third and fourth centuries, the Roman Empire was dealing with a number of significant challenges. For one, the empire had divided in the late third century into Eastern and Western halves, each with its own emperor – one located in Constantinople and the other in Italy. The divided empire brought with it its own unique problems, both political and religious. Beginning in 303, the Roman emperor, Diocletian (284–313), began a series of persecutions against the Christians, perhaps as one way of unifying the empire. These persecutions were most emphatic from 303–305, but they continued on to a lesser degree until the Edict of Milan in 313. One aspect of this persecution involved the decree to turn in all copies of the Christian Scriptures to the magistrates to be destroyed.

Failure to comply resulted in imprisonment, torture, or even death. There was no clear biblical mandate about what Christians were to do in such a situation. On the one hand, the Bible says to obey civil authorities (Romans 13). On the other hand, this was obviously a violation – even a desecration – of the very Word of God. Some church leaders complied; others refused.

After these persecutions ended, concerns arose about what to do with those bishops – referred to as *traditores* (from which the English word *traitor* is derived) – who had turned over the sacred Scriptures to the authorities. Was this an act of apostasy? Was it a betrayal of the Lord himself? And what about other Christians who were not in a position of ecclesiastical authority but had nevertheless also complied with the magistrates and given up the sacred writings? Were they lesser Christians than their brothers and sisters in the faith who held steadfast amidst persecution? Furthermore, there was the issue of whether bishops consecrated by the *traditores* had received a valid consecration. If not, they had no authority to administer the sacraments.

Most of the Christian leaders of North Africa maintained that, while penance was needed by the *traditores,* their official status and authority did not rest on their individual actions, but rather on the office and their official consecration. Others disagreed. This schism came to a head when Mensurius, bishop of Carthage (the capital of Roman Africa), died in 311, and some local Carthaginian bishops ordained a man named Caecilian without waiting for the provincial bishops to arrive and participate. These late-arriving bishops were incensed. What made the situation even more problematic was that one of the local bishops involved in the clandestine ordination, Felix, was suspected of being a *traditore*!

The provincial bishops who arrived after the ordination took it to be an invalid consecration given the situation with "traitor" Felix, so they ordained a different person to be bishop, one Majorinus. He died shortly after this event, so they ordained another to take his place, Donatus. Furthermore, Donatus and his followers (referred to as the Donatists) disagreed with broad catholic teaching about the church and the sacraments. They maintained that a bishop who had lapsed (had turned over the Scriptures to the magistrates, for example, or who had committed some other significant malfeasance) committed apostasy and was no longer capable of administering the sacraments. The Catholics, on the other hand (and this would include the leaders in Rome),

DONATISM

Donatism, founded and led by Donatus (d. c. 311), was a Christian sect which flourished in North Africa in the fourth and fifth centuries. They were rigorists who held that the Church must consist of saints, not sinners, and that the sacraments, including baptism, must be administered by holy and blameless priests and bishops.

maintained that if a lapsed bishop repented, he would be able to continue administering the sacraments. So emerged the Donatist controversy, and by Augustine's time it was reeking havoc on the Church in Africa.

The Donatist controversy was the first major issue on Augustine's agenda as he officially took office in Hippo. He used his position and political power as bishop, as well as his rhetorical skills, to attend to this situation and put an end to the Donatist schism. He wrote letters, treatises, and even songs to rebut their teachings. At first he believed they should not be compelled to conform to Catholic belief on the matter, but he eventually came to strongly favor the use of force to bring this schismatic group back into the Catholic fold.

Both sides – the Donatists and the Catholics – had appealed their case to the Church in Rome. After lengthy inquiries and appeals, a number of councils, and even the emperor himself, came down on the side of the Catholics. Emperor Honorius made several edicts against the Donatists, including surrendering their churches to the Catholics, forbidding their services, and even exiling their leaders. Sadly, both sides ended up using intimidation, violence, and terror in an attempt to win the debate. Imperial troops were eventually brought in to shut down the Donatist churches and to force them to join the Catholic churches. Despite all this, however, the Donatists continued to exist in some segments of Africa, even up to the time of the Arab conquests in the seventh century.[8]

Two significant theological developments surfaced from this controversy. The first was the nature of the Church. Augustine understood the Church to be universal (that's what "catholic" means), and therefore manifest throughout the earth. The Donatists, on the other hand, were a schismatic group restricted to Africa. They had, in effect, cut themselves off from the Catholic Christian Church. In reply, the Donatists argued that some of the Catholic bishops were unholy and so not manifesting proper authority in the Church of Jesus Christ. But Augustine responded that the Church is a holy body, not because of the moral worthiness of its individual members, but because its head is Christ, and its members will be perfected in eternity. What Augustine did, in effect, was introduce the notions of the visible and invisible church, and he was the first to do so. Not everyone within the visible church is a genuine Christian, even though they may be legitimate members. Only God can judge the heart, so we are not in a position to discern who the true and false Christians really are. The visible church is the outward organization, while the invisible church is the true body of believers in Christ.

The second theological development of the Donatist controversy involved the sacraments. Augustine argued, contrary to the Donatists, that the administration of the sacraments should not be based on the moral worthiness of the human agent administering them, and this for two reasons. First, human beings are incapable of accurately making such judgments. There could, for example, be secret sins of a bishop of which no one is aware. Second, the sacraments are efficacious on account of the grace of Christ, not on account of the standing in the invisible church of the one administering them. Augustine made an important qualification, however. A distinction needs to be made between the sacrament itself and

THE CITY OF GOD

The City of God is Augustine's magnum opus. It was motivated by the sack of Rome in 410 and was an answer to the Roman pagans who claimed that Christianity was the primary cause of the decline of the Roman Empire. Consisting of twenty-two chapters, this book is one of the first attempts at writing a theology or philosophy of history and is a detailed, carefully argued defense of the Christian faith. In constructing his apologetic, Augustine develops at great length the notion that the true church is the spiritual city of God, and this is distinct from the material city of Man.

the right to perform the sacrament. Thus, even though a Donatist heretic, for example, may have administered a particular sacrament (such as baptism), it is still valid so long as the recipient is united to the Catholic Church (or becomes so united) in good faith.[9] This understanding of the causal efficacy of the sacraments became the prevailing view in the Western Church.

4 HUMAN NATURE, SIN, GRACE, AND PREDESTINATION

A second controversy which erupted during Augustine's tenure as bishop was also significant in the history of Western Christian thought: Pelagianism. Pelagius was a theologian (and most likely a monk) who was active in Rome in the late fourth and early fifth centuries. Little is known of his biography, including his dates of birth and death. What is known is that he was not pleased with certain aspects of Augustine's theology, most especially his views of God's sovereignty and human will. As Pelagius understood him, Augustine afforded no place in his theology for human will, or effort, or participation in the acts of God.

Pelagius' theology of free will and moral responsibility may well have been a response to the moral determinism of the Manichees.[10] As noted above, they maintained that there are two co-eternal principles: good and evil. They also maintained that an evil human nature could do no good, and a good human nature could do no evil. It was this Manichean

PELAGIUS

Pelagius (c. 354–c. 420) was a theologian who lived during the time of Augustine. His doctrines are known through his own writings (several sources still survive) and quotations in the writings of his opponents. His primary surviving works are *Exposition of the Pauline Epistles* and *Book of Faith*. Much of his career was spent defending himself and his positions against other theologians, most notoriously Augustine.

Manicheanism	Pelagianism	Augustinianism
Absolute sovereignty of God	Denied absolute sovereignty of God	Absolute sovereignty of God
Denied human free will	Total freedom of human will	Freedom of human will

determinism that drove Augustine to write one of his earliest books, *On the Free Choice of the Will*, in which he argued that sin is not eternal with God but arises from the misuse of free will. Pelagius and Augustine were agreed on the importance of human free will, but while Augustine also strongly affirmed the necessity of God's sovereignty, Pelagius believed this doctrine undermined both human will and moral responsibility.[11]

For Augustine, ever since Adam and Eve gave in to the tempter in the garden, and fell into sin, humanity has been in a fallen state. All human beings have inherited this sin, what Augustine called *original sin* (this is one of the earliest mentions of original sin in Christian thought). As a result, human nature, including human free will, is corrupted and bent toward evil. Only God's grace can restore human will, and bring it back to a state of true freedom.

For Pelagius, human beings were created good and were given a will that is good. Even though evil entered the world when Adam and Eve sinned, it was not sufficient to efface the human ability to avoid sin. To put it differently, for Pelagius the original sin of Adam and Eve did not nullify the ability of human beings to do what was right in God's eyes. Original sin did not corrupt human nature in such a way as to eliminate the freedom of will to do the good. On Pelagius' account, human beings have, and always had, the power not to sin – *posse non peccare* (to use the Latin slogan). Furthermore, he argued that God is righteous and would not command what was impossible for humans to do. If God commands us to do the right thing, then it must be in our own power to do the right thing. Humans are born sinless, and sin is an individual affront to God. It is not merely a forensic or legal issue (an abstract concept which is somehow related to humanity) which has been passed down from Adam and Eve. It involves personal choices. Having the example of Christ's life and the instruction of his teaching is sufficient, then, to lead human beings to obey the commands of God.

Augustine disagreed. For him, sin has so corrupted human nature and will that our disposition, even at birth, is toward evil, and we are in need of God's grace both to understand sin's effects and to overcome them and turn to God. Here are his own words on the matter:

> They, however, must be resisted with the utmost ardor and vigor who suppose that without God's help, the mere power of the human will in itself, can either perfect righteousness, or advance steadily towards it. ... We, however, on our side affirm that the human will is so divinely aided in the pursuit of righteousness, that (in addition to man's being created with a free will, and in addition to the teaching by which he is instructed how he ought to live) he receives the Holy Ghost by whom there is formed in his mind a delight in, and a love of, that supreme and unchangeable good which is God ... .[12]

Augustine went even further. Faith is a gift of God. But not all turn to God; some remain unrepentant. So God does not freely offer his gift of grace to everyone. It is for the elect. Addressing God, he puts it this way: "Thou movest us to delight in praising Thee; for Thou hast formed us for Thyself, and our hearts are restless until they find rest in Thee."[13] God, in his grace, chooses to save some, but not all. He predestines some for salvation, but not everyone.

There has been much debate throughout the centuries regarding Augustine's views of grace and predestination, especially, as we will see in later chapters, with the sixteenth century Protestant Reformers.

Augustine was the most influential church father of the Latin or Western tradition. His thinking about such fundamental matters as free will, predestination, the nature of God and the self, to name but a few, has notably affected the way those in the Western Christian tradition conceptualize such matters. For centuries during the Middle Ages he was appealed to as *the* authority on which theological debates were to be settled. However, we should not think, as is sometimes maintained, that the Middle Ages were a long, sterile time which relied only on citing authority. As we'll see in the next part, it was a tremendously creative and fruitful period of Christian thought.

SUMMARY OF MAIN POINTS

1 Augustine sought sophisticated, philosophical answers to fundamental questions about God and human nature, and this led him first to Manicheanism and then to academic Skepticism.

2 By incorporating ideas of Greek thinkers, primarily the Neoplatonists, Augustine overcame his skepticism and acquired philosophical tools which he used to understand and defend orthodox Christian faith.

3 In responding to the Donatists, Augustine developed a distinction between the visible and invisible church and a view of the sacraments in which they are causally efficacious because of the moral purity of Christ rather than the one administering them.

4 Through his responses to Pelagianism – the view that the sin of Adam and Eve did not corrupt human nature and that the human will is capable of following God – Augustine developed the ideas of original sin, the unification of divine sovereignty and human free will, and the predestination of the elect.

FOR FURTHER READING

Peter Brown, *Augustine of Hippo: A Biography* (Berkeley, CA: University of California Press, 2000). A magisterial biography; this is the re-released version with an update by way of an epilogue by Henry Chadwick.

Phillip Cary, *Augustine's Invention of the Inner Self: The Legacy of a Christian Platonist*. (Oxford: Oxford University Press, 2000). Placing Augustine's thought within the Platonist and Christian traditions, Cary argues that Augustine invented the concept of the self as a private inner space which one can enter to find God.

Henry Chadwick, *Augustine: A Very Short Introduction* (Oxford: Oxford University Press, 2001). A helpful introductory guide to the life and thought of Augustine.

William R. Cook and Ronald B. Herzman, *The Medieval World View*, 2nd edition (Oxford: Oxford University Press, 2004). An accessible and engaging introduction to the ideas that shaped the medieval worldview.

Allan D. Fitzgerald, *Augustine Through the Ages: An Encyclopedia* (Grand Rapids, MI: Eerdmans, 1999). Includes entries by leading experts on a variety of relevant subjects and a helpful bibliography.

Part3

Establishment and diversification

The Medieval period 500–1500

12

Monasticism of the early Middle Ages

QUESTIONS TO BE ADDRESSED IN THIS CHAPTER

1 What is the Rule of Benedict?
2 What contribution did monasticism make to Christian thought?
3 What is the significance of Pope Gregory the Great?
4 How did Irish monasticism relate to Roman Christianity?

Epochs in history are the conventions of historians. The flow of time in the daily lives of people is rarely distinguished by the sorts of momentous boundary markers we find in history books. Nevertheless, it is necessary for us to sift through the near-infinity of events that have occurred and select just some of them if we want to tell a coherent story. Similarly we must impose some large-scale structure on the past in order to provide a framework in which individual events cohere and find their meaning. In so doing, we identify epoch-defining events and infuse them with all the portentousness we can muster.

It has been customary to claim that one such event occurred in 529 when Emperor Justinian closed down for good the philosophical Academy which Plato had founded in the fourth century BCE. Not all scholars agree on just what was decreed or what the effect was, but the standard interpretation (of the rather scant evidence) is that the emperor wished to rid society of the adverse influence of pagan ideas, and so he forbade anyone who was not an orthodox Christian to teach the populace. The philosophers in residence at the Academy were exiled to Persia (where they were welcomed with open arms), and Christian thought lost much of the on-going interchange with pagan philosophy. This effectively closed the door on antiquity and ushered in the Dark Ages.

Also in the year 529 some 2,000 kilometers northwest of Athens, fourteen bishops descended on the city of Orange in southern France for an official church council. The Council of Orange concerned itself chiefly with the Semi-Pelagian controversy that had festered in the wake of Augustine. Pelagius, who died about a century earlier, denied the doctrine of original sin and taught that human beings were born in a

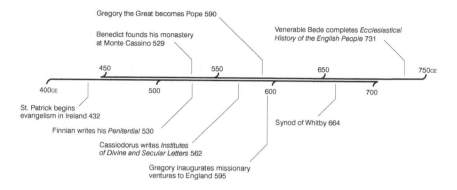

Gregory the Great becomes Pope 590

Benedict founds his monastery
at Monte Cassino 529

Venerable Bede completes *Ecclesiastical
History of the English People* 731

450   550   650   750CE

400CE   500   600   700

St. Patrick begins
evangelism in Ireland 432

Finnian writes his *Penitential* 530

Cassiodorus writes *Institutes
of Divine and Secular Letters* 562

Synod of Whitby 664

Gregory inaugurates missionary
ventures to England 595

Timeline 12 Monasticism of the early Middle Ages

state of innocence. As such, humans would have the capacity and the responsibility for seeking God apart from any grace God imparts to enable them to do so. Semi-Pelagians, as they came to be known, aimed to find a middle way between this and the doctrine propounded by Augustine that the salvation of humans is entirely up to God. Semi-Pelagians claimed that humans must take the first step toward God in repentance, but then God completes the act of salvation by his grace. The Council of Orange came down firmly on the side of Augustine.

Ironically, and fortunately for Christian thought and civilization, another event took place in 529 which in retrospect we see as enormously important: Benedict founded a monastery at Monte Cassino, Italy and developed his Rule of monastic life. We might view this as a kind of antidote to the previously mentioned events: monasticism was hugely

FROM THE COUNCIL OF ORANGE IN 529

Canon 3: If anyone says that the grace of God can be conferred as a result of human prayer, but that it is not grace itself which makes us pray to God, he contradicts the prophet Isaiah, or the Apostle who says the same thing, "I have been found by those who did not seek me; I have shown myself to those who did not ask for me."

(Rom 10:20, quoting Isa. 65:1[1])

influenced by Benedict, and without the culture engendered by these monks, it is difficult to imagine how our knowledge of the classics of antiquity would have survived. Also, without the environment of work that the Benedictines fostered, the understanding of predestination which won the day at the Council of Orange might have easily let Christian thought lapse into fatalism like the ancient pagan schools of determinism.

Perhaps nothing symbolizes medieval times so well as the monk. What was this culture, and how did it affect Christian thought? We begin with Benedict.

1 THE RULE OF BENEDICT

Benedict was born sometime around 480 in the town of Nursia about 100 miles northeast of Rome. He spent his youth at schools in Rome, but grew disgusted with his education and left to pursue God alone, having been "instructed with learned ignorance, and furnished with unlearned wisdom."[2] He moved outside the city to the region of Subiaco and lived in a cave as a hermit for three years. During this time he attracted disciples and afterward started twelve different groups or proto-monasteries, of which he served as a kind of abbot or leader. But the local clergy were not all pleased with his groups, because they upset the local power structures, and eventually their persecution drove Benedict to relocate to Monte Cassino where he founded the most famous of his monasteries and wrote the Rule which became so influential.

Of course there is in Benedict a continuity to be discerned with the desert fathers and mothers of the previous couple of centuries. But his emphasis was on life in community rather than the solitary pursuit of God in the desert. This helped to curb the excesses that tended to arise in the earlier instantiations of the life of a monk and provided a stable institution that did so much to leaven Christian thought and society in general.

We're not going to find in Benedict – nor in monks in general – lives that reflect Orange's interpretation of Augustine's theory of salvation. That is, they didn't live as though God's grace was predetermined for those who would be saved and how holy they might become. Neither will we find carefully argued theological treatises by monks arguing on behalf of the Pelagians or Semi-Pelagians. But their words are squarely in line with the tradition that believes humans to have responsibility for their own spiritual development. And even more, their actions showed that they didn't believe

Figure 12.1 St. Benedict. Fresco. Monastery San Benedetto/CC/Wikimedia Commons

they were merely passive recipients of God's grace. Of course they believed God's grace to be involved in salvation and discipleship, but there was an expectation and responsibility for humans to act in cooperation with his grace. Benedict says in the Prologue to his Rule,

> The Lord waits for us daily to translate into action, as we should, his holy teachings ... We must, then, prepare our hearts and bodies for the battle of holy obedience to his instructions. What is not possible to us by nature, let us ask the Lord to supply by the help of his grace. If we wish to reach eternal life, even as we avoid the torments of hell, then – while there is still time, while we are in this body and have time to accomplish all these things by the light of life – we must run and do now what will profit us forever.[3]

It is not easy to reconcile this attitude with the theory approved at the Council of Orange by those who thought about such things in the abstract. There is work to be done, and the monks believed they needed to take the initiative to do it. The connection between theology and the regulated life of the Benedictines needs to be emphasized here. "To pray is to work, to work is to pray" is the motto of the Benedictine order to the present day. It infuses them with the predisposition to balance the contemplative life with the active.

Benedict had not necessarily intended by writing his Rule to found an order of monks, but rather he was trying to give guidance to those in the monastery he had founded for the sort of life that would be most conducive to bringing about their goal. Most conspicuous about this life is what is called the Divine Office. This is the schedule of services the monastery would follow, which was grounded on the Psalmist's claims, "Seven times a day have I praised you" (Ps. 119:164) and "At midnight I arose to give you praise" (Ps. 119:62). Thus there were prescribed eight services:

Lauds:	Dawn
Prime:	Early morning
Terce:	Mid-morning
Sext:	Midday
None:	Mid-afternoon
Vespers:	Evening
Compline:	Before retiring
Vigils or Matins:	During the night

At each of these services, the community was called to come together by a signal. "On hearing the signal for an hour of the divine office, the monk will immediately set aside what he has in hand and go with utmost speed, yet with gravity and without giving occasion for frivolity."[4] A version of this schedule with only very slight modifications is still followed in Benedictine monasteries today.

In between services, the monks were to have specified periods of manual labor as well as prayerful reading or other devotional activities. Exactly what this consisted of varied by seasons and the local conditions and needs. Many of the rules concern practical matters: how meals are to be served, the number of Psalms to be read at various services, how to welcome visitors, the types of clothing to be worn, and so on. But undoubtedly one of the reasons for the success of the widespread adoption of the Rule was its flexibility. It provides parameters, but leaves much open for adaptability to local circumstances. For example, in selecting an abbot for the monastery, Benedict says that he may be selected by "the whole community acting unanimously in the fear of God, or by some part of the community, no matter how small, which possesses sounder judgment."[5]

The overall impression in reading the Rule is that it is a training exercise for advancing in spirituality. There are stages to be attained, and steps that should be worked toward. Most famously in this regard are the steps of humility to be ascended.

The Rule ends with a reminder that it is only the beginning. The writings of the Scripture and of the fathers, as well as other monastic rules, are also "tools for the cultivation of virtues"[6] and should be followed as the monks "hasten toward [their] heavenly home."[7]

2 OTHER BENEDICTINES/MONKS

When Benedict went to Monte Cassino to found his monastery, his twin sister Scholastica came to meet him and started a convent just five miles south at Plombariola. This functioned loosely under the Rule of Benedict too, thus making Scholastica the first Benedictine nun. The two maintained a close spiritual friendship, and met each year to confer together. At the last of these meetings, when Scholastica believed she was near death, she implored her brother to stay through the night that they might continue their conversation. Benedict staunchly refused on the grounds that it would break the rule that he had set for the monastery. Scholastica turned her entreaty to God, asking him to intervene and keep them together. Although the sky had been completely clear, immediately a severe thunderstorm broke out which kept Benedict and his company from returning. Benedict said to his sister, "God forgive you for what you have done." To which she replied, "I implored you to stay, and you would not grant my request; so I asked our good Lord, and he answered my petition."[8]

Immediately after the death of Benedict around 547, the Benedictine order was only a local phenomenon. In due time, it would become the

THE STEPS OF HUMILITY FROM *THE RULE OF BENEDICT*, CHAPTER 7

1 That a man keeps the fear of God always before his eyes.
2 That a man loves not his own will nor takes pleasure in the satisfaction of his desires.
3 That a man submits to his superior in all obedience.
4 That in this obedience under difficult, unfavorable, or even unjust conditions, his heart quietly embraces suffering.
5 That a man does not conceal from his abbot any sinful thoughts or wrongs committed, but confesses them humbly.
6 That a monk is content with the lowest and menial treatment in whatever work he is given.
7 That a man admits with his tongue and is convinced in heart that he is inferior to all.
8 That a monk does only what is endorsed by the common rule of the monastery and the example set by his superiors.
9 That a monk controls his tongue and remains silent unless asked a question.
10 That he is not given to ready laughter.
11 That a monk speaks gently and without laughter.
12 That a monk always manifests humility in his bearing no less than in his heart.

dominant model for monasteries throughout Europe. And while the Rule encouraged learning and study for the sake of spiritual advancement, there was not immediately an explicit emphasis on intellectual activity.

Cassiodorus, a younger contemporary of Benedict, started a monastery in which monks were expected to pursue a course of study that included non-Christian texts. He was interested in history, literature and philosophy, and believed that so-called pagan learning had already been assimilated into Christian thought, and so should be studied in its own right. His *Institutes of Divine and Secular Letters* summarized the knowledge of antiquity and became the model on which medieval education was based.⁹ His monks were instrumental in that stereotypical activity of copying and preserving manuscripts of antiquity for later thinkers to use.

Another in this same line was the Venerable Bede. He was a Benedictine monk living in a monastery in the Northumbrian region of the British Isles from about 673 to 735. He and his fellow laborers provided an important connecting link with antiquity through their labors of preservation and chronicling. He wrote poems, works on grammar, and biblical commentaries, but is most well known and most valuable to us as the Father of English History. His *Ecclesiastical History of the English People* is the primary lens through which we have access into medieval England and the story of its Christianization. In it we read the story about the impetus for Pope Gregory the Great to start the missionary ventures into the region. Gregory was at a marketplace in Rome when he saw some fair complexioned, blonde-haired boys for sale as slaves. He inquired from what country these boys came and whether they were pagans or Christians. He was told they were from the island of Britain and that they were still pagans. "What a pity," he said, "that the author of darkness should own men of such fair countenances." He asked what they were called, and was told that they were Angles. A traditional – though probably apocryphal – story has Gregory responding, "No, they are not Angles, but Angels." Bede continues his account with Gregory saying, "for they have an angelic face, and it is meet that such should be co-heirs with the Angels in heaven." ¹⁰ From there, he went immediately to make arrangements for missionaries to be sent to the British Isles.

3 POPE GREGORY THE GREAT

Some discussion of Pope Gregory properly belongs to the account of this chapter, for he himself was a monk – the first of which to become pope. Born in 540 to a wealthy, noble family in Rome, he received an education which prepared him for a life of public service. He was given the important post of Prefect of Rome around 570, but shortly thereafter his father died, whereupon Gregory quit the post and spent the family fortune establishing monasteries in Italy. He himself became a monk in the monastery formed out of his father's palace. But public life did not elude him for long. From the years 578–585 he was the ambassador to Constantinople representing Pope Pelagius II. And in 590 when Pelagius II died, Gregory was chosen to be his successor.

Gregory the Great, as he is often called, was a remarkable person whose influence ranged from music (Gregorian chant) and relief efforts among the sick, to defending the city of Rome against Lombard invaders when the public officials proved inept. He was also a prolific writer – about 850 of his letters are preserved. The *Life of Benedict* he wrote was probably the most important factor in the early spread of the Benedictine Rule throughout the Roman world.[11] Sometimes it is said that Gregory is unoriginal and merely an interpreter of Augustine. But he was a major contributor to the medieval understanding of spirituality as well as to theological concepts that bear the mark of monasticism. He is the most significant theologian of the early Latin monastics, and should be accorded an important place in the history of Christian thought.[12]

Gregory's constant mantra was that the goal of human life is to see God. His favorite metaphor for God was light, and he held that vision will tend toward light if properly trained. That humans have the capacity for vision is a gift of God – pure grace. But Gregory also breaks with the sort of fatalism that could have ensued from the Council of Orange: humans must prepare themselves for the vision and develop this gift through their efforts at contemplative prayer and acts of service.

So too with regard to penance. Forgiveness, for Gregory, was given by the grace of God, but humans must prepare themselves through penance to receive that grace.[13] Chief among the penitential activities for Gregory was confession. There had been a question since the first generations of the Christian Church concerning sins committed after the point of conversion and baptism.[14] It had been the practice of the Church in the Mediterranean region that penance was a public act that could be performed only once, after which there was no further recourse for the same offence. The effect was that people delayed penance and persisted in their sins. Gregory saw that this was contrary to the intent of the spiritual life and the goal of seeing God; instead, he advocated the approach to penance that was coming out of Irish monastic tradition whereby there was regular confession of sinful thoughts and deeds to a representative of the church. He believed this helped to preserve the humility that was necessary for advancing in the spiritual vision.

There still remained, though, the question of what would happen to a person who died with sins that had not been officially confessed and forgiven. Gregory was instrumental in the acceptance of the doctrine of purgatory – a place after death in which one's sins would be purged before entering heaven. Augustine had suggested something like this might be the case,[15] but Gregory was the first to dogmatically claim it to be so. He argues for the reality of purgatory for the purging of smaller or more insignificant sins (like idle talk, immoderate laughter, negligence in the care of family, error due to ignorance) based on two passages from the New Testament. Matthew 12:32 speaks of a sin against the Holy Spirit which would not be forgiven, "either in this age or in the age to come;" from which Gregory concludes that there must be some sins that are forgiven in the age to come. And then from a passage in 1 Corinthians Chapter 3 where Paul describes a person's deeds as being refined by fire, Gregory interprets the elements of wood, hay, and straw as lesser sins that will be burned up, but the stone and iron as more significant sins that would remain.

Whoever speaks a word against the Son of Man will be forgiven, but whoever speaks against the Holy Spirit will not be forgiven, either in this age or in the age to come.

(Matthew 12:32)

For no one can lay any foundation other than the one that has been laid; that foundation is Jesus Christ. Now if anyone builds on the foundation with gold, silver, precious stones, wood, hay, straw – the work of each builder will become visible, for the Day will disclose it, because it will be revealed with fire, and the fire will test what sort of work each has done. If what has been built on the foundation survives, the builder will receive a reward. If the work is burned up, the builder will suffer loss; the builder will be saved, but only as through fire.

(1 Corinthians 3:11–15)

So Gregory claimed, "We must believe that before the Day of Judgment there is a purgatory-fire for certain small sins. ... Yet we have here further to consider, that none can be there purged, no, not for the least sins that be, unless in his lifetime he deserved by virtuous works to find such favour in that place."[16] The idea must have caught on and spread quickly. The Venerable Bede, writing just a couple of decades later in England, tells the story of a near death experience in which a man named Drythelm was led by a guide through purgatory, where "the souls of those are tried and punished, who, delaying to confess and amend their crimes, at length have recourse to repentance at the point of death."[17] The similarity of this story with Dante's masterpiece some six hundred years later is striking (and we should note that Bede makes it into Dante's work in the fourth heaven where (the character) Aquinas introduces him as one of a dozen great theologians).

The spread of Roman doctrine to the British Isles was accelerated by Gregory's missionary campaign. In 595 Gregory sent a Benedictine monk named Augustine (not to be confused with Augustine of Hippo) to the region of Kent in southeast England. He was very successful in his evangelistic mission – thousands converted to Christianity on Christmas day in 597, and Augustine became the first Archbishop of Canterbury in 598. A central question for the spread of Christianity so far away from the Mediterranean, was how much Christianity could be accommodated to the local customs and culture. Gregory seemed to take a rather liberal point of view on this issue.

He wrote a letter to Mellitus whom he had sent to England as the leader of a second wave of missionaries around 601. Pope Gregory had been considering the question of what to do with the pagan temples they came across. His advice was to remove the idols from them, but otherwise leave the temples and begin to use them for Christian purposes:

> When people themselves see that these temples are not destroyed, they may put away error from their heart, and knowing and adoring the true God, may have recourse with the more familiarity to the places they have been accustomed to. And, since they are wont to kill many oxen in sacrifice to demons, they should have also some solemnity of this kind in a changed form, so that on the day of dedication, or on the anniversaries of the holy martyrs whose relics are deposited there, they may make for themselves

tents of the branches of trees around these temples that have been changed into churches, and celebrate the solemnity with religious feasts. Nor let them any longer sacrifice animals to the devil, but slay animals to the praise of God for their own eating, and return thanks to the Giver of all for their fullness, so that, while some joys are reserved to them outwardly, they may be able the more easily to incline their minds to inward joys. For it is undoubtedly impossible to cut away everything at once from hard hearts, since one who strives to ascend to the highest place must needs rise by steps or paces, and not by leaps.[18]

The Roman missionaries at the end of the sixth century were not the first to bring Christianity to the British Isles or to wrestle with accommodation of the faith to culture. There is a significant tradition of Irish monasticism that influenced all of the British Isles and predates Gregory's missionary ventures.

4 IRISH MONASTICISM

Patrick (387–c.461), of course, is the patron saint of Ireland, and it is traditionally held that he brought Christianity to Ireland in 432. But there were Christian influences in Ireland before Patrick. Although Ireland was never incorporated into the Roman Empire, the Irish were active traders and not cut off from the rest of the world. It is plausible to believe, then, that Patrick's contribution to Irish Christianity was more along the lines of organizing than introducing.

Ireland in this time period did not have large cities or national organization. Social and political life was organized around local tribal dynasties. As local chieftains converted to Christianity, they would often found a monastery in proximity to their territories. Given this structure and the ascetic influence of Patrick, it was the natural thing for monasteries to become the dominant institution in the land and the chief expression of Christianity. It was the abbot of the local monastery who was the highest authority – not the bishop – and the abbey was responsible for care of the churches in their regions.[19] This sort of arrangement allowed for Christian thought and practice to develop somewhat independently and to take on more of a local flavor than in England where the Roman influence was much stronger.

The monks of Ireland are known to us through their penitential writings. As mentioned above, the development of Christians' understanding of penance took an important step through the contribution of the Irish, and some of the local cultural factors made this possible. There was a legal tradition that demanded payment from the offender to the offended, and each particular offence had its own price; when this was paid, harmony was again established. Second, the tradition of public penance which was so solidly established in the Roman tradition from the times of persecutions of Christians, had no hold on Irish society. So it was far easier in Ireland for penance to become a private affair between people and God (and perhaps a representative of the church).[20] The outgrowth of this was an understanding that sin is an internal matter between an individual and God. Penance was not just about forgiveness; it was a means of reconciliation – not of punishment – which would lead to a restored and stronger Christian who would be less likely to sin again. "Irish law saw penalties as reparations of damage done, not as punishments to inflict suffering on the criminal; and within that framework the penitentials were merely an extension of their basic legal attitude into the realm of the sacred."[21]

One of the works that has survived is the *Penitential* of a monk named Finnian (*c*. 470–*c*. 552). He began the rules of penance by clearly indicating that the purpose was to pursue the sort of life for which people were intended:

> If anyone has sinned by thought in his heart and immediately repents, he shall beat his breast and seek pardon from God and make satisfaction, and (so) be whole. But if he frequently entertains (evil) thoughts and hesitates to act on them, whether he has mastered them or been mastered by them, he shall seek help from God by prayer and fasting day and night until the evil thought departs and he is whole.[22]

Many of the rules in the *Penitential* had to do with the "big" sins like sexual misconduct and murder:

> If any layman has defiled a vowed virgin and she has lost her crown and he has begotten a child by her, let such a layman do penance for three years; in the first year he shall go on an allowance of bread and

water and unarmed and shall not have intercourse with his own wife, and for two years he shall abstain from wine and meat and shall not have intercourse with his wife. If, however, he does not beget a child of her, but nevertheless has defiled the virgin, he shall do penance for an entire year and a half, an entire year on an allowance of bread and water, and for half a year he shall abstain from wine and meat, and he shall not have intercourse with his wife until his penance is completed.[23]

But there were also internal sins or attitudes like envy, gloom, and greed that were identified and for which penance was prescribed. The goal was to "cleanse these faults from our hearts and introduce heavenly virtues in their places."[24]

Of course there would be later misunderstandings and abuses of the practice of penance. But this is an important strand of the way Christians have understood sin, forgiveness, and the pursuit of closeness to God which grew out of the Irish monastic movement.

The interchange that developed between the Irish monastics and the more Roman-influenced Christians in England was bound to cause conflict. The issue which brought this to a head was the dating of Easter: the Celtic Christians followed a different calendar from what had been adopted by Rome and calculated the dating of Easter differently. In 664, a Synod was called by King Osuiu of the kingdom of Northumbria in England to discuss this and other matters of religious practice at Whitby. The synod was held at Whitby where there was a double monastery (one for men and one for women) which was ruled over by Hilda (614–680). She was renowned for the success of the monastery and appeared to have the authority of the office of bishop in the region. At the Synod, Hilda backed the right of the Celtic contingent to celebrate Easter according to their customs. But in the end Wilfrid, the Bishop of York, convinced King Osuiu to conform to the customs of Rome.

The Synod of Whitby was not a watershed for theology itself. There were no significant theological points at issue here; besides the dating of Easter, they discussed how people should be baptized and whether the tonsure (the distinctive haircut for monks) was to have the crown of the head shaved or a vertical stripe down to the forehead. But in retrospect, we can look back at Whitby as an important step in the history of Christian thinking about the Church. Monasticism would continue to play an important role throughout the Middle Ages – almost all of the significant theologians would come from monasteries. But Whitby signals the suppression of local flavors of expression and the assertion of the ecclesiastical authority of a centralized Church.

This process of standardization that occurred in the West at the beginning of the Middle Ages did not fare so well in the East. We pick up that story in the next chapter.

SUMMARY OF MAIN POINTS

1 The Rule of Benedict became the standard guide for the organization of monasteries throughout the Latin Church in the Middle Ages.

2 Monks were the keepers and transmitters of the classical works of antiquity, and they fostered a climate of work that encouraged human participation in spiritual development.

3 Pope Gregory the Great contributed to the spread of monasticism and influenced medieval theology with his ascetically influenced doctrines of penance and purgatory.

4 Celtic Christianity was originally dominated by monasticism and accommodation to its own peculiar cultural expression, but came to accept the pattern of Rome.

FOR FURTHER READING

Benedict, *The Rule of St. Benedict in English*, Timothy Fry, ed. (Collegeville, MN: The Liturgical Press, 1982). A readable translation of the famous Rule which was so influential for medieval monasticism.

Gregory the Great, *Dialogues* (London: Burns and Oates, 1874). Fascinating insight into the spiritual world of the first monastic pope. No editions currently in print, but libraries carry the Henry James Coleridge English edition.

David Knowles, *Christian Monasticism* (London: Weidenfeld and Nicolson, 1969). A classic text surveying the history of Christian monasticism from its origins into the twentieth century. There are numerous pictures of famous abbeys included.

C.H. Lawrence, *Medieval Monasticism* (London: Longman, 1984). A readable history of monasticism from the fourth century through the Middle Ages.

Thomas O'Loughlin, *Celtic Theology: Humanity, World and God in Early Irish Writings* (London: Continuum, 2000). A survey of the distinctive theological contributions to medieval Christianity by early Irish writers.

13

Eastern Christianity splits from the West

QUESTIONS TO BE ADDRESSED IN THIS CHAPTER

1   What was the relation of Rome to the Eastern Church?
2   What was the *filioque* clause and its importance?
3   What was the Iconoclastic Controversy?
4   How did Eastern spirituality contribute to the separation of East and West?

Almost any history of Christianity with a chapter about the separation of East from West tells some version of the following story. On 16 July 1054 at eight o'clock in the morning, Cardinal Humbert, a legate from Pope Leo IX, walked into the Hagia Sophia basilica in Constantinople during the Eucharist celebration and plopped a document on the altar. He then spun around and walked out, stopping at the door to literally wipe the dust off his sandals and to announce, "Videat Deus et judicet!" – "Let God look and judge!" The document was a papal bull (an official written edict, as in "bulletin") which chronicled many errors those in the East had fallen into, and it excommunicated the Patriarch of Constantinople, Michael Cerularius. After a swiftly aborted attempt at resolving the

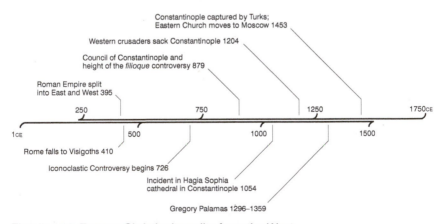

Timeline 13 Eastern Christianity splits from the West

issues, Cerularius responded by excommunicating Humbert and his two companions.

While this story is true,[1] the importance of it is often greatly exaggerated. It was Gibbon in his *Decline and Fall of the Roman Empire* who attached such significance to the scene above, claiming it to be a "thunderbolt" from which the "consummation of the schism" can be dated.[2] Many historians have seemed to follow his lead. But in reality, the Great Schism which obtained between East and West was a process that had been going

East and West were becoming strangers to one another, and this was something from which both were likely to suffer. In the early Church there had been unity in the faith, but a diversity of theological schools. From the start Greeks and Latins had each approached the Christian Mystery in their own way. At the risk of some oversimplification, it can be said that the Latin approach was more practical, the Greek more speculative; Latin thought was influenced by juridical ideas, by the concepts of Roman law, while the Greeks understood theology in the context of worship and in the light of the Holy Liturgy. When thinking about the Trinity, Latins started with the unity of the Godhead, Greeks with the threeness of persons; when reflecting on the Crucifixion, Latins thought primarily of Christ the Victim, Greeks of Christ the Victor; Latins talked more of redemption, Greeks of deification; and so on. Like the schools of Antioch and Alexandria within the east, these two distinctive approaches were not in themselves contradictory; each served to supplement the other, and each had its place in the fullness of Catholic tradition. But now that the two sides were becoming strangers to one another – with no political and little cultural unity, with no common language – there was a danger that each side would follow its own approach in isolation and push it to extremes, forgetting the value in the other point of view.

(Timothy Ware, *The Orthodox Church*, 48–49)

on for centuries before 1054 and would continue a couple of centuries after that date before the separation was complete. If we want to pin the consummation of the schism on one event, we'd do better to look at the Fourth Crusade in 1204 in which Western crusaders sacked the city of Constantinople, causing irreparable damage to East–West relations.

The schism wasn't all about personalities and politics. There were some deep divides on theological issues and approaches which increasingly separated the two sides. And not to be understated in this was the difference of languages – Greek in the East and Latin in the West – and the mindsets that accompanied them. Of course changes in the Roman Empire itself came into play, with its two capitals and two emperors, as did the relationships that evolved between bishops and emperors and between the bishops themselves. We begin this chapter of Christian thought with ideas about the leadership of the Church which were developing in the early Middle Ages (ideas which will include a good dose of politics as well).

1 ROME CLAIMS PRIMACY

When it became apparent that the Christian Church would be around for a while – neither being exterminated by persecution nor gathered up into the skies at the Second Coming of Christ – of necessity, it institutionalized. In the West (roughly, everything west of the Adriatic Sea on the north side of the Mediterranean and west of the Gulf of Sidra in modern day Libya on the south side), this meant taking on the form of the Roman Empire, with one head or monarch: the Bishop of Rome (who came to be called "pope").

Historically, there were five sees (areas of jurisdiction of a bishop) in a class of their own as most important and prestigious for the Church: Rome, Alexandria, Antioch, Constantinople, and Jerusalem. It is not in question at all that the See of Rome and its bishop came to be preeminent among even these. Those in the East who resisted granting authority over the entire Church were quick to acknowledge that the Bishop of Rome was the first among equals. This may seem somewhat surprising since the power structure of the Roman Empire had shifted to the East.

In 330, Emperor Constantine built his new capital city on the site of the ancient village of Byzantium for strategic reasons, so he could

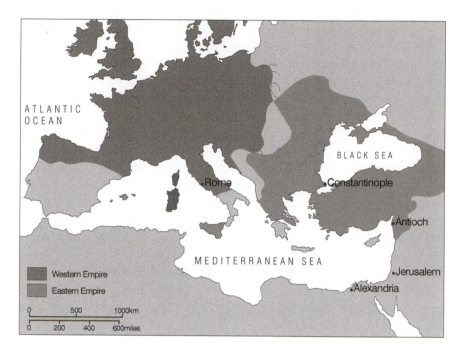

Map 13.1 Eastern and Western empires with five important sees

be closer to the eastern frontier of the empire. He called the city, "New Rome" but didn't seem to object when the name "Constantinople" was retained. In 395, the one empire was divided into two, with emperors both in Rome and in Constantinople. But Rome was invaded and fell in 410 to the Visigoths, and it seemed that the Eastern realm of Christianity would be more influential in the affairs of the Church.

Perhaps, though, because the Bishop of Rome was so far removed from the others and because the Western part of the empire was not strong politically, his importance naturally grew in the power vacuum on that side of the empire. And in the doctrinal disputes throughout the centuries, Rome had tended to come out on the winning side time after time. Especially influential in this was Leo's *Tome* from the time of the Council of Chalcedon (see Chapter 8). In contrast, the great rival of Rome, Constantinople, had harbored many of the worst heretics: Arius, Nestorius, Eutyches, and the Monotheletes – a point which Humbert was quick to point out in his dealings with Constantinople.

Of course the string of doctrinal victories by Rome might be explained sociologically rather than theologically as follows: given the propensity of the East for speculative thought, they often probed ever more deeply into theological mysteries – not inventing or changing what was handed down, but proffering explanations which might be interpreted by others in heretical ways; and given the Western penchant for pragmatism, for brokering deals that would work rather than clinging to an idea or ideal, it is not surprising that they came out on the winning side more often. Supporters of the West might counter that the sociological explanation doesn't really supplant the theological but is derivative from it. And here is the central difference in points of view on primacy of Rome: in the East, the pope was acknowledged to be first among the bishops because of the orthodoxy that had attended the office over the years; in the West, the explanation ran the other way: the continued orthodoxy of the popes occurred because they were in fact the most authoritative of the bishops.[3]

Beyond the bald assertion of authority by the West, there needed to be some justification for why the Bishop of Rome was preeminent. The West's case rested on two claims:

Now when Jesus came into the district of Caesarea Philippi, he asked his disciples, "Who do people say that the Son of Man is?" And they said, "Some say John the Baptist, but others Elijah, and still others Jeremiah or one of the prophets." He said to them, "But who do you say that I am?" Simon Peter answered, "you are the Messiah, the Son of the living God." And Jesus answered him, "Blessed are you, Simon son of Jonah! For flesh and blood has not revealed this to you, but my Father in heaven. And I tell you, you are Peter [*Petros*, in Greek, which means 'rock'], and on this rock I will build my church, and the gates of Hades will not prevail against it. I will give you the keys of the kingdom of heaven, and whatever you bind on earth will be bound in heaven, and whatever you loose on earth will be loosed in heaven.

(Matthew 16:13–16)

1   Jesus said that his Church would be built on Peter, and he gave Peter ultimate authority.
2   Peter's authority is passed on through the office he founded in Rome.

With regard to the second point, there were various objections raised. Some claimed that Antioch had a better claim to priority because Peter had been bishop there before he ever went to Rome. Something about the importance of the city of Rome itself, though, lent more significance to Rome having the place of honor. If the honor was due to the importance of the city, though, some in the East protested that the honor and function should have transitioned to Constantinople when the Roman capital moved there. Defenders of Rome were unmoved by this argument and pointed out that, "the kingdom of the world is one thing and the distribution of ranks in the Church is quite another."[4]

Arguing against the first point proved difficult for the Eastern side, because most Greek theologians acknowledged that Peter was first among theologians owing to his confession of Jesus as the messiah. Still, some argued that Jesus's words about the foundation of the Church were not to be taken as pertaining to Peter himself, but that the confession itself of Jesus as messiah (which Peter happened to make first) was that foundation. Or in a slightly different tack, it was argued that all bishops who kept the faith were imitators of Peter, regardless of whether they stood in a direct line of succession to him.

But the tradition of recognizing the primacy of Rome was too strongly held to be overturned by arguments. This was a significant bone of contention between East and West. The East strove to maintain collegial relations between the different sees and did not accept that one bishop could have authority over the affairs in another see. In their view, disagreements were to be settled by collaborative councils, not by edicts of one person.

The authority of the pope was the major issue which led to the split between East and West. And it must be mentioned that the West didn't always play fair. Sometime in the eighth century a document was produced that purportedly came from Emperor Constantine in the fourth century. The "Donation of Constantine," as it was called, gave Pope Sylvester and his successors authority over the whole Church, specifically mentioning the other historic sees:

Inasmuch as our imperial power is earthly, we have decreed that it shall venerate and honour his most holy Roman Church and that the sacred see of blessed Peter shall be gloriously exalted above our empire and earthly throne. We attribute to him the power and glorious dignity and strength and honour of the empire, and we ordain and decree that he shall have rule as well over the four principal sees, Antioch, Alexandria, Constantinople, and Jerusalem, as also over all the churches of God in all the world.[5]

The primary usage of the document was in securing land for the papacy, but it also was used against the Eastern Church in the debate over the primacy of Rome. It wasn't until the fifteenth century that the document was proved to be a forgery; by then the rift was so deep that there was little hope of reconciliation.

2 *FILIOQUE*

Another important doctrinal debate during the process of schism concerned the *filioque* clause. *Filioque* is a Latin word which translates as "and the son." This seemingly insignificant phrase became the source of a significant theological difference between East and West when taken in the context of the part of the Nicene Creed which states, "The Holy Spirit, the Lord and the Life-giver, that proceedeth from the Father [and the son]."[6]

In the papal bull delivered by Humbert at the Hagia Sophia in 1054, one of the grievances cited was that the Eastern Church had deleted the *filioque* clause from the Nicene Creed. As a matter of fact, it was the Western Church which had added the clause after the creed was

FILIOQUE

A Latin word meaning literally, "and from the son." This word was inserted into the Nicene Creed in its Latin translation so that it was asserted that the Holy Spirit proceeds from the Son as well as from the Father.

finalized at the Council of Constantinople in 381. The issue was debated for centuries between East and West. At one point, the West's Pope Leo III (in office 795–816) tried to compromise by making the distinction between *teaching* that the Holy Spirit proceeded from the Son (which the Roman Church did) and *chanting* the same as part of the official creed (which, he claimed, they did not). In the East, Photius (*c.* 810–893) was the Patriarch of Constantinople during the Council of Constantinople in 879–880. There he thought the East had won the day when it was agreed that any alteration of the Nicene Creed was to be condemned. But although there were representatives from Rome at the council, it is still debated whether Rome ever recognized the decisions there as authoritative. To this day, the Eastern Orthodox Churches call the council the Eighth Ecumenical Council. The Roman Catholic Church claims the Eighth Ecumenical Council to be a prior council in 869 at which Photius was deposed as the Patriarch of Constantinople (he was reinstated in 877).

Besides the political drama that attended the *filioque* controversy, there was a deep theological issue at stake. Central to this was how the relationships between members of the Trinity were to be conceived and explained. For the Latins in the West, to claim that the Holy Spirit proceeded from the Father but not the Son was to drive a wedge between the unity of Father and Son: "When the Holy Spirit is said to proceed from the Father, it is necessary that he proceed also from the Son, because Father and Son are undoubtedly of the same *ousia*."[7] For the Greeks, though, this is missing the fundamental point about the Trinity in which there is one common nature (or *ousia*), but three separate *hypostases* (refer to Chapter 9 for this discussion). And any properties of the divine which do not belong to the common nature must belong to just one of the *hypostases,* not to two of them while excluding the third.

In characteristic Greek fashion, their theologians drove the analysis deeper to make very fine-grained distinctions. They were happy to admit that the Holy Spirit was indeed *sent* from the Son; but this was different from the Spirit's *proceeding* from the Son, which they would not admit as the West did. On this point, there was something lost in translation between the Greek and Latin explanations, as the Latin verbiage did not always account for this subtle difference.

At its core, the disagreement serves to highlight the different starting points that East and West had in considering the Trinity. For the West, the

Trinity was first and foremost a unity; it is much more common in Latin for prayers to be addressed simply to "God" rather than to the individual members of the Trinity. And this unity of the Trinity is preserved by seeing the Holy Spirit as the Spirit of both Father and Son. In the East, the starting point is the communal "three-ness" of the Trinity. To keep this from lapsing into tri-theism, they needed a principle of unity as well. This was found in the Father as the source or cause of both the Son and the Spirit.

Each side appealed to multiple church fathers in support of their interpretations, but ultimately there was stalemate. For the East, however, there was more at stake than just a subtle theological point. Giving in to the Western version of the creed would mean acknowledging that Rome had the authority to revise the decisions of the ecumenical councils on its own. The East would not acknowledge this, and used the *filioque* controversy as further justification for separating from Rome and the West.

3 ICONOCLASTIC CONTROVERSY

Another debate which was ultimately grounded in Christology was the Iconclastic Controversy. This was particularly important in the East because of their tradition of the use of icons in worship, but also because of the ramifications the dispute had for the developing relationship between church and state. The controversy began when Emperor Leo III of the Eastern (or Byzantine) Empire had an image of Jesus removed from the imperial palace in Constantinople in 726. It is difficult for us now to discern clearly the motivation behind Leo's actions, and undoubtedly it was a complex issue. But certainly there was an element of sincere belief on Leo's part that icons of Jesus were idolatrous, and he was acting to purify the Church from this tendency. The second of the Ten Commandments prohibits the construction of idols or images to be worshiped, and this seemed to him to be a rather straightforward application of this commandment.

The iconoclasts used a sophisticated theological argument about the nature of Christ which had been accepted at the Council of Chalcedon (451) to justify their prohibition of images depicting Christ. It is presented in the form of a dilemma. In representing Christ in an image, we must do so either with respect to his humanity and his divinity, or with respect

ICONOCLASM

From the Greek for "image-breaker." The doctrine and practices of those who believed that images should have no place in Christian worship.

to just his humanity. If only his humanity is represented, then his two natures have been separated and we are left with the Nestorian heresy; this is not acceptable. If the divine nature is also to be represented, then his two natures are confused; this too is unacceptable. Therefore there should not be any pictorial depictions of Christ.[8]

The Patriarch of Constantinople, Germanus I (c. 640–733), was strongly opposed to the policy of Emperor Leo. In 730 when he refused to change his position, the emperor essentially forced him out of office and had him replaced by the iconoclast Anastasius, who was patriarch from 730–754. This episode serves to show the very different trajectories that church and state relationships were on in the East as opposed to the West. It was only 70 years later that the pope was appointing the emperor in the West!

After his deposition, Germanus actually appealed to the West for support. Pope Gregory II (in office 715–731) supported Germanus by refusing to acknowledge Anastasius as a legitimate patriarch. Gregory died in 731 and his successor, Pope Gregory III (in office 731–741) continued the support for Germanus. In the East, Emperor Leo retaliated by removing lands that had been under the jurisdiction of the pope and granting them to the Patriarch of Constantinople. Of course, none of this helped the East–West relations.

There were two monks who came out significantly in defense of icons during the iconoclastic controversy in the East. John of Damascus (c. 676–749) was a monk living in the St. Sabbas Monastery outside Bethlehem (a monastery of the Greek Orthodox Church still in operation today). He wrote three influential treatises defending the use of icons in Christian worship.[9] His central argument was that there was a change in the status of God's relationship to the visible world with the coming of Christ; it is only idolatry if we try to represent the invisible God or worship things that are not God. But in the Incarnation, God became visible to us:

Figure 13.1 John of Damascus © Mondadori Portfolio/Electa/Art Resource, NY

Of old, God the incorporeal and uncircumscribed was never depicted. Now, however, when God is seen clothed in flesh, and conversing with men, I make an image of the God whom I see. I do not worship matter, I worship the God of matter, who became matter for my sake, and deigned to inhabit matter, who worked out my salvation through matter. I will not cease from honouring that matter which works my salvation.[10]

Pushing this line of argument even further, John would warn that disdain of visible images could easily lead to disdain of the matter of Christ and be a kind of docetism (the claim that Jesus only seemed to be human).

This was the line of thought adopted by the Seventh Ecumenical Council in Nicea in 787. The Eastern emperor by then was Constantine

VI (third successor to Leo III), who was still in his teens. His mother Irene acted as regent for the minor, and she was a strong supporter of icons. When Tarasius (in office 784–806) was chosen as the new patriarch, she pushed for the council to be called. Irene and Tarasius worked together with Pope Hadrian (in office 772–795) in the West to maneuver the tricky political waters and win over the members of the council. There it was ruled that icons have a legitimate role to play in worship – namely, the beholders of them will be "aroused to recollect the originals and to long after them." It was also stressed, that the images themselves are not to be worshiped.[11] This was only a temporary victory for icons, however.

After a couple of short-lived and turbulent reigns by Eastern emperors, Emperor Leo V hoped to return to the more glorious days of the iconoclastic emperors and so decided to return to the iconoclastic policies predating the 787 council. Theodore the Studite was a monk in charge of the "Studios" monastery in Constantinople. Theodore argued vehemently against this reversal of policy and even engaged in civil disobedience by flaunting the continued use of icons in his monastery. Theodore was exiled and embarked on a massive letter-writing campaign against the emperor's policy. His arguments dealt not only with the legitimacy of icon use in worship, but also with the illegitimacy of emperors deciding theological matters. That it was a monk arguing this point underscores that the debate was not ultimately about power or the elevation of institutions; rather, Theodore was concerned about orthodoxy and upholding the truth.[12]

In 820, Leo V was murdered, and while his successor, Michael II, did not reverse the iconoclastic policies, he greatly eased up on the enforcement of them. Theodore died in 826 without seeing the completion of the resistance movement against the iconoclasts, but at that time things were well on their way. It was another empress acting as regent for a young emperor who brokered the final resolution. Empress Theodora organized a council in 843 which restored the decisions of Nicea II in 787.[13]

4 EASTERN SPIRITUALITY

It should be emphasized that the debate over icons in the East carried more than just academic or intellectual gravitas. The reverence and use of icons was an important way of life for people in the East. John of Damascus had called them "books for the illiterate"[14] – ways in which people could be visually drawn into the mysteries of the faith. Furthermore, icons were an extension of the Eastern way of honoring the material world with a sacramental value. It is only recently that Christians in the West have begun to appreciate the significance of this approach.

In the past couple of decades, the church in the West (both Catholic and Protestant) has rediscovered the vast spiritual resources of the East – many of which date to the time period under consideration here. In particular, the publication of *The Philokalia*[15] has brought to the attention of English speakers the rich tradition of Eastern spirituality. A collection of writings from the fourth through the fifteenth centuries, *The Philokalia*, preserves the important thought of the Hesychast movement in Eastern orthodoxy.

The Hesychasts, a term which translates as "stillness," maintained with the earlier apophatic theologians of the East (see Chapter 6) that God cannot be known in his essence or nature. But they argued that he can be known through the energies which emanate from him. Most often this happens during times of spiritual ecstasy when the Holy Spirit envelops the one praying with light.[16] Symeon the New Theologian (949–1022) reported that while sitting still repeating to himself over and over the words, "God, have mercy upon me, a sinner" a flood of light filled the whole room and indeed transformed himself into light. He was filled with tears and inexpressible gladness, and then his intellect "ascended to heaven and beheld another light, more lucid than the first."[17] These mystical experiences were ridiculed by some, creating what is known as the Hesychast Controversy.

The two principal opponents in the controversy were Barlaam (*c.* 1290–1348) and Gregory Palamas (1296–1359). Barlaam was a Greek-speaking monk from the south of Italy. He had been trained in Western traditions and favored reunification of East and West. Seeing the Hesychast tradition as an impediment to this, he argued that the application of logic and philosophical analysis was what theology needed – not the navel-gazing mantras of the Hesychasts. Gregory Palamas is generally considered the greatest of the Hesychast theologians. He successfully argued against Barlaam that theology ought not to consist in innovation, but in repeating what has been handed down faithfully from the past. Thus the constant repeating of simple phrases like the Jesus Prayer, as well as prostration of the body and attention to breathing, were used to focus the intellect in prayer. Gregory convinced those in the East that Hesychism was a valid approach to spirituality, and Barlaam withdrew to the West.

This episode symbolically captures the final separation between East and West. They had talked and debated, but ultimately found themselves viewing faith in different ways. The East continued in the trajectory of the desert fathers and mothers and the Cappadocians with a strongly ascetic impulse, and they viewed salvation as the process of theosis (see Chapter 6). In the West, as we'll see in the next chapter, the emphasis of salvation came to be understood primarily in a legal sense with the use of concepts like justification and substitutionary atonement. These separate (though perhaps complimentary) approaches were not so much a topic to be debated as they were different vocabularies that had few points of intersection. The East went its own way – especially after its center shifted to Moscow when Constantinople was captured by the Turks in 1453 – and had little exchange with the West until the twentieth century.

SUMMARY OF MAIN POINTS

1   The primacy of Rome was justified by the claims that Jesus gave authority to Peter, and Peter passed his authority on through the office he founded at Rome.
2   The disagreement over the *filioque* clause of the Nicene Creed cut to the heart of different theological approaches between East and West.
3   The Iconoclastic Controversy forced further reflection on Christology and was another source of tension between East and West.
4   Eastern spirituality continued in the mystical tradition of earlier Christian ascetics and gradually had less and less interaction with Roman Catholicism.

FOR FURTHER READING

John Meyendorff, *Byzantine Theology: Historical Trends and Doctrinal Themes* (New York: Fordham University Press, 1979). A standard work that includes good information on how the Eastern Church came to be shaped as it is today.

Jaroslav Pelikan, *The Spirit of Eastern Christendom (600–1700)* (Chicago, IL: University of Chicago Press, 1974). Volume 2 of the monumental series, *The Christian Tradition: A History of the Development of Doctrine*, by one of most learned scholars of historical theology in the twentieth century.

The Philokalia (four volumes), compiled by St. Nikodimos of the Holy Mountain and St. Makarios of Corinth, G.E.H. Palmer, Philip Sherrard, and Kallistos Ware, trans. and ed. (London: Faber and Faber, 1979–1995). A compilation of Eastern Orthodox writings from the fourth to the fifteenth centuries.

Timothy Ware (now known as Bishop Kallistos of Diokleia), *The Orthodox Church* (Baltimore, MD: Penguin, 1964; 2nd edition, 1993). A popular exposition of the history and contemporary practice of the Orthodox Church written by a scholar at Oxford who became a priest of the Greek Orthodox Church.

14

Anselm, Abelard, and Bernard

QUESTIONS TO BE ADDRESSED IN THIS CHAPTER

1   What does Anselm's "faith seeking understanding" dictum mean?

2   How did Anselm's ontological argument relate to this methodology?

3   To what position did rationality lead in the doctrine of the Atonement?

4   How does the Eucharist influence theories of the Atonement?

By the end of the first millennium after the birth of Christ, the center of gravity for the story we are tracing had shifted to Western Europe. With the abatement of successive waves of invaders in Western Europe, the population grew and society became relatively stable in that part of the world. Politically, prominent aristocratic families were the most noticeable powers as they controlled extensive feudal territories and exercised influence over all aspects of society. One practice that became increasingly common around 1000 was the granting of land and endowments by these noble families for the creation of monasteries. Their motivations were mostly selfish: they believed that the prayers of the monks would get them into heaven and lessen the time they had to spend in purgatory. Whether this goal was achieved or not, an unintended consequence for Christian thought during this time was the creation of centers of learning. Most monasteries were sufficiently well endowed to permit many of the monks to devote themselves entirely to intellectual pursuits. One such monk was Anselm.

In 1066, William the Conqueror crossed the English Channel from Normandy and conquered England. Twenty-six years later, Anselm left his Benedictine monastery in Normandy and crossed to England where he was to become the Archbishop of Canterbury at the request of King William II. Anselm's relationship with the English monarch (William II and then his successor, King Henry I) was almost always strained. Anselm held that his allegiance was first and foremost to the pope – a conviction that rarely sits well with kings. There was a lot of drama during his

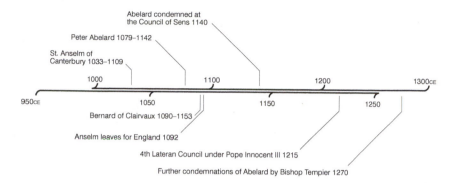

Timeline 14 Anselm, Abelard, and Bernard

tenure as bishop, including secret envoys to Rome, excommunications, and banishments. But ultimately, Anselm fulfilled the duties of his office with a degree of popularity among the people of England until his death in 1109.

1 ANSELM OF CANTERBURY: FAITH SEEKING UNDERSTANDING

Anselm merits a place in the history of Christian thought not for his ecclesiology or political ideas, but because of his doctrine of the Atonement and especially for the influence he had on understanding the relationship between faith and reason. On this latter issue, he saw himself very consciously as standing in the tradition of Augustine.[1] It was Anselm who penned the famous Latin phrase, *credo ut intelligam* – I believe in order to understand.[2] But Augustine had said basically the same thing in his commentary on John 7:17 ("Anyone who resolves to do the will of God will know whether the teaching is from God or whether I am speaking on my own"). Augustine wrote, "For understanding is the reward of faith. Therefore do not seek to understand in order to believe, but believe that thou mayest understand."[3] Augustine's commitment to this methodology is certainly influenced by his biography (see Chapter 11): he had searched through the rationalistic systems of thought and found that these did not live up to the bar of reason. In this sense, reason led him to faith. But understanding the depths of Christian faith could only be achieved after he had committed himself to that faith. Reason could not take him all the way to understanding.

With Anselm too, there seem to be two contrary impulses at work. On the one hand, he affirms the primacy of faith over reason – and he does so consistently throughout his writings. But on the other hand, he employs a strongly rationalistic methodology of proving things by reason. He attempted to show that many of the truths of the faith could be demonstrated by reason without reliance at all on revelation. How does this fit with the primacy of faith over reason and his insistence that he believed in order to understand?

The point of *credo ut intelligam* was that faith is the starting point for understanding. Faith supplied beliefs through revelation, and these were not questioned. But in order to understand what was believed by faith, there was something further that needed to be done with those beliefs. By analogy with scientific methodology, we might say that for the Augustine-Anselm model, faith provided the "empirical" data that had to be explained, and then the theories which did the explaining were the understanding that was sought after.[4]

To say the same thing in another way, faith needed to be worked out in the accepted cultural framework of thought. As such, the explanation or understanding might take different forms in different contexts, but all those who follow in the train of Augustine will begin with the same articles of faith. In the case of Augustine, Christian faith was explained in the context of the Neo-Platonic philosophy which was so pervasive in his day. But Anselm lived some 700 years later and in a different part of the world; his understanding of the same articles of faith would sometimes take on a different look. The argot of the eleventh- and twelfth-century monastery culture was Aristotelian logic.

Anselm started by acknowledging that which was believed by faith, but then wondered whether those beliefs might be proved logically without appeal to faith. It may seem as though he was adopting this approach in order to engage unbelievers on their own terms – using only the tools they would accept as legitimate. But the practice of bracketing off revelation was not done for the purpose of proving to unbelievers that the articles of faith were true. Rather, Anselm's motivation seemed to be to show to fellow Christians that the things they believed by faith were also rationally demonstrable. Even if faith was primary, however, they were not fideists (those who affirm that religious belief should be based on faith alone rather than reason). Their goal was to understand more fully that which they believed by demonstrating that it was logical.[5] According to the twentieth-century medieval scholar Étienne Gilson, this is the process of transforming truth that is merely believed into truth that is known.[6]

To see Anselm's method in action, we turn to his logical explanation of the existence of God.

2 ANSELM'S ONTOLOGICAL ARGUMENT

Anselm is probably best known for his formulation of the ontological argument for the existence of God. The argument is at once ingenious and perplexing, and it has been hotly debated right down to the present day. Essentially, Anselm argued that we can all form a concept of the greatest imaginable being. He purports, then, to show from the concept itself that the greatest imaginable being must exist in reality, not just in the imagination. How is this possible? Consider the following example of deducing something from the mere concept.

Stump has an Aunt Pat. Even those who know nothing at all through experience of his Aunt Pat should be able to figure out some things about Aunt Pat merely from the concept "aunt." Of course Aunt Pat will be a female – otherwise she wouldn't be an aunt. By persevering a bit further into analysis of the concept, it can also be deduced that Aunt Pat must have a sibling who has children (or in the looser sense, she might be married to someone whose sibling has children). When we come to fully understand what is meant by "aunt," we recognize that anything that is an aunt couldn't help but have these properties because that is precisely the sort of thing we mean by "aunt."

In the same way that we can deduce "female" or "has a sibling with children" as properties belonging to the concept "aunt," Anselm claimed to be able to deduce "exists" from the concept "God." His argument rests on two central premises:

1   God is the greatest imaginable being.
2   It is greater to exist than not to exist.

From these, it is merely a matter of comparing two similar concepts: a) the greatest imaginable being that does not exist in reality; and b) the greatest imaginable being that does exist in reality. Then Anselm asks, "Which one is greater?" According to his second premise, it must be the one that really does exist. Therefore, the greatest imaginable being (which is what we mean by God) must exist.

Of course other thinkers objected to the premises, but it is difficult to pin down exactly what the problem is with either premise. Anselm's ontological argument has shown remarkable resilience for almost 1000 years.[7]

For, it is one thing for an object to be in the understanding, and another to understand that the object exists. When a painter first conceives of what he will afterwards perform, he has it in his understanding, but he does not yet understand it to be, because he has not yet performed it. But after he has made the painting, he both has it in his understanding, and he understands that it exists, because he has made it.

Hence, even the fool is convinced that something exists in the understanding, at least, than which nothing greater can be conceived. For, when he hears of this, he understands it. And whatever is understood, exists in the understanding. And assuredly that, than which nothing greater can be conceived, cannot exist in the understanding alone. For, suppose it exists in the understanding alone: then it can be conceived to exist in reality; which is greater.

Therefore, if that, than which nothing greater can be conceived, exists in the understanding alone, the very being, than which nothing greater can be conceived, is one, than which a greater can be conceived. But obviously this is impossible. Hence, there is no doubt that there exists a being, than which nothing greater can be conceived, and it exists both in the understanding and in reality.

(Anselm, *Proslogium*, Chapter 2)

Figure 14.1 Anselm. National Portrait Gallery/Public domain/ Wikimedia Commons

3 THE ATONEMENT

Anselm also has a secure place in the history of Christian thought for re-working the accepted understanding of the Atonement. It was believed by faith that Christ's death was necessary for the salvation of humans. Could this also be understood by reason? Anselm took the same sort of approach here as with the ontological argument. He says in the preface to his *Why God Became Man*, "leaving Christ out of view (as if nothing had ever been known of him), [this book] proves, by absolute reasons, the impossibility that any man should be saved without him."[8] Whether or not his argument constitutes a proof, his thinking on the Atonement marks a significant milestone in Christian thinking.

Prior to the time of Anselm, the death of Christ was conceived primarily in terms that sound more mythological than theological: there was a cosmic battle between God and Satan for human beings, and the death of Christ was understood to be a way of paying off Satan. Satan was tricked, though, by the resurrection, and his ransom escaped. Gregory of Nyssa seems to be the source of this interpretation of the Atonement which came to be shared by (among others) Augustine and Gregory the Great. It is known as the "fishhook" theory in which Satan takes the bait of the death of the second person of the Trinity, but then is tricked by the concealed "hook" of the resurrection.[9]

Such a theory, though, was an affront to the logical analysis of the concept of God according to Anselm. God is righteousness and truth, and he would never stoop to deception even in the service of a good cause. Just as it is a contradiction to think of the greatest imaginable being not existing, so too it is contradictory for God to be a deceiver. Therefore, the account of Atonement by deception could not be correct even though it had many eminent authorities to recommend it. Anselm argued that Satan had no rights over humans and that God was under no obligation to pay him anything for their redemption. So, if Christ did not have to die as a ransom paid to Satan, then why did he have to die? His reasoning was as follows.

Sin has prevented human beings from achieving that for which they were created, namely, a state of eternal bliss with God. Because this was God's purpose for human beings and because God's purposes cannot ultimately be thwarted, there must be a remedy for this situation. Any remedy has to provide satisfaction for sin – it cannot go unpunished. Again deriving his conclusions from a logical analysis of the nature of God, Anselm says, "without satisfaction, that is, without voluntary payment of the debt, God can neither pass by the sin unpunished, nor can the sinner attain that happiness, or happiness like that, which he had before he sinned."[10] So there must be payment, but it is not a ransom payment to Satan; rather it is payment of a debt to God.

But how can the debt be paid? Human beings can't pay the debt themselves by doing what is right, because that is already expected of them. Only a perfect being would have the ability to provide satisfaction for the debt by voluntarily suffering on their behalf; but justice demands that the debt must be paid by human beings. Therefore, because there must be a remedy to allow God's plans for human beings to be realized, it is necessary that there be a God-man – one who has both the ability (as God) and the obligation (as human) to provide satisfaction.

Given the times, some have read Anselm as making God into a feudal lord who had been affronted by his peasants and so demanded satisfaction to restore their relationship. But his logical analysis of the Atonement as satisfying sin has been enormously influential in subsequent Christian thought – well beyond feudal times. Even in his own day, however, not everyone accepted the logic of Anselm's analysis of the situation.

Peter Abelard (1079–1142) was a younger contemporary of Anselm who studied primarily in Paris. He is known outside the realm of theology and philosophy as one of the great tragic lovers. While studying at Notre Dame in Paris (before construction of the magnificent cathedral was started), he lived with Canon Fulbert and tutored his niece Heloise. More than intellectual attraction developed between the two and Heloise was found to be with child. An academic career was not viewed as compatible with marriage in those days, but feeling bound by his duty, Abelard married Heloise secretly. Uncle Fulbert found out and hired some thugs to storm into Abelard's room at night and castrate him. Heloise and child were shuttled off to a convent and Abelard became a monk at St. Denis monastery. Despite the scandal, Abelard had a fairly productive career as a scholar-monk, enjoying great popularity as a teacher and significantly influencing the later scholastic movement.

On the Atonement, Abelard agreed with Anselm that Christ's death was in no way to be construed as paying a ransom to Satan. But neither did he think it correct to construe it as a payment to God. In fact, he found it repulsive to think that a righteous, holy God would demand the blood of an innocent person as some sort of pay-off to let guilty people off the hook. In his commentary on the Epistle of Romans, Abelard wrote:

> Indeed, how cruel and wicked it seems that anyone should demand the blood of an innocent person as the price for anything, or that it should in any way please him that an innocent man should be slain – still less that God should consider the death of his Son so agreeable that by it he should be reconciled to the whole world. These, and like queries, appear to us to pose a considerable problem concerning our redemption or justification through the death of our Lord Jesus Christ.

Abelard continues, offering his own theory of the Atonement:

> Now it seems to us that we have been justified by the blood of Christ and reconciled to God in this way: through this unique act of grace

manifested to us – in that his Son has taken upon himself our nature and preserved therein in teaching us by word and example even unto death – he has more fully bound us to himself by love; with the result that our hearts should be enkindled by such a gift of divine grace, and true charity should not now shrink from enduring anything for him.[11]

According to Abelard, the meaning of Christ's death consists in providing a supreme moral example for us, in order that we might emulate him. The Gospel of John records Jesus saying, "no one has greater love than this, to lay down one's life for one's friends" (15:13). Abelard understood this to mean that Christ died in order to show human beings how to perfectly love each other. "Everyone becomes more righteous – by which we mean a greater lover of the Lord – after the Passion of Christ than before, since a realized gift inspires greater love than one which is only hoped for."[12]

This is significant not just for the emphasis on the more subjective nature of the Atonement that Abelard was advocating, but also for the place that logic took him. For Anselm, the articles of faith – of which one was the claim that Christ died for the sins of humankind – provided the starting point for understanding and these were not to be abrogated. Abelard, however, did not follow the method of faith seeking understanding. In fact, his methodology sounds more at home in the Modern period after Descartes than in medieval scholasticism. In the prologue to his *Sic et Non* he states, "Through doubting we come to questioning and through questions we perceive the truth."[13] This book, the title of which is translated as "Yes and No," consists of asking questions and then lining up what the church fathers had said on the topics – showing their contradictory opinions and attempting to resolve them. In another couple of generations, this sort of disputation would become the standard method of education (most famously, Peter Lombard's *Four Books of Sentences*). But during Abelard's lifetime, his method of doubting and the conclusions he came to were not received well.

Most vocal in opposition to Abelard was an activist monk known as Bernard of Clairvaux (1090–1153). He was abbot of the monastery at Clairvaux in France which was part of the new Cistercian order of monks and which parented about 70 other monasteries during Bernard's supervision. Bernard was very outspoken and had powerful allies. He was so upset with Abelard that he wrote a book entitled *The Errors of*

Peter Abelard and influenced the pope to have Abelard condemned at the Council of Sens in 1140.

The central bone of contention was that Abelard had done away with the forgiveness of sins and replaced it with a positive role model. According to Bernard, Abelard's Christ had only announced the redemption of humankind rather than having achieved it through his work on the cross: "he taught righteousness, but he did not grant it; he demonstrated love, but he did not infuse it."[14]

Undoubtedly, Bernard was interpreting Abelard uncharitably. Abelard still used language like "our redemption through Christ's suffering" which "frees us from slavery to sin."[15] But it was true that Abelard had attempted to significantly change the emphasis of Christ's life and death to be an example rather than a satisfaction for sin which entailed some legal *quid pro quo* on our behalf with God.

Abelard would have fitted more comfortably within the Modern period of theology (see Chapter 25). His methods and conclusions sound like they belong in the nineteenth century rather than the twelfth. It might be argued that he sowed some of the seeds of modernism through his method of doubt, but his contemporaries were not ready to cultivate these to fruition. It is unclear how far Abelard himself pushed the undermining of faith and authority in favor of reason. His opponents portrayed him as going quite far. In 1277 the Bishop of Paris, Étienne Tempier, would condemn 219 propositions, two of which seemed to be explicitly aimed at Abelard:

- The proposition is condemned that one should not hold anything unless it is self-evident or can be manifested from self-evident principles.
- The proposition is condemned that man should not be content with authority to have certitude about any question.[16]

These condemned propositions were not Abelard's, and it is not clear that he would have endorsed them specifically as formulated. But he was definitely pushing toward this sort of methodology. Bernard would have none of it though. Perhaps the logic of the Atonement was difficult to reason out and, contrary to Anselm, he conceded that we might not be able to fully understand it; but Bernard knew as a fact (through faith) that redemption and forgiveness came only through Christ's blood.[17]

4 ATONEMENT AND EUCHARIST

From this it may sound like Bernard's dogmatic insistence on faith shifted Anselm's goal of "faith seeking understanding" to something like "faith regardless of understanding." But again, understanding is a highly contextual operation of the intellect, and there is one facet of the context of eleventh- and twelfth-century faith that needs to be included if we are to do justice to their attempts to understand the Atonement: spiritual practice.

For a thousand years Christians had participated in the Eucharist – a ritual of consuming bread and wine instituted at the Last Supper of Christ before his crucifixion. This was incorporated into the Catholic Mass during which this text from the Gospel of Matthew was used: "Then [Jesus] took a cup, and after giving thanks he gave it to them, saying, 'Drink from it all of you; for this is my blood of the covenant, which is poured out for many for the forgiveness of sins'" (Matthew 26:27–28).

Few chronicles of Christian thought pay much attention to the significance of spiritual practice for shaping thought (though many recognize the influence of theology on practice). But especially when considering the context within which articles of faith are being worked out, the practices of believers contribute significantly to the plausibility structure of their understanding. That is to say, Bernard was speaking for a large portion of Christian thinkers when he rejected Abelard's views because they seemed to run contrary to the article of faith that was inculcated through the Mass: Christ's death was efficacious for the forgiveness of sins. Whether or not this could be understood apart from revelation, it formed a cornerstone of religious life and so it had to be incorporated into any understanding of the death of Christ.

It seems that a more holistic view of reason and understanding could have developed from Abelard's critique which would have recognized the integral place of faith within understanding but also allowed for some way of subjecting the articles of faith themselves to evaluation. But rather than viewing Abelard's use of reason as a healthy feedback loop for faith, Bernard saw it only as an attack on an article of faith – an article which was constantly reinforced by the Eucharist.

It was Bernard's view which would prevail, ensuring that the Middle Ages and its elevation of faith would not yet give way to the Modern period. Symbolic of this was the Fourth Lateran Council In 1215. Pope

Innocent III called for an ecumenical council and presented a number of canons (ecclesiastical decrees). The first of these established the doctrine of transubstantiation. This asserts that during the celebration of the Eucharist, the bread and wine are literally transformed into the body and blood of Christ. All appearances and reason may testify to the contrary, but this is to be believed by faith. Here we have faith being upheld not just when reason can't bring about understanding, but faith being upheld even when reason and understanding seem to say otherwise.

Pope Innocent III and the Fourth Lateran Council represent the pinnacle of the powerful Church of the Middle Ages. The authority of the Church and its pope was asserted over any other source of information; it was claimed that there is no salvation for anyone who is outside the Church (and Jews and Muslims were required to wear special clothing distinguishing themselves); the foundations were laid for the Inquisition whereby the official interpretations of the Church would be forcibly upheld. Faith and reason seemed to be pitted against each other, and reason could get you into trouble. This was the direction Christian thought in general seemed to be headed. But there were other forces at work.

SUMMARY OF MAIN POINTS

1   For Anselm, "faith seeking understanding" means that Christians accept the data of revelation unswervingly, then work out and explain how these things are so.

2   Anselm's ontological argument is an attempt to explain in the language of logic that it is impossible for God not to exist and still be God.

3   Anselm's view of the Atonement was that Christ as God and man was the only one who could provide satisfaction for sins through his death, but this was questioned by Abelard.

4   Bernard reacted strongly to Abelard and held to the dictates of faith which were reinforced by the practice of the Eucharist.

FOR FURTHER READING

Eugene R. Fairweather, ed., *A Scholastic Miscellany: Anselm to Ockham* (Philadelphia, PA: Westminster Press, 1956). A good collection of primary sources of the time period.

Etienne Gilson, *Reason and Revelation in the Middle Ages* (New York: Charles Scribner's Sons, 1938). A classic work on the relationship of faith and reason in the work of medieval theologians.

Alister E. McGrath, *Iustitia Dei: A History of the Christian Doctrine of Justification*, 3rd edition (Cambridge: Cambridge University Press, 2005). A scholarly tome on the history of the concept of Atonement by a leading theologian of our day.

Jaroslav Pelikan, *The Growth of Medieval Theology (600–1300)* (Chicago, IL: University of Chicago Press, 1978). Volume three of Pelikan's monumental history of the development of doctrine.

15

Islam and Judaism in the Middle Ages

QUESTIONS TO BE ADDRESSED IN THIS CHAPTER

1   What is Islam?
2   In what ways did Islamic philosophy influence Christian thought in the Middle Ages?
3   What were some central tenets of Jewish thought in the Middle Ages, and how did they influence Christian ideas about God's nature and existence?
4   What were some of the major issues involved in Christian encounters with these other faiths?

Throughout the first five centuries of the Christian Church there were ongoing internal theological debates as the orthodox battled the heterodox regarding who had the authentic teachings of Jesus and the early apostles. As we have seen in earlier chapters, in attempting to understand, clarify, and articulate Christian teachings (which later developed into Christian doctrines), the Church often utilized the language and conceptual schemes of the classical Greek philosophers.

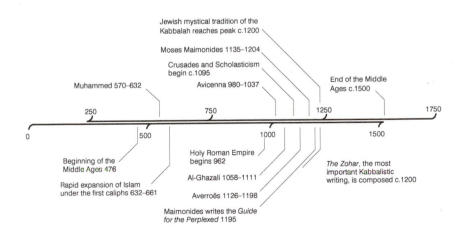

Timeline 15 Islam and Judaism in the Middle Ages

But Christianity was not the only tradition in antiquity to appropriate classical ideas. The Islamic and Jewish traditions were also shaped, to some extent, by the works of Plato, Aristotle, and other ancient Greek thinkers as well as other classical beliefs, ideas, and experiences which emerged during this period of history. As Christianity expanded into new territories and was confronted with Judaism and Islam, fresh ideas and challenges arose for the Church. Thus, in order to understand medieval Christian thought, it is imperative to be acquainted with some of the central figures and ideas of these religious traditions during this formative historical period.

1 ISLAM – A NEW RELIGION EMERGES

In the sixth century, Arabs in the Arabian Peninsula were clustered into families, clans, tribes, and cities. Two of these cities, Medina (then called Yathrib) and Mecca, were wealthy commercial settlements – the latter being on the western coast of the Red Sea. In 570, a boy was born in

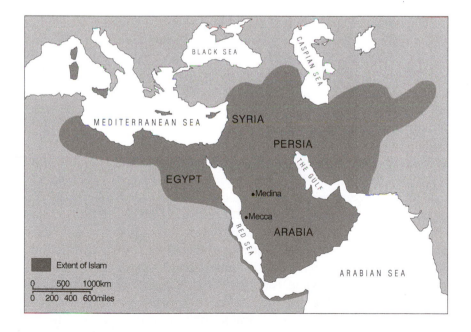

Map 15.1 Extent of Islam by 661CE

Mecca who would forever change Arabian thought and religious practice. His name was Muhammad.

Muhammad Ibn Abdullah (c. 570–632) was born a member of the clan of Hashem, a prestigious Arabian group in Mecca at that time. Muhammad's father died shortly after he was born, and his mother died when he was six. He was then raised by his uncle, a leader of the Hashem. Little is known of Muhammad's later youth or early adulthood. It seems that he became a merchant involving sea trade.[1] In his mid-twenties, he married an older widow named Khadija who became a close companion and spiritual advisor to him. In the year 610, at the age of 40, he was dissatisfied with life and withdrew to a cave in the mountainous region surrounding Mecca to spend time in solitude and meditation. According to Islamic tradition it was here in this cave, during the month of Ramadan, that Muhammad began to receive revelations from God through the mouth of an angelic being. At first he was fearful that he was hearing from a deceiving spirit, or demon. But his wife, Khadija, counseled him that these were, in fact, the very recitations, or revelations, of God. These recitals continued until his death in 632.

Several years after first receiving the revelations, Muhammad began proclaiming them publicly in Mecca. His primary declarations were that God (Allah) is one, that a person must be fully surrendered to God, and that he (Muhammad) was a true prophet of God – an early form of what would develop into the fundamental pillars of Islam (see box below). He gained an early following in Mecca, but not everyone was receptive to his teachings. Arabia was primarily polytheistic at the time, and his strict monotheism was an odd, if not sacrilegious, belief. So he and his early band of followers experienced persecution and fled to Medina in 622 – an event that marks the beginning of the Islamic calendar.

In Medina, Muhammad united many of the warring tribes and in less than a decade this newly formed religion swelled to over 10,000 followers. With a substantial Islamic army, in 630 he returned and conquered Mecca. Islam then spread quickly throughout Arabia and by 632 – the year of Muhammad's death – virtually all Arabs had become Muslims, acknowledging the leadership and authority of the Prophet.

The central teachings of Islam are based on the various revelations which Muhammad received from that initial cave experience in 610 until his death. These revelations (in Arabic the term is *Ayat*, which literally means "signs of God") form the verses of the Islamic holy book, the

THE FIVE PILLARS OF ISLAM

1   **Bearing of witness**. This is where a Muslim publicly and with all sincerity declares that "There is no God but Allah, and Muhammad is the messenger of Allah."

2   **Prayer**. An activity which is to be performed by Muslims five times daily.

3   **Giving of alms**. Muslims believe that everything belongs to God, and so they should provide out of their surplus for those in need.

4   **Fasting**. For the month of Ramadan, Muslims are to abstain from food and drink from the first light of dawn to sunset.

5   **Pilgrimage**. If possible, all Muslims must make the pilgrimage to Mecca at least once in their lifetime.

Qur'an, which was written down by Muhammad's companions while he was alive. There are many areas of agreement between the Qu'ran, the Hebrew Bible, and the Christian New Testament. Because of this, Muslims in the Medieval period understood Jews and Christians to be "people of the book" – a phrase recognizing their status as those who were also recipients of God's revelation. And they tolerated Christians and Jews, although giving them a lower status in Islamic society. However, Muslims also viewed the Jewish and Christian "revelations" to be significantly corrupted and include dangerous falsehoods; it was only the Qur'an which could be trusted as inerrant divine revelation.

Islam became, in short order, a powerful movement which conquered some of the largest and most influential cities and empires in the world at that time, including the Persian Empire and major Byzantine cities such as Antioch and Jerusalem. It quickly expanded into North Africa, western Asia, Sicily, and Spain. This religious, political, and intellectual offensive had a significant impact on Christianity, for not only were mosques replacing churches at a rapid rate across vast regions and empires, but in many instances Islam was supplanting Christian thought and practice at the highest intellectual levels. Great Islamic thinkers emerged during

THE QUR'AN

Muslims believe that the Qur'an was revealed by God to Muhammad through angels who recited the words orally, verse by verse, over a period of twenty-two years. This work consists of 114 *suras*, or chapters, and is divided into two parts, the Meccan *suras* which were revealed while Muhammad was in Mecca between 610 and 622, and the Medina *suras* which were revealed while he was in Medina between 622 and 632. The Qur'an instructs Muslims how to live in accord with God's will.

this period who developed their own philosophical theology and brought great challenge to, as well as insights for, Christian and Jewish beliefs.

2 ISLAMIC INFLUENCES: AVICENNA AND AVERROËS

With the breakup of the Roman Empire, major portions of Greek writings in science, philosophy, medicine, and astronomy were lost to the West in the Middle Ages. Fortunately, many of them were preserved in Islamic societies. After the death of Muhammad, these Islamic societies formed into what could rightly be called the Muslim Empire – an empire led by caliphs (successors of Muhammad as spiritual heads of Islam). By the end of the seventh century this empire extended from Persia to Spain and over the next few centuries could boast of a cultural and intellectual sophistication which superseded that of Western Christianity. Two of its greatest minds were from these times and places: Avicenna from Persia and Averroës from Spain.

Avicenna

Avicenna (Ibn-Sina 980–1037) was a Persian (Iranian) Muslim philosopher, theologian, physician, and statesman. He is considered by many scholars to be one of the great thinkers of the Medieval period. He

Figure 15.1 Avicenna. Source: Wellcome Images/CC/ Wikimedia Commons

wrote numerous works on a wide range of topics, including medicine, science, and philosophy, and many of his writings have survived to this day.

Avicenna's philosophical ideas drew from the wells of many great minds before him, including Aristotle, Plotinus, other Neo-Platonists, and earlier Islamic thinkers such as Al-Farabi (*c.* 875–*c.* 950). His ideas were influential among the Scholastics (Scholasticism is the view connected with an intellectual movement in the Middle Ages in Europe which gives prominence to reason and rational justification of Christian theology), including Thomas Aquinas, who were indebted to him.

One important debt is the metaphysical distinction he developed between the essence of a thing (what it is) and a thing's existence (that it is).[2] To explain what a human being is, is not the same thing as saying that a human being exists. This led to the further notion that there are logically two kinds of being: one whose existence belongs to its essence, and another whose existence is accidental to its essence. The former Avicenna called "necessary being" and the latter "contingent being." He further reasoned that, while one contingent being could cause another contingent being to exist, and so on indefinitely, this does not account for the contingent series as a whole. Since the contingent series needs a cause, this implies the existence of a necessary being, God. Thus Avicenna developed a philosophical argument for the existence of God (see box) which later Christian Scholastics also used as a proof for God's existence.[3]

Another important contribution was Avicenna's view of faith and reason. He maintained that through proper reasoning, or rational reflection, a person can attain knowledge of ultimate truths regarding being, reality, and God – perhaps even achieving mystical union with God. But he also left room for the role of the prophet. Just as there is a fundamental place for reason, there is also a fundamental place for divine inspiration. The prophet receives illumination from God which enables him to establish religious and moral laws necessary for a properly functioning society. Thus despite his heavy emphasis on philosophical reasoning, the prophet Muhammad was no less important than Plato or Aristotle to him.

AVICENNA'S FIRST CAUSE ARGUMENT FOR GOD'S EXISTENCE

1   There are contingent beings (that is, beings which come into existence and need a cause for their existence) which exist.

2   All contingent beings have a cause of their existence (they do not explain their own existence).

3   There cannot be an infinite series of causes of contingent beings, for unless there was a causal basis for the series, there would be no beings there to be caused.

4   Therefore, there must be a first cause for all contingent beings (i.e. for all beings that come into existence).

5   Therefore, since the cause of all contingent beings cannot itself be a contingent being, it must be a necessary being.

6   This necessary being we call "God."

Nevertheless, by utilizing the works of pagan philosophers to develop his views about God and reality, Avicenna was accused by some Muslims of his day of denying Qur'anic teachings and even of being an unbeliever. He viewed himself, however, as a devout Muslim who was endeavoring to make philosophical sense of the world around him and of the religious truths offered in the Qur'an.

Averroës

Probably the most famous Arabic thinker of the Middle Ages was Averroës (Ibn Rushd 1126–1198), a Spanish Muslim philosopher, physician, scientist, theologian, and Qur'an scholar. He was raised in a family of judges and served for some time as a judge himself. He is best known in the West for his commentaries on Aristotle and for his work entitled *The Incoherence of the Incoherence* (*Tahafut al-tahafut*), in which he defends the importance of philosophy in understanding the world created by God. He held Aristotle in high regard, going so far as to say that he provided the "supreme truth" to humanity and that he was "the model that nature produced to show the ultimate in human perfection."[4] Averroës's commentaries were considered by many Scholastics, including Aquinas, to be the best available; so brilliant was his commentary work, in fact, that Aquinas and others referred to him as "the Commentator."

Throughout Averroës's writings runs the theme that religion and philosophy, when rightly understood, are not in conflict. Not everyone agreed, however, so he spent much time defending philosophy against the attacks of fellow Muslims. One such attacker was Al-Ghazali (1058–1111) who wrote a book entitled *The Incoherence of the Philosophers* (to which *The Incoherence of the Incoherence* was a response) claiming that Aristotelian philosophy contradicts Islamic theology and should therefore be rejected.

One way Averroës attempted to reconcile philosophy and theology was through his theory of double-truth. He maintained that the Qur'an was written for the masses, and the masses are not intellectually equipped to understand deep philosophical truths. Thus the Qur'an was written allegorically in order to capture the imagination and pique the emotions of intellectually inferior and uneducated people. The task of the philosopher, on the other hand, is to peer into the deeper, inner meanings of things, and once this is done properly (in other words, once this is

AL-GHAZALI

Al-Ghazali was another significant Islamic thinker of the Middle Ages. In his method of reasoning he brought together logic, teachings from the Qur'an, and Sufi mysticism. Al-Ghazali had a different view from Avicenna and Averroës regarding science and the laws of nature. For him, the very notion of "laws of nature" contradicted the existence of a sovereign God who was in control of all events. So much the worse for laws of nature! Thus while Islamic countries led the world in scientific matters in the tenth and eleventh centuries, Al-Ghazali's views caught hold and by the eleventh and twelfth centuries both science and philosophy were in a decline in Islamic culture – one from which it has not yet fully recovered.[5]

done with the right training in Aristotelian philosophy and logic), truth will be discovered. If there is a conflict between Scripture or religious tradition and philosophy, one can be assured that the conflict is only with the apparent meaning of the Scriptures or tradition.

Many Christians of the thirteenth century misunderstood Averroës on this point, for they took him to mean that two claims – one philosophical and the other theological – could both be true even if they contradict one another. One Christian who interpreted him this way was Siger of Brabant (1240–1284). In an attempt to affirm certain Aristotelian views which contradicted teachings of the Church, Siger split philosophy and theology into two disparate realms – realms so separated that a claim could be true in one and not true in another. Thus he could keep his philosophical views without being accused of being a heretic.

But truth be told, this was not in fact Averroës's view of the matter. For him, double-truth meant that a claim could have a different meaning at different levels – a literal philosophical meaning and an allegorical or figurative theological meaning. One example of this has to do with the universe. According to Islamic teaching, God created the universe. But on Averroës's view, philosophy demonstrates that the universe is eternal.

For him, the idea of "creation" is a religious and figurative one, not a philosophical one, and the two meanings should be kept distinct.

Averroës's influence on Christian thought was significant and stretched through the Middle Ages and even well into the Renaissance. His commentaries on Aristotle were highly respected by Scholastics and widely utilized in European universities. By the second decade of the thirteenth century, virtually all of Aristotle's works had been translated into Latin for the first time and were being widely read by Christians. This had the effect of displacing Platonic and Neoplatonic ideas in Christian thought with the insights of Aristotle.

3 JEWISH INFLUENCES: MAIMONIDES'S RATIONALISM AND KABBALISTIC MYSTICISM

Much of Judaism in the Middle Ages existed within the boundaries of Islamic political rule. Perhaps this explains why Jewish thought was to some extent dependent on Islamic ideas. During the tenth through the twelfth centuries, Jewish philosophy forked into two very different streams. On the one hand was rationalism, spearheaded by the most important Jewish philosopher of the Middle Ages: Moses Maimonides. On the other hand was mysticism, reflected in the various texts of the Kabbalah – an esoteric school of thought focusing on the mystical aspects of Judaism. While neither of these streams had as much influence on Christian thought as the Islamic philosophers, they did exert some influence on medieval Scholasticism, and their effects on Christian thought can be seen even today.

Jewish rationalism

Moses ben Maimon (1135–1204), known by Jewish authors as Rambam and by Latin writers as Maimonides, was born in Córdoba, Spain. In his mid-twenties, when Córdoba was overrun by a fanatical Muslim sect, he and his family moved to Cairo, Egypt. Maimonides was educated by his father and other teachers. He became a physician, a medical writer, and an expert in Jewish law. He wrote extensively, particularly works in logic, medicine, and theology.

As with certain earlier Jewish thinkers of medieval times, Maimonides strove to integrate his Jewish faith with classical Greek thought. He highly valued the wisdom of the Greeks; after all, they had given the ancient and medieval world science, philosophy, art, and a host of other important disciplines. But he was also a devout Jew; he revered the Tanakh, or Hebrew Bible (see box), and for him there could not be an actual conflict between his religious faith and scientific or philosophical reason – at least reason rightly understood. As with Averroës, if there are apparent conflicts between them, they must be due to a misinterpretation of either the Scriptures or the works of the philosophers. His own work reflected his continual pursuit of integrating faith and reason.

Maimonides wrote a number of theological works and commentaries on the Mishnah (an important work of Rabbinic Judaism consisting of interpretations of the Jewish scriptures). He interpreted the Jewish scriptures metaphorically, utilizing Aristotelian philosophy (as put forth by Avicenna) to aid his understanding of the various passages. He believed that a figurative reading of the texts made more sense than a literal interpretation. For example, anthropomorphic language is often used of God in the Tanakh. God is described as having eyes that see and ears that hear. But these attributes cannot be taken literally, argued Maimonides, for then God would not be indivisible.

Maimonides's primary theological/philosophical work, the *Guide for the Perplexed*, had two purposes: first, "to explain certain words occurring in the prophetic books" and second, "to explain certain obscure figures which occur in the Prophets … ."[6] While Maimonides was a philosopher through and through, he was also a devout Jew, and he hoped to help fellow Jews who were perplexed with certain scriptural passages which seemed at first glance to be obscure or contradictory.

TANAKH

"Tanakh" is a Hebrew acronym formed from its three components: The Torah ("Teaching," the Five Books of Moses), Nevi'im ("Prophets"), and Ketuvim ("Writings") – hence *TaNaKh*. The Tanakh is also called the "Hebrew Bible" and is included in the Christian Bible as the "Old Testament."

In his *Guide* he objected to a univocal understanding of God's attributes, for since God is transcendent we cannot truly know what he is like. When we refer to God's attributes, such as his being good, for example, this goodness is not identical to the goodness attributed to a human being. When we say God is good, we mean that God is not evil. When we say God is omnipotent, we mean that God is not powerless. This led him to adopt a negative theology or *via negativa* – the notion that one can only negate attributes of God, not offer positive descriptions of them. Some attributes are negations by definition, such as God's immutability (God does not change), but a conclusion of such thinking is that we are left with no way of describing God; God is beyond our conceptual capabilities. While God's *nature* is beyond human understanding, Maimonides, like his Islamic counterparts, argued that God's *existence* can be demonstrated by rational argument. He developed several versions of the cosmological argument for God's existence, including arguments for a first mover, a first cause, and a necessary being – each of which was utilized by Aquinas and other Scholastics. Along with Avicenna, Maimonides also developed the idea that only God has existence necessarily and that all other beings exist only contingently.

Maimonides marks the finale of Jewish engagement with Greek thought in the Middle Ages. His arguments for negative knowledge of God and God's existence did have significant influence on the Scholastics, perhaps most especially on Thomas Aquinas who referred to him as "Rabbi Moses." Indeed, Aquinas's famous Five Ways arguments for God's existence sometimes use Maimonides's words verbatim.[7] But rationalism was only one significant stream within the Judaism of the Middle Ages.

Jewish mysticism

There exists in all of the major world religions esoteric, mystical traditions, and there is a long history of Jewish mysticism stretching back to at least the first few centuries of the Common Era; possibly even back to the time of Moses or Abraham. Perhaps partly due to a reaction to Maimonides's rationalism in the thirteenth century in Spain (which seemed to place more emphasis on philosophy than Torah), these mystical teachings reached a climax and became systematized in a tradition known as Kabbalah (from the Hebrew meaning "received" or "tradition"). While probably based on much earlier writings, a number of

Kabbalistic works were composed during the Medieval period, including the *Book of Creation* (*Sefer Yetzirah*), the *Book of Illumination* (*Sefer ha-Bahir*) and, most importantly, the *Book of Splendor* (*Sefer ha-Zohar*). The *Zohar*, as it is often called, is the most well-known of the Kabbalistic writings, and it teaches that the Torah was the outer garment of an inner mystery. It offers commentary and mystical interpretations of the Torah (or Pentateuch, as it is also called, which comprises the five books of the law of Moses: Genesis, Exodus, Leviticus, Numbers, and Deuteronomy) in an attempt to reveal deep spiritual truths. A shared theme among these Jewish mystical teachings is that the external, visible, finite world is only a dim reflection of a higher, invisible, infinite realm. Kabbalists desired access to this higher plane of spiritual reality to understand the relationship between the infinite God and the finite creation and to experience God through contemplation and illumination (as opposed to reason or rational reflection).

Kabbalistic teachings include elements of Neoplatonic and Gnostic thought, but their primary emphasis is on Torah. Central to the Kabbalah tradition is the notion, in agreement with Maimonides, that God in his essence is unknowable. This unknowable aspect of God is referred to as Ein Sof, which is translated as "the Infinite." This is God-in-himself; God who is ultimately transcendent and beyond human comprehension. But there is a second aspect of God, his *sefirot* (emanations of the divine essence), which are the attributes and activities that reveal the divine essence and by which human beings can come to know God. There are ten *sefirot* which emerge from Ein Sof, each one reflecting different aspects of God's creative nature or essence (see box).

According to Kabbalah, through studying the attributes and activities of the *sefirot*, along with proper meditation on Torah and mystical insights, the soul can reunite with God and thus receive the salvation it longs for. Thus the Kabbalah provided a guide to spiritual growth and understanding from within the Jewish tradition, offering mysticism rather than rationalism as the way to see and experience the divine.

Kabbalah was considered to be a crucial part of orthodox Judaism from the thirteenth through the seventeenth century. A number of Christians of the Medieval and Renaissance periods adopted mystical elements of Kabbalistic teachings, including the famed Italian philosopher Giovanni Pico della Mirandola; and in one form or another versions of Kabbalistic mysticism continued on through the centuries in both Judaism and Christianity.[8]

THE TEN *SEFIROT*, OR EMANATIONS OF EIN SOF, IN THE JUDAIC KABBALAH

Hebrew name	Conventional English name
1 Kether	Crown (or Will)
2 Chokmah	Wisdom
3 Binah or Tabum	Understanding (or Intelligence)
4 Chesed	Mercy
5 Geburah	Judgment
6 Tifareth	Beauty (or Harmony)
7 Netzach	Victory
8 Hod	Splendor (or Majesty)
9 Yesod	Foundation
10 Mulkuth	The Kingdom

4 CHRISTIAN ENCOUNTERS WITH ISLAM AND JUDAISM

In the Middle Ages the three great "threats" to Christianity were the Jews, the heretics, and the Muslims. While defending Trinitarian monotheism had been an ongoing intellectual battle for Christians with non-orthodox Christians and Jews for centuries, the new religion of Islam posed an even greater threat. Christian abbot Peter the Venerable (c. 1092–1156) described "the heresy of Muhammad" as being worse than any heresy "in the 1,100 years since the time of Christ."[9] Indeed, Islam had probably made more inroads into Christian thought than Arianism had. Christian apologists emerged once again to take on this new challenge, with Peter being one of the most important among them.

Theologically, the Muslims as well as the Jews charged the Christians with blasphemy, for the Christians were worshipping Jesus and the Father (as well as the Holy Spirit). In effect, they were worshiping more than one God. The Christian doctrine of the Trinity seemed to them more like tritheism (the belief in three gods) than monotheism. For Muslims, as well as for Jews, there is only one God – period. This accusation forced

Christians to continue to clarify and defend their Trinitarian dogma. Christian apologists such as Nicetas Choniates of Byzantium and John VI Cantacuzenus did just that – wrote polemics defending Trinitarian monotheism. So significant was this issue that if a Muslim converted to Christianity, he or she was asked to declare: "I anathematize ... all these things that I have stated, as well as Muhammad himself .... And I believe in the Father and the Son and the Holy Spirit."[10]

Debates between Christians and Muslims and Jews over the doctrine of God spawned a wide range of topics beyond Trinitarian issues, including theological determinism and free will (the Christians argued that the Muslims were absolute determinists who denied free will of any kind), establishing parameters for determining who was a true prophet (Christians denied that Muhammad was a true prophet of God), and determining what makes something Scripture (Christians affirmed that the Old Testament was from God, but denied that the Qur'an was so). Furthermore, since in the minds of Muslims a father is only a father through sexual union, it was blasphemous to believe that Jesus of Nazareth was the son of God the Father, for this entailed the notion that God had sexual relations with Mary. The Christians argued that, while Jesus was the begotten Son of God, he was not a created "son" of God. He was God eternal, second person of the Trinity, incarnate in human flesh.

It was also during this time that Jerusalem was occupied by Muslims, who were making religious and political advances throughout the Byzantine Empire. So there was not only theological debate in the air but military battles were occurring as well. The Crusades first began when the Byzantine emperor Alexios I appealed to Pope Urban II for help regarding invading Muslims in his empire. The Crusades turned from an early attempt to halt invading Muslims to a religious conquest. They continued in the Middle East, with the violent fury of many Christians unleashed against those who opposed orthodoxy, whether Muslim or Jew or, in some cases, even schismatic Christians, through the thirteenth century.

By the end of the twelfth century the influx of Greek, Islamic, and Jewish philosophies raised again the overarching question of whether Christian thought could, and if so should, integrate these powerful non-Christian ideas. It was up to some of the most brilliant Christian minds of the next few centuries to attempt an answer.

SUMMARY OF MAIN POINTS

1   Islam is a monotheistic religion, founded by Muhammad in the sixth century, which is based on the Qur'an and which emphasizes the Five Pillars.

2   Two of the greatest Islamic thinkers of the Middle Ages, Averroës and Avicenna, developed philosophical methods of integrating religion and philosophy.

3   There were two great strands of Jewish thought in the Middle Ages which had some influence on later Christian theology and practice: a rationalism based on Greek philosophy and promulgated by Moses Maimonides, and an esoteric mysticism rooted in various texts of the Kabbalah.

4   In the Middle Ages Christians were confronted with radically different religious beliefs, and these encounters – both intellectual and political – required new apologists to defend the orthodox faith against new heresies and non-Christian religion.

FOR FURTHER READING

John L. Esposito, *Islam: The Straight Path* (Oxford: Oxford University Press, 1991). An excellent introduction to Islamic beliefs.

Moses Maimonides, *The Guide for the Perplexed*, 2nd edition (New York: Dover, 1956). The classic work of medieval Jewish philosophy and theology.

Armand A. Maurer, *Medieval Philosophy*, revised edition (Toronto: Pontifical Institute of Mediaeval Philosophy, 1982). A great introduction to the topic.

Seyyid Hossein Nasr, ed., *Islamic Spirituality: Foundations* (New York: Crossroad Publishing, 1987). A helpful collection of essays about Islam by Islamic scholars.

G.S. Scholem, *Major Trends in Jewish Mysticism* (New York: Schocken Books, 1941). A classic work in the history of Jewish esoteric spirituality.

Eliezer Segal, *Introducing Judaism* (London: Routledge, 2008). A concise introduction to Jewish belief and practice focusing on Jewish history and geography.

16

Women and theology in the Middle Ages

QUESTIONS TO BE ADDRESSED IN THIS CHAPTER

1   How was Hildegard of Bingen an example of the way in which women could have a voice in theological matters in the Middle Ages?
2   What did Julian of Norwich contribute to the medieval understanding of God's nature and relationship to humans?
3   What gave Catherine of Siena the platform from which to challenge ecclesiastical authorities?
4   How did Teresa of Ávila bring reform to Carmelite spirituality and become the first female "doctor of the Church?"

Many histories of Christian thought do not include much on the role of women. There is the impression that Christianity has been a hierarchical religion in which males were the only ones to contribute. There is no doubt that with the influence of the Roman Empire on Christianity during its formative years, as well as the patriarchy of Judaism, a hierarchical model dominated. But because so much of the history we have has been written from the male-dominant perspective, women's influence

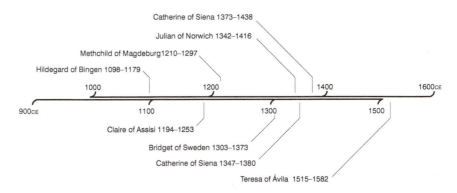

Timeline 16 Women and theology in the Middle Ages

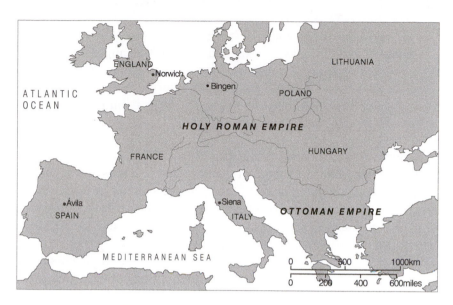

Map 16.1 Medieval Europe

on Christian thought and practice has not received the attention it should have. Throughout this book we have attempted to include the voices of significant women where they have typically been neglected. Additionally, we thought it important to draw attention to women in the Middle Ages who were especially important and influential for the narrative of Christian thought.

1 HILDEGARD OF BINGEN

Hildegard (1098–1179) was the tenth child of a noble family who lived near Bingen on the Rhine River to the west of Frankfurt and Mainz. At eight years old, her parents dedicated her to God (not uncommon in those days), and she was raised in a monastery. At the age of fourteen, she took monastic vows and joined a Benedictine community in Mainz called St. Disibod. She claims to have been uneducated, but showed wide interests and abilities ranging from science to music and drama.

When she was 43 years old, Hildegard reports that she had a vision in which God instructed her to communicate to others what was revealed to her in visions:

Say and write what you see and hear. But since you are timid in speaking, and simple in expounding, and untaught in writing, speak and write these things not by a human mouth, and not by the understanding of human invention, and not by the requirements of human composition, but as you see and hear them on high in the heavenly places in the wonders of God.[1]

Evidently she had been having spiritual visions since her childhood. Some commentators today explain the occurrence of these by her sickly nature and frequent migraines.[2] But the presence of a physiological basis need not explain away the spiritual experience. In her time, there was much less of a tendency to discount the veridical nature of her message on account of physical causes than there was to discount it because she was a female. She understood her standing in society, and the possibility of her visions being taken as the flights of female fancy, or even as satanic,

Figure 16.1 Hildegard of Bingen © Br. Robert Lentz/ Trinity Stores

was real. Therefore she had to emphasize all the more that it was not she herself who was giving these messages, but that they were direct and unmediated from God. She deemphasized her own education so that her teaching would not be seen as standing on that.[3]

Hildegard's status as a "seer" was widely accepted in her own day. This gave her an authority that was rare for women, and she was able to leverage it against the dominant sex. She had become the abbess of the community, but desired to found a new monastery in Rupertsberg. The abbot opposed her intentions, and as a result Hildegard was overcome with a paralyzing sickness and confined to bed; the only cure for her ailments was for the abbot to admit that it was the will of God for the new monastery to be founded as reported by Hildegard. The abbot gave in. Hildegard became healthy again and the new monastery was founded.

On another occasion when her sisters were banned from singing, Hildegard explained to the church officials in Mainz that sung prayer was a way of cooperating with the Spirit of God in an external form so that they might be inwardly instructed in his ways. The songs were imitations of the celestial harmonies that pervaded creation before the fall of Adam and were sung by angels. She warned her superiors that anyone who blocked this divine work was only contributing to the work of the devil and would not themselves sing with the angels in heaven.[4] The singing was allowed to continue.

As this emphasis on singing illustrates, Hildegard's approach to theology might be described as more holistic than was typical of the dry, word-centered theological texts of the Middle Ages. Besides the rich and reflective music she wrote as a way of teaching the theology communicated in her visions, she also used pictures to stimulate a different sense with theological truth. As might be expected, the theology to be extracted from the work of Hildegard is highly metaphorical.

Hildegard used her visions as teaching tools. She saw her work to be that of cultivating a garden in which the spiritual lives of those under her charge could grow. The goal of spiritual development for these "spiritual plants" was greenness and fragrance. This comports well with one of the more prevalent and distinctive concepts she uses for God, which is developed in her most important theological work, *Scivias* (taken from the Latin phrase, *scito vias domini*, Know the Ways of the Lord).

Scivias was written over a period of ten years beginning in 1141. It reads very much like the prophetic or apocalyptic writings of the Bible.

EXCERPT FROM *SCIVIAS*

I saw a great mountain the color of iron, and enthroned on it One of such great glory that it blinded my sight. On each side of him there extended a soft shadow, like a wing of wondrous breadth and length. Before him, at the foot of the mountain, stood an image full of eyes on all sides, in which, because of those eyes, I could discern no human form. In front of this image stood another, a child wearing a tunic of subdued color but white shoes, upon whose head such glory descended from the One enthroned upon that mountain that I could not look at its face. But from the One who sat enthroned upon that mountain many living sparks sprang forth, which flew very sweetly around the images. Also, I perceived in this mountain many little windows, in which appeared human heads, some of subdued colors and some white.

(Book I, Vision I)

There are a number of visions, which are described as literally as possible, and explanation of these. The book begins with a vision of God and then gives a retelling of the creation and fall narrative in the Garden of Eden. The guiding theme for her narrative is life itself. This is an outgrowth of the attribute of God that she calls "viriditas," which is translated variously as vitality, fertility, greenery, fecundity, and similar terms. It was the "viridity" of God which gave rise to creation itself. It was the "viridity" of the Virgin Mary into which the Only-Begotten of God was placed for the Incarnation. And it is "viridity" to which Christians should aspire.[5]

Hildegard's place in the history of Christian thought comes not from carefully argued treatises, but from the originality with which she used metaphors from the organic world to interpret the Christian story and from the influence she exercised on her contemporaries. Despite the extreme disadvantage of her gender, she became one of the most well-known and sought-after Christians of her day. She corresponded with popes and emperors, and countless pilgrims came to be taught by her. She lived to the age of 81, continuing to have visions and teaching others through them.

MAIN THEOLOGICAL WORKS OF HILDEGARD

- *Scivias* (Way to Know), record of 26 visions and explanations
- *Liber vitae meritorum* (Book of Life's Merits), a book of instruction about morality
- *Liber divinorum operum* (Book of the Divine Work), her final book, describes the relationship between God and humans

2 JULIAN OF NORWICH

Julian of Norwich (*c.* 1342–*c.* 1416), also known as Juliana, was an English anchorite who spent most of her later life in seclusion in a small hut (or cell, as they are called) which was attached to St. Julian's Church in Norwich, England. While Julian is heralded as one of the greatest English mystics, little is known of her personal life beyond what she describes in her own writings. Even her name is uncertain, "Julian" possibly being derived from her home church in Norwich.

In her writings Julian notes that when she was thirty years old she became gravely ill and was expected to die. She recovered, however, and toward the end of her infirmity she had what she describes as fourteen "showings" or revelations – intense visions of Jesus Christ. She

ANCHORITE

A person who enters into a life of seclusion and solitude, in a fixed location, for spiritual purposes. Anchorites were distinct from hermits for while the latter went into the "desert" for complete isolation and to test their physical fortitude, anchorites usually were walled into a small cell which was attached, or "anchored," to a church. Sometimes anchorites were nuns or monks, sometimes not.

subsequently had two additional revelations, making a total of sixteen, and she recorded all of them shortly thereafter. Twenty years after the original revelations she wrote them down again, this time including her own theological reflections on the experiences. She then combined both her earlier and later writings into a book, *Revelations of Divine Love*.

It is believed that the *Revelations*, widely regarded as one of the most remarkable texts of medieval religious experience, is the first confirmed female publication written in the English language.[6] It is filled with theological insight and reflection, covering such profound mysteries as the problem of evil, divine foreknowledge, and predestination. But it is also an affectionate meditation on God's eternal and universal love.

A prominent theme throughout the first thousand years of the Christian Church was that Jesus was the great victor who had defeated a formidable enemy, Satan, thus conquering sin and death. It also emphasized God's role as a just judge and divine punisher of sin. Current events of Julian's day, including the Black Death and other pestilences and plagues which wiped out a third of Europe's population, seemed to many to accentuate the justice and wrathfulness of God. However, beginning in the eleventh and twelfth centuries new theological developments, spawned by such theologians as St. Anselm and Bernard of Clairvaux, shifted the emphasis from God as warring conqueror and wrathful judge to a loving, suffering servant as demonstrated in the Incarnation of Jesus.

Julian's visions are consistent with these theological developments and throughout them there is a strong emphasis on God's love. She spent many years contemplating the meaning of these visions before finally putting pen to paper and commenting on them.

> For truly our loving God wants our souls to cling to him with all their might, and wants us to cling to his goodness forever. For of everything the heart could devise, this is what most pleases God and most readily benefits us; for our soul is so specially loved by him that is highest that it surpasses the knowledge of all beings – that is to say there is no being made that can know how much and how sweetly and how tenderly our Maker loves us.
>
> (Julian of Norwich, *Revelations of Divine Love*[7])

And from the time that this [series of revelations] was shown, I often longed to know what our Lord meant. And fifteen years and more later my spiritual understanding received an answer, which was this: "Do you want to know what your Lord meant? Know well that love was what he meant. Who showed you this? Love. What did he show you? Love. Why did he show it to you? For love. Hold fast to this and you will know and understand more of the same; but you will never understand or know from it anything else for all eternity." This is how I was taught that our Lord's meaning was love. And I saw quite certainly in this and in everything that God loved us before he made us; and his love has never diminished and never shall. And all his works were done in this love; and in this love he has made everything for our profit; and in this love our life is everlasting.[8]

Julian's understanding of God's nature and role in human history went beyond that of lover and giver of love, however, for she describes

Figure 16.2 Statue of Julian of Norwich, Norwich Cathedral. Source: David Holgate/Public Domain/Wikimedia Commons

God and Christ as a loving mother, thus graphically promoting feminine attributes of the divine.

> I saw and understood that the great power of the Trinity is our father, and the deep wisdom of the Trinity is our mother, and the great love of the Trinity is our lord; ... . And so our Mother ... works in us in various ways; for in our Mother, Christ, we profit and grow. ...[9]

During her lifetime, Julian became a well-known and respected spiritual counselor, and many persons sought out her wisdom and guidance. Her influence was widespread throughout medieval times, advancing the loving and gracious nature of God, and continued on throughout the centuries. Even today her influence is still felt as a number of contemporary Christian mystics, theologians, and feminists consider her a harbinger of their own theological understandings of God's nature and loving role in human history.[10]

3 CATHERINE OF SIENA

Born just a few years after Julian, Catherine of Siena (1347–1380) was another well-known Christian mystic in the Middle Ages. She was part of a very large family (by some accounts, she was the twenty-fourth child!) from Siena in Tuscany, Italy. From an early age she reported having visions, and like Julian became an anchorite for a time during her youth. Then after an experience of "mystical marriage" to Christ, she returned to live with her family as a tertiary – a member of a religious order who participates in its work, but lives outside the religious community of other monks or nuns as a lay person.

Late in (her short) life, Catherine composed a dialogue which was called *The Book of Divine Providence* (also known simply as the *Dialogue*). It recounts petitions made to God along with God's replies. Reportedly, the work was dictated to a secretary while Catherine was in a state of spiritual ecstasy. But it shows considered insight and thoughtfulness about the Christian life. The book was influential in her own generation, and now is regarded as a classic of fourteenth-century Italian literature.

Consistent with her station in life, she did not urge that all people renounce the world and live as hermits. There is the way of greater perfection which consists in such a renunciation, but the world and its goods are not sinful in themselves; they only become such if one has an improper relationship to them. The key to a proper relationship with the world is the will. She reports in her *Dialogue* that God said, "In whatever situation people may be, let their will be good and holy, and they will be pleasing to me."[11]

The opposite of this good and holy will is a perverted and selfish will, and it should be the desire of those who would follow Christ to be rid of this and to be subjected to his will. To this end, she urged Christians in Pauline language to, "learn to keep your body in check by disciplining your flesh when it would war against the spirit."[12] But these works of discipline or penance, which are valued above empty words that might be offered in their stead, are not to be seen as an end in themselves, but only as a means to the perfect love enabled by the good and holy will.

We must not mistake her theology here as some sort of works righteousness or Pelagianism. Like those orthodox ascetics in the desert (see Chapter 6), she understands the paradox or tension that the Apostle Paul maintains in his charge to "work out your own salvation with fear and trembling; for it is God who is at work in you, enabling you both to will and to work for his good pleasure" (Philippians 2:12–13). After pleading with people to do their work, Catherine ends her *Dialogue* with an entreaty to God to do his work:

> Though you created us without our help, it is not your will to save us without our help. So I beg you to force their wills and dispose them to want what they do not want. I ask this of your infinite mercy. You created us out of nothing. So, now that we exist, be merciful and remake the vessels you created and formed in your image and likeness; re-form them to grace in the mercy and blood of your Son.[13]

Catherine's theology was formed not just in times of mystical ecstasy. Because she lived in the world, she saw the effects of the selfish will even among those who were supposed to be models of Christ for others. Corruption and sinfulness drove her to confront people with a directness of speech and authority that was remarkable for a lay woman, and to urge them to change their ways. She wrote some 380 letters to various people including queens and popes. Her letters and visit to Pope Gregory XI (in office 1370–1378) were crucial in his decision to return the Papal Court to Rome from Avignon (see Chapter 18 for a description of these events). In the scandal of rival popes which followed, Catherine saw clearly the selfish human wills involved and did not shirk from pointing this out. She wrote to three Italian cardinals:

> Dearest brothers and fathers in sweet Jesus Christ, I, Catherine, the slave and servant of the servants of Jesus Christ, write to you in His precious blood, in the desire of seeing you return to the true and most perfect light, of seeing you leave the great darkness and blindness into which you have fallen. Then you will be fathers to me; otherwise you will not be.[14]

Although she died at the young age of 33, Catherine's charismatic personality endeared her to many and exerted considerable influence on both the Church and local Italian politics. She was canonized in 1461 by Pope Pius II. More significantly as a testimony to her place in the history of Christian thought, Catherine was designated as a Doctor of the Church in 1970. There are only 33 people who have been universally recognized by the Roman Catholic Church as such. It is a title given to those from all ages whose writings have had a profound effect on the Christian Church. There have only been three women to date to receive this honorific title. Catherine was the second, and we turn now to the first.

4 TERESA OF ÁVILA

Teresa of Ávila (1515–1582), known in Spanish as Teresa de Cepeda y Ahumada, was born and brought up in Ávila, Spain. The daughter of a large aristocratic family, she lived a childhood typical of wealthy families in her day. She enjoyed reading (especially romances) and dancing. In her later teens she was educated at an Augustinian convent, and then at age twenty she entered a Carmelite convent in Ávila as a novice (also called a *novitiate*, a novice is one who has entered a religious order but has not yet taken final vows). She spent many years as a Carmelite nun in obscurity, including hours each day in prayer, but continued to live an active social life. She had frequent bouts of illness, and at one point in her twenties she fell into a kind of trance which left her paralyzed for many months. She recovered, but the paralysis recurred intermittently for a number of years. Later in life, she began to see visions – what she took to be revelations from God.

CARMELITES

The Carmelites are a Roman Catholic religious order which began in the twelfth century by a group of devout hermits who adopted a solitary lifestyle on Mount Carmel in Palestine. Sometime after 1200 these hermits asked the Patriarch of Jerusalem, Albert, to create a Rule of Life. This Rule directs them to celebrate the Eucharist together each day in a place near their cells and to gather every week for encouragement and offer each other correction. Carmelites still follow this Rule today.

JOHN OF THE CROSS

John of the Cross (1542–1591) became a Carmelite monk in Spain in 1564. Three years later, when he was ordained, he met with Teresa. She was immediately impressed with his devotion, rigorous lifestyle, and leadership qualities, and put him in charge of the order. Even though Teresa was much older than he, they became close friends, and John was deeply influenced by her. He wrote what has become a devotional classic: *The Dark Night of the Soul*.

In her mid-forties Teresa began to see that a stricter regimen was needed for spiritual growth. The ascetic and rigorous Carmelite rule had become lax and permissive: nuns could see visitors regularly, could go into town and visit with others, and pursue non-cloistered activities. Teresa felt these activities were too distracting and not pleasing to God. With her bishop's permission (which was required, of course), in 1562 she founded a new, more demanding, convent of Reformed (Discalced) Carmelites. The new community was small, with just four novices to begin with, but she was later granted permission to travel and began other similar communities. Two monks were recruited to join her, one of them being John of the Cross, who founded Reformed Carmelite communities for men. Before becoming gravely ill and finally unable to travel, she founded thirty-two Discalced Carmelite communities.

Teresa desired through her life and writings to guide others toward spiritual perfection. She wrote a number of books along these lines, the most well-known being the *Interior Castle* – one of the most celebrated works of mystical theology in Western literature. In this work she offers an account of the soul's journey toward God. After a brief preface, she begins the book this way: "I began to think of the soul as if it were a castle made of a single diamond or of very clear crystal, in which there are many rooms, just as in heaven there are many mansions."[15] She then continues her description of the soul, and describes entrance into its inner sanctuary:

> Now let us return to our beautiful and delightful castle and see how we can enter it. I seem rather to be talking nonsense; for, if this castle is the soul, there can clearly be no question of our entering it. For we ourselves are the castle: and it would be absurd to tell someone to enter a room when he was in it already! But you must understand that there are many ways of "being" in a place. Many souls remain in the outer court of the castle, which is the place occupied by the guards; they are not interested in entering it, and have no idea what there is in that wonderful place, or who dwells in it, or even how many rooms it has. You will have read certain books on prayer which advise the soul to enter within itself: and that is exactly what this means.[16]

The many rooms of the castle represent stages of development in the spiritual life of believers. Teresa encourages her readers to push through the outer rooms toward the center where God and the soul can unite. While her writings (including this one) influenced many in her own day and countless others throughout history, in her humility she didn't perceive them as being all that significant; not even bothering to reread them once they had been written down.

It is really quite astonishing that such a meek woman, living in the sixteenth century in a cloistered community, writing under orders of her superiors amidst the onerous duties of devout religious life, could have attained such international fame among both laity and scholars. She was highly revered even while she was alive for her deep devotion, spiritual

THE SEVEN STAGES (MANSIONS) OF SPIRITUAL PROGRESSION IN TERESA OF ÁVILA'S *INTERIOR CASTLE*

1 State of grace and humility
2 Practice of prayer
3 Discipline and penance; acts of charity
4 Supernatural element of the mystical life; pure divine grace begins
5 Temporary union through prayer; infused contemplation
6 Extended intimacy with the divine; increasing afflictions (interior or exterior)
7 Spiritual marriage; the soul and God become completely united

rigor, and reformation, and she was canonized only forty years after her death. Because of her amazing influence in the Church, as mentioned earlier she was the first woman elevated to "doctor of the church."[17] Her works are even today widely read and considered to be among the most remarkable of the mystical writings of the Roman Catholic Church.

5 CONCLUSION

St. Teresa is often regarded as the most prominent of the women mystics in the Medieval period. This claim is no doubt defensible, but should not cloud the fact that there were many more women who contributed to Christian thought in important ways. Besides those featured in this chapter, we should also mention women such as Clare of Assisi (1194–1253), Methchild of Magdeburg (1210–1297), Bridget of Sweden (1303–1373), Margery Kempe (c. 1373–1438), and others – many of whose contributions have sadly been lost from the annals of history.

SUMMARY OF MAIN POINTS

1   Hildegard de-emphasized her own intellectual contribution and attributed the message of her visions to God himself.
2   Julian emphasized God's all-encompassing love and the feminine attributes of the Trinity.
3   Catherine was able to have a prominent voice in the Church because of her status as a mystic who received direct revelation from God.
4   Teresa taught that through rigorous discipline and devotion along with divine grace one could achieve union with God.

FOR FURTHER READING

Julian of Norwich, *Revelations of Divine Love*, Elizabeth Spearing, trans. (New York: Penguin Books, 1998). The classic work by Julian of Norwich in which she describes her revelations and then offers theological reflection on them.

Barbara Newman, *Sister of Wisdom: St. Hildegard's Theology of the Feminine* (Berkeley, CA, University of California Press, 1987). A discussion by one of the leading Hildegard scholars of today.

Amy Oden, ed., *In Her Words: Women's Writings in the History of Christian Thought* (Nashville, TN: Abingdon, 1994). A collection of primary sources and commentary on writings by the women highlighted in this chapter.

Elizabeth Alvilda Petroff, *Body and Soul: Essays on Medieval Women and Mysticism* (Oxford: Oxford University Press, 1994). Examines the writings of medieval women mystics from England, Germany, France, and Italy, among other countries.

Teresa of Ávila, *Interior Castle*, E. Allison Peers, trans. and ed. (New York: Image Books, Doubleday, 1989). St. Teresa's classic and inspirational work on the soul's journey to God.

17

Thomas Aquinas

QUESTIONS TO BE ADDRESSED IN THIS CHAPTER

1   What was the focus of Thomas's thought?
2   How does Thomas argue that God exists?
3   What is the relationship between reason and revelation in his thought?
4   How do reason and revelation fit into the broader nature and grace relationship?
5   What is the beatific vision?

St. Thomas Aquinas (1225–1274) is perhaps the archetype of medieval monks who quietly toiled away at their books by candlelight. But his career would have taken a very different turn if his family had gotten their way. They were a noble family from Aquino, Italy and had planned a respectable career for Thomas as the abbot of Monte Cassino monastery (the one founded by Benedict, see Chapter 12). Thomas had no taste, however, for what would have been a more formal and bureaucratic post in the hierarchy of the church, and instead wanted nothing but a life of study as a friar in the relatively new order of Dominicans. These were not the most respectable monks in the eyes of the gentry, as they depended on begging for their existence. So after declaring his intentions and leaving for Rome, his family kidnapped him and imprisoned him in a castle tower where he was kept for two years as they tried to persuade him to give up this crazy notion.

Characteristically, he used the time alone to read and think. At one point, a prostitute was sent to his cell with the hopes that he might be distracted from his singularly intellectual pursuits. He grabbed a flaming log from the fire and chased her from the room, slamming the door behind her and burning the sign of the cross into it with the ember; thereupon he put the log back in the fire and returned to his studies. His family resigned themselves to his chosen future and allowed him to escape, thinking that he was throwing away his life. Thomas went on to become one of the greatest thinkers in the history of Christian thought.

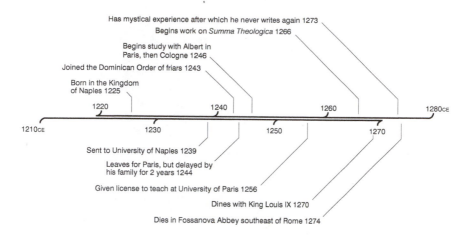

Timeline 17 Thomas Aquinas

1 THE NEW ARISTOTELIANISM

Sometime around 1270, Aquinas was taken to the court of King Louis IX in Paris for dinner. Already quite well-known, though somewhat controversial, Thomas was a kind of curiosity for the courtly dinner guests who inhabited a very different world than the Dominican friar. For his part, Thomas was ill at ease in society and became sullen and withdrawn in such environments. This tendency together with his large physical size earned him the nickname in school of "the dumb ox." At some point during King Louis's dinner party with conversations going on around him, Thomas suddenly came to life, pounding his massive fists on the table and exclaiming, "And that will settle the Manichees!" At once Thomas realized that his interior life had broken out into the external world in an awkward way at an inopportune time. He was embarrassed and apologetic for causing such a scene, but his gracious host (who later was venerated as St. Louis) responded by sending one of his secretaries to Thomas with a tablet to write down the argument, because it must have been a good one and he didn't want Thomas to forget it.

We don't know now what argument had come to Thomas in that moment of inspiration, but in a sense all of his work was directed against Manicheism.[1] We met the Manichees briefly in Chapter 11 when the pre-converted Augustine had turned to them in hopes of understanding the problem of evil in the world. They were a starkly dualistic sect, positing

Figure 17.1 St. Thomas Aquinas. Source: Carlo Crivelli/National Library/Public domain/Wikimedia Commons

that there were two eternal forces in the world, one for good and one for evil. And according to them, evil definitely stems from the physical, created order.

It is plausible to suppose that Aquinas had in mind not some remnant group of Manichees themselves, but the Manicheistic influence that had crept into Christianity through Gnostic and Platonic associations. Plato too held that the physical was a degraded state of reality and that the spiritual goal of people should be to escape the prison of the flesh and so free their souls to the spiritual reality of the heavenly Forms. Platonism in the Church had become the established orthodoxy since the time of Augustine. Just as Aristotle challenged Plato's thinking back in Greece in the fourth century BCE, so too the reintroduction of Aristotle in the thirteenth century altered the intellectual landscape.

Some texts of Aristotle had been available in Latin translation in the West since the sixth century, but these were primarily works on logic. It wasn't until the late 1100s and early 1200s that Aristotle's philosophical and scientific texts made it into the hands of medieval Christian thinkers, and they caused quite a stir. Not only was Aristotle regarded with suspicion because these new texts had come primarily through Muslim scholars (and some were available only by translating them from Arabic); but also as more and more of his thinking was understood, it became clear that the whole Platonic system of thought – which had provided the basic framework of Christian thinking since Augustine – was being challenged. There was a massive shift, then, in appropriating Aristotelianism for the Christian faith. This shift began with the starting point for rational reflection. As illustrated in Raphael's famous painting, *The School of Athens*, Aristotle brought philosophy from the heavens back down to the earth. For Thomas, then, even our thinking about God begins by thinking about the physical world.

2 SENSE, BEING, GOD

Thomas's greatest book is the massive *Summa Theologica*, or Summary of Theology. It contains some 2 million words in a systematic configuration of questions and articles ranging over the whole of theology in his day. Within the first few pages, he jumps right into arguments for the existence of God. These are the famous Five Ways of proving that God exists, but they do not feel like other proofs. Today we are accustomed to thinking about God by starting with the concept of an entity to which things like omnipotence, omniscience, and so on are attributed; then we offer various evidences that such an entity really exists. Even Anselm's ontological proof (discussed in Chapter 14) proceeds this way, starting with an idea and staying very theoretical.

For Aquinas, however, there is a very different starting point for showing that God exists. According to Aquinas, "Our natural knowledge takes its beginning from sense."[2] The Manichean mindset would go as far as possible away from our sensation of the natural world to look for the divine. And for the Platonists, truth is to be found in the intelligible world of unchanging ideas or Forms – not the sensible world of changing things. But in the commonsense mindset of Aristotelians, we start with what we're most immediately aware of. If we look out the window of

THE WRITINGS OF THOMAS AQUINAS

More than seventy-five different writings are attributed to Thomas Aquinas. The greatest of these is the *Summa Theologica*, which is a summary of theology in the style of scholastic disputation. That is, a question is asked, like whether existence of God can be known by reason, and Aquinas first lists the most relevant and difficult objections to the answer he will give; then he'll cite an authority who agrees with the answer he will give; then he'll give his answer and the reasons for it; and finally he provides a direct response to each of the objections that were raised.

The second greatest and most enduring work is his *Summa Contra Gentiles*, which responds to objections that non-Christians make to the faith. Besides these two "Summas," Aquinas wrote numerous commentaries on individual books of the Bible and on the works of Aristotle. Many of his other works, then, are shorter pieces on specific topics in theology like the Eucharist or Angels or the Trinity.

On Being and Essence
Disputed Questions on Truth
Commentary on the Sentences of Peter Lombard
Commentary on De Trinitate of Boethius
On the Unicity of the Intellect
Many commentaries on the works of Aristotle
Many commentaries on the Bible
Summa Contra Gentiles
Summa Theologica

our study, we see things – trees, animals, and so on. This is the first and most profound insight of common sense if we attend to it: there are things that exist in the world. Pushing the analysis of these commonsense experiences further in the vein of Aristotle, Thomas would say that existence itself, or Being (*ens*, in Aquinas's Latin) imposes itself upon us. That is to say, we cannot help but be confronted with Being – understood not as just the existence of individual things, but existence in general. The next point, however (and we're still in the realm of common sense), is that we notice that these objects of our senses do not remain the same. They change and develop; they become what they were not: the acorn grows into a tree, a tadpole into a frog. And yet their Being remains. At least according to Aquinas their Being remains.

For those in the Manichean and Platonist tradition, the only way they saw to understand change was by concluding that things must not really exist as we had supposed. Individual existences for them must be something less than real. It is the commitment to value thinking over experience that leads them to conclude that physical things must be mere shadows or otherwise degraded realities since they are not stable. But in the face of our unmistakable evidence of near-constant change, Thomas brings us back to the first, empirical insight: there are things! Trees, tadpoles, and the like. Their changing leads us instead to the more reasonable conclusion that at any given moment they are not all that they could be. A lump of ice is not somehow unreal because it changes into water and then steam; its being is merely limited and incomplete. Things must change because they cannot be all they can be at once. Their incompleteness, however, can only be understood in reference to Being that is complete. That is God.[3] It is against this very Aristotelian metaphysical backdrop that Thomas gives his Five Ways as proofs that we must believe that God exists because of what our senses tell us about the world.

The empirical data he gives is indisputable, so the fact that not everyone accepts the Five Ways as proving the existence of God shows that there must be something more controversial going on in the proofs than bare empirical data. Each of the Ways has also a metaphysical principle upon which the conclusion of God's existence rests no less than the empirical premise. This will take some careful explaining.

The First Way is generally translated as the proof from "motion." And it may sound as though the argument runs as follows: since things are in motion, something else had to put them in motion and so ultimately there will have to be a First Mover, which is God. But this reading is only superficially correct.[4] Thomas uses the Latin word *motu*, which can mean motion or change, and he clearly has in mind the second more comprehensive meaning, because the example he gives is that of a piece of wood growing hotter because of fire. That is to say, it is undergoing change. His empirical premise, then, is that in our experience of the world, we recognize that things change – they change in position (which would be movement) and in quality (the wood grows hotter) and size (an ice block melts and becomes smaller). His commonsense analysis of these situations is that things that change become what they previously were not. The only way this could happen, according to Aquinas, is if there is something else which makes possible this new reality coming to be in the object which changed. So this is not the sort of mechanistic cause that we might think of today, like when a billiard ball is caused to move because it was struck by another. What Aquinas has in mind is more along the lines of understanding the motion of the billiard ball because of the existence of the game of billiards. The billiard ball's motion (and, we might add, even its existence) depends on the fact that there is a game of billiards.

If we were to take the mechanistic read, then God is more like the first domino to start things going. This is the deistic God of modernism, not the God Aquinas is defending.[5] Aquinas is not talking about sequences of events in time. Aquinas is not claiming something happened earlier which caused the change, and then something happened prior to that, and so on. That could only prove that God existed sometime in the past. Rather, there exists something in the hierarchy of being which explains the change in the object. The fire explains the wood getting hotter; the billiard game explains the motion of the ball. Now, if these other things (the fire and the game) are also incomplete and changing things, there must be an explanation for them too; and it is this chain of causes that Aquinas says cannot go on forever.

We might render this point more understandable by talking about existence instead of change – for the point amounts to the same thing for Aquinas. The billiard ball only exists because there is a game of billiards – the game is the ball's ground of being. If there were no game of billiards, there would be no billiard ball. But then the game itself exists only because of something else, namely the people who invented it. And these

EXCERPT FROM THE FIRST WAY

The first and more manifest way is the argument from motion. It is certain, and evident to our senses, that in this world some things are in motion. Now whatever is in motion is put in motion by another, for nothing can be in motion unless it is in potency [that is, potential] to that towards which it is in motion. But a thing moves in so far as it is in act. For motion is nothing else than the reduction of something from potency to act. But nothing can be reduced from potency to act, except by something in a state of act. Thus that which is actually hot, as fire, makes wood, which is potentially hot, to be actually hot, and thereby moves and changes it. Now it is not possible that the same thing should be at once in act and potency in the same respect, but only in different respects. For what is actually hot cannot simultaneously be potentially hot, though it is simultaneously potentially cold. It is therefore impossible that in the same respect and in the same way a thing should be both mover and moved, that is, that it should move itself. Therefore, whatever is moved must be moved by another. But this cannot go on to infinity. ... Therefore, it is necessary to arrive at a first mover which is moved by no other. And this everyone understands to be God.

(*Summa Theologica*, I.2.3)

people only exist because their being too derives from something else. The existence of all these things is derivative. Aquinas says, "All beings apart from God are not their own being, but are beings by participation."[6] It is God alone which is Being in itself, not derived from any other source. The existence of God stops the infinite regress of being and is therefore called the First Cause or the First Mover in the sense of being the ultimate grounding of all change and existence.

Put another way, God is not something about which we can state a lot of qualities and then ask whether it exists. For example, we can state fully what it is for something to be a unicorn and then legitimately wonder whether such a thing really exists in the world. This is not the case for God.[7] According to Aquinas, if we were to enumerate all of the things in the universe that exist, God would not be counted among these existing things; rather, he is the source or ground of all these existing things. Again, this is not a deistic God who started things up and then kept his hands off. So long as things exist, God (as existence itself) must be present to them. Just as the effect of fire is to ignite things, so the effect of God is to cause them to exist:

> Now since God is being itself by his own essence, created being must be his proper effect; just as to ignite is the proper effect of fire. Now God causes this effect in things not only when they first begin to be, but as long as they are preserved in being. ... Therefore as long as a thing has being, God must be present to it, according to its mode of being.[8]

3 REASON AND REVELATION

The other four ways of proving God's existence that were presented by Aquinas are similarly metaphysical in nature. These are not easy to understand without extensive study, and Thomas conceded that such study is not available to everyone – some are probably incapable of understanding, some must be concerned with other more practical affairs, and some are just intellectually lazy by nature and won't put forth the effort.[9] Since many people do have at least some knowledge about God, then it must be the case that there is another source of knowledge about God besides reason.

Furthermore, reason cannot show us some of the truths about God. Reason may be able to show us that God exists, but these proofs do not bring to light all that God is. This is because we can only reason from the effects we observe through our senses to what must be true of the cause of these effects. But we are not warranted in ascribing any more to the cause than is necessary for the effects. For example, if we discover a broken window, we can infer a cause sufficient to bring that about, but no more; if a small rock being thrown by a child is sufficient to cause the break, then we can't infer the existence of a cannonball shot from a cannon to explain the broken window. In the same way, Thomas thought that reason could show the existence of God, but the effects upon which we reason are not sufficient for us to infer that God is a Trinity, for example. In order to know this about God, then, our natural reason must be supplemented with what has been revealed to us supernaturally.[10]

So if we need revelation because not everyone can come to knowledge of God by reason, and if some things about God are knowable only by revelation, then what is the purpose of reason? Why not just rely entirely on revelation? There is a use for reason, argued Aquinas, in showing others who may not accept the truth of revelation. But we have to be careful here in ascribing more to Aquinas than he claimed. It just doesn't seem to be the case that Aquinas was writing in order to prove to people of no faith that Christianity is true. In his second greatest work, the *Summa Contra Gentiles*, he claims that his intent is to show "how the truth that we come to know by demonstration is in accord with the Christian religion."[11] That is to say, the things we can prove with reason are consistent with revealed truths. These two can never contradict each other, as they both must be true. But that is not to say that the Christian faith can be proved by reason. Similarly, in the *Summa Theologica* he discusses the need for reason to proceed from common ground:

> Sacred Scripture, since it has no science above itself, can dispute with one who denies its principles only if the opponent admits some at least of the truths obtained through divine revelation. Thus we can argue with heretics from texts in Holy Writ, and against those who deny one article of faith we can argue from another. But if our opponent believes nothing of divine revelation, there is no longer any means of proving the articles of faith by reasoning, but only of answering his objections – if he has any – against the faith.[12]

We may not be able to prove every article of faith by reason, but we should be able to satisfactorily answer every possible objection to an article of faith through the use of reason alone. Too often Aquinas is read as a modern apologist for the faith, but it seems better to see him fitting into the mold of Anselm and others of "faith seeking understanding" as discussed in Chapter 14. Within the framework of revealed faith, understanding that faith is worked out through reason – and in the case of Aquinas, through a heavy dose of Aristotelian metaphysics. Reason by itself is not considered sufficient for Christian faith. It is faith which completes reason, just as the changing, natural things are incomplete in themselves and need the existence of God for their being.

4 NATURE VS. GRACE

The relationship between reason and revelation is a sort of sub-species of the relationship between nature and grace for Aquinas; nature and grace are not opposed to each other in the thought of Aquinas like they were in Augustine. Aquinas tries to follow Augustine in everything he can – there are more references to Augustine in the *Summa Theologica* than to anyone else. But it seems that Augustine was never able to shake the influence of the Manichees enough for Thomas's liking. According to Augustine, the gulf between nature and grace was absolute. The natural world suffered from the consequences of the Fall no less than the spiritual, so it was useless to look at nature in hopes of finding any knowledge of God. Besides that, our sensory systems, as part of fallen human nature, couldn't be trusted as reliable. So, knowledge of God could only come through grace as revealed to us.

But according to Aquinas, the effects of original sin were not as severe. Original sin does not eradicate virtually all that is good from humans, nor does it efface the effects of the creator from the natural order. He says, "Now sin cannot entirely take away from man the fact that he is a rational being, for then he would no longer be capable of sin. Therefore it is not possible for this good of nature to be destroyed entirely."[13] And because the good is not entirely destroyed, there is not the stark opposition between the realms of nature and grace. Just as there can be no contradiction between the truths of reason and revelation, so too there is no contradiction between nature and grace. Aquinas certainly agrees with Augustine that humans can only be saved from their sins by the grace of God. But that grace does not abolish and destroy the natural state of humans; rather it perfects it. He connects the relationship between these two pairs in a passage from his commentary on Boethius's *De Trinitate*:

> Gifts of grace are added to those of nature in such a way that they do not destroy the latter, but rather perfect them; wherefore also the light of faith, which is gratuitously infused into our minds, does not destroy the natural light of cognition, which is in us by nature.[14]

The same understanding is also seen in Aquinas's treatment of the flesh in relationship to sin. Speaking of the actual meat of which we're composed (in distinction to St. Paul's sometimes metaphorical use of "flesh"), Aquinas says that flesh cannot be the subject or inheritor of original sin – this distinction is left for the soul.[15] Here again, there is a marked difference in attitude toward the natural body from those in the wake of Plato and Augustine. The doctrine of the resurrection always sat uneasily with the Platonic understandings of Christian doctrine. Why would we want bodies again at the culmination of time if our goal had been to break free from the prison of the flesh? Aquinas brings back an understanding of the relationship of soul and body that is more in line with Christian Scripture. Following Aristotle again, he maintains that the soul is the form of the body. Upon death, the soul has some sort of independent existence; but this is incomplete and awaits the resurrection in order to bring back that essential unity of body and soul.

Nature, the body, and reason are not evil and completely corrupted in the thought of Aquinas. They are incomplete, though, and lacking in certain respects. And so grace – sometimes in the form of revelation, sometimes as forgiveness of sin in the soul – is needed to complete and perfect the natural state. Only by this grace can created things move toward their perfect ends in God.

5 BEATIFIC VISION

As down-to-earth as Thomas was, there is a sort of irony that his life ends with a mystical experience. This need not be cast as anti-Aristotelian, though, because following Aristotle, Thomas took the greatest good to be contemplation of the divine. The greatest essential feature of human beings is their intellect, and as the purpose or goal of anything is to fulfill its essential nature, it becomes the goal of human life to exercise that intellect in its knowledge of God. Aquinas claims:

> Some [have] held that no created intellect can see the essence of God. This opinion, however, is not tenable. For as the ultimate happiness of man consists in the use of his highest function, which is the operation of the intellect, the created intellect could never see God, it would either never attain to happiness, or its happiness would consist in something else beside God, which is opposed to faith.[16]

Seeing God with the intellect is the beatific vision. But here again, in our natural state and with our incomplete natural powers, we will not be able to fully achieve this sight. Nor should we expect that it is possible to achieve such a vision in this life while we are still constituted by matter which is incomplete. We can't help wondering, though, whether Thomas changed his mind on this last point due to personal experience.

As the story goes (on rather well documented grounds), Thomas was in the church of St. Dominic in Naples in 1273 when a voice spoke to him from the crucifix. It said that Thomas had written correctly in his works and offered the reward of anything he wanted. In response to this voice, which he took to be Christ's, he simply said, "I will have Thyself." In December of 1273, he had some sort of mystical experience during the celebration of the Mass which left him profoundly affected. He couldn't return to his rigorous schedule of writing, of finishing the *Summa Theologica*. His brother friar Reginald inquired why. Thomas answered, "I can write no more. I have seen things which make all my writings like straw." He never did write another word.

In early 1274 the pope sent for Thomas to attend a council being held in Lyon. He set out on the journey, but was stricken with an illness from which he didn't recover. He was taken to a monastery where he lay in bed and asked that the Song of Solomon be read to him. He confessed his sins and passed into eternity in March 1274, having already been united with the lover of his soul.

Thomas's family thought that he was throwing away what could have been a promising ecclesiastic career and was wasting his life by donning the friar's habit and spending all his time poring over books. It was his teacher, Albert the Great, who had the better insight into Thomas's future: when his school friends were still calling him "the dumb ox," Albert claimed, "The bellow of this dumb ox will one day be heard throughout the world." And so it has been.

The thought of Aquinas was not uncontroversial at first, but he was immediately recognized as an intellectual force to be reckoned with. In 1323 Pope John XXII canonized Thomas, and in 1567 Pope Pius V gave him the title "Universal Doctor of the Church." There was a lull in the popularity of Thomism (as the thought of Thomas is widely referred to) during the eighteenth and nineteenth centuries, but in 1879, Pope Leo XIII declared that Thomas's teaching was to be counted as the official teaching of the Catholic Church. He has certainly been one of the two or three most influential Christian thinkers of all time.

SUMMARY OF MAIN POINTS

1   Aquinas appropriated the thought of Aristotle in service to Christian theology.

2   Since our senses show the reality of incomplete beings, he argues that there must be a Being which is complete in itself. This is God.

3   Reason can be used to obtain some knowledge of God, but revelation is needed to supplement reason.

4   The relationship of reason and revelation is an instance of the more general relationship by which nature, in all its guises, is perfected by grace.

5   The beatific vision is an intellectual "vision" of God which is the proper goal of all people.

FOR FURTHER READING

G.K. Chesterton, *Saint Thomas Aquinas* (New York: Doubleday, 1956). A thin volume providing an overview of Aquinas's life and thought that is unsurpassed in insight and style.

Brian Davies, *The Thought of Thomas Aquinas* (Oxford: Clarendon Press, 1992). A treatment of Aquinas with more depth and sophistication, yet still readable for the non-specialist.

Anthony Kenny, *The Five Ways: St. Thomas Aquinas' Proofs of God's Existence* (Notre Dame, IN: University of Notre Dame Press, 1980). A thorough treatment of Aquinas's famous proofs by one of today's leading historians of philosophy.

Peter Kreeft, *Summa of the Summa* (San Francisco, CA: Ignatius Press, 1990). An edited and annotated summary of Thomas's *Summa Theologica*.

18

Preparation for reform

QUESTIONS TO BE ADDRESSED IN THIS CHAPTER

1 What did Meister Eckhart teach and how did he encourage reform?
2 What role did Ockham and nominalism play leading up to the Reformation?
3 How did the realism of Wyclif contribute to a climate of reform?

There is a common conception that the late Middle Ages prior to the Protestant Reformation was populated with monkish academicians and corrupt churchmen. On the academic side of this caricature, Scholasticism and its endless disputations over minutiae had devolved to where learned monks sat around with their students and debated how many angels could dance on the head of a pin; and on the clerical side, the Church had sunk into systemic corruption and abuses, like selling indulgences to the poor ignorant masses in order to fund their extravagant building projects. As in most caricatures, there is some truth to this picture. But the over-emphasis of this fact obscures other important elements. The story should be told of the social and cultural influences that contributed to making the climate ripe for Reformation. However, since this book is primarily an account of the history of thought, in this chapter we'll highlight some of the crucial ideas and their progenitors that formed the background for the momentous episodes of the sixteenth century.

1 MEISTER ECKHART

The person known to us today as Meister Eckhart (*c.* 1260–*c.* 1328) was born as Johann Eckhart in the province of Thuringia in present-day Germany. In his mid-to-late teens he joined a Dominican order and studied for the priesthood. After attending schools in Cologne and Paris where he was trained as an academic theologian, he returned to Germany in 1294 to become the vicar of his home province. In 1302 he went back

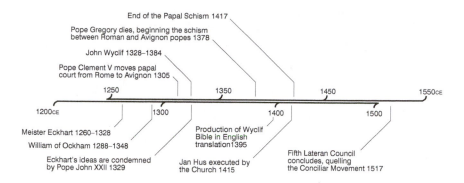

End of the Papal Schism 1417

Pope Gregory dies, beginning the schism
between Roman and Avignon popes 1378

John Wyclif 1328–1384

Pope Clement V moves papal
court from Rome to Avignon 1305

1250   1350   1450   1550CE

1200CE   1300   1400   1500

Meister Eckhart 1260–1328

William of Ockham 1288–1348

Eckhart's ideas are condemned
by Pope John XXII 1329

Production of Wyclif
Bible in English
translation1395

Jan Hus executed by
the Church 1415

Fifth Lateran Council
concludes, quelling
the Conciliar Movement 1517

Timeline 18 Preparation for reform

to Paris where he occupied the same chair at the university as his fellow Dominican Thomas Aquinas had the generation before. It was there that he became known as "Meister" (or Master, in German) Eckhart. The last fifteen years of his life were spent back in Germany in Strasbourg and Cologne where he found his niche as a preacher, but it was here that he fell out of favor with the Church.

Eckhart left two different sets of writings, and the harmonization of these is not always easy. On the one hand, he had projected a massive systematic work in Latin called the *Opus Tripartum* (A Work in Three Parts). In it he had intended to explain the teachings of faith and Scripture with the help of philosophy. It is doubtful that he ever completed the work; and the only extant parts are prologues, some outlines, and several pieces from part three. On the other hand, there are numerous writings in his native German – primarily sermons – which are more devotional and pastoral in nature. At the time, these two sets of writings created some confusion about what exactly he believed, since the translations in and out of German were not yet standardized.[1]

Eckhart's dominant idea which pervades almost everything he wrote was the theme, common to so many mystics, of union with God. For Eckhart, though, it is more of a re-union, a coming back to being one with God. And here is one of the sources of the heresy charges that would come against Eckhart, for it is very easy to interpret him in a pantheistic sense. All things, according to Eckhart, have their being in God. He says, "If we were to know the smallest object as it is in God – say, if we were to know only a flower that has being in God – this object would be more

PANTHEISM

A religious belief system which identifies God and the universe; pantheists take the material world to be a manifestation of the divine rather than a creation which is distinct from God.

noble than the whole world."[2] And, "From time to time I have said – and it is true – that to get all the world together with God is to get nothing more than God alone. All creation without God could have no more Being than a fly would."[3] From such statements alone, a pantheistic interpretation of Eckhart seems warranted.

But the language of a mystic is difficult to pin down. Eckhart's individual claims can't be judged in isolation from the broader context of the whole of his thought.[4] In attempting to describe spiritual experience, arguments will almost necessarily give way to metaphor and poetry. His challenge in remaining orthodox was to show that he really did uphold a distinction between creatures and the creator. In this vein, a sympathetic reading would show that Eckhart's point in imbuing all of creation with God was not that God and his creation are one, but that creatures are nothing in themselves. This point is less controversial, and passages like the following might even be consistent with some interpretations of Aquinas: "Creatures have no Being of their own, for their Being is the presence of God. If God withdrew from them even for a moment, they would all perish."[5]

But Eckhart pushed the notion further than this in claiming that the being of all things was in God from eternity past. He took creation to be an overflow of the being of God, which spilled out as particular objects. It is the goal of the mystic, then, to rise above this createdness and return to the sort of undifferentiated being that he or she formerly had in God. "Through creation God addresses, counsels and orders all creatures, by the very fact that he has created them, to follow him, to make him their end, to return quickly to him, the cause of all their being."[6]

The method prescribed for returning to God is by the practice of what Eckhart called "detachment." Detachment is not a series of ascetic exercises or rituals approved by the Church. "To seek God by rituals is to get the ritual and lose God in the process, for he hides behind it."[7] Instead, it is a sense of abandonment that takes place deep within a person's being – an abandonment of all creaturely-ness. And in this detachment, God is allowed to inhabit that being again and be reunited with us. He says,

> God desires urgently that you, the creature, get out of his way – as if his own blessedness depended on it. Ah, beloved people, why don't you let God be God in you? What are you afraid of? You get completely out of his way and he will get out of yours – you give up to him and he will give up to you. When both [God and you] have forsaken self, what remains [between you] is an indivisible union. It is in this unity that the Father begets his Son in the secret spring of your nature. Then the Holy Spirit blooms and out of God there comes a will which belongs to the soul."[8]

Eckhart was not the first Christian theologian to discuss religious experience in these mystical terms, but he is significant for disseminating it to the masses. The important idea here for our story is that union with God, the goal of the Christian life, is taken to be possible through personal experience. This sort of mystical teaching was a concern to the Church. If people can come to know God or enter into a relationship with him apart from the mediating role of the Church, then what is the point of the ecclesiastical hierarchy? Especially in a culture where abuses and excesses of the Church were becoming more apparent, people were ready to receive Eckhart's message of personal religion. But such a message could be dangerous to deliver in those days.

In 1326 Eckhart was charged with heresy by the Archbishop of Cologne. Eckhart wrote a careful defense against the charges – this time in Latin – but was not able to overcome the momentum against him. Pope John XXII wrote a papal bull dated 27 March 1329 condemning seventeen of Eckhart's propositions and labeling eleven others as susceptible to being construed heretically. Eckhart never got the news. His death is a bit of a mystery, occurring sometime between 22 February 1327 and the 1329 bull.

Meister Eckhart wasn't trying to start a reformation. He wasn't openly challenging the Church in either doctrine or practice. In his "Defense" he wrote, "I am able to err, but I cannot be a heretic, since one has to do with the intellect and the other with the will."[9] In evidence of his good will, he had written to the Church that he would submit his ideas to their authority; so he died in their good graces.

> The Reformation can be traced back to Eckhart spiritually and intellectually – if not ecclesiastically. There was enough matter for any reformation to work on in what Eckhart said plainly to whoever would listen to him. He could not be satisfied until he had made certain of the creative, ultimate source of all being, in the only place where it can be immediately known: in the depths of the immaterial self of a man. This is Protestantism.
>
> (Raymond Blakney, *Meister Eckhart*, xxi)

Besides anticipating a more personal mode of religion, Eckhart is significant in that he reversed some of the Aristotelian tendencies of Aquinas and other Scholastics. Like most mystics, he was inclined toward Platonism (or Neoplatonism) and its emphasis on the unseen spiritual realm at the expense of the physical world. Later devotional writers like Thomas à Kempis (*c.* 1380–1471) and Teresa of Ávila (1515–1582) were deeply influenced by Eckhart and would push this Neoplatonic tendency even further. There is another debate between the Platonists and Aristotelians of the day which played out in the Christian thought of the late Middle Ages. Both sides contributed to the intellectual climate which gave rise to the Reformation.

2 UNIVERSALS, OCKHAM, AND THE *VIA MODERNA*

The central issue in the debate between Aristotelians and Platonists in the late Middle Ages was over the meaning of universal terms. Aquinas held on to a kind of realism about universals and so maintained a version of the long-established realist position. But in the next generations, Oxford Franciscans Duns Scotus (1266–1308) and William of Ockham (*c.* 1288–1348) turned the tide against realism by defending nominalism, and this is reflected in several doctrines that were important for the Reformation. Before discussing these, however, we must try to understand the metaphysical debate. What are universals, and what is the difference between taking a nominalist approach and a realist approach toward

JOHN DUNS SCOTUS

John Duns Scotus (*c.* 1265–1308) was probably from Scotland and taught at Oxford University. He opposed many of the positions of Aquinas, particularly his use of reason. Scotus emphasized the freedom of the will over reason, both for humans and for God. This means that things are the way they are not out of conformity to some rationality which pervades all things, but rather because of the free choices of God and people. Scotus did not write a systematic summary of theology like many of his contemporaries, but did write two commentaries on the *Sentences* of Peter Lombard.

them? The issue becomes very technical, but in simplified terms it can be illustrated with the function of proper and common nouns in language.

Proper nouns such as "Napoleon" or "Marengo" (Napoleon's favorite horse) refer to the individual objects that are named. If these were the only kinds of nouns there are in language, we would be severely limited in what we could say efficiently (think of how long it would take to say you were going out to rake the leaves if you had to refer to each leaf individually!). So language is equipped with other kinds of nouns that apply to many different individual objects which belong to certain classes or groups. The common noun "animal" can be used to talk about both Napoleon and Marengo (and lots of other individual objects) such as in the sentence, "All animals are mortal."

The central question in the debate under consideration is, "To what do these common nouns refer?" They seem to be pointing to something that is common or universal among a given set of objects. But we might ask whether we only treat some individual objects similarly because the same common noun is applied to them. Or is it the other way around, and we apply the common noun to those individuals because there is something about them that they have in common – namely, they are all animals? To ask the same questions in a different way: is the universal term 'animal' just a convention of language that we have accustomed ourselves to, or does it really correspond to some objective feature of the named objects? Realists since the time of Plato have invoked the existence of a "Form" or "universal" to explain the objective order in the world that our language reflects. All things that we call "animal" in some sense share in the Form of animal.

Nominalists, on the other hand, have found real universals to be too fantastic of a postulation and have held that only particular things exist; anything else is just a linguistic convention – a name. And the collection of individual objects which fall under that general name is a decision of the community of language-users rather than a reflection of some order or structure that is built into the universe. For example, a community living in Arctic regions may have need to distinguish between many different types of snow and so the people there have made several different groupings and applied different names to them; whereas communities in more temperate regions get along fine with one general word covering all kinds of snow. Realists would claim that our language (to the degree that it is accurate) reflects the real nature of things; nominalists claim that what we take to be real is a reflection of our language, and there is no degree of accuracy that should be attributed to language, only degrees of usefulness. These simplified descriptions of the theories slide over many nuances but capture the essential point in the debate.

Aquinas had started moving toward nominalism, but stopped at a sort of middle position. With the Aristotelian crowd, he denied the separate existence of universals; but he did claim that universals exist in particular things and do in fact reflect an objective order of reality that God had planned all along. It is because of this, he maintained, that we can apply our reason in discerning this order.

William of Ockham, continuing in the tradition of Duns Scotus, feared that this sort of conception of God was too limiting. To his mind, positing an objective order to the universe forced God to conform to some standard external to himself. Thus Ockham claimed that we should begin our theology by accepting that God can do anything he wants. When we do this, theology will not spend so much time trying to discern by means of arcane theorizing what God must do; we must trust instead that divine revelation has revealed what God has in fact done, and look at each and every particular rather than assuming that they conform to a larger pattern. There is a sense in which nominalism supports an empirical approach to nature as well as to theology. Nature does not exist as the necessary creation of God, but as his voluntary and contingent choice. Thus again, scientists must actually look at nature and experiment on it in order to find out the way things are rather than deducing it as part of a rationalistic system.[10]

WILLIAM OF OCKHAM

William of Ockham (c. 1288–1349) was born in England and educated at Oxford. He ran afoul of Pope John XXII for siding with the Franciscans and their commitment to poverty. He took refuge with Emperor Ludwig of Bavaria, who agreed to defend William with the sword so long as William would defend him with his pen. Ockham's name is most widely recognized for the principle known as "Ockham's Razor" which urges parsimony in theories – cutting away all that is not necessary to explain the phenomena. Ockham wrote extensively in philosophy, theology, and political theory.

This nominalist approach is often credited as playing a significant role in doctrines which led to the Protestant Reformation. One aspect of that is the nominalists' conscious break from the traditional realist position of the Church. To emphasize this, they called their position the *via moderna* – the modern way. Against the realists of the past, the nominalists would claim that there is no objective order in the universe to which our language and structures conform. So even an institution like the Church could be taken to be a mere convention used by people for a certain purpose rather than something that exists necessarily. We can see Ockham's movement toward this position in his comments about the papacy:

> Although papal rule is divine in that Christ decided that it should exist in the Church, in many respects it seems to be human. For it is for men to decide who should be appointed to it, and who should elect, and who should correct the one appointed if he needs correction, and the like. Therefore, similarly, it will be human in this respect, that it should be decided by men whether one only, or, when beneficial, many, should be appointed to such rulership.[11]

Such a position chipped away at the authority that the papacy and the institution of the Church had acquired in society throughout the Middle Ages. If the particular form of the papacy was not something that conformed to a divine plan for all times, then people should be able to reform the institutional and authoritative structure of the Church to suit the needs of the present age.

This sentiment became increasingly popular when a crisis in the papacy developed at the end of the fourteenth century. In 1302, Pope Boniface VIII issued a papal bull declaring that popes had supreme authority not only in ecclesiastical affairs, but also in secular ones; kings were subordinate to the pope in all matters. This bull was aimed particularly at King Philip IV of France, with whom Boniface had conflicted over the right to tax the clergy. Philip would have none of it. He sent an army into Italy to capture the pope and bring him to trial, accusing him of gross immorality and heresy. Boniface did not stand trial, but died just a month after the ordeal.

Not surprisingly, a Frenchman was elected pope to replace Boniface: Pope Clement V (in office 1305–1314). In further obeisance to the king, Clement moved the papal court from Rome to Avignon in the south of France where there was a papal-held territory. The next pope, John XXII (in office 1316–1334) was also French and continued to reside at Avignon – as did popes for the next seventy years. After pressure from many quarters, Pope Gregory XI (in office 1370–1378) returned the papacy to Rome in 1377. After his death, the cardinals convened to elect the next pope and settled on a monk from Naples – geographically a part of Italy, but pro-French. Before this decision was announced, a Roman mob burst into the conclave, prompting the cardinals to flee in terror. That same year, the cardinals regretted their choice and elected a new pope, Clement VII (in office 1378–1394), claiming that the mob had influenced their first choice (Urban VI). Urban, of course, didn't accept the decision and deposed all of the cardinals and appointed new ones from Rome. Clement took up residence at Avignon and had the support of the French crown. So there were now two popes – one in Rome and one in Avignon – and two sets of cardinals who claimed authority to elect popes. This situation persisted through four Roman popes and two in Avignon – each one excommunicating his rival.

Besides fomenting more calls for reform, this situation brought to a head the ongoing question of authority within the Church. Drawing on Ockham's nominalism, a movement to place the pope under the authority of a council gained support. The Conciliar Movement, as it came to be known, had some adherents who saw the need for a governing council only in times of crisis; others, though, pushed further and wanted what we might call today a system of checks and balances for the pope even during more normal times. These Conciliarists regarded the Church as a human institution and so able to be restructured in order to meet the needs of changing circumstances.[12]

The Conciliar Movement was ultimately defeated at the Fifth Lateran Council (1512–1517) called by Pope Julius II to oppose the council which had been called without his sanction in Pisa in 1511. There the council had suspended Julius, but the decisions of that council were declared to be null and void by the "official" Lateran Council. Although the attempts at reform were stamped out for the time, seeds of discontent had been sown which could not be kept from growing. It was only a few months after the close of the Fifth Lateran Council that Martin Luther would tack his ninety-five theses to the church door in Wittenburg – leading to the Protestant Reformation. Before continuing with this story, however, we jump back to follow another thread which contributed to the climate of reform – this time from an adherent of realism.

3 WYCLIF

John Wyclif (c. 1328–1384) was born in the late 1320s to a well-to-do family in Yorkshire, England. He was trained as an academic and lived the life of a scholar in Oxford, gaining quite a reputation as one of the finest philosophers and theologians there. He had argued for a theory of lordship or dominion according to which only the godly can legitimately exercise authority over others. So on his theory, because the monastic orders were supposedly committed to poverty, their massive wealth (monasteries owned about one third of all property in England) disqualified them from fulfilling their duties. Such claims found ready ears in English society, and this propelled Wyclif into public life in 1371. For a time he enjoyed support from the English crown. England needed money for the Hundred Years' War, and his theories were useful in the king's argument with monasteries about their tax exemptions. In 1378 Wyclif returned to academic life and pursued increasingly radical and subversive doctrines. In 1381 he was banished from Oxford, and lived until 1384 under the protection of noble patrons in Lutterworth.

During Wyclif's years in Oxford, it was the *via moderna* of Ockham which had won the day. It is somewhat ironic, as we'll see, that the

Radical Reformation doctrines of Wyclif grew directly out of the more conservative Platonic philosophy. This is apparent in his attacks on the accepted doctrines of transubstantiation, the Church, and the Bible.

Wyclif was committed to the realist position, and it had profound influence on the reforming doctrines he propounded. For example, on the issue of transubstantiation, his beliefs stem directly from his metaphysical commitment to realism. Remember for realists, any individual objects, like specific pieces of bread, have the properties they do because they share in the real universal essence of bread. Wyclif never denied that the bread and wine became the body and blood of Christ, but he was concerned to explain this in a way that was not an affront to the realist principle he took for granted. And he believed strongly that it couldn't be along the lines that had been accepted in the Fourth Lateran Council (see Chapter 14). The properties of the bread – its taste, appearance, etc. – could not have remained the same, if the underlying substance had changed from bread into the actual flesh of Christ. Furthermore, Wyclif reasoned according to realist principles that the substance of the bread could not just be annihilated when it was blessed by the priest.[13] He maintained instead, that the true body and blood of Christ is added to the substance of bread and the wine in the Eucharist celebration. Especially late in his life, he argued this point with considerable vehemence against the Church's official position (and not always with tact and diplomacy).

In the same way, the Bible was accorded an exalted status by Wyclif because he took it to be the repository of eternal truth which exists for all times.[14] As such, the Bible became the final authority for Wyclif and so was held to be above the authority of the Church. Wyclif spearheaded a movement to translate the Bible into English and advocated that people ought to read it for themselves. They were told that everything they

TRANSUBSTANTIATION

The doctrine officially established by the Roman Catholic Church in 1215 asserting that the bread and wine are transformed literally into the body and blood of Christ during the celebration of the Eucharist – though their outward appearance remains unchanged.

Oure fadir that art in heuenes, halewid be thi name; thi kyngdoom
come to; be thi wille don in erthe as in heuene; yyue to vs this dai
oure breed ouer othir substaunce; and foryyue to vs oure dettis, as
we foryyuen to oure dettouris; and lede vs not in to temptacioun,
but delyuere vs fro yuel. Amen.

(Matthew 6:9–14, The Wyclif Bible (1395))

needed for salvation was contained in it. This was a recipe for reform
when people were given license to interpret the Bible for themselves
apart from the Church.

The problem with the Church in Wyclif's estimation was that it
wasn't really the Church. Recall from Chapter 11 that Augustine had
distinguished between the visible and invisible churches. He had claimed
that the visible church on earth is composed of both elect and non-
elect people (according to the predestination of God) and that we can't
determine who are and who are not. For Augustine, this wasn't a problem
for things like administering sacraments or ordaining priests, because he
taught that the efficacy of these rituals depended on the grace of God as
conveyed through the proper office – not on the spiritual standing of the
one who held the office and administered the sacraments.

Following Augustine and his own realist principles, Wyclif held that
the invisible church – like the Bible – is an eternally existing entity. It
is composed of all those who were predestined by God to be members.
But the visible church for Wyclif wasn't really the Church. Whereas
the mixture of elect and non-elect in the visible church didn't trouble
Augustine too much, this situation undermined the legitimacy of the
visible church for Wyclif. He claimed that Scripture could be used as a
guide to judge who was really a member of the elect; were they following
the dictates of Scripture and did their lives bear the fruit of the Spirit? In
this way, he judged that many among the clergy were clearly not included
in the invisible church. He said, "Neither place nor human election makes
a person a member of the Church but divine predestination in respect of
whoever with perseverance follows Christ in love, and in abandoning all
his worldly goods suffers to defend His law."[15] The visible church, and
especially the institution of the Papacy, were human inventions and not

grounded in Scripture. Therefore, they were illegitimate and irrelevant to the work of God on earth.

Although Wyclif himself never saw the sorts of reforms he was calling for, his thought had an important impact on subsequent generations leading up to the Protestant Reformation. He particularly influenced Jan Hus (c. 1372–1415) on the continent of Europe and a group known as the Lollards in England. Both continued to emphasize that spiritual authority is not derived from a particular office, but rather from people who led virtuous and holy lives. These reformers also continued to hold that Scripture was a higher authority than the Church. In the fifteenth century they were openly calling for an end to the hegemony that the Roman Catholic Church had on religion in Europe. For his role, Hus was burned at the stake by the Church; the Lollards were also persecuted and driven into hiding. But the seeds of reform had taken root. It was only a matter of time until they came to fruition.

Jan Hus, a reformer and preacher in Prague in the first part of the fifteenth century said:

If he who is to be called Peter's vicar follows in the paths of virtue, we believe that he is his true vicar and chief pontiff of the church over which he rules. But, if he walks in the opposite paths, then he is the legate of antichrist at variance with Peter and Jesus Christ. No pope is the manifest and true successor of Peter, the prince of the apostles, if in morals he lives at variance with the principles of Peter and if he is avaricious.

(*De Ecclesia*)

SUMMARY OF MAIN POINTS

1 Eckhart pushed the masses toward accepting a personal brand of religion which did not depend on the Church as mediator between people and God.

2 Nominalism and the *via moderna* undermined the belief that the Church was an objective feature of the structure of reality, and that there were other models which could serve the same purpose.

3 Wyclif's realism produced doctrines of Bible, Church, and Eucharist that were open challenges to the authority of the Roman Catholic Church.

FOR FURTHER READING

Oliver Davies, *Meister Eckhart: Mystical Theologian* (London: SPCK, 1991). An introduction to the life and thought of Eckhart which provides a sympathetic account of his orthodoxy.

Anthony Kenny, *Wyclif* (Oxford: Oxford University Press, 1985). A short and accessible introduction to the central ideas of Wyclif that gave encouragement to the Protestant Reformers.

Steven Ozment, *The Age of Reform 1250–1550: An Intellectual and Religious History of Late Medieval and Reformation Europe* (New Haven, CT: Yale University Press, 1980). A good overview of the period, including all the figures treated in this chapter.

G.H.W. Parker, *The Morning Star: Wycliffe and the Dawn of the Reformation* (Grand Rapids, MI: Eerdmans, 1965). Despite its title, also included are good discussions of Hus, Lollardy, the mystics, and the period up to Reformation.

Part *4*

Protest and revolution

The Reformation period
1500–1700

19

Martin Luther

> ## QUESTIONS TO BE ADDRESSED IN THIS CHAPTER
>
> 1   What was the controversy over indulgences?
> 2   How did Luther understand the righteousness of God?
> 3   What was the issue in Luther's debate with Erasmus?
> 4   What is the foundation of Luther's thought and of the Protestant Reformation?

On 31 October 1517 a monk nailed a document onto the church door at the university in Wittenberg, Germany. It began as follows:

> In the desire and with the purpose of elucidating the truth, a disputation will be held on the underwritten propositions at Wittemberg [sic.], under the presidency of the Reverend Father Martin Luther, Monk of the Order of St. Augustine, Master of Arts and of Sacred Theology, and ordinary Reader of the same in that place. He therefore asks those who cannot be present and discuss the subject with us orally, to do so by letter in their absence. In the name of our Lord Jesus Christ. Amen.[1]

Martin Luther was not trying to start the Protestant Reformation. He was inviting debate. That's what churchmen did in those days. The document has become known as the "Ninety-Five Theses." It was written in Latin and intended only for the students and other theology faculty who were associated with the university.

Luther was upset about some things in the Church, and he did want to see reform. Many of his theses were about the corruption that had become all too commonplace among the clergy. So he sponsored debates, and over the next couple of years, Luther found himself increasingly in the public eye pushing for reform. The recent invention of the printing press and its rapid dissemination of writing helped to fan into flame the controversies Luther sparked. Luther himself published five significant books just in the year 1520 and grew increasingly bold in his accusations. Ultimately he claimed that the Church of Rome was actually inhibiting

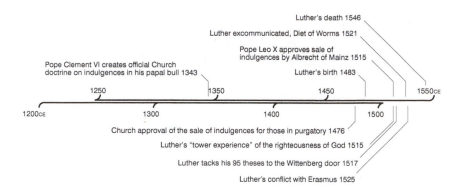

Timeline 19 Martin Luther

the spiritual development of parishioners and urged them to break their ties with Rome. Luther was excommunicated by Pope Leo X on 3 January, 1521.

Later that year, Luther was summoned to the small city of Worms down-river from Strasbourg where Charles V, the Holy Roman Emperor, would meet him in a "diet" (a formal imperial assembly). This was a crucial moment for Luther and for Church–state relations. Would Luther defy the civil authorities as he had the religious authorities? Could Charles be persuaded that Luther was correct in his judgment of the Church? When Luther was asked if he would recant the positions he had published, he first gave an evasive answer, and so was pressed further. He then replied:

> Since Your Majesty and your lordships desire a simple reply, I will answer without horns and without teeth. Unless I am convicted by Scripture and plain reason – I do not accept the authority of popes and councils, for they have contradicted each other – my conscience is captive to the Word of God. I cannot and I will not recant anything, for to go against conscience is neither right nor safe. God help me. Amen.[2]

Some reported Luther also to have added the words at the end of his speech that have become iconic for the Reformation, "Here I stand. I cannot do otherwise."

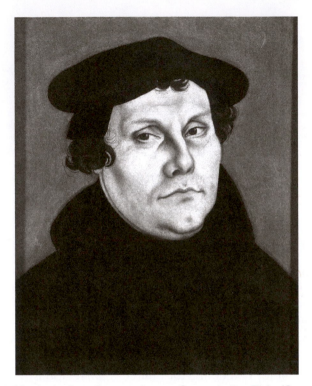

Figure 19.1 Martin Luther. Source: Lucas Cranach the Elder/Cranach Digital Archives/Public domain/Wikimedia Commons

Charles responded that he had descended from a long line of emperors who had been faithful to the Catholic Church and that he had resolved to follow in their steps. He said, "A single friar who goes counter to all Christianity for a thousand years must be wrong."[3] Luther's statement and Charles' response bring out the very real consequence that Luther was not just arguing against doctrine and practice of the Church; rather he was instituting a methodology by which individuals decide the truth for themselves in their own consciences instead of accepting it from an external authority.

Although he didn't persuade Charles, Luther had convinced enough people of his position. The time was ripe for reform. Prince Frederick the Wise of Saxony gave Luther protection and allowed him to live in a castle at Wartburg. There he translated the Bible into German so that people could read it for themselves. Thus began the Protestant Reformation.

1 INDULGENCES

The chief target of Luther's ninety-five theses was the practice of indulgences. Thesis number twenty-one reads, "Those preachers of indulgences are in error who say that, by the indulgences of the pope, a man is loosed and saved from all punishment."[4] By the time of Luther, an indulgence could be purchased from the Church in order to buy out time spent in purgatory working off sins – one's own or someone else's. To our ears today this sounds like some sort of ruse, but there is a theological tradition which underlays this practice and which must be described in order to understand Luther's objections.

There are two concepts in particular upon which indulgences are based: purgatory and the treasury of merits. Recall from Chapter 12 that the doctrine of purgatory was advanced by Pope Gregory in the sixth century as a way of purging people's post-baptismal sins which had not been forgiven before they died. While they lived, there were acts of penance that could be performed which triggered the forgiveness of sins, and it came to be accepted that additional penance assigned by a priest would allow one to "work off" time that would have had to be spent in purgatory. Then the equivalency or exchange of good works for penance – which would come to be called an indulgence – was developed when Pope Urban II declared in 1095 that participation in the crusade to free Jerusalem from its Muslim conquerors was equivalent to completing penance.

Second, the concept of the treasury of merits developed in the thirteenth century through the thought of Alexander of Hales, Albertus Magnus, and Thomas Aquinas. Essentially, it was claimed that the saints and the Virgin Mary did good works, performed penance, and suffered so much more than was required for the forgiveness of their own sins that there was a stockpile of these left over for use by others. And once the sufferings of Christ himself were added to this "treasury of merits" it was infinite and inexhaustible. Aquinas wrote:

> Indulgences hold good both in the Church's court and in the judgment of God, for the remission of the punishment which remains after contrition, absolution, and confession, whether this punishment be enjoined or not. The reason why they so avail is the oneness of the mystical body in which many have performed works of satisfaction exceeding the requirements of their debts.[5]

By 1343, there was official church doctrine to support the treasury of merits when Pope Clement VI set it forth in the papal bull, *Unigenitus*. The Church, then, could distribute these excess merits in exchange for certain good works. And in the 1476 papal bull of Sixtus IV, members of the Church could buy indulgences for souls which were currently in purgatory in order to free them from their suffering. It was this latter move which became so susceptible to abuse by preying on the emotions and good will of the relatives of the deceased. This created the situation which precipitated the abuse Luther would rail against.

In 1515 Pope Leo X authorized the sale of indulgences by Albrecht, the Archbishop of Mainz in Germany. Albrecht needed to raise money because of the debts he incurred in becoming archbishop, and Leo wanted money to complete the building of St. Peter's basilica in Rome. So "collectors" were hired to travel to towns all over Europe announcing the beneficence of the Church in that they had agreed to appropriate merits from the treasury which would completely cancel all time spent in purgatory for oneself, or immediately release from purgatory someone already there. This was available for a modest cash contribution, which would be split 50-50 between Albrecht and Leo.

The enterprise took on the character of a scam, and the collectors were the salesmen (receiving a handsome salary for their work). The slogan "As soon as the coin in the coffer rings, the soul from purgatory springs" was used as a sales pitch, and was cited specifically by Luther in his ninety-five theses.[6] The most notorious of the salesmen was a Dominican monk named John Tetzel (1465–1519). It is recorded that he would drum up interest in indulgences with the following message to people in the towns he entered:

> Don't you hear the voice of your wailing dead parents and others who say, "Have mercy upon me, have mercy upon me, because we are in severe punishment and pain. From this you could redeem us with a small alms and yet you do not want to do so. ... We created you, fed you, cared for you, and left you our temporal goods. Why are you so cruel and harsh that you do not want to save us, though it only takes so little? You let us lie in flames so that we only slowly come to the promised glory."[7]

Tetzel was as unscrupulous in his methods as he was successful in his results. But once the public controversy over indulgences had broken out, he was received with less alacrity. The story is told that after collecting a substantial amount of money in Leipzig and preparing for his departure, a nobleman approached him and asked whether he could receive an indulgence for a sin that might be committed in the future. Tetzel responded that this was possible, but the money had to be paid for it immediately. The nobleman paid the price and received his official letter of indulgence. Then when Tetzel was on his way out of the city, this same nobleman attacked him and stripped him of his money, saying that this was the future sin he had in mind![8]

The corruption which attended the sale of indulgences was a concern to Luther, but this was just a symptom of a deeper problem. The real target of Luther's reforms was the theology of works which he came to regard as unbiblical and therefore wrong.

2 THE RIGHTEOUSNESS OF GOD

Thesis number sixty-two of the famous ninety-five reads, "The true treasure of the Church is the Holy Gospel of the glory and grace of God."[9] This is an overt statement against the treasury of merits and its replacement with one of the key concepts for Luther's thought: gospel. The gospel for Luther is the good news that people are saved from eternal death and justified before God not by anything they might do, but solely as a gift of God which is accepted through faith alone. This was not always Luther's position, and in the process of coming to it, he gave new meaning to these terms and provided innovation in the history of Christian thought.[10]

Recall from Chapter 3 that the Apostle Paul's understanding of justification was not about individuals and how they become "saved." Rather, justification was the mark that one had been included in the promised vindication of God's people. The resurrection was this mark for Christ; for the early believers it was the receiving of the Holy Spirit which showed that they too had been justified. Then throughout the Middle Ages from at least the time of Augustine, justification was regarded as the process which began at conversion and culminated after death with one's entrance to heaven. At the point of baptism and entrance into the Church, the sins of believers are forgiven and washed away. Then through subsequent sacraments and penance, perhaps extending all the way through purgatory, Christians are transformed into actually holy and righteous people and therefore justified before God and admitted to heaven.

It cannot but be admitted that some of the practice of Christianity in the Middle Ages was the driving force behind the direction that theology went. The Church had become very powerful and exerted tremendous influence over people. The inevitable corruption that attends such a situation came to skew people's understanding of what was required of them for eternal salvation. When temporal projects like the crusades or building cathedrals became the chief concerns of popes, official church doctrine was produced to support these which had only very tenuous support from Scripture. And the humanism of the Renaissance had been a major influence in subtly shifting the emphasis from the collective entity of the Church to individuals. So, the question in people's minds became, "What must we do to be saved?" Whatever official church doctrine was, it seemed to the masses that there was a series of good works required of them in order to have any hope of going to heaven when they died.

Luther himself was a child of this theological environment. He tried very hard to do the things that he believed were required in order to make himself righteous. He went to ascetic excesses like severe fasts, sleeping on the cold stone floor of the monastery, and even whipping himself. And then from his reading of Scripture he saw that one would have to be *extremely* good in order to become righteous enough to earn God's favor. But he realized he could never be good enough. In his mature theology, Luther sees the proper function of the law of God to produce just such a realization in us. The law reveals our sin and points out the condemnation we deserve for it. Then its positive function is to lead us to the gospel. At the time, though, the law only led him to despair.

At the end of his life, Luther reflected back on the crisis point of his theological development. In Romans Chapter 1, the Apostle Paul speaks of the "righteousness of God." Luther recalls this being an impediment for his understanding of justification:

> For I hated that word 'righteousness of God,' which, according to the use and custom of all the teachers, I had been taught to understand philosophically regarding the formal or active righteousness, as they called it, with which God is righteous and punishes the unrighteous

sinner. Though I lived as a monk without reproach, I felt that I was a sinner before God with an extremely disturbed conscience. I could not believe that he was placated by my satisfaction. I did not love, yes, I hated the righteous God who punishes sinners.[11]

This is the dilemma that Luther felt: God could accept only righteous people, but these people could try as hard as they might and never become righteous through their efforts. In fact, the law given by God seemed only to heighten their awareness that they could never live up to the standard that was expected by God. The law condemned. God's righteousness only served to show how unrighteous and unworthy people are.

But then a new insight into the meaning of the "righteousness of God" dawned on Luther. This event has come to be known as the "tower experience" for he was meditating on the Romans 1 passage while in a tower at the monastery. Luther himself reports it to have happened in 1518, after the reaction to his ninety-five theses had begun. This would suggest that it was Luther's debate with the churchmen which led him to this new understanding. Many Luther scholars, however, believe that Luther incorrectly remembered the timing of events (it was, after all, 30 years after the fact that Luther wrote his account). They claim that it must have been about 1515 when Luther had his tower experience, and it was this which fomented his dissatisfaction with the Church and its practices. In chronicling the history of Christian thought, it is not important for us to decide the issue of timing. What concerns us here is the new understanding of God's righteousness which Luther came to and which continues to typify Lutheran thought.

Luther came to see that the righteousness of God is not what condemns sinners, but rather it is what saves them. It is true that God accepts and justifies us by righteousness. But it could not be by our own righteousness, for this is what could never be achieved. Rather, it is the heart of the gospel message that God gives to us his own righteousness. God the judge looks upon us sinners and sees the righteousness which was placed upon us because of the sacrifice of Christ on the cross. Upon this realization Luther reported, "Here I felt that I was altogether born again and had entered paradise itself through open gates."[12]

Sinful human beings are justified before God as righteous people on account of the righteousness of God which has been imputed to them. Justification, then, is something external to humans. Contrast this to the

"IMPUTE" AND "IMPART"

Impute

To attribute the qualities or characteristics of one person to another.

Impart

To give the qualities or characteristics of one person to another.

> Through faith in Christ, therefore, Christ's righteousness becomes our righteousness and all that he has becomes ours; rather, he himself becomes ours. Therefore the Apostle calls it "The righteousness of God" in Rom 1. ... This is an infinite righteousness, and one that swallows up all sins in a moment, for it is impossible that sin should exist in Christ. On the contrary, he who trusts in Christ exists in Christ; he is one with Christ, having the same righteousness as he.
>
> (From Luther's sermon, "Two Kinds of Righteousness")[13]

earlier position in which people really become righteous. That would be an internal state in which righteousness is *imparted* to humans. But it is Luther's view that righteousness can only be external and *imputed* for us sinful creatures. To think otherwise in his opinion would be to attribute some merit to our works and lead us back into Pelagianism.

3 THE ROLE OF THE WILL

Pelagianism was the heresy opposed so strongly by Augustine (see Chapter 11) in which people are held to be able to choose the good for themselves. On this view, there is no fallen condition which is propagated through the species because of the original sin of Adam and Eve, so people are not born in sin or otherwise innately sinful. In Luther's estimation, this is tantamount to a denial of human sinfulness altogether. He thought that the espousal of such a doctrine is proof that its defenders have not had an encounter with the law of God, for that could not help but expose their complete sinfulness. Luther believed that the theologians of the Catholic Church in the Middle Ages had allowed this heresy to creep back into Christian thought by preaching works' righteousness. In his *Disputation against Scholastic Theology*, Luther wrote that man can only do evil, and that apart from the grace of God the will can only produce evil and perverse actions. Further, the will on its own cannot even accept the truth when presented with it, for it is "innately and inevitably evil and corrupt."[14]

There was a famous dispute between Luther and the Dutch Renaissance scholar Desiderius Erasmus on the topic of free will. According to Erasmus and his Christian humanism, freedom of the will was necessary for a life of virtue. There is no virtue if it is not freely chosen. So he urged people to turn from their sinful ways by applying their will to the good actions they knew they should be doing. This was not done apart from the grace of God, though. Rather, he claimed that, "A good will cooperates with the action of grace."[15] In Erasmus's humanist view it was a return to Manicheism to insist, as he took Luther to be implying, that the will was evil by nature. Yes, the free will had been wounded through sin, Erasmus would acknowledge, but it had not been destroyed.

Luther responded to Erasmus with his impassioned *The Bondage of the Will* in 1525. Luther recognized Erasmus's literary superiority, but could not countenance the substance of Erasmus's work. Speaking directly to Erasmus in the introduction, Luther says,

> Your book struck me as so cheap and paltry that I felt profoundly sorry for you, defiling as you were your very elegant and ingenious style with such trash, and quite disgusted at the utterly unworthy matter that was being conveyed in such rich ornaments of eloquence, like refuse or ordure being carried in gold and silver vases.[16]

Essentially, Luther's argument was that as sinful, fallen creatures we are held captive to the will of Satan so that we can only will what Satan wills. He uses an image (not original to him) of our will as a beast of burden standing between two riders: God and Satan. If God rides it,

DESIDERIUS ERASMUS

Desiderius Erasmus (1469–1536) was a Christian humanist scholar from Rotterdam. He was sympathetic with the impulse for church reform, but pushed for this to come from within. He remained loyal to the Catholic Church his whole life. His work with ancient texts in their original language was a major resource for Reformation-minded people who were not content to merely receive interpretations from the Church. Most significantly was his publication of the first complete Greek New Testament (1516). This became the source from which many vernacular translations were made – including Luther's German New Testament. Erasmus wrote,

> I am totally against those who do not want the Holy Scripture to be read by the laity in their vernacular, as if Christ had taught so obscurely that he can be hardly understood even by a few theologians or as if the defense of the Christian religion depended on its not being known! Perhaps it is better if the secrets of kings are concealed, but Christ desires that his mysteries be known as widely as possible. I desire that everyone including women read the gospels and the Pauline letters. These ought to be translated into all languages so that not only the Scots and the Irish but also the Turks and the Saracens could read and understand them. The first step is certainly to learn them in whatever manner. … Thus I would like the farmer to sing Scripture as he plows, the weaver to hum it as he weaves, the traveler to pass the boredom of his journey with such stories. Let the conversation of all Christians therefore relate to the Scripture.
>
> (Erasmus, *Paracelis*)[17]

it goes and wills as he desires; if Satan rides it, it goes and wills as he desires. And the problem for humans is that we do not get to choose the rider. "The riders themselves contend for the possession and control of it."[18] Since the Fall caused by original sin, the default rider for all human wills is Satan. As such, the will can do nothing good. It cannot even turn to God for help, for this is nothing that Satan would ever permit. In order to be saved and justified, then, there is nothing that we can do. Here again, Luther brings us to the point in which the law exposes our total and utter sinfulness and helplessness. But then this also is the point at which the gospel takes over.

4 JUSTIFICATION BY GRACE THROUGH FAITH

Christ clothes us with his righteousness. There is nothing we can do to bring this about ourselves. We cannot even ask for it apart from God's grace. The good news of the gospel for Luther is that God will do for us what we could not do for ourselves. This is the doctrine of justification by grace which counters any hint of works righteousness. It is this doctrine more than any other which is the foundation of the Protestant movement.[19] Luther himself claimed that the doctrine of justification is the one article of faith which,

> preserves the church of Christ; when it is lost, Christ and the church are lost, nor is there any knowledge of doctrine or of the Spirit left. This article is itself the sun, the day, the light of the church and of all believers.[20]

Luther's rhetorical flourish masks the innovative move he's made. Justification now becomes the center of Christian thought in Luther's theology. Only when Augustine or Aquinas are reread in the light of Luther does the doctrine assume such a central role for them. There are several implications that come from this new emphasis.

First, there is the question about how it is that such grace comes to be given to a particular individual. Why is it that God's grace brings about the justification of some and not others? Luther's disagreement with Erasmus has ruled out the sinner's ability to choose Christ or otherwise align himself with God through an act of the will. But Luther also understands from Scripture that the believer must have faith. Faith is not to be understood on his account as some sort of act of will or even as belief. Rather, faith is the response to the gospel. "Faith is produced and preserved in us by preaching why Christ came, what he brought and bestowed, what benefit it is to us to accept him."[21] But it is not the sinner's choice to respond in a particular way. That too is the gift of God. "Faith, however, is something that God effects in us."[22] So justification comes to us by grace through faith. We can take no credit for any of this. Justification is purely a gift of God, and we can receive it only by responding in faith to the message of the gospel. That response itself is only possible because God brings it about in us.

Luther spends very little time reflecting on the consequences of this doctrine with regard to personal responsibility or our involvement in the event. (We'll see in the next chapter how John Calvin worked through these implications which were very much a result of Luther's thought.) Luther's emphasis was to guarantee that humans and their efforts toward righteousness and justification could amount to nothing. All our works are sin and death. Whatever righteousness we possess is what has been imputed to us. This results in perhaps the most cogent summation of Luther's theology: "The saints (believers) are at the same time sinners while they are righteous."[23]

Another consequence of this understanding of justification may be troubling. If we are justified only externally, is there any point in following the dictates of the Christian life? Luther seems reluctant to address this question because he wants to keep the focus completely on God's grace to us sinners. And sometimes a caricature of Luther's theology is presented in which he actually encourages people to continue sinning.[24] Careful examination of the whole of Luther's thought, however, shows that he is concerned about believers' good works so long as we understand they have nothing to do with justification. In the preface to his *Commentary on Romans*, he says:

> [Faith] changes us and we are reborn from God, John 1 [:13]. Faith puts the old Adam to death and makes us quite different men in heart, in mind, and in all our powers; and it is accompanied by the Holy Spirit. O, when it comes to faith, what a living, creative, active, powerful thing it is. It cannot do other than good at all times. It never waits to ask whether there is some good work to do, Rather, before the question is raised, it has done the deed,

and keeps on doing it. A man not active in this way is a man without faith.[25]

True faith in Christ does lead the sinner to change. But works are the fruit of justification, not its root. They are not done for ourselves as a means to our justification before God. The purpose of good works is to benefit others, that they may see our good works and be drawn to the gospel.[26]

Finally, justification by grace through faith has another important consequence: the priesthood of all believers. If grace alone through the faith of individuals is responsible for their justification, then there is no need for a privileged class of priests who are mediators between God and the people. Luther did not dissolve the office of the minister of local congregations, but he did hold that all believers have access to God. Such an understanding calls into question one of the chief roles of the Church, and shifts authority to individuals and their own interpretations of Scripture and theology. Once this step is taken, the floodgates for reform are opened wide. We see in the following chapters that reform and factions within the Christian tradition did not stop with Luther and his followers.

SUMMARY OF MAIN POINTS

1 Indulgences were a way of appropriating the excess good works of the saints as penance in exchange for good works or money, and the misuse of this practice was one of the major impetuses of the Reformation.

2 The righteousness of God does not condemn, but is that which saves when imputed to sinners.

3 Luther claimed against Erasmus that our human will is not free to choose any good thing apart from the grace of God.

4 Justification comes by grace from God through faith alone.

FOR FURTHER READING

Roland H. Bainton, *Here I Stand: A Life of Martin Luther* (Nashville, TN: Abingdon Press, 1978). The classic twentieth century biography of Luther's life.

John Dillenberger, ed., *Martin Luther: Selections from his Writings* (Garden City, NY: Doubleday, 1961). A standard collection of Luther's writings, including the ninety-five theses, *The Freedom of a Christian*, *Two Kinds of Righteousness*, *The Bondage of the Will*, and many others.

Carter Lindberg, *The European Reformations* (Oxford: Blackwell Publishers, 1996). A survey of the various reform movements of the sixteenth century.

Bernhard Lohse, *Martin Luther's Theology: Its Historical and Systematic Development* (Minneapolis, MN: Fortress, 1999). A comprehensive exposition of Luther's thought by one of the leading Luther scholars of the late twentieth century.

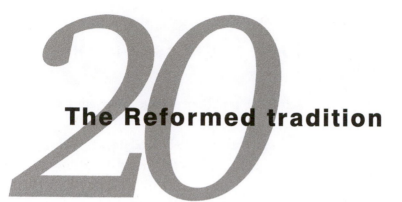

The Reformed tradition

QUESTIONS TO BE ADDRESSED IN THIS CHAPTER

1 How did the Reformed tradition emerge as distinct from Lutheranism?
2 What was Calvin's contribution to Reformed theology?
3 What were some significant developments in Reformed thought after Calvin?
4 How was disagreement between Calvinists and Arminians resolved in Holland?

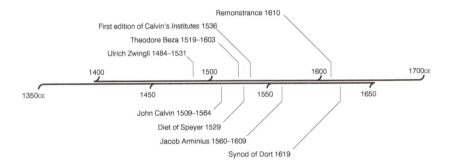

Remonstrance 1610
First edition of Calvin's *Institutes* 1536
Theodore Beza 1519–1603
Ulrich Zwingli 1484–1531

1350CE   1400   1450   1500   1550   1600   1650   1700CE

John Calvin 1509–1564
Diet of Speyer 1529
Jacob Arminius 1560–1609
Synod of Dort 1619

Timeline 20 The Reformed tradition

In March of 1529 an Imperial Diet was convened in the city of Speyer (about 110 km south of Frankfurt). The Holy Roman Emperor, Charles V, did not attend but sent his brother Ferdinand in his place. The object of the meeting was to consolidate support of the territorial princes behind Charles in order to present a united defense against the Turks who had advanced to the eastern edge of the empire. The method of Ferdinand (which probably would not have been the same as Charles's) was to repeal the religious toleration that had been extended in 1526 whereby each prince was allowed to follow the dictates of his conscience regarding religion. The 1529 edict decreed that all territories within the Holy Roman Empire would be loyal to Roman Catholicism. In response to this, six German princes along with representatives of fourteen free cities within the empire officially protested the decision. It was from this incident that people dissenting from Catholicism were called "Protestants."

There were differences among Protestants, but they were largely united in doctrine by three great *sola* statements (*sola* means "alone" in Latin):

sola gratia (grace alone):	justification is by God's gift of grace, not because of any merit on the part of humans
sola fide (faith alone):	this gift is received through faith, not by doing any good works
sola scriptura (Scripture alone):	the final authority of doctrine and practice is the Bible, not the Church

Sola scriptura had some interesting consequences for the Protestant movement. In Catholicism, Scripture is accepted as an authority; but on an equal level of authority are the rulings of the Church. It is characteristic of the Protestant Reformation that the rulings of the Church were to be subjected to the message of the Bible. As it turns out, though, not everyone agrees just what that message is. Without any higher authority which might enforce a particular interpretation of Scripture, there is no common judge between those who disagree. They are left to go their own ways. So, *sola scriptura*, which begins as a unifying factor among the Protestants, becomes the grounds for further divisions between those who interpret the Bible differently. At last count, the number of distinct Christian denominations worldwide exceeds 33,000![1] Of course this denominational explosion took some time, but even in the middle of the sixteenth century there were several distinct Reformation movements apart from the Lutherans. In this chapter, we focus on what is (confusingly) called the Reformed tradition.

1 ZWINGLI

Ulrich Zwingli (1484–1531) was a Swiss theologian and pastor who exercised significant influence on the Reformed tradition. The same year as the Diet of Speyer, Zwingli entered into debate with Luther on the nature of the Eucharist. This proved to be a watershed event for the Protestants because their inability to agree led to further splintering.

Luther continued to hold that Christ was literally present in the bread and wine of the Eucharist, but his was not the transubstantiation view of the Catholic Church by which the elements are transformed into the body and blood of Christ (though retaining their appearances). Luther's view would come to be call "consubstantiation" because he held that the real presence of Christ's body and blood joined with the substances of bread and wine during the Lord's Supper. Zwingli takes another step further away from the Catholic position by interpreting the bread and wine as wholly symbolic.

The debate between Luther and Zwingli boils down to the same Christological controversy that raged between the Alexandrians and the Antiochenes in the fourth and fifth centuries (see Chapter 8). As the representative of the Antiochene Christology, Zwingli emphasized the dual nature of Christ. So he claimed that the body of Christ must be that of a human, and as such it could not be in different places at the same time. Since Christ now resides at the right hand of the Father, that must be where his body stays, and therefore his body cannot be in the bread of the Eucharist. In response, Luther charged Zwingli with being a neo-Nestorian.[2] Luther took the words of Jesus, "This is my body" (Matthew 26:26) literally – too literally in Zwingli's estimation. For Zwingli, Scripture must be understood in its proper context rather than according to church tradition, and on his view the context mandated a non-literal interpretation. In taking this position, Zwingli shows the strong humanist bent that he acquired in his education.

Zwingli went to school in Vienna and then Basle which had become an important center for humanism. He met Erasmus there in 1516 and was deeply impressed with the humanist approach of returning to the original sources. Especially for the proper understanding of Christian doctrine, he believed that we ought to recapture the original meaning of Scripture itself rather than relying on a tradition of interpreting it. He preached straight through the New Testament (using Erasmus's Greek New Testament) to his congregation in Zurich so that they might hear the gospel directly, rather than mediated through the lessons of the church calendar. In this way his emphasis on Scripture went beyond Luther's. Zwingli took the entirety of Scripture to be inspired and useful, while Luther held to a sort of "canon within the canon" by elevating those portions of Scripture which particularly emphasized his understanding of Christ and the gospel above those that did not.

In other ways, though, Luther took the more conservative line regarding the interpretation of Scripture. He was strongly against the importation of philosophical ideas into Scripture, and was perfectly content to allow Scripture to speak for itself and not attempt to force it into explanatory theories or otherwise rationalize the message. Despite his claims to the contrary,[3] Zwingli was strongly influenced in his theology (and interpretation of Scripture) by the philosophical ideas he encountered in his humanist training. Nowhere is this more evident than in the doctrine of predestination.

John Calvin is better known than Zwingli for defending a strong version of predestination, and we shall tend to his thought in the next section. But it is worthwhile to spend some time on Zwingli's version for it has priority in the history of Christian thought and was the source of the Reformed position on the issue. For this reason it is all the more enlightening to see how it developed.

In 1530 Zwingli wrote "On the Providence of God" as a transcript from memory of a sermon he had delivered in October of 1529. It is a detailed treatise which runs to more than 100 pages of text. Most relevantly for our purposes, he began not from Scripture or other Christian traditions, but from a philosophical conception of God as the supreme good. He brought in some proof texts from Scripture (e.g. "Why callest thou me good? There is none good but God" (Matthew 19:17)), but just as often appealed to Plato or Seneca in establishing that this supreme good is above all things. Next he argued that all created things derive their existence from and are dependent on God, for God would be deficient if there were things that escaped his supervision. This supervision extends even to minute or seemingly insignificant matters. God has the hairs of our heads numbered and knows when a sparrow hits the ground (Matthew 10:29–30), so from this "we learn that even the things which we call fortuitous or accidental are not fortuitous or random happenings, but are all effected by the order and regulation of the Deity."[4] This sort of all-encompassing and all-controlling providence leads to a picture of God and the world which comes very close to pantheism or at least the blurring of the line of distinction between creature and creator. Zwingli says:

> Since all things have their being, existence, life, movement and activity from one and in One, that One is the only real cause of all

things, and those nearer things which we call causes, are not properly causes, but the agents and instruments with which the eternal mind works, and in which it manifests itself to be enjoyed.[5]

Very explicitly, Zwingli attributes all the actions of humans as merely secondary causes. They are only instruments through which God as the primary cause effects his will – as the farmer uses a plow to turn the soil. Of course this raises questions about some of the sinful actions of humans and whether they are properly attributed to God. Zwingli does not shrink from these questions, but notes the distinction that humans are under law and therefore guilty, whereas God is not bound by any law and so cannot be judged by it. He says:

> But what God brings about through man's agency is imputed a crime to man, but not also to God. For the one is under the law, the other is the free spirit and mind of the law. And when we say that Divine Providence did this or that wrong which one man or another has perpetrated, we speak improperly. For in so far as God does it, it is not sin, because it is not against the law. The law has certainly not been imposed upon Him as the Righteous One. ... One and the same deed, therefore, adultery, namely, or murder, as far as it concerns God as author, mover and instigator, is an act, not a crime, as far as it concerns man is a crime and wickedness.[6]

Despite his earlier attachment to Erasmus, Zwingli decries free will as being incompatible with providence. Then there is an easy transition from providence to predestination. Once it is established that the providence of God determines every detail of creation, election and predestination follow easily and seem to comport well with the Reformation doctrine of justification by grace. God chooses – or elects – some people to bestow grace upon. What of those who are not the recipients of God's grace? Zwingli doesn't want to say that they are "elected" to damnation, but concedes that God makes a choice regarding them too that their damnation might be examples of his righteousness.[7]

So it is that the doctrine of God's sovereignty becomes the center of Zwingli's theology. It is not sovereignty merely in the sense of being the Lord of the universe to whom all shall be subject. This Reformed version puts sovereignty more into the category of the supreme autocrat who leaves no room for any will but his own. It is derived from the concept of God he began with, which appears to have more in common with ancient Greek notions of deity than with the God of Abraham, Isaac, and Jacob.

Of course the terms "providence," "election," and even "predestination" are found in Scripture and used extensively by Christian theologians throughout the ages. So it is difficult to understand the innovation in Christian thought that has taken place here. For reference, Augustine held to predestination, but his understanding was that all people are sinners and so deserve damnation. God in his mercy elects some for salvation; the others get what they deserve. Notice the difference between this and Zwingli's doctrine: for Augustine, people are not damned because God chooses to damn them. God allows them to go to hell, but he does not choose for them to do so. Zwingli does not recognize or agree with this distinction. His version is sometimes called "double predestination" because he holds that God predestines both the elect and the reprobate.

Aquinas, too, upholds a doctrine of predestination. But for him, God bases predestination on foreknowledge. God foreknows who will respond positively to the gospel and therefore predestines just those as the elect.[8] Zwingli rejects this and claims the situation to be the other way around: God's foreknowledge of the future is certain because he has predestined what will happen.

It is Zwingli's version that was adopted by the greatest articulator of Reformed theology. We turn to him now.

2 CALVIN

John Calvin was born in France in 1509 but spent most of his adult years in the independent city of Geneva (which later became part of Switzerland). He wrote his magnum opus, *Institutes of the Christian Religion*, in 1536 while studying in Basle and received immediate acclaim for it. As a result, some people from Geneva compelled Calvin to assume leadership of the city as it had recently converted to Protestantism. He became the chief pastor of the city and essentially the ruling authority on all matters, instituting a strict lifestyle based on his understanding of the Bible – including the death penalty for heretics.[9]

Without a doubt Calvin has been the most influential theologian of the Reformed tradition. It is often charged, however, that he was unoriginal, drawing his thought from Zwingli and his successor in Zurich, Heinrich

Figure 20.1 John Calvin. Source: Georg Osterwald/Public domain/Wikimedia Commons.

Bullinger. And not all that goes by the name of Calvinism today can be found in the thought of Calvin himself. He was willing to let some things be mysterious and unknown, whereas the later Reformed tradition attempted to work out everything systematically to fill in the gaps. But it was Calvin who was the great organizer and mouthpiece of the Reformed tradition. His *Institutes* went through numerous editions during his lifetime and remains one of the most influential texts for Christian thought today.

Predestination is perhaps the doctrine most commonly associated with Calvin, but he contributed nothing to the doctrine that wasn't already found in Zwingli. Calvin was adamant that predestination was not the centerpiece or foundation of his theology. In fact, double predestination isn't even mentioned in the first edition of the *Institutes*. But with each successive edition, more space is allocated to the doctrine, as though Calvin keeps trying to come to terms with and explicate what he admits is a "dreadful" decree.[10]

His objective seems to be one of producing Scriptural support for the idea of God that Zwingli had derived from natural theology and ancient Greek philosophy. Quoting the Psalms, Calvin shows that the creator God continues his active involvement in the world as preserver, sustainer, and superintendent of even the most inconsequential details.[11] As such, God is the ultimate cause of everything and the all-determining reality, but Calvin wants to make sure that he distances himself from the pagan philosophical sources to which Zwingli appealed:

> We do not with the Stoics imagine a necessity consisting of a perpetual chain of causes, and a kind of involved series contained in nature, but we hold that God is the disposer and ruler of all things, – that from the remotest eternity, according to his own wisdom, he decreed what he was to do, and now by his power executes what he decreed.[12]

The ultimate purpose of all these decrees is God's own glory. This extends not only to the inanimate order of stars and seas, but also to the living plants and animals and even to human beings. So just like Zwingli, Calvin's understanding of providence easily transitions into predestination. All things go according to the will of God, and there is no distinction to be made between what God allows and what he ordains. So the behavior, beliefs, and ultimate destination of each human being are chosen by God according to his will and for his glory. "The first man fell because the Lord deemed it meet that he should: why he deemed it meet, we know not. It is certain, however, that it was just, because he saw that his own glory would thereby be displayed."[13]

By predestination we mean the eternal decree of God, by which he determined with himself whatever he wished to happen with regard to every man. All are not created on equal terms, but some are preordained to eternal life, others to eternal damnation; and accordingly, as each has been created for one or the other of these ends, we say that he has been predestinated to life or to death.

(Calvin, *Institutes*[14])

The election of some for eternal life and some for eternal damnation is an obvious truth of Scripture for Calvin. True to the spirit of the reformers discussed to this point, this election admits no hint of merit on the part of those who are to be saved. Election resides completely in the free choice of God, the decree he made before all time as to whom God would love and whom God would hate. It may be difficult for us to understand and accept, but the reprobate display the glory of God no less than the saved. Beyond this, Scripture is silent and we cannot probe any deeper into the secret will of God.[15]

It is only natural that congregants hearing this message would begin to wonder whether they were among the elect. Salvation comes by grace through faith, but how can people know if they have faith? This is a new sort of question that had not been an issue before the Reformation. Conversion to Christianity for Catholics was an external affair: one went through the rituals of baptism and communion.[16] But with Luther and now the Reformed tradition, true saving faith is something internal. Calvin says that faith is, "a firm and sure knowledge of the divine favour toward us, founded on the truth of a free promise in Christ, and revealed to our minds, and sealed on our hearts, by the Holy Spirit."[17] Luther does not appear to have claimed that we can have firm and secure knowledge; for him all we can do is hold on to the gospel today and hope that tomorrow we will still hold on to it and thus persevere in faith. For Calvin, though, if you have been called by God (what he'd later call the "conversion experience"), you can have assurance that you are among the elect. Of course many will have some doubts and psychological uncertainty about their election. But it is unfruitful to explore within oneself for the certainty of faith. That certainty comes from the promise of the gospel and our own communion with Christ.[18]

It can't be disputed that there will be those who seem to have been called of God but subsequently fall away from Christian faith. To this situation Calvin says, "I deny not that they have signs of calling similar to those given to the elect; but I do not at all admit that they have that sure confirmation of election which I desire believers to seek from the word of the gospel."[19] He admits that there are some biblical passages which seem to suggest that people who have faith do not persevere. But he concludes that these people must not have had a true saving faith. In support of this he notes that Christ prayed for Peter that his faith would not fail (Luke 22:32), and Calvin believes it reasonable to assume that

Christ must pray the same thing for all the elect and that his prayer must be effective since the "Son of God ... never meets with a refusal."[20]

Calvin has taken the doctrines he inherited from Luther, Zwingli, and Bullinger and produced support for these from Scripture (and Augustine). There are gaps and troubling implications in the systematic exposition of these doctrines, and Calvin admits these. But he is content to claim that they are reflective of the revelation that has been given to us. To try to push further into the mystery and hidden will of God would be churlish. Calvin's successors in the Reformed tradition did push further to bring more comprehensiveness to the Reformed system.

3 BEZA AND ARMINIUS

Theodore Beza (1519–1603) was the successor of Calvin in Geneva with regard to duties associated with the church and the school Calvin had founded. He accepted Calvin's doctrines and sought to bring greater clarity and systematization to them. One element of this was to understand the logical order of God's eternal decrees. All the Reformed thinkers mentioned so far agreed that God's decree for creation included the provision that humans would fall through sin, and they also agreed that the predestination of some to heaven and some to hell was an eternal decree. The question was which had logical priority. The supralapsarians (which literally means "above the fall") held that the decree of predestination was above the decree for creation and fall. That is to say, they held that God's higher priority was that some would be saved and others damned, and that then creation and fall was a means to this end. Others, called infralapsarians ("below the fall"), reversed this logical priority so that God's higher priority was to glorify himself through his creation, and that predestination was a consequence that needed to be decreed because of the sin that humans fell into.

Jacob Arminius (1560–1609) was a Dutch Protestant educated under Beza in Switzerland. As a pastor back in Holland, he came increasingly into conflict with the Reformed Church because he criticized the supralapsarian position. He believed that human beings must exercise their free will in accepting the gift of salvation which is offered by the grace of God. So he was more in line with Aquinas's version of predestination in which predestination rests on God's foreknowledge. Because humans have free will,

> It is unavoidable that the free will should concur in preserving the grace bestowed, assisted, however, by subsequent grace; and it always remains within the power of the free will to reject the grace bestowed, and to refuse subsequent grace; because grace is not an omnipotent action of God which cannot be resisted by man's free will.[21]

This brings out another set of theological positions which were hotly debated in the Reformation period: Arminius is here advocating synergism – the doctrine that salvation is effected by God in cooperation with human will. The opposing doctrine, monergism, states that it is God alone who brings about salvation for humans. Many Reformed theologians of the time held that only monergism was consistent with the Reformation pillar of justification by faith. They believed that synergism was a Catholic understanding and dangerously close (if not equivalent) to Pelagianism. The Reformed community of Holland was more independent and open minded than the Geneva of Calvin and Beza. Many were persuaded by Arminius's claims that the strict Calvinist interpretation made people into something no better than a "stock or a stone."[22]

Arminius was able to take a chair of theology at the University of Leiden in 1603. But another professor of theology at the university was not happy. Franciscus Gomarus, a strict and fractious supralapsarian, charged Arminius with heresy and incited a public inquisition. Arminius died in 1609 of tuberculosis while the inquisition was still going on, but the debate continued and included theologians, pastors, and public officials.

4 THE REMONSTRANCE OF 1610 AND THE SYNOD OF DORT

In 1610 a group of pastors and officials, many of whom had been students of Arminius, wrote a remonstrance (or formal expression of protest) and presented it to the government. It consisted of five articles which detailed their disagreement with strict Calvinist theology. In summary these are as follows:[23]

1   God predestines for salvation those who will believe and persevere in their faith.
2   Christ's death was for all people, but only those who believe benefit from it.

3   People cannot do, think, or will anything that is truly good apart from the grace of God.
4   The grace offered by God to people can be resisted.
5   It may be that true believers could abandon their faith and so lose the saving grace they once had.

In response to this document, which came to be known as the Remonstrance of 1610, the government gave an edict of toleration that allowed the "Remonstrants" to teach their doctrine and hold office. The supporters of Gomarus did not give up the fight, however. Pamphlets were distributed accusing the Remonstrants of all sorts of heresy and crime, and this led to a time of public unrest. Prince Maurice of Nassau, who controlled the army and sided with the Calvinists, stepped in and ordered the leading Remonstrants to be jailed until an international synod could be held to decide the matter.

In late 1618 the Synod of Dort (or Dordrecht) convened under the presidency of an extreme Calvinist named John Bogerman. There were delegates from the Reformed Church traditions in England, Scotland, France, Switzerland, and Germany. Thirteen of the Remonstrants were allowed to present their case, but then were dismissed for deliberation. The synod closed in May of 1619 and presented their responses to each of the points of the Remonstrance. These have become known as the five points of Calvinism. We give the points in summary here in order of their response to the Remonstrance (rather than the more common way they are listed now according to the mnemonic device TULIP formed by the first letter of each point):

1   **Unconditional election**: God's predestination is not based on his foreknowledge, but completely on his own choice.
2   **Limited Atonement**: Christ did not die for the sins of all, but only for the elect.
3   **Total depravity**: since the Fall, every person inherits a corrupt nature that makes them incapable of any good.
4   **Irresistible grace**: God's saving grace offered to the elect cannot be refused.
5   **Perseverance of the saints**: once saving faith has been given to people, it cannot be revoked.

These became the official statements of Reformed Churches. The leaders of the Remonstrance were condemned as heretics and either imprisoned or exiled (and at least one was beheaded). After the death of Prince Maurice, the Arminians were shown more tolerance and formed the Remonstrant Reformed Church, which still exists today. Arminian theology, however, would have its greatest impact outside Holland through the thought of John Wesley in the eighteenth century (see Chapter 24).

There are many denominations today who look at the decisions of the Synod of Dort as authoritative or otherwise take Calvinist or Reformed (which are often used interchangeably now) theology as their heritage. There was another branch of the Protestant Reformation, however, that sought a different path – one which undercut the tight relationship between the civil and ecclesiastical authorities which continued to mark the Lutheran and Reformed traditions of the sixteenth and early seventeenth centuries. We look next at these Radical Reformers.

SUMMARY OF MAIN POINTS

1   Zwingli disagreed with Luther on the Eucharist and developed an understanding of God influenced by his humanist education.
2   Calvin became the greatest articulator of the Reformed doctrines, interpreting Scripture to be fully supportive of them.
3   Beza was influential in developing the stricter supralapsarian version of Calvinism; Arminius considered himself Reformed but objected to Calvinist doctrines.
4   The Arminian Remonstrance of 1610 was condemned by the Synod of Dort, which identified the "Five Points" of Calvinism.

FOR FURTHER READING

Carl Bangs, *Arminius: A Study in the Dutch Reformation* (Nashville, TN: Abingdon Press, 1971). The classic biography of the life of Jacob Arminius.

John Calvin, *Institutes of the Christian Religion*, Henry Beveridge, trans. (Grand Rapids, MI: Eerdmans, 1975). A large, two-volume work that set the tone for the Reformed tradition.

Roger Olson, *The Story of Christian Theology* (Downers Grove, IL: Intervarsity Press, 1999). A very readable one-volume history of theology that gives a more balanced treatment of the Reformation period than most.

Ulrich Zwingli, *On Providence and Other Essays*, Samuel Macauley Jackson and Clarence Nevin Heller, eds. (Durham, NC: Labyrinth Press, 1983). Contains most of Zwingli's important papers.

21

Protesting against the Protestants

Anabaptism and the Radical Reformation

QUESTIONS TO BE ADDRESSED IN THIS CHAPTER

1   Who were the Anabaptists and where did the term "Anabaptist" come from?
2   What did the Anabaptists believe that was distinct from the Magisterial Reformers?
3   Who were important figures in the Anabaptist movement?
4   What were the other significant movements of the Radical Reformation?

It is common practice to divide the Protestant Reformation into two groups: the Magisterial Reformation and the Radical Reformation. Those Reformers we have discussed in the last few chapters fit into the former category, for they sought to utilize the support of the magistrates (public officials) and governing authorities to advance their reform movements. These Reformers worked with the secular state authorities to champion their own religious views and to expel those they deemed heretics.

There were other Protestants of the sixteenth century who didn't agree with the church/state views of the Magisterial Reformers. This latter group – the Radical Reformers, as they are often called – believed that there should be a separation of church and state. They didn't think it was right for the government to coerce individuals to affirm certain religious beliefs or engage in certain religious practices. Furthermore, they disagreed with a number of the Lutheran, Reformed, and Anglican (and Roman Catholic) doctrines, most notably their views of infant baptism.

The Radical Reformation (also called the Left Wing of the Reformation) can be divided into three categories: Anabaptists, spiritualists, and anti-trinitarian rationalists. With a few exceptions, the latter two groups are typically understood to have strayed outside the bounds of orthodox Christian thought, so emphasis here will be placed on the Anabaptists.

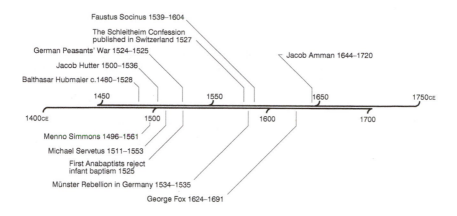

Faustus Socinus 1539–1604

The Schleitheim Confession
published in Switzerland 1527

German Peasants' War 1524–1525

Jacob Hutter 1500–1536

Balthasar Hubmaier c.1480–1528

Jacob Amman 1644–1720

1450   1550   1650   1750ce

1400ce   1500   1600   1700

Menno Simmons 1496–1561

Michael Servetus 1511–1553

First Anabaptists reject
infant baptism 1525

Münster Rebellion in Germany 1534–1535

George Fox 1624–1691

Timeline 21 Protesting against the Protestants

1 ORIGINS OF ANABAPTISM

One of the most important sacraments, or rites, in the history of Christianity is baptism. The New Testament describes Jesus himself being baptized by John the Baptist, and in the Great Commission, where Jesus offers his final words to his disciples, he says this:

> All authority in heaven and on earth has been given to me. Go therefore and make disciples of all nations, *baptizing* them in the name of the Father and the Son and the Holy Spirit, and teaching them to obey everything I have commanded you.
>
> (Matthew 28:18–20, italics added)

This practice has been continued by Christians down through the centuries. So what is the significance of baptism? Why should a person be baptized, and when?

Historically, Christian baptism has been practiced as an initiation rite into the Christian Church. It signifies a washing, or cleansing, of the individual from sin and an ushering into the body of faith. In Catholicism, baptism holds special sacramental significance and is distinguished from the other sacraments in that through it one finds regeneration – "baptismal regeneration." As the Roman Catholic catechism puts it: "Baptism is the sacrament of regeneration by water in the word."[1] Most Protestants, too, have always considered baptism to be of fundamental importance. But in the Reformation era a number of Protestants disagreed with the Catholic view of baptism, both its meaning and those for whom it is intended. A brief history of the matter here might be helpful in understanding the disagreement.

In the first two centuries of the Common Era it was the norm for Christian adults to be baptized. It is unclear whether children were baptized, but infants were probably not included in the rite. While all unambiguous references to persons being baptized in the Bible refer to adults, the Bible is not definitive about whether only adults can be baptized. There are, for example, biblical references to a "household" being baptized (Acts 16:15), but it does not mention children specifically. Even if there were children in the house, the term "household" could well have meant only the adults (parents, grandparents, servants, etc.). In addition, the earliest extra-biblical Christian source on baptism – the *Didache* (c. 100) – requires that the person being baptized should fast, thus perhaps implying that it is for adults rather than small children.[2] Toward the end of the second century a debate arose among Christians about infant baptism, and Tertullian briefly addressed the issue in his book, *On Baptism*, where he suggested that baptism is not something to be rushed into: "According to the circumstances and disposition, and even age, of each individual, the delay of baptism is preferable; principally, however, in the case of little children."[3] However, by the middle of the third century, infant baptism had become a common practice.[4] It continued to be widely performed by Christians, and by the time of the Protestant Reformation it was virtually a universal practice.

But here is where problems emerged. As noted in previous chapters, Protestant leaders such as Luther, Zwingli, and Calvin affirmed *sola fide* – "faith alone." Some of Zwingli's followers in Zurich, called the Swiss Brethren, believed that the baptism of infants was in contradiction to this Reformation credo. The Brethren, led by Conrad Grebel (c. 1498–1526), maintained that baptism is a sign signifying one's personal commitment to faith in Christ, not a means of regeneration or coming to faith. Grebel and others had conversion experiences as adults – experiences they took to be regenerative (being born again), as described in the New Testament book of John. Since small infants are unable to have a faith of their own, unable to make that kind of decision for God, they believed such infants should not be baptized. On the Brethren view, baptism taught by the

Catholics and the Magisterial Reformers was a magical practice, and as such needed to be purged from the Church.

These Radical Reformers, with Luther and Calvin, also affirmed *sola scriptura* – "the Bible alone." But as the Swiss Reformers searched the Bible, they didn't find infant baptism anywhere in its pages. So despite its lengthy role and widespread practice in Christian tradition, these Reformers in the sixteenth century maintained that infant baptism was unbiblical, theologically suspect, and even spiritually deceptive and harmful. Only adult baptism, or what they called "believer's baptism," was a legitimate form of the practice on their view. So after careful consideration, study, and prayer, in 1525 several Swiss Christians baptized themselves. Hence they were called "Anabaptists," which literally means rebaptism. This was no small matter, for it was understood by the authorities of church and state (both Catholics and Reformed) to be an act of heresy and sedition. For all intents and purposes, this event marked the birth of the Anabaptist movement.[5]

Swiss Anabaptist belief was then ratified in 1527 in the Schleitheim Confession – a published document which offered seven declarations of Anabaptist belief. One of its declarations was that baptism is to be administered only to those who have consciously repented and believed that Christ died for their sins. The Anabaptist movement quickly spread throughout Switzerland, Germany, Austria, and Holland as these young firebrands spread their message of the need for repentance and faith before baptism. Thousands of people, both Catholics and Protestants, became convinced of the necessity of believer's baptism and joined the fledgling Anabaptist movement. As we will see below, this was a Radical move with revolutionary ramifications regarding one's understanding of what it means to be a Christian, and even for social order.

2 ANABAPTIST BELIEFS AND PRACTICES

The Anabaptists experienced dreadful persecution for their beliefs and their practice of believer's baptism. They were tortured on the rack; they were executed by being burned at the stake, drowned, strangled, and thrown from cliffs. The consensus of thought on the historical development of Anabaptist belief and practice has undergone an important shift over the last half-century or so. From Luther until the mid-twentieth century, the reigning opinion was that Anabaptism began with certain social revolutionaries in Germany – most notably the Zwickau prophets and Thomas Müntzer (*c.* 1489–1525). This would at least partly explain their persecution; they were dangerous Radicals attempting social revolution, so their movement needed to be squelched.

Recent research, however, has demonstrated that these German revolutionaries had little, if any, influence on Anabaptist thought. It is now believed that there were a number of Reformation and evangelical impulses involved in the development of early Anabaptism. Given their Protestant belief that it is the right of every Christian to interpret the Bible as he or she understands it (since the Bible is the final authority for matters of faith and practice), a number of Anabaptist groups emerged. This makes it difficult to glean a set of beliefs that all and only Anabaptists affirmed. Nevertheless, there are several beliefs and practices that were (and are) held by virtually all Anabaptists. Besides the point just noted about the Bible as the final arbiter, there are three other themes which were central to the early Anabaptist movement that we will focus on here: believer's baptism; a personal, devoted relationship with Christ; and the communal nature of Christian life.

The Zwickau prophets were a small band of Radical Reformers in Saxony who claimed to be directly led by the Spirit of God. They disparaged the written word and professional ministry and rejected the Catholic view of the sacraments, including infant baptism. They also envisaged the overthrow of the existing social order and predicted the immanent return of Christ. In 1521 they moved to Wittenberg to propagate their ideas, but were fiercely opposed by Martin Luther. Within twelve months Luther had them banished from Wittenberg, and they dissolved soon thereafter.

Thomas Müntzer, a Reformed pastor and former student of Luther, claimed to be directed by the Spirit of God to lead a violent revolution. He became one of the leaders of the German Peasants' War, and in 1525 he led thousands of peasants at the battle of Frankenhausen. Defeated, Müntzer was tortured and beheaded on 27 May 1525.

The Anabaptists objected to the "rebaptizers" label; they denied that they were rebaptizing anyone. In their view, the believer's baptism was the first genuine baptism one could receive; infant baptism wasn't baptism at all. Balthasar Hubmaier (1480–1528; more on him below), an early Anabaptist leader, wrote the following description of baptism, which he believed more faithfully followed the biblical teaching on the matter:

> Baptism signifies not the putting away of the flesh but the certain knowledge of a good conscience toward God through the resurrection of Jesus Christ. ... From this every pious Christian sees and grasps that the one who wants to be baptized with water must beforehand have the certain knowledge of a good conscience toward God through the Word of God. That is, that he is certain and sure to have a gracious and favorable God through the resurrection of Christ. From that we still have the custom of asking at baptism: "Do you believe in God the Father, etc. and in Jesus Christ, etc. Do you believe in the forgiveness of sin, the resurrection of the body, and eternal life?" And he who wants to be baptized answers: "Yes."
>
> Then water baptism follows. Not that the same cleanses the souls but rather the "yes" of a good conscience toward God which preceded inwardly in faith.
>
> For that reason water baptism is called a baptism *in remissionem peccatorum*, Acts 2:38, that is, in forgiveness of sins. It is not that only through it or in it sin is forgiven, but by the power of the internal "Yes" in the heart, which the person proclaims publicly in the reception of water baptism, that he believes and is already sure in his heart of the remission of sins through Jesus Christ.
>
> (Balthasar Hubmeier, "On the Christian Baptism of Believers"[6])

In infant baptism there is no "'yes' of a good conscience toward God," so it should not be practiced. Only those persons of sufficient age and ability to make an informed decision about following God should be baptized.

This view of believer's baptism was radical, for it meant for all intents and purposes that all of those Catholics and Reformers who had been baptized as children were not really baptized after all! This had two significant results. First, it was impossible to distinguish between true Christians and false ones since both had been baptized as infants. Second, it meant that the Catholic and Reformed Churches were not truly Christian Churches. Christendom, rather than being the bride of Christ, had become simply an arm of the state. For Balthasar Hubmaier and the other Anabaptists, this was unacceptable. Becoming a part of the true Church – the *ecclesia* (those called out) – should not be (and literally could not be) imposed on someone by church and governmental authorities. Being a follower of Christ and a member of his Church required a personal decision. Thus, for the Anabaptists, the need for personal repentance and faith was a fundamental aspect of being a Christian. Simply being baptized as a child didn't produce faith, nor did it ensure a life devoted to God and his righteousness.

This raises another major theme of Anabaptist belief and practice: the necessity of a personal, devoted relationship with God. Several points are in order here. First, regarding this notion of a personal relationship with God, the Anabaptists disagreed with the Lutheran and Reformed Protestants with respect to faith and human will. Contrary to the monergism of Luther and Calvin, the Anabaptists affirmed a synergism in which human wills cooperate with God's grace in their salvation. Hubmaier, for example, wrote a pointed defense of free will in which he takes issue with Luther's "bondage of the will."[7]

Second, this personal relationship with God meant a life of discipleship to Christ and his teachings – primarily as expounded in the Gospels. The Anabaptists rejected the Reformed distinction between justification and sanctification for, on the Anabaptist view, they are an indivisible continuum – both significant dimensions of the process of being conformed to the character of God. While they didn't teach spiritual perfectionism (that is a later development of Methodist thought), they did affirm that the life of a Christian was a life of discipleship. If you were not a devout Christian, you were not a Christian. Menno Simons (1496–1561; more on him below), another leader of the early Anabaptist movement, put the point this way:

> I declare, Did you ever in all your days read in the Scriptures that an orthodox, born-again Christian continued after repentance and conversion to be proud, avaricious, gluttonous, unchaste, greedy,

hateful, tyrannical, and idolatrous, and continued to live after base desires of the flesh? You must say No, must you not?[8]

Furthermore:

> they are the true congregation of Christ who are truly converted, who are born from above of God, who are of a regenerate mind by the operation of the Holy Spirit through the hearing of the divine Word, and have become the children of God, have entered into obedience to Him, and live unblamably in His holy commandments, and according to His holy will all their days, or from the moment of their call.[9]

This leads to a third major theme of Anabaptist thought and practice: the communal nature of Christian life. The Anabaptists took the New Testament to be the literal Word of God for faith and life. They were often called "Sermon on the Mount Christians" by both friends and enemies for their view that faith and life are inseparable. Consistent with the book of Acts, there was a strong emphasis on Christian community (see, for example, Acts 2, where it describes the Christians living together and having all things in common). Meeting in small groups for Bible study, prayer, and fellowship, the Anabaptists believed they were following the biblical practice of living in unity in Christian community.

In addition, they believed that the Christian community – the church – should be separate from the world, for the true Church consisted of regenerate believers devoted to Christ and his teachings, whereas the state (and the state church) consisted of believers and unbelievers. Most of the early Anabaptists would have no association with state churches and were adamant about a complete separation of church and state. (It is worth noting that while a separation of church and state seems an obvious notion in our day, in the sixteenth century it was indeed a radical idea.) Many of them were also devout pacifists. In Jesus's Sermon on the Mount, Jesus commands his followers to love their enemies (rather than kill them!). He describes turning the other cheek when someone strikes you (rather than striking them back). He talks about a kingdom of righteousness that his followers were to follow which goes far beyond even that of the Pharisees. The Anabaptists tried to live out these kingdom principles, and in their view this included not harming others, whether individuals or nations. War was not an option.

Because of these beliefs and practices, the Anabaptists were considered by both Catholics and Magisterial Reformers to be a threat to Christendom. The Anabaptists were attempting to redefine the religious and social boundaries of Christian Europe, and they would pay a great price, for they were persecuted – mercilessly so. Thousands were tortured, and many were executed, either burned at the stake, drowned, decapitated, or even thrown off cliffs onto sharp iron stakes. Their children were often passed

The **Mennonites**, named after Menno Simons (1496-1561), descended from the Swiss, German, and Dutch Anabaptists. In keeping with their spiritual heritage, they continue to emphasize believer's baptism, holiness of life as a basis for faith, and pacifism. But they represent a wide array of backgrounds and beliefs. Today the Mennonites are the largest group of Anabaptists, with about a million followers in 75 countries.

The **Amish** movement originated in Switzerland under the leadership of Jacob Amman (1644–1720) as a reform group within the Mennonites. In the early eighteenth century many Amish migrated to Pennsylvania, where a large number of them live today. They are perhaps best known for their simple living, plain attire, and their resistance to utilizing many of the conveniences of modern society. Their current membership is roughly 180,000.

The **Hutterites** were founded by Jacob Hutter (1500–1536). Hutter was a hat maker in northern Ireland who became the leader of an Anabaptist movement in Italy, Austria, and Moravia. He and his followers – the Hutterites – practiced believer's baptism, the communal ownership of property and goods, and nonviolence or pacifism. Hutter was tortured and burned at the stake in 1536. While the Hutterites were nearly extinct in the nineteenth century, their move to North America in the 1870s proved effective. Today they have roughly 50,000 followers, primarily centered in the Midwestern United States and Western Canada.

on to members of the "official" church. Nevertheless they persevered, and the more they were persecuted, the faster they multiplied.

Over time, disagreements emerged among some of the Anabaptist leadership, which led to offshoots of the movement including the Amish, the Hutterites, and the Mennonites. Yet the core Anabaptist beliefs and practices remain to this day in all their various streams: a rejection of infant baptism, personal holiness and devotion to Christ, church unity and community separated from the state, and for many, nonviolence and pacifism.

3 ANABAPTIST HEROES

As noted above, one of the early important figures in the Anabaptist movement was Balthasar Hubmaier (c. 1480–1528). Balthasar was born and raised in Friedberg, in the south of Germany. He studied theology at the University of Friedberg and then at the University of Ingolstadt, where he was trained in Catholic theology and received a doctorate in 1512. Four years later he became priest of a new cathedral in Regensburg in southern Germany. In 1521 he moved to a new parish in Waldshut – a small town on the Rhine River. As a trained scholar, active priest, and effective communicator, Balthasar was a highly influential apologist of the Catholic faith during the time when Luther was propounding his Reformation ideas in the north.

About the time he moved to Waldshut, however, he began studying the ideas of the Reformers, and in 1522 he converted to Protestantism. It appears that he studied the ideas of the Swiss Brethren, for he began to question the role of government in religious matters and certain theological issues, including infant baptism. The following year he met with Zwingli in Zurich and engaged in a disputation (a public dialogue/ debate) with him. It was during this event that he publicly abandoned infant baptism.

In 1525, on Easter Sunday in Waldshut, Balthasar baptized over 300 adults using a milk pail. Within a month after this event Zwingli published an attack on the Anabaptist's view of baptism, and Balthasar immediately replied with a treatise entitled "The Christian Baptism of Believers" – now recognized as a classic Anabaptist defense of believer's baptism – which was widely read in Switzerland and stirred quite a controversy.

In December, 1525, Austrian soldiers invaded Waldshut, and Balthasar fled to Zurich. There the city council, however, had him arrested. In prison, he requested a disputation on baptism, which was granted. About a dozen men were present for the disputation, including Zwingli and four men whom Balthasar requested be present. In his presentation, he quoted from none other than Zwingli himself, where he asserted that children should not be baptized until they had been instructed. Zwingli responded by saying that his words had been misunderstood. Balthasar, taken aback because Zwingli had earlier agreed that infant baptism had no biblical warrant, agreed to recant by the end of the disputation. He was invited to do so publicly the next day after Zwingli's sermon, but he changed his mind and when in front of the crowd uttered these words: "Oh what anguish and travail I have suffered this night over the statements which I have myself made. So I say here and now, I can and will not recant."[10] He went on to defend believer's baptism until Zwingli entered the other pulpit and quelled the event. Refusing to recant, Balthasar was thrown back into prison. He was tortured by being stretched on the rack and finally gave in to Zwingli's demands of recantation in writing. Disgraced, he left Zurich and traveled quietly to Nikolsburg in southern Moravia. The year was 1526.

While the recantation in Zurich was a disappointing time for Balthasar and the Anabaptists, it was followed by one of the most fruitful. Many Moravian Christians were open to his Anabaptist message, and it is estimated that some 6,000 adult believers were baptized in just one year between 1526 and 1527. Now experiencing much freedom in Moravia (but still a hunted man in Austria), Balthasar preached openly and wrote a number of books and treatises on a variety of subjects, including works on the Lord's Supper, free will, and the burning of heretics, as well as the believer's baptism.

Although the mandate of the Diet of Worms was relaxed at this time for those choosing to align with Luther, the Radical Reformers were still subject to arrest and persecution. In 1527 Balthasar was captured by Austrian authorities and taken prisoner to Vienna. He was tried for heresy, convicted, and tortured on the rack once again. This time, however, there was no recantation; he remained steadfast. Then, on March 10, 1528, he was taken to the public square and, with his wife exhorting him to remain resolute in his beliefs, burned at the stake. Three days later, his wife was drowned in the Danube River by the same authorities.

Figure 21.1 Dirk Willems. Courtesy of the Mennonite Church USA Historical Committee. This etching was created by Dutch Mennonite artist Jan Luiken for the Martyrs Mirror, specifically the second edition, published in 1685

The Anabaptists were persecuted mercilessly, and countless stories of heroism and nonviolence exist in the annals of Anabaptist history. Another Anabaptist martyr was Dirk Willems. Under the auspices of the Roman Catholic Church in Holland, where he lived, Dirk was placed in prison for his beliefs about baptism and awaited trial with the death sentence an inevitability. In the cold of winter he escaped from his prison cell and was pursued by a guard. After he crossed over a thinly frozen pond, the guard who followed him broke through the ice and fell into the frigid waters. In a typical act of Anabaptist love and compassion for enemies, Dirk turned back and rescued his pursuer. Upon being freed from the icy waters, the guard – under orders of the burgomaster (chief magistrate) who had appeared on the scene – immediately seized him and led him back to captivity. Soon thereafter, on May 16, 1569, Dirk Willems was tortured and burned at the stake for his Anabaptist convictions.[11]

Another towering figure in Anabaptist history is Menno Simons (1496–1561). While little is known of his early background, it seems that he was raised by his parents on a dairy farm in Witmarsum – a small town in the Dutch province of Friesland. He became a Catholic priest in 1524 but, as he describes himself, spent much of his time doing such "useless" things as playing cards and drinking. Even in his first year of the priesthood, he notes that he was troubled with certain Catholic doctrines, most notably at that time transubstantiation.

Sometime in the early 1530s Menno began to study the works of Zwingli and Calvin as well as some from the more Radical wing of the Reformation. In 1535 his brother Peter, who had joined the Anabaptist movement, was killed in a tragic battle often referred to as the Münster Rebellion – an event which had a profound impact on Menno.

Soon after the death of his brother, Menno broke from the Catholic Church and converted to Anabaptism. He was convinced, through his own study of the Bible, that his Anabaptist view of the sacraments, including baptism, was correct, but he had remained silent for some time. After the Münster tragedy, however, he believed that many Anabaptists were being misled by deceitful leaders, and he could keep silent no longer. He decided to publicly join the movement.

THE MÜNSTER REBELLION

From 1534 to 1535, the city of Münster, Germany, had become a haven for the Anabaptist movement. An attempt to create a theocracy in the city was made by a group of fanatical Anabaptists during this time who believed that Christ would soon return and that Münster was the New Jerusalem from which he would rule. They chased off the bishop, who was ruling the city, and set up their own prophet as ruler and king. When Christ's return didn't happen as prophesied, the prophet was killed in a battle and a new king was put in his place. After eighteen months, the city was besieged and many were killed in the battle. The king and two other leaders were executed and hung in cages on the spire of the church. These same cages (minus the skeletons) hang in Münster to this day.

Following the calamity at Münster, Menno assumed leadership of the Dutch Anabaptists. Early on he was allowed to freely preach his new beliefs in Holland and elsewhere. And preach he did. He says the following about his own activities during the first year of his conversion to Anabaptism:

> In consequence, I began in the name of the Lord to preach publicly from the pulpit the word of true repentance, to direct the people unto the narrow path and with the power of the Scriptures to reprove all sin and ungodliness, all idolatry and false worship, and to testify to the true worship, also baptism and the Lord's Supper according to the teaching of Christ. ... I also ... voluntarily forsook my good name, honor and reputation which I had among men and renounced all the abominations of Antichrist, mass, infant baptism and my unprofitable life, and willingly submitted to homelessness and poverty under the cross of my Lord Jesus Christ.[12]

Menno was quite persuasive in convincing others of his Anabaptist ideas, and though a devout pacifist, he was soon seen as a dangerous man by those opposed to Anabaptist ideas. Even Emperor Charles V became concerned about him and put out a warrant for his arrest. Menno went underground and continued to build Anabaptist congregations. He persisted in promoting his views of pacifism, believer's baptism, separation of the church from the world, and the need to follow a holy life – loving and serving even those who mistreated him. He died of natural causes in 1561.

While Menno Simons did not officially found the Mennonite Church (that was done in Zurich in 1525 by Conrad Grebel and others), it does bear his name – and for good reason. For he led the early movement during one of the most difficult times in Anabaptist history. His writings, message, and convictions, as well as his character, are to this day revered not only by Mennonites worldwide, but by Anabaptists of all persuasions.

4 OTHER MOVEMENTS IN THE RADICAL REFORMATION

While the Anabaptists were the most influential element of the Radical Reformation, there were other groups as well who are subsumed under this category. One of these groups was called the spiritualists.

Spiritualists

Beginning in the sixteenth century in Germany and Holland, the wing of the Radical Reformation denoted as "spiritualists" or "spiritualizers" or "spiritual reformers" emphasized the role of the Holy Spirit and inner illumination which took precedence over a literalist understanding of the Bible as a guide for their lives and for their reform program. They also tended to reject, or at least significantly downplay, the external forms and social aspects of the church, focusing on the invisible rather than the visible church.

One leading spiritualist, Caspar Schwenkfeld (c. 1490–1561), so emphasized the inner witness of the Spirit that he completely rejected the external practices of baptism and the Lord's Supper. Another, Sebastian Franck (1499–1542), rejected entirely the notion of the external church and instead maintained that the true Church of Jesus Christ was invisible and would remain so until the second coming of Christ. The spiritualist stream branched in different directions, including one form founded by George Fox (1624–1691) which arose in seventeenth-century England under the title Quakerism (see Chapter 22 for more on the Quakers).

Anti-trinitarian rationalists

Another group of Protestant Radicals was the anti-trinitarian rationalists. As their name implies, this group placed much weight on human reason as the source of ultimate authority, in addition to Scripture – often doing so against the church fathers, creeds, and tradition. They ended up rejecting fundamental aspects of traditional Christian thought, most notably the doctrine of the Trinity.

Michael Servetus (1511–1553) and Faustus Socinus (1539–1604) were leading figures of this movement. Servetus was a Spanish theologian, scientist, and humanist who developed a non-trinitarian theology, publishing *De trinitatis erroribus* ("On the Errors of the Trinity") using a pseudonym to avoid persecution. But his identity was later discovered and he was burned at the stake as a heretic under the auspices of the governing body in Geneva. Socinus was an Italian theologian and founder of the movement known as Socinianism, which denied the deity of Christ and understood the Atonement of Christ as an example for us rather than a satisfaction paid to God the Father. In the eighteenth century this rationalist form of Christianity evolved into Unitarianism – a denomination which to this day affirms that God is one person, not three.

Given the fact that many of these spiritualists and anti-trinitarian rationalists went beyond the bounds of what the Anabaptists took to be orthodox Christian faith, the Anabaptists typically found themselves closer theologically to the Magisterial Reformers than to them. But what makes all three of these groups unified under the rubric of the Radical Reformation is primarily their disdain for infant baptism and for the state's authority in matters of faith.

SUMMARY OF MAIN POINTS

1   The Anabaptists were a group of Protestant Reformers in the sixteenth century who were called "Anabaptists" because they were baptized again as adults – rejecting their infant baptism as unbiblical.

2   In contrast to the Roman Catholics and Magisterial Reformers, the Anabaptists held to believer's baptism and a freedom of religion from the state.

3   Balthasar Hubmaier and Menno Simons provided doctrinal and practical leadership to Anabaptist groups during times of intense persecution.

4   Besides the Anabaptists, two other major movements within the Radical Reformation were the spiritualists and the anti-trinitarian rationalists.

FOR FURTHER READING

Cornelius J. Dyck, *An Introduction to Mennonite History,* 3rd edition (Scottdale, PA: Herald Press, 1993). A recent and thorough account of Mennonite history.

William R. Estep, *The Anabaptist Story: An Introduction to Sixteenth Century Anabaptism*, 3rd edition (Grand Rapids, MI: Eerdmans, 1996). A standard introduction to the Anabaptists.

Walter Klassen, ed., *Anabaptism in Outline* (Scottdale, PA: Herald Press, 1981). A selection of primary Anabaptist sources on a number of theological issues.

George Hunston Williams, *The Radical Reformation,* 3rd edition (Kirksville, MO: Truman State University Press, 1992). An excellent and extensive history of the Anabaptists and other "Radical Reformers."

22

Reformation continues
The English and the Catholics

QUESTIONS TO BE ADDRESSED IN THIS CHAPTER

1   What was the English Reformation?
2   Who were the Puritans?
3   What were some of the primary and enduring offshoots of the Puritan movement?
4   What was the Catholic Counter-Reformation?

The reform movements in the Christianity of the fifteenth and sixteenth centuries were not limited to the Magisterial and Radical Reformations in Germany and Switzerland – far from it. There were also major reforms occurring in the Church of England, from which Anglicanism and the Puritans emerged. Key reforms were also occurring within the Roman Catholic Church, some in response to Protestant objections, some having nothing to do with the Protestant Reformation. Through these various reform movements, the Christian Church would advance throughout Europe, and it would be divided once again – fracturing into multiple denominations which would scatter throughout the Western world.

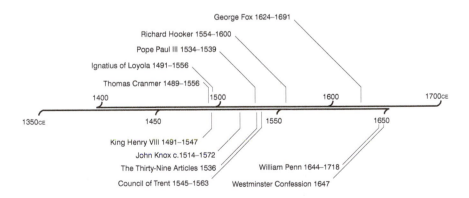

Timeline 22 Reformation continues

1 THE ENGLISH REFORMATION AND ANGLICANISM

England in the sixteenth century was marked by political and ecclesiastical turbulence and upheaval. In 1509 Henry VIII (1491–1547) became king of England, continuing the Tudor monarchy which lasted from 1485–1603. Henry VIII, unable to bear a son by his first wife, Catherine of Aragon, strongly desired a male heir to continue the monarchy after his death. He decided to divorce Catherine and marry his new-found love, Anne Boleyn, by whom he hoped to bear a son. But one problem loomed: the Catholic Church, of which he was a member, forbade divorce by canon law. Despite the fact that Henry was a devout Catholic who opposed the Protestant movement, through a series of events he ended up breaking with Rome in 1533, and took England with him.

Prior to England's break with Rome, the pope and other ecclesiastical authorities in Rome decided Church doctrine and law and appointed bishops. Church taxes in England also went to Rome. But after the separation, the monarch of England – Henry VIII, in this case – became "Supreme Head" of the Church of England, which became the new national church. Now doctrinal and legal disputes were handled by the king, and English Church revenue remained in England. It was still Catholic in form and practice (minus the pope) rather than Protestant, but it was through these unusual circumstances that the Protestant Reformation of England took root.

While the Church of England remained Catholic under Henry VIII, he went to work crafting a new ecclesiastical structure, excluding Rome entirely. He made Thomas Cranmer (1489–1556), Protestant theologian at Cambridge University, Archbishop of Canterbury. Cranmer supported Henry's decision to divorce and remarry, which he did soon thereafter. Unfortunately, Anne bore Henry no sons either, so through trumped up charges of high treason he had her executed and then remarried once again. Through this marriage with Jane Seymour, he finally received the son he longed for, whom he named Edward.

As archbishop, Thomas Cranmer worked diligently to "Protestantize" England as much as Henry VIII would allow. After Henry's death, his nine-year-old son became King Edward VI and reigned through a regency council. During this time there was even more openness to Protestant advances than under Henry. In September 1548, a commission was established to guide the development of a uniform order of service throughout the Church of England. From this commission emerged the Act of Uniformity (March 1549), which required all members of the Church to use a new worship manual: the Book of Common Prayer. This book, crafted by Cranmer, contained the morning and evening offices and the administration of the sacraments of Baptism and the Eucharist. The first edition of the Prayer Book (as it is often called) met with little favor as it was not Protestant enough for many English theologians, so in 1552 Cranmer wrote a second edition which reflected key ideas from Reformed theologians in Switzerland and Germany.

When Mary I succeeded to the throne in 1553 after her half-brother Edward's death, she basically put an end to the book's usage and brought about a temporary return to Roman Catholicism in the land during her five-year reign. As she restored England to the Church of Rome, she was merciless to Protestants. She had over three hundred of them put to death, including Thomas Cranmer, hence earning the title "Bloody Mary."[1] Other Protestant leaders fled to more friendly neighboring countries until Mary's death.

After Mary's death, her half-sister Elizabeth ascended to the throne and reigned from 1558–1603. Elizabeth, a Protestant, longed to unite the various factions of the English Church. Under what is known as the Elizabethan Religious Settlement, she pushed for a *via media* (middle way) between Protestantism and Catholicism. She assumed the title "Supreme Governor of the Church of England"; she had the Book of

The Book of Common Prayer is the book of prayers and services used since the sixteenth century in the Church of England with only minor revisions. It has gone through many editions, both in England where it originated and in other places where the various Churches of the Anglican Communion are active, including the Episcopal Church in the United States and elsewhere. It is widely recognized as a major work of English literature and its present use, both within and without churches of the Anglican Communion, includes over fifty countries in which it has been translated into more than 150 languages.[2]

WILLIAM TYNDALE

William Tyndale (c. 1492–1536), an English scholar and reformer, published two editions of his English New Testament – the first English translation to be based on the Greek text – thus making it available to the people in England in their own tongue. He was tried, found guilty of heresy, and martyred in 1536, but his work continued to be a significant force of the English Reformation.

Common Prayer revised once again, which all the Churches of England were compelled to use; and under her leadership a document entitled the "Thirty-Nine Articles" was written as a doctrinal statement, whereby it was mandated that all bishops and priests be in agreement with its teachings.

There was not enthusiastic support of the Thirty-Nine Articles, either by the Catholics (it was condemned by Rome) or by the Protestants (many considered it to be too Catholic). It wasn't long before schism erupted in the English Church as high-church and low-church groups each defended their own theological and ecclesiological viewpoints. Those among the low-church group wanted to follow the developments of Reformed Protestantism in Scotland – to remove bishops and other Catholic structures, practices, and teachings. Those among the high-church group wanted to keep the Catholic-style liturgy, church administration, and even some of the Catholic teachings. A split ensued; the low-church group became the Puritans, and the high-church group was known as the Anglicans.[3]

In Scotland, a clergyman named John Knox (c. 1514–1572) led the Protestant Reformation there. He was influenced by the Swiss Reformers, most notably John Calvin. He co-authored the *Scots Confession*, which was the confessional foundation of the Scottish Church, and a precursor to the Westminster Confession. But perhaps his most notable contribution to the history of Christianity was his view on polity and the right of dissent from a tyrannical government. This view was instrumental in ushering in a Presbyterian polity, first to Scotland and eventually to England and elsewhere.

The Thirty-Nine Articles, a revision of the Forty-Two Articles of 1553 crafted by Archbishop Cranmer, were established in 1563 and are the defining set of statements of Anglican doctrine, primarily with respect to the various controversies surrounding the English Reformation. They were intended to be conciliatory to both Catholics and Protestants, and as such do not provide a dogmatic definition of faith. Their statements are obviously vague in many places, allowing for a variety of interpretations. They do, however, explicitly reject the Roman Catholic doctrine of transubstantiation (XXVIII) and the sacrifice of the Mass (XXXI) and explicitly affirm the Reformed doctrines that Scripture is the final authority on salvation (XXX) and of justification by faith alone apart from works (XI–XIII). The Church of England still requires its priests/ministers to publicly affirm their faithfulness to these Articles.[4]

Back in England, while Thomas Cranmer is generally recognized as the central leader of the English Reformation, Richard Hooker (1554–1600) was undoubtedly the most significant theologian in the early development of Anglicanism. He wrote a number of works, including the influential *The Laws of Ecclesiastical Polity* in which he, in effect, replied to the Puritan challenge for a Reformation of English church government. The Puritans claimed that a truly Christian form of polity should be structured in a way similar to congregationally-run government manifested in Calvin's Geneva. Fundamental to Hooker's multi-volume reply was the notion of natural law which God has placed in creation. Laws of church and state, established properly, are derived from biblical revelation, tradition, reason, and experience. Both the Roman Catholic and the Puritan approaches, he argued, were flawed. What was needed was a *via media*.

When all was said and done, it was the middle way of Hooker's Anglicanism that won the day for Christianity in sixteenth-century England, and it has carried on – with smaller groups of Reformed Protestants and Roman Catholics co-existing – as the leading Christian

English body even to our own day. Today, the Church of England is the established church in England and the Mother Church of the worldwide Anglican Communion.[5]

2 THE PURITANS

Some of the Calvinist theologians and leaders in the Church of England believed that the Anglican reforms were not far-reaching enough. For them, there was too much capitulation to the Catholics, so they thought it necessary to purify the church even more. These Puritans, as they are called, wanted further reform in terms of doctrine, ecclesiology, and even personal piety. They desired to cleanse the church to make it more in line with what they took to be the biblical portrait of the early Christian church, maintaining that it should only include those things mentioned in the Bible itself. These Puritans believed that a number of practices in the English Church were unbiblical (or at least non-biblical) – including kneeling, wearing of vestments, and bishops' authority over other ministers – and therefore must be eliminated. They further believed that personal religious experience with God was fundamental for a minister and held that society should be a unified whole. It was their hope to model the English Church/government on the polity established in Scotland and Geneva (basically Christian Reformed commonwealths).

In the seventeenth century, religious and political conflict permeated the English landscape. In 1603 the Scottish king, James VI (1566–1625; known as King James I in England), succeeded to the throne in England as well. He attempted to unify the Church of England by bringing together scholars from a variety of perspectives to create a new translation of the

The "Golden Age" of Elizabethan literature, which included such authors as John Donne, Francis Bacon, and William Shakespeare, continued to flourish under King James I. The King James Bible is considered to be a masterpiece of English prose of this time. The translation was accomplished by several dozen scholars who were all members of the Church of England.

The Westminster Confession of Faith was a document commissioned by the English Parliament in Westminster Abbey for the purpose of reorganizing the Church of England along Puritan principles. Various positions of church government were represented, with Presbyterianism being the prevailing view. Regarding theological positions, however, there was uniform agreement on Reformed, Calvinistic theology.

Bible free of strong Calvinistic and Catholic influences. The final product was the King James Bible.

The political conflict under King Charles I (successor to King James) culminated in the English Civil War – an armed struggle between the king and Parliament. In 1649 Parliament executed the king, abolished the monarchy, and established the Commonwealth of England. It also organized the Westminster Assembly[6] (1643–1649) in an attempt to delineate and define religious faith. From this Assembly came the Westminster Confession of Faith which was never fully accepted by the Church of England yet became a fundamental statement of faith for Presbyterians in England and Scotland. Parliament and the Puritans did succeed, however, primarily through the leadership of Oliver Cromwell (1599–1658), in creating religious toleration for all Protestants throughout England. Nevertheless, after the death of Cromwell, the monarchy was restored by Charles II (ruled 1660–1685). The English Puritan heydays were over, but the doors to religious toleration and diversity had been opened.

3 PURITAN OFFSHOOTS: BAPTISTS AND QUAKERS

Some Puritans continued to work within the English Church, attempting reform from the inside. There were disagreements in the midst of this reform, primarily having to do with church governmental structure. The primary Anglican polity of sixteenth-century England was an episcopal state church. Those Puritans who wanted to keep this form were known

FORMS OF CHURCH GOVERNMENT IN THE SIXTEENTH CENTURY

One of the central debates in the sixteenth century involved church organization and authority. There were three primary positions which emerged.

- **Episcopal**: from the Greek term for "overseer" or "bishop," the episcopal form of church government is one in which bishops govern. Roman Catholics, Orthodox, and Anglicans all have episcopal polities, and they all maintain that their bishops are in direct succession of the New Testament apostles and so share in Christ's authority to govern the Church.
- **Presbyterian**: from the Greek term for "elder," the presbyterian form of church government is one in which a group of elected lay elders or presbyters govern. Presbyterian and Reformed Churches have presbyterian polities.
- **Congregational**: the congregational form of church government is one in which every local congregation is independent or ecclesiastically autonomous. Many Puritans have this form of polity, as do Baptists, Anabaptists, and in recent times many non-denominational churches.

as the *Low Church* wing of the Church of England. Other Puritans wanted to establish a Presbyterian or Congregationalist polity instead, and were referred to as Presbyterian Puritans and Congregational or Independent Puritans, respectively. There were still others who separated from the Church of England, seeing internal reform as beyond hope. These *Separatists*, as they were called, evolved into different denominations – primarily the Baptists and Quakers.

Baptists

One group of Separatists was strongly opposed to infant baptism. Like the Anabaptists in Switzerland, this group of "Baptists," as they came to be called, rejected baptismal regeneration and affirmed the believer's baptism.[7] They also believed in religious freedom and toleration. In 1609, Anglican minister John Smyth (c. 1570–c. 1612, often recognized as the founder of the Baptist denomination) and his friend Thomas Helwys took a group of followers to the Netherlands and began the General Baptist movement. They were called "General Baptists" due to their view of the "general atonement" in which the death of Christ makes salvation available to all who come to God by faith. They also believed that a person could "fall from grace," and so they were more in agreement with Arminian theology than with the Reformed theology of John Calvin.

Another group of Baptists emerged in England, however, which was more in line with Calvinistic thinking. These "Particular Baptists" adhered to the "particular atonement" view in which Christ died only for the elect. No particular individual is credited with founding this branch of the Baptist denomination, and it was illegal to be a Baptist in England when the movement first began. But by the end of the seventeenth century the Baptists had become a significant voice in England on matters of religious freedom. Both the General and the Particular Baptists had members who emigrated to America in the seventeenth century where they founded churches in the new colonies. There they began a rapid rate of expansion which continued for over two centuries.

While Baptists do not have a central governing body, and so have a wide range of theological viewpoints, there are several distinctive beliefs typically affirmed by most Baptist Churches. The following popular acronym, BAPTIST, delineates eight common core beliefs:

- **B**iblical authority – this is the *sola scriptura* position that the Bible alone is the final authority on all matters of faith and practice.
- **A**utonomy of the local church – each local church is an independent, self-governing body; church leadership and doctrine are decided by democratic vote within the local congregation.
- **P**riesthood of the believer – every Christian is a "priest" of God – one who is authorized to perform the sacred rites and who has immediate access to God and God's truth via revelation – and so no other mediator is needed between God and human beings.
- **T**wo ordinances – there are two official ordinances (rites) recognized by local Baptist Churches: (1) Believer's Baptism, a baptism for

professing believers by immersion in water, and (2) Communion or the Lord's Supper, which commemorates Christ's death.

- **I**ndividual soul liberty – every person, believer or unbeliever, should have the freedom of conscience to choose what he or she believes is right and true in the domain of religion.
- **S**eparation of Church and state – church and civil governments should be distinct and free from the control of the other.
- **T**wo offices of the church – there are only two official offices established in the Bible: pastor (which is synonymous with overseer, elder, and bishop) and deacon.

Today the Baptists are one of the largest Protestant denominations, numbering over 100 million in membership in over 200,000 congregations, and have established churches across the globe.

Quakers

In the mid-seventeenth century another Separatist or Non-conformist group emerged from the English Puritans known as the Religious Society of Friends, also called the Quakers (so named, as the story goes, due to the spiritual trembling and shaking which often occurred at prayer meetings). The Society was founded by George Fox (1624–1691) who in 1647 had a religious experience which changed his life. He came to believe that God could speak to any person directly, through what he called the "Inner Light." Unlike the Calvinist doctrine of total depravity in which a person needs to become born again to be open to God and God's guiding Spirit, Fox and his Friends (as they were often called) maintained that every human being has the voice of God within, and this voice can be heard if a person quiets herself and listens to the guiding presence.

This Inner Light was central to Quaker belief; it was so important, in fact, that all outward religious signs were abolished, including sacraments and ritual. They sought to live simple lives, to include women as eligible for all ministerial roles, and to emphasize peace and unity regardless of race, class, or sex. The Quakers stood strongly for religious freedom and became leaders in the anti-slavery movement in England. They refused to participate in wars or to swear oaths, and like the Anabaptists they were fiercely persecuted. The Friends movement spread quickly to Scotland, Ireland, and Wales.

Figure 22.1 George Fox. Courtesy of the Library of Congress

Perhaps the most well-known Quaker was William Penn (1644–1718), a close friend of Fox. Penn joined the Quakers at the age of twenty-two, and was forthrightly expelled from Christ Church, Oxford, for his religious views. He was also arrested on several occasions as the persecutions against the Society of Friends grew in intensity. The persecution became so severe, in fact, that Penn decided to found a new Quaker settlement in North America.

At first, however, the Puritans in New England were just as opposed to the Quakers as the Puritans back in England, and getting land to establish such a settlement was difficult. But fortune was on the side of the Friends, for King Charles II – who owed William's deceased father a hefty sum of money – granted him a large area of land close to New Jersey. Penn called it Sylvania, and King Charles changed it to Pennsylvania in honor of William's father. Because of the religious freedoms offered in the new colony, religious pilgrims from England, Germany and elsewhere – Quakers, Mennonites, Amish, and others – flocked there. The religious ideals established in Penn's Charter for his colony were to be influential in America's future; religious diversity and liberty had moved to the New World.

4 THE CATHOLIC COUNTER-REFORMATION

By the mid-sixteenth century, it seemed that Protestants were winning Europe north of the Alps. But as Protestantism was spreading, reform was occurring within the Roman Catholic Church as well; indeed, Catholic reforms had begun before the Protestant Reformation, with Catholic leaders such as Erasmus of Rotterdam working for internal reform. Many Catholic bishops and leaders of this time period believed that reform was much needed in the Church. The Protestant Reformation had also raised many theological and political questions, and on a number of issues there was no clear and officially stated delineation in Catholic dogmas (affirmations of official Church belief) between Catholic and Protestant beliefs. A new council was needed.

In general, we can identify three primary catalysts of the Catholic Reformation (or Counter-Reformation, as it is often called): the Council of Trent, the Inquisition, and the Society of Jesus.

Council of Trent

Early in the second decade of the sixteenth century there had been a growing consensus among leaders in the Catholic Church to take steps toward reform through a new council. But there was resistance to a general council, primarily due to disagreements between the Holy Roman Emperor, Charles V, and the Catholic popes. There is a long story to be told here, including political factors in which the emperor and the pope were vying for control of the council, but for the sake of brevity it can simply be noted that Charles and Pope Paul III ultimately agreed to initiate a general council of the Catholic Church.[8]

After much deliberation between Pope Paul and Charles, they agreed on a location of the council – a town in northern Italy called Trent. The Council of Trent lasted from 1545 to 1563, being interrupted by wars, plagues, and other internal debates and controversies. It consisted of hundreds of church leaders, including archbishops, bishops, abbots, cardinals, and other delegates who were given the task of reforming the customs and laws of the Catholic Church, dealing with theologically contentious issues raised by the Protestants, and working toward overall institutional and administrative reform.

The council established as dogma many standard Catholic issues of belief and practice, and it roundly rejected the Protestant doctrines of *sola fide*, *sola gratia*, and *sola scriptura*. Regarding the issue of justification, for example, the chairman of the council wrote that "the significance of this council in the theological sphere lies chiefly in the article on justification, in fact this is the most important item the council has to deal with."[9] Contrary to the Protestant mantra, *sola fide*, *sola gratia* ("faith alone, grace alone"), the council decreed that while God's grace is fundamental, so too is human effort; the latter should not be left out of the justification process. Indeed, unlike the Reformed view of justification as a forensic event – a kind of legal transaction of God toward an individual for the remission of sins and the imputation of righteousness – the council saw justification as a process closely associated with sanctification:

> This disposition or preparation is followed by *justification itself, which is not only a remission of sins but also the sanctification and renewal of the inward man* through the voluntary reception of the grace and gifts whereby an unjust man becomes a friend, that he may be an heir according to hope of life everlasting.[10] (italics added)

The Council went so far as to pronounce condemnations of contrary views on the matter, including the Protestant claim that a sinful person is justified by faith alone. Protestants understood this Catholic view of justification to be adding human works to salvation – a form of works righteousness – and so to be contradicting the Bible when it says "For by grace you have been saved through faith, and this is not your own doing; it is the gift of God – not the result of works, so that no one may boast" (Ephesians 2:8–9).

Regarding the Protestant view of *sola scriptura*, the council concluded that Church tradition should have an authority independent of Scripture. After all, the very earliest Christians had no New Testament, and yet they were able to keep orthodoxy advancing through the authority of tradition (oral or otherwise). In addition, as there are a number of liturgical practices in the Church believed to go back to the apostles themselves, why shouldn't such customs be continued, even if they are not mentioned in the Bible? "Scripture and tradition," as opposed to Scripture alone, was a clarion call of Trent. Furthermore, the council specified that the Latin Vulgate version of the Bible is the authentic one, and so officially adopted what are called the deuterocanonical books as legitimately belonging alongside the other thirty-nine books of the Old Testament (see Chapter 10 on the canon).[11] The Protestants thoroughly rejected these books as a part of the biblical canon since they are, as they called them, "Apocryphal" works.

The council also reaffirmed the basic theological and organizational positions of the Catholic Church, including its religious orders and the seven sacraments of Baptism, Confirmation, Eucharist, Penance, Anointing of the Sick, Holy Orders, and Matrimony. Other common Catholic observances which the Protestants opposed were also reaffirmed by the council, including the practice of indulgences and the veneration of saints, relics, and the Virgin Mary. At the same time, the council was also willing to admit that changes were needed and that some of the complaints leveled against the Church were valid and some practices needed to be modified or extricated from the Church, including the sale of indulgences for money.

The decisions of the Council of Trent were quite important for the history of Christian thought, for they became binding on all Catholics and continue to be so to this day. Trent articulated what Roman Catholics were and are to believe; to reject any of the council's decisions amounts to heresy.

Inquisition

The Catholic reforms instigated by Pope Paul III included not only the Council of Trent but also the Roman Inquisition, which was designed to purge false ideas and teachings. The Inquisition had originated in France in the thirteenth century in an attempt to deal with the Albigenses. It was established in Spain in the late 1400s in order to deal with heresy there, even going after devoted Catholic mystics, such as Teresa of Ávila. Then in 1542 Pope Paul established the Inquisition in Rome under the title "The Roman Congregation of the Holy Office of the Inquisition." Consisting of cardinals and other Church officials, its purpose was to defend the Catholic faith and examine and eradicate false teachings. It was used in Italy to suppress the growing Lutheran movement. Having named Luther and other Reformers at the Council of Trent as heretics and their beliefs anathematized, the Catholic Church went after all manner of "false teachers," and those found guilty were punished by harsh means, including imprisonment and even execution if they refused to recant. This Inquisition continued until its abolition in 1854.[12]

Society of Jesus

A related catalyst of the Catholic Counter-Reformation was the Society of Jesus, also known as the Jesuits. Its founder, Ignatius of Loyola (1491–1556), studied at Barcelona, Spain in the 1520s where for a brief period he was imprisoned by the Inquisition. He was cleared of charges, however, and continued his studies. He eventually earned the status "Master Ignatius" and gained a following. He shared with his followers

Figure 22.2 Ignatius of Loyola. French School, anonymous. Public domain/ Wikimedia Commons

his own ideas of attaining spiritual perfection, which he developed into a work entitled the *Spiritual Exercises*. He was ordained in 1537, and in 1540 Pope Paul III approved his fledgling society – the Society of Jesus – as a new religious order.

Ignatius was made the first Superior General, an elected position which lasted for life. The members of the society, referred to as the "Jesuits," served the pope as missionaries. To the traditional vows of chastity, poverty, and obedience, they added a fourth vow of express loyalty to the pope. Their mission under Ignatius was bold and twofold: convert non-Christians to Christian faith around the globe, and bring Protestant Europe back to Catholic faith.

The Jesuits were a dedicated lot. Through their personal, spiritual discipline and devotion they quickly gained the respect of Christian and non-Christian alike. Their influence was widespread, reaching four continents by the time of Ignatius's death and converting many to the Christian faith. They were also a powerful and effective tool for the Council of Trent and the Counter-Reformation, slowing the spread of Protestantism in Central Europe and France, and at times even reversing it.

Through articulating Catholic orthodoxy and reforming the Church hierarchy, the Council of Trent and the Catholic Counter-Reformation made great advances in countering the Protestant Reformers and in advancing Roman Catholic faith and practice. These events also marked the birth of the modern Roman Catholic Church.

5 CONCLUSION

By the end of the seventeenth century, the religious and political unity of Western Christendom was permanently destroyed. There was now a myriad of Christian Churches and denominations scattered throughout Europe, including Roman Catholics, Anglicans, Anabaptists, Puritans, Baptists, and Quakers. Delegates from each of these groups eventually traveled to America and became significant players in its own religious and political history.

SUMMARY OF MAIN POINTS

1   The Church of England initially separated from Roman Catholicism over purely political motives, but matters of religious dissent were also key factors in its eventual move toward a middle way between Protestant and Catholic faith and practice: Anglicanism.

2   The Puritans began as a group of Calvinists in the Church of England in the sixteenth century who believed that the Anglican reforms did not go far enough in purifying the Church in faith and practice.

3   The Baptists and the Quakers were two offshoots of the Puritans which have endured as their own traditions.

4   The Catholic Counter-Reformation was a series of theological and practical reforms which occurred in the Roman Catholic Church in the sixteenth century – some in response to Protestant Reformation challenges, others unrelated to Protestant ideas and critique.

FOR FURTHER READING

Book of Common Prayer (many editions).

A.G. Dickens, *The English Reformation*, 2nd edition (University Park, PA: Pennsylvania State University Press, 1991). A helpful overview of the English Reformation.

John H. Leith, ed., *Creeds of the Churches*, 3rd edition (Louisville, KY: John Knox Press, 1982). An excellent collection of important historical documents, including the Thirty-Nine Articles and the Creed of the Council of Trent.

Michael Mullett, *The Catholic Reformation* (New York: Routledge, 1999). A comprehensive history of the Counter-Reformation.

Part 5

Enlightenment and evolution

The Modern period 1700–2000 and beyond

23

The challenge of modernism

QUESTIONS TO BE ADDRESSED IN THIS CHAPTER

1   What effect did the religious wars of the seventeenth century have on Christian theology?
2   How did the scientific and philosophical revolutions influence the trajectory of Christian thought?
3   How did the deists develop religious thinking in this new climate?
4   What is the challenge that modernism posed to orthodox Christian thought?

The twentieth-century historian of science Edwin Burtt remarked in his *Metaphysical Foundations of Modern Science*, "It is the ultimate picture which an age forms of the nature of its world that is its most fundamental possession. It is the final controlling factor in all thinking whatever."[1] The picture that Europeans had of their world underwent incredible revision during the sixteenth and seventeenth centuries. There were many factors driving the change, including the widespread use of the printing press, the discovery of new "worlds" by sea-faring explorers, political reorganization and revolution, and the scientific and philosophical revolutions. These were at the same time causes and effects of the changes during this period of intellectual history we now call modernism, and they fundamentally shaped the world picture of the time.

There were geographical discoveries that had to be incorporated into the picture: it was realized that the regions around the Mediterranean were not the only centers of civilization in the world; there were highly developed cultures on the "bottom" of the globe as well (and the people there didn't fall off!); and rather than being the center and focal point of the universe, the earth itself turned out to be a medium-sized planet orbiting one of an unfathomable number of stars.

More subtle but no less impacting than geography was the shift in authority that occurred during these centuries. The Church lost its central position of authority in society. Science and philosophy were

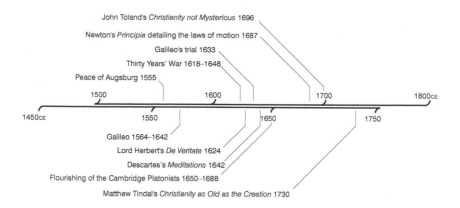

Timeline 23 The challenge of modernism

increasingly being pursued independently of the strictures of the Church, and these disciplines came to be treated with authority. But there was also a sense in which external authority itself came under suspicion. Individuals relied on reason and their own experience above what was handed down through institutional structures. Of course none of this happened overnight, but from the beginning of the sixteenth to the end of the seventeenth century, the change was remarkable.

So if Burtt is right, this new picture of the world should have had significant effects on all aspects of the thought of the time period. We'll see in the following chapters the different directions that Christian thought went in response to the new world view. The purpose of the present chapter is to show the development of that picture itself and the challenge it presents to traditional Christian thought in this time period known as modernism.

1 THE THIRTY YEARS' WAR

In 1555 Europe took a step toward the religious pluralism that would eventually dominate the scene. An Imperial Diet was convened in the city of Augsburg, and there it was conceded that the break of the Lutherans from the Catholic Church (occasioned less than 40 years earlier) was irreparable. Holy Roman Emperor Charles V saw himself as a loyal defender of the Catholic faith and so couldn't bring himself to be in attendance at the Diet. But needing to consolidate support of the German princes who were divided between Catholics and Lutherans, he allowed his brother Ferdinand I to broker the peace deal which culminated with the slogan, *cuius regio, eius religio* – "whose region, his religion." That is to say, the religion of any particular region would be determined by the local ruler. Of course at the time there was a rather restricted set of religious options to choose from: Catholicism or Lutheranism. But still, the overarching political body (the Holy Roman Empire) would not be dictating to the local rulers which of these they had to follow.

What the Peace of Augsburg did not do, however, was sever the ties between religious and political interests of the people. It is difficult for us to understand today just how tightly these two aspects of life were interwoven. Their separation was only effected by the long and bloody conflict from 1618–1648 known as the Thirty Years' War.

Two principal personalities brought to a boil the conflict that had been simmering for some time. First, Ferdinand II (grandson of Ferdinand I of the previous paragraph) was designated King of Bohemia and then elected as Holy Roman Emperor in 1618. As a staunch Catholic, he planned to consolidate the empire under Catholicism again. This led to revolt in Bohemia, which had been uncomfortable with its forced Catholicism ever since many there had followed Jan Hus in his attempts at Reformation in the fifteenth century (see Chapter 18). The revolt culminated in the Estates of Bohemia deposing Ferdinand as their king and replacing him with the second of the major players – Frederick V, a Calvinist and head of the Protestant Union which was committed to defending Protestantism militarily within the empire. Frederick's Calvinism challenged the Peace of Augsburg since Calvinism was not officially recognized, but more troublesome for the stability of the empire was the fact that his position gave Protestants a majority among those who elected the emperor. With such high stakes involved, it was inevitable that fighting would ensue.

A history of Christian thought need not include the gory details of the war and the atrocities that were committed in the name of religious allegiances; suffice it to say that the cemeteries of Europe are littered with the graves of Christians who were killed by other Christians. It is tempting for us now to interpret this conflict as being more about power than religion, but that betrays a modern viewpoint that religion can be separated off from other human activities and treated as a secondary social phenomenon. Perhaps today it is only the radical or fundamentalist sects which will fight and terrorize in the name of religion. But in the seventeenth century the main powers of "civilized" Europe were all embroiled in the conflict and condoned the brutal actions of their armies against even civilians and children – all the while believing themselves to be the best of Christians and acting on behalf of what they believed to be the one true version of Christianity.[2] Nothing else could have been expected, according to one commentator:

> The barbarity of the Thirty Years' War represents the logical conclusion of insisting that Christ's kingdom is indeed "of this world" (thereby rejecting a fundamental precept of Christ) and that Christianity was therefore a formula for ruling it.[3]

By the end of the war, Spain, France, Sweden, and the Netherlands had become involved in the conflict in the Holy Roman Empire. Of course more was at stake here than which version of Christianity could be practiced, but the religious motivations continued throughout. In 1648 when the Peace of Westphalia ended the war, Calvinism was added to Catholicism and Lutheranism as one of the religions from which local rulers might choose. This sounds like a feeble gain for the price paid, especially by the German people whose population was reduced by at least 25 percent by the war. But (perhaps ironically) there was also a new attitude which emerged among the populace as a result of the war: religious tolerance.

The Thirty Years' War was the last effort by Roman Catholicism to restore unity through political means. Had they succeeded, something like the powerful combination of emperor and pope that marked the Middle Ages and defined Christendom may have continued. But times had already changed too much for the Catholic Church to succeed at this.[4] The Peace of Westphalia guaranteed a new sort of society – a secular society in which religious confessions were of less interest to the political state. This is a significant factor leading to the modernist challenge to which Christian thought would have to respond – not least because tolerance has a way of leading to irrelevance. Did Christian thought matter any more?

Mirroring the displacement of the Church from its role in society, theology was also shifting out of the center of intellectual life. The breakdown of religious unity paved the way for people to shift their

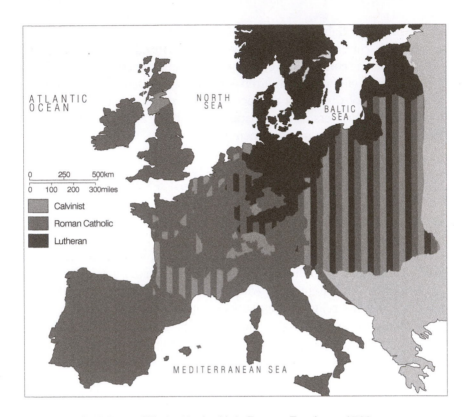

Map 23.1 Religious affiliation in the Holy Roman Empire *c.* 1560

allegiance away from theology as the authority on the way things are in the world (which, in turn, accelerated the breakdown of religious unity).

2 SCIENCE AND PHILOSOPHY APART FROM THE CHURCH

During the Thirty Years' War, the hegemony of the Catholic Church was under attack on another front besides the Protestant Reformation. In 1609 the Italian scientist Galileo Galilei (1564–1642) had heard about the invention of the telescope in Holland and made one for himself. The following year he pointed it at the heavens and made several discoveries which challenged the picture of the universe that the Church had held for centuries. First, the objects in the heavens were held to be perfect spheres, and Galileo's discovery of mountains and craters on the moon challenged this.[5] Next, he saw four moons which orbited Jupiter, undermining the belief that all celestial objects orbited the earth. Finally, the discovery that Venus displays phases similar to our moon was significant evidence that it circles the sun in an orbit inside the earth's orbit of the sun. With advances in the technology of the telescope, there was no denying the appearances of these phenomena, but the Church disputed the conclusions being drawn by Galileo. Why should we trust the data produced by a tube with lenses at each end when it contradicts the obvious evidences of our senses which were designed by God to give us the information we need about the world? It also contradicted the plain interpretation of Scripture on which the Church relied for its picture of the world. Galileo attempted to take a step toward separating off the authority of the Church from science by responding that the Bible tells us how to go to heaven, not how the heavens go.[6] The Church, however, was not ready to relinquish its authority. In 1633, under threat of excommunication, Galileo was forced to recant his positions and live the rest of his life in house arrest.

René Descartes (1596–1650) was a younger contemporary of Galileo and was deeply influenced by Galileo's scientific theories and by the Church's treatment of him. Descartes too was a Catholic and sought to remain in the Church's good graces even while pursuing the new science that was emerging and challenging the authority of the Church. He professed to be working in service to the Church, but one of the great ironies in the history of Christian thought was that in claiming to set the teachings of the Church on firmer footing, Descartes actually undermined those teachings. Descartes' true intentions remain a matter of scholarly debate.

In 1628 Descartes attended a meeting in Paris in which a French philosopher proposed a new philosophy that would supersede the Scholastic philosophies. Everyone gave the speech a rousing ovation except Descartes. When pressed for a reason for his response he said, "I praise the address, but do not praise the assembly because they allow themselves to be satisfied with what is only probable."[7] He was set, then, on a mission to develop a system that could defeat the skeptics and atheists once and for all by putting the claims of theology on firmer footing and so achieving certainty.

GALILEO'S FORCED RECANTATION

I, Galileo, son of the late Vincenzo Galilei, Florentine, aged seventy years, arraigned personally before this tribunal and kneeling before you, Most Eminent and Reverend Lord Cardinals Inquisitors-General against heretical pravity throughout the entire Christian commonwealth, having before my eyes and touching with my hands the Holy Gospels, swear that I have always believed, do believe, and by God's help will in the future believe all that is held, preached, and taught by the Holy catholic and apostolic Church. But, whereas – after an injunction had been judicially intimated to me by this Holy Office to the effect that I must altogether abandon the false opinion that the Sun is the center of the world and immovable and that the Earth is not the center of the world and moves and that I must not hold, defend, or teach in any way whatsoever, verbally or in writing, the said false doctrine, and after it had been notified to me that the said doctrine was contrary to Holy Scripture – I wrote and printed a book in which I discuss this new doctrine already condemned and adduce arguments of great cogency in its favor without presenting any solution of these, I have been pronounced by the Holy Office to be vehemently suspected of heresy, that is to say of having held and believed that the Sun is the center of the world and immovable and that the Earth is not the center and moves: Therefore, desiring to remove from the minds of your Eminences, and of all faithful Christians, this vehement suspicion justly conceived against me, with sincere heart and unfeigned faith I abjure, curse, and detest the aforesaid errors and heresies.[8]

Descartes' most enduring work is the *Meditations on First Philosophy* (1641). It is separated into six days and written as journal entries in which he works through the problem of knowing with certainty. The work is dedicated to the theology faculty of Paris, but in the dedicatory letter he says, "I have always thought that two issues – namely, God and the soul – are chief among those that ought to be demonstrated with the aid of philosophy rather than theology."[9] This is a significant step on the way to the problem modernity presents Christian theology. Theology and its methods are deemed insufficient for grounding our knowledge of God, and therefore Descartes looks to a different method.

Descartes famously aimed to purge himself of all the beliefs he had acquired that might possibly have been false, so he began with doubting all that could possibly (not just plausibly) be doubted. Most audaciously, he invoked the logical possibility that there could be some great but malign power (an evil genius or demon) which constantly deceived him so that any belief he formed was in fact wrong. This seemed to land him in complete skepticism until he realized that even if he was constantly deceived, he had to exist. Either some of his beliefs were true, or he was completely deceived. On either option, there was an awareness of his mental life that could not be eliminated. And so he utters the most famous words in philosophy, "I think, therefore I am."[10] With this claim he found a certain foundation for all knowledge in the realization that there could be no doubting that he experienced his own mental states in a way that was immune to doubt, and therefore he himself must exist as a center of consciousness. Thus the foundation of all certainty was located in the subjective psychological realm. As a result, reality was bifurcated

FROM DESCARTES' *MEDITATIONS*

Here I make my discovery: thought exists; it alone cannot be separated from me. I am; I exist – this is certain. But for how long? For as long as I am thinking; for perhaps it could also come to pass that if I were to cease all thinking I would then utterly cease to exist. At this time I admit nothing that is not necessarily true. I am therefore precisely nothing but a thinking thing; that is, a mind, or intellect, or understanding, or reason – words of whose meanings I was previously ignorant. Yet I am a true thing and am truly existing; but what kind of thing? I have said it already: a thinking thing.[11]

into two clear and distinct realms: the subjective realm of consciousness and the objective world that is external to one's consciousness. Descartes called the internal, mental realm of thoughts and feelings "mind"; the external world of trees and tables and bodies was called "matter."

According to Descartes, we can't be wrong that we experience various things in our inner mental lives. As such, there can be no doubt that we have various ideas in our minds about the external, material reality; but the question which launches modern epistemology is whether we can know if these ideas are accurate representations of the objects in the external world. Descartes claims to have answered this question by proving with mathematical certainty that God exists and that this God would not allow us to be deceived about our ideas if we think about them carefully. His answer to the problem was not accepted by later thinkers, but they were left with his question.

There are two implications of Descartes' project that are particularly relevant for the story we're telling here. First, Christian theism became philosophical theism. The centrality of the person and work of Christ was relegated to a non-essential and even overly restrictive component of theism. In fairness to Descartes, the process of defending Christian theology with reasoning that was devoid of anything specifically Christian was not unique to him. Leonard Lessius (1554–1623) and Marin Mersenne (1588–1648) were theologians and contemporaries of Descartes who had appropriated the work of Aquinas as purely philosophical arguments rather than seeing it as part of a larger theological system as Aquinas had intended.[12] Still, it was Descartes who was the epoch-defining figure and the one who influenced Christian thinkers into taking the idea of God – the god of the philosophers – as the object of Christian reflection rather than the Christian Trinity. In their Western European culture, which was still profoundly Christian, there was barely a mention of Christ in the seminal writings of modernism.

The second implication of Descartes' work for the future of Christian thought stems from his bifurcation of reality into two separate realms. The external world of matter could be treated mathematically and so became the object of scientific thinking. This new scientific methodology proved to be very fruitful, and by the end of the seventeenth century Isaac Newton had discovered the mathematics that brought together the heavens and the earth. The same sets of equations which describe the flight of a projectile in a parabola could be used to describe the elliptical orbits of planets around the sun. The precision with which Newton demonstrated his theories silenced those who still dissented from the heliocentric system on theological grounds. The Church's capacity to speak with authority about affairs in the external world was removed and replaced by science. The celestial realm was stripped of its unique status and incorporated into the terrestrial realm.

The dualism between heaven and earth was replaced with the new Cartesian dualism of mind and matter. There were many parts of life and experience which seemed recalcitrant to the mathematization of material bodies. Emotions, will, and even our experience of color were not able to be subsumed under scientific theories, so these were relegated to a secondary status. They were subjective features of our mental lives and couldn't be treated as objective facts of the "real" world. Descartes's dualism morphs into the fact-value distinction which became so firmly entrenched in the modern mind. The world that can be described by mathematical science and reasoned about is the world of facts. For example, two bodies are attracted to each other proportionally to their mass and inversely proportionally to the square of the distance between them. There are experiments that can be performed to confirm or disprove such claims, and their truth does not depend on subjective elements. Values, however, are subjective. They are not features of the external world, but are ways that individuals (or groups) experience and interpret the external world. On this understanding, values are not true or false any more than cultures are true or false.

Religious belief, then, has elements of fact and elements of value. Those elements which were able to be treated with reason were esteemed to be the part of religious belief that was worth saving. It seemed to many at the time that certain moral precepts could be arrived at through reason. It was unnecessary, then, to depend on revelation, which seemed to belong to the value realm. This shift had an enormous effect on the religious thought that was developing in the centuries after the Reformation. Given this trajectory, the most natural development in thinking about God was deism.

3 DEISM

Popularly, deism is often termed the "clockmaker" theology and posits God as the supreme engineer who constructed a mechanical system, wound it up, and now stands back and watches it go. While such a picture seems to fit well with the scientific and industrial revolution, there is very little in the Christian writing of the time period to substantiate the common usage of the term today. Deism as classically understood has less to do with God's approach to the world than it does with people's approach to believing in and understanding God. The term "deist" first comes into wider usage with the publication of Pierre Bayle's *Dictionary* at the end of the seventeenth century. In it the coinage of the term is attributed to Pierre Viret (1511–1571), a follower of Calvin, who described deists as those who believe in God on the grounds of reason, but reject the divinity of Christ and Christian revelation.[13] They still considered themselves Christians, but the distinctiveness of Christianity fell by the wayside as the deists attempted to transcend denominational strife and determine what religion might look like if it were founded entirely on the natural use of reason rather than on any sort of revelation.

Lord Herbert of Cherbury (1583–1648) is the first in line of the English deists when the term is understood as just defined. He typifies many of the thinkers of the age who were not professional academics. He was a soldier and an ambassador; he wrote history and poetry; and he was an accomplished player of the lute. His most influential work was his *De veritate* (On Truth) which was published in 1624. In it he developed a system or method of discovering truth which is based on the natural capacities or faculties of humans. By doing so, he determined the set of religious beliefs he thought all reasonable people should come to by application of their reason. These beliefs were called the "Five Articles" or "Common Notions of Religion" and can be summarized as follows:

1   There is a supreme God.
2   People have an obligation to worship this deity.
3   Worship is to be identified with a practical morality.
4   People must repent of sin and abandon it.
5   There will be rewards and punishments in the afterlife.

The Common Notions set the stage for further development of natural religion and allowed for people to profess belief in God (it was still a crime to admit to atheism in most countries) without having to take sides in the sectarian strife of the early seventeenth century.

Benjamin Whichcote (1609–1683) was one of the leaders of a group of Christian thinkers in Cambridge known as the Cambridge Platonists. They too were concerned to transcend the individual claims to revelation as the way to know God, and instead they professed to rely solely on reason. So strongly did they turn to reason, it became not just a substitute for revelation but almost the personification of God. Whichcote said, "To go against reason, is to go against God: it is the self same thing, to do that which the Reason of the Case doth require; and that which God Himself doth appoint: reason is the Divine Governor of Man's Life; it is the very Voice of God."[14]

We should note at this point that the emphasis on reason would be developed in two very different ways throughout the Modern period. With the stark bifurcation between reason and revelation which mirrored the fact-value distinction that Descartes helped to create, there were also those who attempted to use reason to establish the traditional picture of God that had been left in the value compartment. Of course this natural theology approach has roots going back at least to Aquinas, but there seemed to be a new urgency to start from completely natural premises about the world and reason to the existence and attributes of God. This impulse reached a high point in the natural theology of William Paley (1743–1805) and continues right to the present day in various forms of Christian apologetics.

That use of reason is very different, however, from the natural religion that developed out of the deistic impulses of the likes of Herbert and Whichcote. Their tendency was to accept that reason could not establish

NATURAL THEOLOGY

Natural theology uses reason to attempt to demonstrate the existence and attributes of God (typically through the traditional "proofs" like the Cosmological Argument or Teleological Argument) often as a supplement to revelation. Natural religion denies that reason can prove most of what is accepted in traditional Christian theology and asserts that religion should confine itself only to what reason can prove.

the traditional concept of God (and especially of Christ as the divine Son of God), and that this was so much the worse for that traditional picture. Reason demanded that religion be developed in a different direction than the irrational varieties of revealed religion. John Toland (1670–1722), an Irish critic of established and institutionalized Christianity, is most well-known for his 1696 book, *Christianity not Mysterious*. In it he claimed that all so-called revelation must be submitted to the bar of reason. There are no genuine mysteries in Christian dogma because anything that cannot be understood by reason must be regarded as gibberish. He believed that Christianity should come to be seen as a form of the universal natural religion which is available to all who will exercise their intellects.

In Toland's wake we find the Englishman Matthew Tindal (1657–1733) who wrote the work that came to be referred to as the Deists' Bible: *Christianity as Old as the Creation* (published in 1730). Tindal claimed that reason tells us everything that God could require of us, and therefore Christianity becomes nothing more than a sort of rational system of ethical dictates. These ethical dictates point no further than to the achievement of our own good. He said, "Nothing can be a part of the divine Law, but what tends to promote the common Interest, and mutual Happiness of his rational Creatures; and every thing that does so, must be a part of it."[15] Understood as such, religion no longer has anything to say about God or our duty toward God. The natural trajectory for this type of thinking, then, is atheism. If religion is really about a system of ethics, if all we need to know about ethics is discoverable through reason, and if all our system of ethics aims at is human flourishing, then what is the point of God?

4 THE CHALLENGE OF MODERNISM

In the line of thinking we've been tracing through the Modern period, reason has become the focal point for human understanding. This has a couple of profound implications for Christian thought. First, the world had proved to be an ordered place where things happen according to laws that are discoverable by humans through application of reason (along with experimental observation). If miracles are taken to be an exception to this regular order, they would actually inhibit our ability to discern what we must know to live happily in the world. Furthermore, the acceptance of miracles would make God to be capricious. So the miraculous is deemphasized in modern thought.

Of even greater import for the traditional understanding of Christian theism is that the emphasis on grace which so typifies the Reformation period is largely lost. God endowed humans with reason and expected them to use it not only to discover things about the natural world, but also about their moral duties. Perhaps this attitude is a reaction to the highly charged and intricate doctrinal debates of the sixteenth and seventeenth centuries over grace, free will, and predestination; moderns hunger for a more theologically streamlined system.[16] At any rate, God has much less to do in modern thinking.

Once the Thirty Years' War drove theology out of the central place it occupied in life, it had to be forced into one of the realms that Descartes' project helped to created. But there was a dilemma. If it went into the subjective realm of values in order to account for the vast differences in personal conviction that came out of the Reformation, then there would no longer be any point in talking about theological truth; but if it went into the objective realm of fact, it seemed that the inner logic of modern Christian theism quickly became deism, which pushed precariously close to atheism. This is the crisis or challenge that modernism creates for Christian thought. What are the alternatives? The next chapters of this section detail several different responses that were made in reaction to the challenge of modernism.

SUMMARY OF MAIN POINTS

1 The separation of Church and state encouraged religion to be placed in the private, subjective category of life and thought.
2 Reason replaced revelation as the foundation of theology, and so Christian theism became philosophical theism.
3 Deism was an attempt to develop a rational religion which ultimately had exemplary moral conduct as its aim.
4 The commitments of modernism seem to force Christian thinking into subjectivity or atheism.

FOR FURTHER READING

Michael Buckley, *At the Origins of Modern Atheism* (New Haven, CT: Yale University Press, 1987). An extensive study of the pivotal points in Christian thought which allowed atheism to become the default worldview of intellectuals in Europe.

Edwin A. Burtt, *The Metaphysical Foundations of Modern Science* (Atlantic Highlands, NJ: Humanities Press, 1992). A classic description of the interplay between philosophy, religion, and science during the Modern period.

James M. Byrne, *Religion and the Enlightenment: From Descartes to Kant* (Louisville, KY: Westminster John Knox, 1997).

René Descartes, *Meditations on First Philosophy* (many editions). The most enduring work of the father of modern philosophy.

Charles Taylor, *A Secular Age* (Cambridge, MA: Harvard University Press, 2007). A sweeping chronicle of intellectual history which charts the transition from religious society to secular society.

24

Pietism and revivalism

QUESTIONS TO BE ADDRESSED IN THIS CHAPTER

1   What theological development in seventeenth century German Lutheranism sparked a major Protestant renewal movement?
2   How did a revivalist movement in Oxford University and the Church of England give birth to a separate religious group called the Methodists?
3   Who was Jonathan Edwards, and what events did he foster which spread throughout the American colonies in the eighteenth century to change the face of colonial Christianity?

In the last chapter we saw that modernism – with its emphasis on reason and the scientific method – created a crisis in Christian thought. The Protestant Reformation had provided the needed avenue for the scientific revolution, and science had in some cases challenged or even disproven certain long-held beliefs and assumptions of the Church. A deep respect for science and human reason began to replace faith and dogma, and the period of the late seventeenth/early eighteenth century exhibited a significant decline in religious interest and devotion. Sometimes the response to this crisis in Christianity is described as a head/heart split in which the deists emphasized reason and the revivalists emphasized

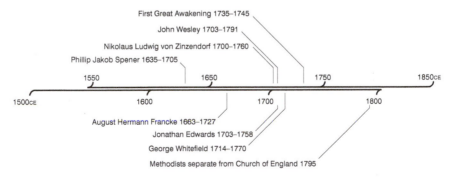

Timeline 24 Pietism and revivalism

emotion. As we'll see in the following chapters, this distinction is oversimplified and incomplete as a characterization of the response of Christian thinking to the modernist challenge. But there certainly was a response to the modernist challenge in terms of the heart and religious experience. This chapter explores three manifestations of this response.

1 THE PIETISTS

The rationalist ideals which were part and parcel of the scientific revolution had a significant impact on Protestant theology. The doctrine of faith that Luther had believed, practiced, and shouted from the rooftops began, for many Protestants in the seventeenth century, to become more of an academic program for discussion and debate. Faith was often intellectualized as Protestant theologians and pastors entered into a new form of medieval scholasticism. In Lutheran Germany this intellectualism was especially pronounced, and Pietism arose from within this milieu as a response to what some saw as a cold orthodoxy, moral laxity, and godless secularism. Several men stand out as important figures in a new Protestant movement of the heart: Phillip Jakob Spener, August Hermann Francke, and Nikolaus Ludwig von Zinzendorf.

Phillip Jakob Spener (1635–1705) was reared as a young boy under the tutelage of a pious countess who lived in a castle near his home. She schooled him in devotional works, including a book by Johann Arndt (1555–1621) entitled *True Christianity*. This book, which many historians consider to be the founding book of Pietism, focuses on the experience of an individual's new life in Christ and the need for genuine repentance of the heart.

Spener became a Lutheran pastor in Frankfurt in 1666. Several years later he organized private prayer meetings and Bible studies in homes, known as the *collegia pietatis* (assemblies of piety). Their purpose was not merely to help people grow in knowledge of the Bible; rather, they were designed from the start to be a means by which serious Christians could cultivate personal piety and devotion. Spener was more concerned with the proper feeling of the heart than with doctrinal purity, and focus on the heart he did. His groups later became known as the Pietists.

In 1675 Spener wrote a small work entitled *Pia Desideria* (*Pious Desires*) in which he critiqued the Lutheran state church and offered guidance for its reform. His teachings were condemned by the Lutheran church, though they were quite influential even in his own day. By the time of his death in 1705, Pietism had spread in Lutheran churches throughout Germany and Scandinavia.

He encouraged a friend, August Hermann Francke (1663-1727), to help him found the *collegium philobiblicum* ("group of Bible lovers") in 1686, and they devoted themselves to God and the study of the scriptures. Francke had studied as a Protestant scholastic and found it leading him to atheism. Through a religious experience (a "struggle of repentance"), however, he was transformed in his thinking about God and conversion, actually becoming certain of God's existence and his own salvation. In 1690 he cofounded the Pietist University of Halle and served there as a university professor while pastoring a church in a nearby town. He also founded several charitable institutions, including orphanages and missionary centers. Francke quickly gained prominence as a central leader of the Pietist movement and became widely known throughout Europe as a leading Protestant authority. He challenged the Lutheran (and Reformed and Catholic) idea that being baptized and believing Christian doctrines are enough for being assured of having real faith. One must also have had a genuine, heart-felt, born-again experience in order to be certain that he or she is a true Christian. This experience was central not only for conversion, but even for proper theological reflection. As he says: "What is to be looked for first of all and above all in a theological student is that his heart be right with God."[1]

A third major Pietist figure, Nikolaus Ludwig von Zinzendorf (1700–1760), born and reared by his grandmother, Henrietta von Gerstoff, a remarkably gifted, Pietist woman – was a child prodigy. He tended toward spiritual matters, writing poems and letters to Christ before he was ten years old. Given his talents and religious devotion, his grandmother's piety, and his close relationship with Jakob Spener (who was his godfather), it was all but fated that he would be an influential religious leader one day. He studied under Francke and was strongly influenced by his emphasis on personal piety.

In 1722 a group of Moravian Protestant refugees, fleeing persecution, founded Herrnhut (a municipality) on Zinzendorf's estate in Saxony. Five years later Zinzendorf became the leader of these Moravians, and in 1742 the Moravian Church was established with him at the helm. Central to the Moravians' teaching was a deep, emotional devotion to Christ and reverence for his sacrifice on the cross. Their devoutness was contagious to many, including the Englishman John Wesley.

Three themes of Pietism had lasting influence on Christian thought and practice: conversion as manifest in a heartfelt, inward experience; a focus on the Bible and its application to daily life and spiritual growth; and personal holiness, reflected both in one's inward thoughts and

Nikolaus Zinzendorf wrote over two thousand hymns. The following is entitled "Jesus, the Lord, our Righteousness," translated by John Wesley:

> JESUS, the Lord, our righteousness!
> Our beauty Thou, our glorious dress!
> Midst flaming worlds in this arrayed,
> With joy shall we lift up the head.
>
> Bold shall we stand in that great day,
> For who ought to our charge shall lay,
> While by Thy blood absolved we are
> From sin and guilt, from shame and fear?
>
> Thus Abraham, the friend of God,
> Thus all the saints redeemed with blood,
> Saviour of sinners, Thee proclaim,
> And all their boast is in Thy name.
>
> This spotless robe the same appears
> In new creation's endless years;
> No age can change its glorious hue;
> The robe of Christ is ever new.
>
> Till we behold Thee on Thy throne,
> In Thee we boast, in Thee alone,
> Our beauty this, our glorious dress,
> Jesus the Lord, our righteousness.

outward lifestyle. While Pietism began in Germany as a reform movement within Lutheranism, its tentacles spread far and wide in Protestantism, influencing Lutheranism and other denominations and even inspiring the formation of new ones, including Methodism.

2 JOHN WESLEY AND METHODISM

In eighteenth-century England, a third religious awakening followed on the heels of the Protestant Reformation (sixteenth century) and the Puritan movement (seventeenth century). As we saw earlier, the attempt by the Puritans to transform the Church of England's theology and polity into something akin to Geneva's Calvinism was ultimately unsuccessful. Instead of radical internal reform, it birthed new denominations. But there would be yet another attempt to reform the English Church from within. Indeed, just as Pietism emerged as a reform movement within Lutheranism, Methodism emerged as such a movement within Anglicanism. The Methodists, who rocked England's spiritual moorings in the eighteenth century, developed out of a small band of devoted students at Oxford University, and their story begins with the central figure and founder, John Wesley.

John Wesley (1703–1791) was born to Samuel Wesley, an Anglican clergyman, and Susanna Wesley, daughter of a Nonconformist minister. Reverend Samuel and Susanna had nineteen children, ten of whom survived infancy. Two among them became historically significant: John and Charles.

As a young child, John was educated by his parents, primarily his mother (as was the custom in eighteenth-century England). Susanna taught him reading, writing, and arithmetic, but her instruction went far beyond the fundamentals of a typical education of the day. It also included in-depth spiritual instruction and practices such as daily prayers, Bible stories, and regular service to others. A remarkable and intelligent woman, every week Susanna devoted specific time of religious instruction to each child individually, and she was spartan in her discipline and daily routine. She has been called the Mother of Methodism, for her rigid and methodical lifestyle was adopted by her sons as they developed and structured the new denomination.

At eleven years of age, John was sent off to Charter House School in London. When he was seventeen he went to university at Christ Church, Oxford. While studying there he was especially impressed with

CHARLES WESLEY

Charles Wesley (1707–1788), brother of John Wesley, attended Westminster School and Christ Church, Oxford. In 1735 he took holy orders in the Anglican Church so he could travel with John on a mission to the New World. After what he and John perceived to be a failure in the American colonies, they traveled together back to England. Soon after their return Charles and John had religious experiences that would transform their lives and ministry. Together they oversaw the Methodist revival which transformed England.

Charles was a powerful preacher, but he is most known for his more than 7,000 hymns which proved to be an effective force for advancing the fledgling Methodist movement. Among some of his most well-known hymns are "Hark the Herald Angels Sing," "Jesus, Lover of My Soul," "O for a Thousand Tongues to Sing," and "Christ the Lord is Ris'n Today." Many of his hymns continue to be included in hymnals across denominational lines around the world.

the writings of the church fathers and other classical devotional work – most notably Thomas á Kempis's *Imitation of Christ* and William Law's *A Serious Call to a Devout and Holy Life*. About the latter's writings Wesley said this:

> Mr. Law's *Christian Perfection* and *Serious Call* were put into my hands. These convinced me, more than ever, of the absolute impossibility of being half a Christian; and I determined, through his grace, (the absolute necessity of which I was deeply sensible of; [sic]) to be all-devoted to God, to give him all my soul, my body, and my substance.[2]

While at Oxford John joined a small group that his brother Charles and a few close friends, including George Whitefield, formed in response to the growing deism at the university. The purpose of the group was to study the Scriptures and encourage one another to live holy lives devoted to God. John soon became the group's leader, and each member agreed

GEORGE WHITEFIELD

George Whitefield (1714–1770) was a friend of John and Charles Wesley and a co-founder of the Holy Club. While he was a Calvinist theologically, he was also formative in the development of Methodism. His doctrinal differences with the Wesleys eventually led to a division in Methodism, with Whitefield and others forming the Calvinistic Methodist Association.

Whitefield became an astounding preacher in England and the American colonies and could hold large crowds (sometimes 20,000 or more) spellbound with his open-air sermons. He preached three and four times a day from the age of twenty-two until his death, traveling throughout England, Scotland, Ireland, and America. He was unyielding in his preaching; he preached more than 18,000 sermons over the course of his life, averaging over 500 a year! His tireless efforts provided astounding dividends, especially in America, for he ushered in a spiritual revival in the colonies equivalent to the Methodist revival in England and Ireland.

to follow certain rigid spiritual practices and to engage in regular social action, including frequent visitations to the sick and preaching to the incarcerated. The group was called the "holy club," and because of their methodological approach to spiritual life and personal holiness, they became known as "Methodists."

In 1728 John was ordained a priest in the Church of England. In 1735 he and Charles were invited to serve God and put their Holy Club ideas into practice on a grand scale in the new colony of Georgia. Charles would be secretary to General James Oglethorpe – leader of the colony – and John would be the colony's chaplain. Excited to preach to the Indians and reach a new world with the gospel, they took the offer. Their short stay in the colonies (less than two years), however, proved to be a fiasco. First, John's attempt to impose some of his views on the colonists was met with contempt. Then he found himself embroiled in a love affair with

Figure 24.1 John Wesley. Frank O. Salisbury / Public domain / Wikimedia Commons

one Sophy Hopkey. When Sophy eloped with another man, John ended up in a legal battle with Sophy's husband over defamation of character (it seems that John barred her from Holy Communion, an act which she and her husband did not much appreciate). Confused, frustrated, and embarrassed after six months of legal battles, John returned to England with his brother.

John had been a deeply religious person most all his life, but the Georgia experience left him questioning his own faith and direction. However, not long after his return to England he met with a Moravian named Peter Bohler, and he visited the Moravians at Herrnhut, Germany. The Moravian brethren challenged him with a new understanding of the essence of true Christianity: true faith comes about through new birth, and this is an individual experience that happens to a person in such a way that one is filled with assurance. Something did indeed happen to John soon after this, for on May 24, 1738, John had an experience which would change his life forever. He was attending a prayer meeting (called a "society")[3] when he had a deeply moving religious experience. He describes it this way in his journal:

> In the evening I went very unwillingly to a society in Aldersgate Street,
> where one was reading Luther's preface to the Epistle to the Romans.
> About a quarter before nine, while he was describing the change which
> God works in the heart through faith in Christ, I felt my heart strangely
> warmed. I felt I did trust in Christ, Christ alone, for my salvation; and
> an assurance was given me that he had taken away *my* sins, even
> *mine*, and saved *me* from the law of sin and death.[4]

Following this warming of his heart, John set out on a ministry of
preaching to and serving the common people across the British Isles. He
preached this gospel of forgiveness, assurance, and holiness, traveling
thousands of miles on horseback and preaching to crowds large and
small. He helped the unemployed devise ways of earning a living, cared
for the poor, denounced slavery, and advocated prison reform. John, his
brother Charles, and George Whitefield unleashed a revival in England
– one that became viral, spreading throughout England and elsewhere,
including the American colonies. By the time of his death Methodism had
become, in many ways against John's will, a flourishing denomination
unto itself, completely separated from the Church of England.

John's theological work was no doubt hindered by his relentless social
activism which precluded the time necessary to formulate a systematic
theology or to organize and publish a compendium of his theological
views. As we noted, Wesley was a fan of the church fathers, and he
undertook to ensure that his new movement reflected the theological
integrity and communal vigor of the early Christian Church. While
strongly influenced by the ideas and ideals of the Magisterial Reformers,
some of Wesley's theological positions were also at odds with them – and
in significant ways!

For one, while he affirmed the Reformed dogma, *sola scriptura*,
and believed that the Bible was the supreme authority of doctrine and
practice, he also agreed with the Anglican theologians that tradition
and reason are crucial in understanding and interpreting Scripture. And
he agreed with the Pietists and Moravians that personal experience is
central to fully grasping Christian faith and truth. These four sources of
theological understanding are now commonly referred to as the Wesleyan
Quadrilateral.[5]

Furthermore, while he affirmed the Reformed dogma, *sola gratia et
fides*, and maintained a robust understanding of an individual's desperate
need for God's prevenient grace, he also affirmed the Arminian emphasis

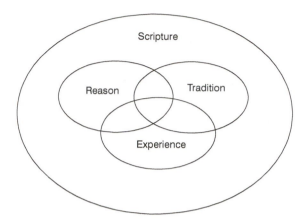

Figure 24.2 Wesleyan Quadrilateral

of the role of human will and responsibility in religious life.[6] He denied, even abhorred, the theological determinism and predestination of Luther, Zwingli, and Calvin, for he believed such views entailed certain negative and unbiblical conclusions with respect to good works and love for others.

> This uncomfortable doctrine [of Calvinistic predestination] directly tends to destroy our zeal for good works. And this it does, First, as it naturally tends (according to what was observed before) to destroy our love to the greater part of mankind, namely, the evil and unthankful. For whatever lessens our love, must so far lessen our desire to do them good. This it does, Secondly, as it cuts off one of the strongest motives to all acts of bodily mercy, such as feeding the hungry, clothing the naked, and the like – viz., the hope of saving their souls from death. For what avails it to relieve their temporal wants, who are just dropping into eternal fire?[7]

Another significant contribution by Wesley to the history of Christian thought and practice is his view of sanctification, in particular perfection via entire sanctification. Unlike the Protestant Reformers' view(s) of sanctification, most especially that of Martin Luther in which a person – even a mature Christian believer – is always both righteous and sinner (righteous in Christ and a sinner in himself) – Wesley believed one could, in principle at least, reach a state of entire sanctification, or Christian perfection.

There is much debate about what exactly Wesley meant by this. He did not mean sinless perfection, as he clarified in his book, *A Plain Account of Christian Perfection*. But this much seems clear. He maintained that a Christian could attain "perfection in love" – having one's heart set toward God and God's righteous laws and a freedom from impure intentions. This is not necessarily a permanent state one achieves. Nevertheless, there can be – no, there *should be* – real growth in a true Christian. And he recognized that this kind of spiritual advance would require a close examination of conscience and a life of methodic discipline in all spheres of life. It's also important to note that while he argued for the need for rigorous self-discipline and spiritual training, he taught that true Christianity was the most deeply satisfying way to live, and that such a life made the person truly happy and fulfilled.

For Wesley, the goal of Methodism was the spread of scriptural holiness throughout the land. In important respects his goal was achieved, for his emphasis on sanctification became a central trait of the Methodist movement, and historians have claimed that he was one of the leading social reformers of his century. Some scholars have even affirmed that his revolutionary work so impacted England that it prevented a bloody revolution similar to the French Revolution.[8] One thing is sure: John Wesley ushered in a spiritual revival in England which transcended England and the eighteenth century – a revival which emphasized a personal experience of conversion, continual sanctification, and zealous good works.

3 JONATHAN EDWARDS AND THE GREAT AWAKENING

On the American scene, things were heating up as well in the eighteenth century. As we saw in a previous chapter, a number of Puritans left England for the American colonies. Here they and other Christian "pilgrims" found refuge in various places on the Eastern seaboard, and their communities quickly grew and flourished. By the eighteenth century, the Puritan ideal of personal and corporate piety had lost much of its force. There is, no doubt, a number of reasons for this, including social and political independence (those on the frontier depended on themselves and rejected authoritarian control, including ecclesiastical hegemony), growing mercantilism (interest in making money can supersede even the most devout interest in religious matters!), and the developing sense of religious freedom and toleration. After several generations, these factors and others contributed to a radical decline in church membership throughout the colonies. It was in the midst of this waning, slumbering religious milieu that an awakening would emerge in the American colonies and set ablaze a great revival that spread throughout the land. A leading figure in this spiritual revival was a Puritan scholar and preacher, Jonathan Edwards.

Jonathan (1703–1758) was born and raised in the colony of Connecticut. He was a precocious child, learning Hebrew, Greek, and Latin in his early teens and graduating from what is today known as Yale University (where the curriculum at the time emphasized classical studies and strict adherence to orthodox Puritanism) at the top of his class. His father, Timothy Edwards, was a Puritan minister in East Windsor, Connecticut, who took very seriously both the call to ministry and the significance of education.

Jonathan graduated in 1720 and soon thereafter had a mystical religious experience often described as his conversion to faith in Christ:

> As I read the words [of the biblical passage of I Timothy 1:17], there came into my soul, and was as it were diffused through it, a sense of the glory of the Divine Being; a new sense, quite different from any thing I ever experienced before. Never any words of scripture seemed to me as these words did. I thought with myself, how excellent a Being that was, and how happy I should be, if I might enjoy that God, and be rapt up to him in heaven, and be as it were swallowed up in him for ever! I kept saying, and as it were singing, over these words of scripture to myself; and went to pray to God that I might enjoy him; and prayed in a manner quite different from what I used to do, with a new sort of affection. ... From about that time I began to have new kinds of apprehensions and ideas of Christ, and the work of redemption, and the glorious way of salvation by him.[9]

He went back to Yale in 1722 and studied divinity for two years, receiving the Master of Arts Degree. He took the position of tutor at Yale for two years and then became an assistant minister to his grandfather, the well-known Solomon Stoddard – "pope of the Connecticut valley" – at a church in Northampton. In 1729 Jonathan became the senior pastor there.

Edwards's sermons were meticulously manuscripted, based on reflective exegesis and careful study. He frequently preached on human sinfulness and the absolute dependence on God for salvation. His most well-known sermon, "Sinners in the Hands of an Angry God," includes the following famous lines:

> There is nothing that keeps wicked men at any one moment out of hell, but the mere pleasure of God. ... The God that holds you over the pit of hell, much as one holds a spider, or some loathsome insect over the fire, abhors you, and is dreadfully provoked: his wrath towards you burns like fire; he looks upon you as worthy of nothing else, but to be cast into the fire; he is of purer eyes than to bear to have you in his sight; you are ten thousand times more abominable in his eyes, than the most hateful venomous serpent is in ours. You have offended him infinitely more than ever a stubborn rebel did his prince; and yet it is nothing but his hand that holds you from falling into the fire every moment. It is to be ascribed to nothing else, that you did not go to hell the last night; that you were suffered to awake again in this world, after you closed your eyes to sleep. And there is no other reason to be given, why you have not dropped into hell since you arose in the morning, but that God's hand has held you up.[10]

Edwards's theology was influenced by Reformed and Puritan theologians and was strongly Calvinistic. While for John Wesley God's *love* was central to his theology, for Edwards it was God's *glory and sovereignty*. For Edwards, God is the absolute sovereign over all creation. Unlike the synergism of the Arminians (including Wesley), in which God works along with human free will to bring about their salvation, Edwards affirmed a Calvinistic monergism in which God, as sovereign, determines all things, including who is saved and who is not (see Chapter 20).

> *What God's sovereignty in the salvation of men implies.* In answer to this inquiry, I observe, it implies that God can either bestow salvation on any of the children of men, or refuse it, without any prejudice to the glory of any of his attributes, except where he has been pleased

to declare, that he will or will not bestow it. ... [C]oncerning some, God has been pleased to declare either that he will or that he will not bestow salvation on them; and thus to bind himself by his own promise. And concerning some he has been pleased to declare, that he never will bestow salvation upon them.[11]

On Edwards's view, human will is so deeply affected by the Fall and by human sin that it is totally depraved. This depravity of will, coupled with God's absolute sovereignty, entails a denial of human free will – at least a libertarian free will as affirmed by the Arminians (that is, a self-determining will that is able to freely choose good or evil). Edwards opposed the Arminians on this count, fearing that they were espousing heresy and theological inconsistency. For him, the only free will we human beings have is the freedom to do what we want.[12] But as depraved sinners, the only thing we ever want is evil. So how then can we ever choose the good? How can we ever decide to be saved? Only through divine election. God elects or foreordains some, unconditionally, for salvation. Others he does not. So much the worse for the latter.

While Edwards's sermons taught Calvinism through and through, and emphasized the point that there is nothing a person can do to earn God's favor or to move God to action to bring one to salvation (for salvation is ultimately in the hands of God), people responded in droves. As one wag noted, he literally "scared the hell" out of his congregants! Although his sermons are sometimes characterized as dry, sophisticated, exegetical lectures (and it seems they were), they were filled with both head and heart. His treatise, *Religious Affections*, suggested that true Christianity is the product of a redeemed heart, not a matter of intellect or will. He is recognized as a great theologian (some consider him the greatest American theologian), but he was also a revivalist to the core.

A revivalist movement had already started through the preaching of other ministers in the colonies in the 1730s, including powerhouse communicator George Whitefield. But Edwards was its most famous leader, and he was no doubt the one primarily responsible for the great revival in New England. In the midst of the revival he fostered, he describes the situation this way:

There was scarcely a single person in the town, old or young, left unconcerned about the great things of the eternal world. Those who were wont to be the vainest and loosest, and those who had been disposed to think and speak lightly of vital and experimental religion, were now generally subject to great awakenings. And the work of conversion was carried on in a most astonishing manner, and increased more and more; souls did as it were come by flocks to Jesus Christ.[13]

The periods of revival which occurred in the colonies between the late 1730s and 1740s are referred to as the Great Awakening, and they spread like wildfire – even across denomination lines.[14] It influenced the thinking of church-state relations; it challenged the authority of the clergy of established churches; it challenged people to live holy lives. Before the Great Awakening came to an end, the American colonies had been socially and religiously transformed.

Through the tireless efforts of the Pietists, John Wesley and the Methodists, and Jonathan Edwards and the Puritans, one branch of Christian thought took a radical turn in the eighteenth century. The impact on English and American Christianity was significant, for it rejuvenated Christian faith, it brought the heart back into religion, and, as we will soon see, it spawned Evangelicalism. But next we will explore another response to the rationalism of the eighteenth century: Romanticism.

SUMMARY OF MAIN POINTS

1   Pietist Lutherans – most notably Phillip Spener, August Francke, and Nikolaus Zinzendorf – began to focus more on the subjective experience of salvation than on its objective characteristics.

2   Several Oxford students experienced a religious awakening which, under the leadership of John Wesley, provided the basis for Methodist prayer meetings, classes, and eventually a separate denomination with thousands of members.

3   Through his preaching and convictions, Jonathan Edwards, a Puritan theologian and preacher, played a central role in ushering in the Great Awakening – a series of revivals in the colonies that brought about a renewed religious enthusiasm and personal conviction and had a lasting impact on American Christianity.

FOR FURTHER READING

Kenneth J. Collins, *The Theology of John Wesley: Holy Love and the Shape of Grace* (Nashville, TN: Abingdon Press, 2007). Helpfully organizes Wesley's views on a number of important themes.

A.C. Coulter, *John Wesley* (Oxford: Oxford University Press, 1980). An excellent representative selection of theological writings by Wesley.

Peter C. Erb, *The Pietists: Selected Writings* (Mahwah, NJ: Paulist Press, 1983). A rich collection of Pietist writings.

Thomas S. Kidd, *The Great Awakening: The Roots of Evangelical Christianity in Colonial America* (New Haven, CT: Yale University Press, 2007). An impressive and clearly written work on the Great Awakening and its influence on American Evangelicalism.

George M. Marsden, *Jonathan Edwards: A Life* (New Haven, CT: Yale University Press, 2003). A magisterial biography.

Harold Simonson, ed., *Selected Writings of Jonathan Edwards*, 2nd edition (Long Grove, IL: Waveland Press, 2004). A compilation of important essays, sermons, and other writings of Jonathan Edwards.

Romanticism's response to Enlightenment theology

QUESTIONS TO BE ADDRESSED IN THIS CHAPTER

1   What was Lessing's approach to religious knowledge?
2   What were Kant's central contributions to theology?
3   How did Schleiermacher meet the challenge of modernism?
4   What is the relationship of doctrine to the Christian life for Schleiermacher?

The Revivalists of the previous chapter made an enormous impact on the way many people understand and practice their religion. In this regard there can be no doubt that they contributed to the overall mosaic of Christian thought. But their enthusiasm didn't particularly influence the more intellectual currents of theology in the eighteenth and nineteenth centuries. To follow this branch of thinking, the first half of this chapter continues further into the heart of Enlightenment theology to the figures of Lessing and Kant. Then we will consider Friedrich Schleiermacher, Christianity's chief representative of the Romantic Period, and his response to the challenge of modernism.

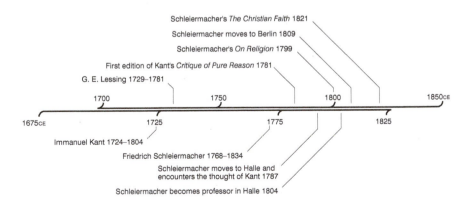

Timeline 25 Romanticism's response to Enlightenment theology

1 LESSING

Gotthold Ephraim Lessing (1729–1781) was a German writer who deeply influenced the Enlightenment movement. His understanding of Christianity continued in the trajectory of the Deists and their emphasis on reason. He was adamant that religious truths are truths of reason. That is to say that we come to religious knowledge through the application of reason, and its certainty rests on the certainty of reason. By contrast, contingent truths are learned through experience or by reliance on the testimonies of the experiences of others.

In 1777 Lessing wrote a short essay called "On the Proof of the Spirit and of Power." In it he began by ruing the fact that the miracles and prophesies connected with Jesus of Nazareth are confined to the pages of history, for which we must depend on the testimony of others. Even if these testimonies are of the highest caliber of historical accuracy, they will never amount to the sort of proof we expect from rational demonstrations.[1] He had no problems affirming the "historical certainty" of miracles and fulfilled prophesies recorded in the Bible. But historical certainty is something very different from rational certainty. So he doesn't deny that the things recorded about Jesus of Nazareth really happened because he has no other historical proof that they didn't. But Lessing denies that these historical contingencies can provide any basis for believing in the teachings of Christ with certainty. If those teachings are to be believed, we must arrive at them using a different method than the revelation of the biblical records. Religious truth had become moral truth for the thinkers of the Enlightenment, and moral truth was to be founded on reason. For Lessing, then, it is a category mistake to adduce historical truths in support of moral truths. He says, "Accidental truths of history can never become the proof of necessary truths of reason."[2]

Pushing further his antipathy for a historical foundation of religious beliefs, Lessing famously invoked the metaphor of an impassable ditch which separates us from the events of the past. This ditch prevents us from using the past to ground the traditional beliefs of orthodox Christianity. He says, "That, then, is the ugly, broad ditch which I cannot get across, however often and however earnestly I have tried to make the leap."[3] Such a position moves Lessing away from the validity or importance of dogmatic creeds. Apart from such distinctives, Christianity will be regarded as just one of several different religions which are the

LESSING ON THE PURSUIT OF TRUTH

The worth of a man does not consist in the truth he possesses, or thinks he possesses, but in the pains he has taken to attain that truth. For his powers are extended not through possession but through the search for truth. In this alone his ever-growing perfection consists. Possession makes him lazy, indolent, and proud. If God held all truth in his right hand and in his left the everlasting striving after truth, so that I should always and everlastingly be mistaken, and said to me, "Choose," with humility I would pick on the left hand and say, "Father, grant me that. Absolute truth is for thee alone."

(*Lessing's Theological Writings*[4])

creations of humans rather than the revelation of God. To illustrate this concept Lessing wrote a play, *Nathan the Wise*, in which the story is told of a father who had a magic ring that caused its wearer to be most loved by God. The father's dilemma was that he had three sons – each of whom he wanted to inherit the ring. After their father's death, the three sons (who represent Judaism, Christianity, and Islam) discover that each of them has been given a ring identical to the others, so they take their case to a judge to determine who has the "true" ring and is most loved by God. The judge concludes:

Oh, then, all three of you have been deceived,
And are deceivers too; and all three rings
Are spurious alike – the genuine ring
Was lost, most likely, and to hide its loss,
And to supply its place, your father caused
These three to be made up instead of it …
… My advice is this:
Accept the case precisely as it stands;
If each of you in truth received his ring
Straight from his father's hand, let each believe

His own to be the true and genuine ring.
Perhaps your father wished to terminate
The tyranny of that especial ring
'Mid his posterity. Of this be sure,
He loved you all, and loved you all alike.[5]

We don't see in this passage the claim that there is no one true religion, but rather that such truth is inaccessible to humans. Whether Lessing would ultimately claim that there is no truth or just that we can never know the truth, he encouraged a deep skepticism about claims to religious knowledge. This skepticism received its grandest treatment in the work of Immanuel Kant – the Enlightenment's greatest figure. It is he who sets the stage, then, for a different sort of reaction to the problem modernism created for Christian thought.

2 KANT

Immanuel Kant (1724–1804) was born, lived, and died in the Prussian city of Königsburg, where he was a professor of philosophy. His influence is felt widely in almost all areas of modern thought, but particularly in philosophy and, what interests us here, theology. He continued in the modernism of the Deists and Lessing in that morality was taken to be the chief concern of religion, but in some ways Kant had the sensibility of a Pietist. For both the Pietists and Kant, religion was not a matter of knowing some creed, but rather of doing the right thing. Kant was raised and educated in a family of Pietists and never lost respect for the seriousness with which they approached their duty to live devout lives of moral excellence. Like Lessing, though, he came to question the basis on which their moral certainty was founded, namely, a literal interpretation of the Bible. Morality needed a more secure foundation than historical anecdotes no matter how reliable the witness may have been. Kant sought instead to ground morality in reason alone. The title of one of his important books thus alludes to the great *sola* statements of the Reformation, but with an Enlightenment twist: *Religion Within the Limits of Reason Alone* (1793).

Kant's defense of this approach to religion comes from his epistemological project as found in his most famous and influential book, *Critique of Pure Reason* (1781). There are two points that come out of it

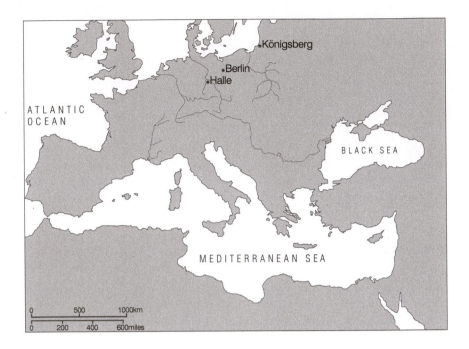

Map 25.1 Kant's Germany

which are most relevant for our story. The first is that we can't look for knowledge outside the limits of our own experience. He was convinced by the skeptical Scottish philosopher David Hume (1711–1776) that the speculations of philosophers were made in vain when they reached beyond confines of experience. But then second, even careful attention to experience does not give us absolute truth about reality, because our experiences themselves are shaped by the way our minds work. That is to say, our minds are hard-wired to work in predictable ways or to provide certain forms that our knowledge of the external world must conform to. Kant called this position his "Copernican Revolution" in knowledge.

So we can never say that we have discovered something about the world, but only about how we *perceive* the world to be. Kant had an argument that all rational beings would perceive the world in the same way, so there would be consistency among these in their experiences (a point that would later be challenged in postmodernism). But his position added to the difficulty of Lessing's ditch with another unbridgeable gap. Kant's stands between the way things are independently of us (what

KANT'S COPERNICAN REVOLUTION

Just as Copernicus was better able to understand the movements of the heavenly bodies by attributing motion to our point of view on earth, so too Kant took what had always been attributed to objects in the "external" world and attributed it to our minds. That is, instead of our having knowledge when our concepts conform to the way the external world is, knowledge occurs when the objects of the external world conform to the forms of our concepts.

Kant called the noumenal realm) and the way things appear to us (the phenomenal realm). Recall from Chapter 23 that Descartes framed the problem of whether our mental representations are accurate depictions of reality; now Kant's "solution" entails that there can be no representations of some supposed external reality, but only of the internal constructs of our minds.

So of course the traditional arguments for the existence of God prove nothing objectively about the way things really are for Kant. He argues that each of these fails to substantiate the claim that God exists. Lessing had eliminated supernatural revelation that was handed down through history; Kant went a step further and eliminated the possibility of coming to know things about God through nature and reason. But even though theoretical knowledge of God and religion is not possible on Kant's system, that is not his final word on the subject. Kant thought that there was another sphere of human activity – the sphere of practical morality – which points to the existence of God.

Reason dictates that we ought to act virtuously and that happiness is the ultimate goal of our actions. Experience shows us, however, that there are times when acting virtuously does not bring about happiness. This dilemma indicates that the present order of things must not be the end of all things. Sometimes in this life bad people are rewarded and good people do not see their reward. Reason and experience can take us no further. But Kant believed that it is morally necessary that we postulate the existence of a God who can guarantee that all the wrongs will be righted in an age that is to come. Religion, therefore, had a positive role to play in society in providing an ethical foundation. But in Kant's view it was relegated to the ethical sphere, the category of values over against the category of fact which was the province of knowledge.

There were some who followed in Kant's theological footsteps. But his position is really the culmination of the process which ends in the dissolution of theology as a systematic discipline. There is no point in theorizing about God when one's epistemological position prevents any objective connection with a deity. The Pietists and Revivalists considered in the previous chapter had largely ignored the epistemological challenge of Descartes's philosophical revolution which Kant continued. For theology to be brought back into intellectual circles, another sort of revolution was needed – a revolution which could overcome the fact-value distinction and its proscription of theology from serious consideration as a species of knowledge in the scientific conception of the world.

3 SCHLEIERMACHER AND THE FEELING OF ABSOLUTE DEPENDENCE

In an intentional nod toward Descartes' purported fatherhood of modern philosophy, Friedrich Schleiermacher (1768–1834) is often called the father of modern (Protestant) theology. He self-consciously attempted to set theology on a different footing so that there would not be the conflict between modernism's scientific conception of the world and religious claims. In 1799 Schleiermacher published a small book called *On Religion: Speeches to its Cultured Despisers*. In it he addressed squarely those who had given up on theology as a legitimate area of inquiry and argued for a different understanding of religion. This new understanding drew its breath from the Romantic period and overcame the fact-value distinction by suggesting that there is a more fundamental unity of feeling or intuition.

Life

Schleiermacher began his life on the path to Pietism. His father was deeply concerned that Friedrich be protected from the skeptical currents of the day and so sent him to a boarding school run by the Moravian Brethren when Friedrich was fifteen years old. Friedrich was impressed with the piety of the Moravians but was troubled that they could not answer his more theoretical questions. He admitted his doubts of the traditional Christian theology in letters to his father. In January of 1787 he wrote that he must announce something that would cause great pain:

> Faith is the regalia of the Godhead, you say. Alas! dearest father, if you believe that, without this faith, no one can attain to salvation in the next world, nor to tranquility in this – and such, I know, is your belief – oh! Then, pray to God to grant it to me, for to me it is now lost. I cannot believe that He who called himself the Son of Man, was the true, eternal God: I cannot believe that His death was a vicarious atonement, because He never expressly said so Himself; and I cannot believe it to have been necessary, because God, who evidently did not create men for perfection, but for the pursuit of it, cannot possibly intend to punish them eternally, because they have not attained it.[6]

Friedrich realized that his doubts would prevent him from taking up a clerical position within his conservative community and so he asked that he be allowed to continue his theological studies at the more liberal University of Halle. The father responded with something less than understanding and compassion: "Alas! into what a state of delusion has the wickedness of your heart plunged you!"[7] He even went so far as to disown his son, but gave him permission to pursue his studies at Halle with the understanding that they could not be reconciled under such circumstances. Friedrich went to Halle and the two never saw each other again. But they did continue to correspond through letters, and despite their differences of belief Friedrich seemed to receive continuing support from his father.

After a couple of years studying at Halle, Friedrich became a Reformed minister and took a job as a tutor. The publication of *On Religion* thrust him into the public consciousness and achieved its aim of reclaiming for theology a legitimate place in intellectual life. Schleiermacher was made a professor and university preacher at Halle in 1802 and enjoyed enormous popularity. His criticism of the Enlightenment's dismissal of religion caught the wave of Romanticism and provided a legitimate option for intellectuals to engage in theological discussion again.

In 1807 Schleiermacher moved to Berlin and was appointed the pastor of Trinity Church. He was influential in the founding of the University

Figure 25.1 Friedrich Schleiermacher. Public domain/Wikimedia Commons

of Berlin and took a chair in theology there. In 1821 he published his monumental work, *The Christian Faith*, which took a place alongside Calvin's *Institutes* as the most important texts of Protestant theology. His thinking about Christianity and theology always maintained a connection to the Church. He was a strong advocate of the union of Lutheran and Reformed Churches in Prussia which occurred in 1817. He was also a charismatic preacher who attracted people everywhere he went. When he died in 1834, his coffin was carried through the streets of Berlin followed by a line of mourners more than a mile long – among whom were the king and crown prince of Prussia.[8]

Religion's foundation in feeling

The foundation of religion for Schleiermacher is not some sort of propositional knowledge that has been revealed to us by God or agreed upon by some church council. He agreed with Kant that religion is not a matter of theorizing, but rejected Kant's conclusion that put religion into the practical sphere of value and reduced religion to a code of ethics. Instead, there is another more fundamental realm of human consciousness, the realm of feeling. By this we shouldn't take Schleiermacher to put religion on a foundation of subjective emotion. For the Romantic period, feeling was understood more in the sense of a direct intuition. He explains:

> Religion's essence is neither thinking nor acting, but intuition and feeling. It wishes to intuit the universe, wishes devoutly to overhear the universe's own manifestations and actions, longs to be grasped and filled by the universe's immediate influences in childlike passivity. … Thus religion maintains its own sphere and its own character only by completely removing itself from the sphere and character of speculation as well as from that of praxis. Only when it places itself next to both of them is the common ground perfectly filled out and human nature completed from this dimension. Religion shows itself to you as the necessary and indispensable third next to those two, as their natural counterpart, not slighter in worth and splendor than what you wish of them.[9]

The father of modern theology echoes Descartes in positing self-consciousness to be the starting point of his new methodology. Descartes looked within himself and saw a thinking thing; Schleiermacher analyzed self-consciousness further and found a feeling of absolute dependence, which he believed to be just another way of saying consciousness of being in relation with God. The opening sections of *The Christian Faith* where this is laid out are very dense and difficult, but in simplified version we could say that Schleiermacher develops his points as follows.

In our consciousness of ourselves, we are aware both of a constant and abiding self, and of this same self as susceptible to change and development. The change cannot come from within the constant self (or there would be no constant self), and so must be the result of being acted on by something other than myself. Thus there is a subject–object relationship between myself and the other-than-self. I am an object that is acted on by another subject, but I am also a subject which acts on other objects. Insofar as I act on the other, I have a feeling of freedom; I can effect change on something else. Insofar as I am being acted on, I have a feeling of dependence; something else is causing me to change. All of these subject–object relationships are reciprocal to some degree. In the process of acting on something else, that other object affects my own consciousness and so makes me dependent on it.[10] This reciprocity attends all relationships I have with other finite things – including my relationship to the universe as a whole – so there is never a feeling of absolute freedom or absolute dependence in relationship to these other things.

We see so far that Schleiermacher should not be taken to be some sort of pantheist or nature worshiper. Despite what others in the Romantic period may have claimed, for Schleiermacher religious sentiments are not the result of feeling awe at nature. His argument clearly rules out the natural and finite from generating the feeling of absolute dependence which he takes to be the foundation of religion.[11] So that feeling must come from something else. But it can't be just another thing in universe, or it too would enter into the reciprocal subject–object relationship we have with things. Singular finite things may be responsible (at least in part) for making me what I am; but the fact that I am at all requires a different sort of explanation. Schleiermacher recognized that the whole of my conscious existence, that my being itself, must come from some other source besides myself and that this source is not in any way dependent on me. This is the feeling of absolute dependence.

There is a strong resemblance of this argument to Aquinas's (discussed in Chapter 17). In both of these, God is not just one more object among the many objects of the world that impinge upon our consciousness at any given moment. He is the ground of Being itself. But we have not yet connected Schleiermacher's feeling of absolute dependence with *God*. He says, "to feel oneself absolutely dependent and to be conscious of being in relation with God are one and the same thing."[12] It is not that Schleiermacher has some idea of God and in unpacking that idea discovers that it is a feeling of absolute dependence. Anselm's Ontological Argument does begin with such an idea (see Chapter 14), but Schleiermacher works the other way: it is the feeling that is fundamental, and then the recognition that such a feeling could not come from any finite thing results in its identification with God.

By appeal to this fundamental feeling, Schleiermacher has pulled the rug out from under the conflict that modernism brought about between a supernatural conception of the world and the scientific conception. Science has to do with the human activity of knowing, which is very different from feeling. Science and religion, then, are two different ways of talking about the world and they do not stand in opposition to each other. It is as though we asked an artist and a chemist to talk about a painting in the language of their disciplines. The artist would talk about perspective, mood, and the feeling that is evoked; the chemist would talk about the different wavelengths of reflected light from the canvas as a function of the chemical composition of the different paints. For Schleiermacher the miraculous is not some kind of suspension of the laws of nature which are discovered by the physicist. He is happy to admit that scientists can in theory explain all the workings of the world in their language. But just like the chemist's description of the painting does not preclude the artist's description, neither does the scientific view of the world preclude adopting a miraculous point of view:

> "Miracle" is merely the religious name for event, every one of which, even the most natural and usual, is a miracle as soon as it adapts itself to the fact that the religious view of it can be the dominant one. To me everything is a miracle, and for me what alone is a miracle in your mind, namely, something inexplicable and strange, is no miracle in mine. The more religious you would be, the more you would see miracles everywhere; every conflict as to whether individual events deserve to be so named only gives me the most painful impression of how poor and inadequate is the religious sense of the combatants.[13]

The religious sense in no way conflicts with the scientific outlook for Schleiermacher. The Moravian community in which he was brought up (as well as many other Pietist communities) dealt with the conflict between science and their religious beliefs by ignoring science as a godless enterprise that contributed nothing to the important knowledge of eternal things. Schleiermacher developed a way to let science pursue its ends without conflicting with religion.

Now, even if the origin of religion is more in tune with the Romantic period, Schleiermacher would recognize that it is the natural impulse of people to conceptualize and organize what is felt into systems of thought. And so far nothing that has been said about his religious thought is distinctly Christian. But Schleiermacher was a member of a Christian community and believed that the conceptualizations that happen within that community were not unimportant. In *The Christian Faith*, then, he wrote from within the confessional Christian community, trying to give expression to the doctrines they believed.

4 DOCTRINE AND CHRISTOLOGY FROM BELOW

Schleiermacher believed doctrines to be second-order expressions of the more fundamental feeling of dependence. They are culturally dependent attempts to bring conceptual order to the deep feelings that all can have of God. There is, however, a uniqueness of Christianity compared to the other monotheistic faiths, and this stands on two points which are common to all different expressions of Christianity: first, at the center of religious consciousness there is redemption from an evil condition to a better condition; and second, that redemption was accomplished for all by Jesus of Nazareth.[14] There are many ways of unpacking these two notions, and this accounts for the many different Christian communions. But they are united by these two common elements, and all the rest of Christian doctrine must flow from these points.[15] Whatever is not able to be related to this is accorded a secondary place in Christian doctrine. Perhaps most notably in this latter category for Schleiermacher is the doctrine of the Trinity. He notes the historic definitions of the Trinity in the various creeds and councils, but then comments, "Since the doctrine of the Trinity is neither presupposed in every Christian religious experience nor contained in it, these definitions do not belong to our present discussion."[16] This is not to say that the doctrine of the Trinity is irrelevant for the conceptualizations of the Church about God. But it is the fruit rather than the root of Christian thought.[17]

Schleiermacher accords Christology a more foundational place within Christian theology, but here too his thinking is somewhat beyond the pale of orthodoxy. As seen throughout history, there are heretical excesses in emphasizing too far either the humanity or divinity of Christ. Schleiermacher readily acknowledges this. Yet for him the "two natures" solution of Chalcedon (see Chapter 8) cannot be taken to be an adequate description of the reality of Christ. First, he believes that attributing two natures to the one person of Christ actually perpetuates the sorts of heresies it was meant to combat. In attempting to understand this formula, people have inevitably vacillated between the opposite errors of mixing the two natures to form a third or emphasizing the unity so much as to make one nature more important than the other.[18] Even more troubling for him is that by accepting this creedal formulation on faith, we reverse the proper order of understanding who Christ is. We do not first experience what sort of being Christ is, and then from that come to understand what he had done for us in the act of redemption. No. First and foremost we experience what Christ has done for us in the act of redemption, and from this we can infer what sort of person he must be.

Here is an important turning point for Christian thought. It is the difference between doing Christology "from above" and "from below." Schleiermacher has exposed the pretensions of discerning the attributes and nature of Christ from within the world of thought as though he were some abstract concept that could be dissected in isolation from the religious life which gave rise to the concept in the first place. There can be no Christology in this sense which is worked out from above. Rather, we approach our understanding of who Christ is based on our experience of him. We work up to our concepts about him from below. Schleiermacher claims that this is what the first Christians did. It took five centuries for the formulation of Chalcedon to emerge from their reflection on the work of Christ. According to Schleiermacher, Christians today should still be working up to their knowledge of God from below rather than confining Christian thought to abstract notions which have little relevance to Christian experience.

For Schleiermacher, reflection on the corporate life of Christians and their redemption brings us to the understanding that in the person of Christ, God has completed his creation of human nature. In this sense Christ was the perfect man – but he was still a man. Using the Apostle Paul's terminology for Christ as the "Second Adam" Schleiermacher says of Christ, "This Second Adam is altogether like all those who are descended from the first, only that from the outset He has an absolutely potent God-consciousness."[19] Redemption, then, takes on a different guise than the Reformation's atonement and justification language. More in the vein of Abelard (see Chapter 14), the purpose of Christ for Schleiermacher was to be the perfect example for others, drawing them into higher consciousness of God. In this way people are able to participate in the eternal life of God in the midst of their other occupations.

5 CONCLUSION

In Schleiermacher the foundations are laid for modern, liberal Christian thought. Miracles and eternal life are transformed into attitudes; Christ is shorn of metaphysical complexities and made an exemplar. This is an important position in the history of theology, and we'll hear its echoes in the liberal Protestant theologians of the twentieth century (see Chapter 27). But a more conservative strain has not thrown in the towel yet. Perhaps working up "from below" is not as straightforward as we were led to think. Maybe our experience itself is shaped to some extent by prior beliefs and assumptions. In the next chapter we'll see a different response to the challenge of modernism, one which questions the larger framework and assumptions of the Modern period. The Neo-orthodox position, as it is called today, finds a way back across Lessing's ugly ditch to more traditional beliefs.

SUMMARY OF MAIN POINTS

1 Lessing discounts revelation and the historic creeds of Christianity; instead, religious truth becomes moral truth which is discovered through reason.
2 Kant precluded theology from the realm of knowledge but held God's existence to be morally necessary.
3 Schleiermacher's religion is ultimately founded on a feeling of absolute dependence.
4 Schleiermacher relates all of doctrine to the redemption effected by Jesus, and attempts to understand who Jesus was "from below" by his work of redemption.

FOR FURTHER READING

Keith Clements, *Friedrich Schleiermacher: Pioneer of Modern Theology* (Minneapolis, MN: Fortress, 1991). A helpful introduction to Schleiermacher, including substantial excerpts of his writings organized around themes.

B.A. Gerrish, *A Prince of the Church: Schleiermacher and the Beginnings of Modern Theology* (Eugen, OR: Wipf & Stock, 2001). A short book with a good overview of Schleiermacher's thought.

G.E. Lessing, *Lessing's Theological Writings*, H. Chadwick, trans. (Stanford, CA: Stanford University Press, 1957). A small volume which captures the essence of Enlightenment religious sentiment.

Friedrich Schleiermacher, *The Christian Faith*, H.R. Mackintosh and J.S. Stewart, eds (Edinburgh: T&T Clark, 1999). This large book is difficult reading at times, but is the magnum opus of Schleiermacher and deserving of careful attention.

Allen Wood, *Kant's Moral Religion* (Ithaca, NY: Cornell University Press, 1970). An eminent Kant scholar shows how Kant's views on religion are consistent with and an integral part of his overall philosophy.

26

Neo-orthodoxy

Karl Barth and others

QUESTIONS TO BE ADDRESSED IN THIS CHAPTER

1   How was existentialism a precursor to Neo-orthodoxy?
2   Who was Karl Barth and why is he considered one of the most important theologians in history?
3   What are the main points of Barth's Neo-orthodox theology?
4   What are some ways that Neo-orthodoxy has had a lasting influence?

Modernism and Enlightenment thinking permeated much of Western culture in the nineteenth century and challenged a number of central Christian doctrines and dogmas. Some Christians, as we saw in the last chapter, affirmed the rationalist assumptions of the day and sought to align their religious positions with them. These liberal theologians were challenged by two very different groups of Christians: the conservative fundamentalists on one side and the Neo-orthodox thinkers on the other. In this chapter and the next we explore each of these responses.

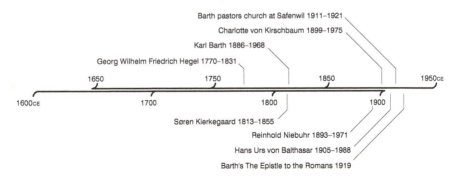

Timeline 26 Neo-orthodoxy

1 SØREN KIERKEGAARD: EXISTENTIALIST AND FORERUNNER TO NEO-ORTHODOXY

The influence of modernism on Christianity was perhaps nowhere more evident than in Denmark. Kantian Transcendentalism and Hegelian Idealism had made their mark, and it was here that a Danish Christian philosopher, Lutheran theologian, and cultural critic reacted to the rationalistic approach to faith and ushered in a focus on individual consciousness and response. Our story in this chapter begins with this Danish thinker – the father of existentialism and a central forerunner to Neo-orthodoxy.

Søren Kierkegaard (1813–1855) – widely recognized to be one of the most influential thinkers of the nineteenth century – was deeply concerned about the moral and religious laxity of the people of Denmark, and he took it as his personal task to "reintroduce Christianity into Christendom."[1] He spent most of his life as a pastor in Copenhagen and saw himself as a religious poet more than a theologian or philosopher. His religion was a very pious, Lutheran form of Christian faith. He developed a Christian existentialist philosophy which emphasized the individual and the role of choice and the will over and above abstract philosophical speculation.

For Kierkegaard, Christian faith is not merely an affirmation of church doctrine and dogma. Rather, it is primarily a matter of subjective passion. What is fundamental to Christianity is faith, for it is only by faith that one becomes a true self. "Truth is subjectivity," he claims; it is what a person ultimately bases her or his life on in a personal decision.[2] Each individual's existential choice, then, is determinative of his or her own eternal destiny.[3]

Christian doctrine and dogma contain paradoxes which are an affront to reason on Kierkegaard's view. For example, with the claim that God is both infinite/transcendent on the one hand (Yahweh) and finite/human on the other (Jesus Christ), we are asked to believe the unbelievable, the paradoxical. We are thus confronted with a choice: believe by faith or reject by reason. If we believe, we believe the absurd, but all the better for faith! Just as Abraham trusted God when asked by God to do the unthinkable (sacrifice Abraham's own son, Isaac, on the altar), so too we are asked by God, by virtue of the absurd, to make a "leap of faith" toward God.

So Kierkegaard sought a Christianity of real subjective faith – one in which a transcendent God confronts individual persons in Jesus

Christ who must then choose either for or against him. His existentialist Christianity can be seen as a response to the work of the German philosopher G.W.F. Hegel (1770–1831), considered to be the father of modern historicism and idealism. Hegel attempted to develop a rational, objective, systematic theology in order to understand and explain the world (his famous line is "the real is the rational, the rational is the real"). His system, known as "objective idealism," includes the notion that world history is the template through which we can understand human nature and destiny. History unfolds dialectically (through a logic of thesis, antithesis, and synthesis), and this is the rational unfolding of absolute, universal Spirit toward its own self-consciousness. In other words, history is the great evolution of the collective spirit (or Spirit or God) becoming aware of itself. This is divine immanence in spades (God is the world!), and Kierkegaard would have no part of it. For him, as already noted, God is "wholly other."

Kierkegaard was highly influential in Denmark during his own lifetime. But because his writings were written and published only in Danish at the time, it was not until Karl Barth made reference to them in his commentary on the book of Romans that Kierkegaard's works became known internationally. Most prominent among these are *Fear and Trembling*, *Either-Or*, and *Concluding Unscientific Postscript*. Kierkegaard's existentialism was later co-opted by atheist thinkers such as Friedrich Nietzsche and Jean-Paul Sartre. But a number of Christian theologians of the twentieth century continued down Kierkegaard's existentialist path in developing their own theological systems. The first of these we consider is Karl Barth.

2 KARL BARTH: NEO-ORTHODOX THEOLOGIAN

Karl Barth (1886–1968) is widely held to be one of the most significant theologians since the Protestant Reformation, and his influence extends far beyond his own Reformed tradition. More than any other figure, Barth brought European and North American Christian theology out of the grip of rationalist Enlightenment thinking in the nineteenth and twentieth centuries. His theological insights and original comprehensive account of the Christian faith have influenced Christian thought in myriad ways up through our own day. Before expounding on his ideas and influence, let's first take a brief look at his life.

Figure 26.1 Karl Barth © Album/Art Resource, NY

Barth was raised in a family with strong Christian affirmations, his parents being affiliated with a conservative wing of the Reformed Church of Switzerland. His father was lecturer at the University of Berne and taught New Testament and early church history. Continuing this theological lineage, he insisted that Karl study theology at Berne. He did attend there, but he also attended schools in Berlin, Tübingen, and Marburg, studying philosophy and theology under some of the most significant liberal thinkers of the day, including Adolf von Harnack (see Chapter 27) and Wilhelm Herrmann. In his university experience he was immersed in the "Modern school" of theology, and for a time he affirmed the liberal, humanistic ideology of his teachers.

He completed his education without earning a doctorate, and soon after college he took an assistant pastoral role in a church in Geneva. This lasted only a short time, and from 1911 to 1921 he worked as a parish pastor in Safenwil, a small border town between Switzerland and Germany. Several life-altering events occurred during this period of Barth's life. First, in 1913

ADOLF VON HARNACK

Adolf von Harnack (1851–1930) was a leading German proponent of liberal theology. His work emphasizes a rigorous historical-critical theological method in which one searches for the "timeless kernel" of Christianity independent of the "husk" of church history and faith. His most important works include *Christianity and History* and *History of Dogma*.

he married Nelly Hoffman, an accomplished violinist, and they had five children together. Second, in 1914 he became disillusioned by his theology teachers in that virtually all of them had signed a statement of agreement with the war policies of Kaiser Wilhelm II. If their liberal theology could so easily allow them to concede to such an expansionist ideology, he wanted nothing to do with it. From this point forward he made up his mind to begin dismantling liberal theology.[4] The third event was an awakening he had as he read the Bible and prepared sermons for his congregation. Contrary to the rationalist theology of Harnack and others, Barth saw a God who was mysterious and unable to be discovered by the unaided human mind. This God was alive and speaking forth to humanity, not a thing that philosophers and theologians could dissect using human experience and reason. This led to a fourth event: a commentary he published on the book of Romans entitled *Der Romerbrief* (*The Epistle to the Romans*). This was a tumultuous work in that it provided a robust criticism of liberal theology. The book was widely criticized by liberal theologians, but others hailed it as a necessary return to Reformation thought and an essential correction to twentieth century theology.

In 1921 he moved out of the ministry to teach theology, which he did until 1935 when his opposition to the Nazis (including his refusal to salute Hitler before class each day) forced him out of the country and back to his native Switzerland. Barth's entanglement with the Nazis began when, in the early 1930s, a group of Protestant pastors in Germany launched a movement called the "German Christians." They were sympathetic to Hitler and the Nazis' anti-Semitism and their desire to unify Protestant Churches under a single Reich Church and bishop. By 1933 this group had grown to include 3,000 pastors (there were about

17,000 total in Germany at the time) – one sixth of the entire Protestant pastor population! In response to the German Christian movement, the Pastors' Emergency League was formed, spearheaded by theologian and Lutheran pastor Martin Niemöller (1892–1984). They set up a church government called the Confessing Church, and in 1934 (at about 3,000 as well) they spelled out their views in a document entitled the *Barmen Declaration*. This *Declaration*, whose primary author was Barth himself, opposed the dictatorial and oppressive positions of the German state, rejected subordinating the Church to the state, condemned the German Christian movement as heretical, and reaffirmed the central teachings of Christianity, calling German Churches back to orthodox faith. Sadly, the leaders of the Confessing Church were harassed by Nazi authorities, and over 700 of them were eventually arrested. Some, including Niemöller, were sent to concentration camps, and some, most notably Dietrich Bonhoeffer (1906–1945; a student of Barth's), were executed.[5]

Barth fled to Basel, the city of his birth. He took a position at the University of Basel in 1935 and taught there (assuming the Chair of Systematic Theology) until 1962. He had been working on his magnum opus for a number of years, the *Church Dogmatics*. It was intended to be a complete systematic theology – one based on God's Word in Christ as revealed in the Bible. After retiring from his university post, he worked

CHARLOTTE VON KIRSCHBAUM

Charlotte von Kirschbaum (1899–1975) was a theologian and student, secretary, and confidant of Karl Barth. She was fluent in Greek, Hebrew, and Latin, and well-studied in theology. In 1929 she moved in with Karl and Nelly Barth and remained with them for thirty-five years. Much intrigue has ensued with respect to their relationship. Recent scholarship indicates that she made a significant contribution to Barth's *Church Dogmatics*.[6] A collection of her lectures is published in *The Question of Woman: The Collected Writings of Charlotte Von Kirschbaum*, edited by Eleanor Jackson (Eerdmans Publishing Company, 1996).

diligently on the *Dogmatics* until the time of his death. At that point, however, it was still incomplete, and thirteen volumes (and six million words) long! While the highly influential *Dogmatics* was primarily written by Barth himself, there is some debate about the influence on the work by Barth's student and secretary, Charlotte von Kirschbaum.[7]

3 CENTRAL THEMES OF BARTH'S NEO-ORTHODOXY

There are many central themes to Barth's Neo-orthodox theology or, as it is sometimes called, dialectical theology, theology of crisis, or even existential theology. His Neo-orthodoxy is rich and complex and cannot receive full treatment here. But we can, perhaps, get a clear sense of it by focusing on several major themes.

Rejecting liberalism

As we mentioned, soon after his theological training Barth rejected the liberal theology of his professors. The horrors of war and the recognition of human depravity as reflected in Nazism had challenged the liberal optimism of human advancement and moral progress apart from divine intervention. As Barth saw things, "nineteenth century theology no longer held any future."[8] He rejected not only human progress absent from God, but also the primary role that higher criticism had played in theological understanding, the uniting of faith and culture, and the dismissal of miracles, among other things.

Barth desired to move theology away from the influence of modern philosophy and the historical-critical method and shift it back to Reformation principles. In one sense he was affirming orthodoxy – a commitment to the authority of the Bible through which God speaks his Word, the sinfulness of human beings, the centrality of Christ in election, and a humble dependence of God in prayer – yet, as we will see, in another sense he was moving beyond orthodoxy, attempting to revitalize and to some extent rethink it.

Affirming God's transcendence, human fallenness, and the event of divine revelation

As he crafted his commentary on Romans, Barth emphasized the radical distinction and separation between God and human beings.[9] In doing this he created his own theological "ditch," but it was quite different from Lessing's ditch noted in the previous chapter. For Barth there is indeed a great gulf or chasm, but it is one between a transcendent God and fallen human beings. While the gulf is impassible from our side, nevertheless it is not impassible from God's side. God can and does reveal himself to fallen humanity, and this is accomplished through the Word of God. The following four emphases capture this essential aspect of Barth's theology:

- The absolute transcendence of God.
- The absolute separation of God and human beings due to human sin.
- The inability of human beings to know God apart from divine revelation.
- The gift of divine revelation through God's self-disclosure (the event of Scripture).

These can be further explained as follows. For Barth there is an "infinite qualitative distinction" between God and human beings. God is mystery – "wholly other" – infinitely beyond human beings. As such, the human mind is incapable of grasping the divine nature on its own accord. This does not mean that nothing can be said or understood about God, however. Indeed, there is much that can be known about God on Barth's view, including that God is a Trinity.[10] But such knowledge is not derived from natural theology. In fact, Barth was opposed to the entire project of natural theology, denying any positive role to general revelation in nature. Knowledge of God (that is, theological knowledge, even knowledge of our own sin) is revealed only through the special revelation of God.

Barth's theology is a theology of the Word. Knowledge of God can only be obtained through divine revelation – the Word of God. The Bible is the written Word, in one sense merely a human book written by human beings, not inspired revelation from God. It is the human witness of the event of God's revelation in Jesus Christ. The Bible *becomes* divine revelation, the revealed Word, to an individual when he or she is encountered by God as the words are read or preached. So God's true

Word is not a set of propositions written on pages, but rather an event – something that happens between God and an individual person. It is the event of God speaking to us.

> The Word of God is the Word that God *spoke*, *speaks*, and *will speak* in the midst of all men. Regardless of whether it is heard or not, it is, in itself, directed to all men.[11]

It is here that Kierkegaard's "leap of faith" – a personal decision and commitment to a transcendent God apart from human reason – reappears as central in Barth's theology. For Barth, God's Word confronts us not as a thing, an object, that can be discovered, analyzed, and evaluated, but rather as a subject which does the discovering and which demands a response. When it does so, we must choose to respond. It is through God's initiative that we can have an authentic (existential) encounter with God through the Word of God. And this Word of God is Jesus Christ. As the Bible is read or preached, God speaks (when He chooses to speak) to us in Jesus Christ.

To all the works and strivings of fallen human beings, God says "No!" But the good news is that God also says "Yes!" We cannot find God on our own, but God finds us as we respond to God's Word in Jesus Christ.

Rethinking divine election and salvation in Christ

While basically affirming a Reformed theology, Barth reconceived the Reformed doctrine of election as it had been developed by Zwingli and Calvin. He saw a number of references in the Bible that he believed identified the *Messiah* as the only elected individual.[12] So he reckoned that God's "election" was an election of Christ, and by joining with the elected one – or, to use the Apostle Paul's phrase, by being "in Christ" – fallen humanity could be a part of that election.[13] Election turns out not to be a hidden decree of the saved and the damned, but an eternal decree of God's "yes" to the Chosen One, and to humanity as well. As with Barth's overall theological paradigm, his doctrine of election is also Christocentric.

Given his view of election in Christ, what is somewhat surprising is Barth's affirmation of the Reformed views of monergism and the sovereignty of God. Barth even affirmed the Calvinistic doctrines of supralapsarianism – the view that God's decrees of election and reprobation logically preceded the decree of the Fall – and double predestination! (For discussion of these themes, see Chapter 20.) However, Barth's understanding of these terms is quite different from Calvin and the Reformers, for he interprets them through the grid of God's election in Christ based on God's universal love. It is through the election of Christ that humanity receives the love and grace of God.

So God's "yes" is to Christ, but his "no" is also to Christ, for Christ is both the elect and the reprobate:

> If the teachers of predestination were right when they spoke always of a duality, of election and reprobation, of predestination to salvation or perdition, to life or death, then we may say already that in the election of Jesus Christ which is the eternal will of God, God has ascribed to man ... election, salvation, and life; and to Himself He has ascribed ... reprobation, perdition, and death.[14]

Of course a central question remains, given this understanding of election. Will everyone experience salvation, or is it only for some? Barth has been accused by some of being a universalist. Others argue that he affirmed the Arminian view that those who choose to follow Christ are in Christ (and therefore elect), and those who choose not to follow are not in Christ (and so not elect). On this question Barth himself was rather elusive. Nevertheless, the universal love of God and Christ are clearly at the core of Barth's views of election and salvation.

In contrast to the liberal Christological views of the nineteenth century (a Christology "from below"), this is a Christology "from above." Barth agreed with traditional Christian thought that Christ was God come in the flesh to humanity, affirming the classical formulations of Chalcedon. This is a paradox on Barth's view: the omnipotent became powerless in order to save the helpless. God chose to save those who were unable to choose him on their own, and God did so by choosing Christ. In choosing Christ, God chooses humanity as well.

Barth's work and impact are often underappreciated by those on the theological right and left, so we take up this issue of lasting influence in the next section.

4 NEO-ORTHODOXY'S LASTING INFLUENCE

The sustained significance of Barth's Neo-orthodoxy is immense, and while one would be hard pressed to find an open adherent of "Barthianism" today, his ideas have infiltrated Protestant and, to a lesser extent, Catholic theology.[15] As one recent theologian aptly put it, "The influence of Karl Barth has been so extensive as to be virtually coterminous with the history of theology during and since his lifetime."[16]

One prominent Catholic theologian affected by Neo-orthodoxy was Hans Urs von Balthasar (1905–1988), a Swiss theologian and Jesuit priest who was invited by Pope John Paul II to be a cardinal.[17] Recognized as one of the most important Catholic theologians of the twentieth century, Balthasar attempted to respond to modernism through his voluminous theological works. He engaged extensively with Barth, and in 1951 published *The Theology of Karl Barth: Exposition and Interpretation*. Barth himself described this book as the best work in print on his own theological views. While they had their disagreements, Balthasar came to agree with Barth's central notion of theology as a witness of God's self-revelation. Many other Catholic theologians were affected by Barth's work as well, and no less than Pope Pius XII himself described him as "the greatest theologian since Thomas Aquinas."

On the Protestant side, one significant thinker who was highly influenced by Barth's theology was the Swiss theologian Emil Brunner (1889–1966). Ordained in the Swiss Reformed Church, Brunner was Professor of Systematic and Practical Theology at the University of Zürich. In the spirit of Barth he reaffirmed core Reformation teachings against the theological liberalism of his day and became a leading advocate of Neo-orthodoxy across Europe and the United States. He saw liberalism as a reflection of human pride, but nonetheless sought to engage humanistic culture through points of contact for the gospel in the natural world and human nature.[18] His Neo-orthodox influence came primarily through his three-volume systematic theology, *Dogmatics*, and his book *Truth as Encounter*.

Probably the most significant Neo-orthodox Protestant theologian in the United States was Reinhold Niebuhr (1893–1971), Professor of Practical Theology at Union Theological Seminary from 1928 until his retirement in 1960. Niebuhr saw liberalism as inadequate from spiritual, moral, social, and political perspectives. For him, only the love of God through Christ could answer the central issues of human life.

A God without wrath brought men without sin into a kingdom without judgment through a Christ without a cross.
(H. Richard Niebuhr, brother of Reinhold Niebuhr, describing liberal theology in the nineteenth century[19])

He defended "Christian realism" – the view that the kingdom of heaven is to be sought, even though it cannot be fully realized on earth due to the fallenness of human beings. For him as with Barth, "theology is ethics," since knowing God entails doing God's will. One simply cannot truly know God (knowledge in the biblical sense involves more than mere "head knowledge;" it entails experiential awareness) and yet not do what God invites one to do. Niebuhr lived out his Neo-orthodox Christian realism, being socially and politically liberal and active while maintaining theological conservatism.

In sum, Barth's impact on Christian thought is inestimable, and his ideas and works – focused as they are on Jesus Christ as the living revelation of God – continue to have a major influence on students, scholars and pastors across the theological spectrum.

Other prominent theologians impacted by Barth's Neo-orthodoxy include Rudolf Bultmann, Paul Tillich, Karl Rahner, and Hans Küng. What unifies them all as Neo-orthodox thinkers is their reaction against the liberal theology of the nineteenth century and their emphasis on the transcendence of God and revelation as a divine encounter between Christ and human beings.[20]

SUMMARY OF MAIN POINTS

1   The Christian existentialism of Søren Kierkegaard required not a rational systematic account of Christian theology, as with liberalism, but rather an authentic faith manifested in a passionate encounter with the living God in Jesus Christ – a central theme of Neo-orthodoxy.

2   Karl Barth was a Swiss Reformed theologian who turned from liberal theology and brought about a return to orthodoxy – or what is better dubbed Neo-orthodoxy or a "theology from above" – in Christian theology.

3   Some of the central tenets of Barth's Neo-orthodoxy are the rejection of liberal theology, the sovereignty, transcendence and the universal love and grace of God, God's self-disclosure through the event of Scripture, and election in Christ.

4   The influence of Barth's Neo-orthodoxy continued throughout the twentieth century and down to our own day, impacting both Catholic and Protestant theological luminaries.

FOR FURTHER READING

Karl Barth, *Church Dogmatics: A Selection* (Louisville, KY: Westminster John Knox Press, 1994). Key selections from Barth's magnum opus.

Geoffrey William Bromiley, *An Introduction to the Theology of Karl Barth* (Grand Rapids, MI: Eerdmans, 1979). A helpful introduction to Barth by a major editor of his *Dogmatics*.

C. Stephen Evans, *Kierkegaard: An Introduction* (Cambridge: Cambridge University Press, 2009). An accessible and authoritative introduction.

Douglas John Hall, *Remembered Voices: Reclaiming the Legacy of "Neo-Orthodoxy"* (Louisville, KY: Westminster John Knox Press, 1998). Argues for the continued relevance of some of the twentieth century's leading Neo-orthodox theologians.

Liberal Protestantism

QUESTIONS TO BE ADDRESSED IN THIS CHAPTER

1   What was Ritschl's contribution to liberal theology?
2   How did Harnack seek to shift Christian theology?
3   What was the Social Gospel according to Rauschenbusch?
4   How did Bultmann and Tillich reorient liberal theology after the Wars?

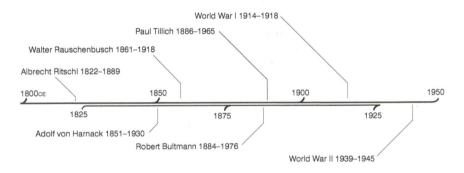

Timeline 27 Liberal Protestantism

Today the term "liberal" is often applied to one's opponents who are thought not to properly endorse the traditional values and beliefs of a community. Even in theological discussions, "liberal" often has a negative connotation. But among academic theologians, "liberal theology" typically refers to a specific historical period and group of theologians in the nineteenth and early twentieth centuries. During this time period, several prominent Protestant theologians adopted the term "liberal" for their own approach to theology. They freely admitted that they were reappropriating theological terms and concepts so as to fit within the context of the modern world as they understood it. Perhaps most distinctive in their approach is an emphasis on the practical implications of Christian faith as flowing out of the moral teachings of Jesus and the role of the Church in helping to effect the realization of this morality in culture. The massive wars of the twentieth century largely undermined their ideal of cultural progress, but the "liberal" approach to Christian thought remains an active strand of theology today. In this chapter we'll see the roots and development of that approach.

1 RITSCHL AND THE KINGDOM OF GOD

The dominant figure of the Liberal Protestant movement was Albrecht Ritschl (1822–1889). He was a theology professor in Germany at Bonn and then Göttingen from 1846 until his death. Especially for the fifty years spanning the last quarter of the nineteenth century and the first quarter of the twentieth, his influence was second to none among the theologians. His work provided the context for theological discussion, and he was enormously successful in establishing a school of thought that was pervasive and dominant. Writing in 1897 James Orr (himself no disciple of Ritschl) called the rise of Ritschl's viewpoint, "the most remarkable phenomenon in the recent history of religious thought."[1]

Like Schleiermacher (see Chapter 25), Ritschl was concerned to understand the claims of Christianity in relation to the scientific worldview that was steadily gaining momentum in his society. And in agreement with Schleiermacher, he took pains to distinguish the scientific approach to knowledge from the religious approach. But Ritschl's account is more subtle and in some ways anticipates the philosophy of science of the second half of the twentieth century. The distinction between the categories of fact, value, and feeling is not as absolute for him. So he cannot simply identify religion with feeling as Schleiermacher did and hope to solve the problem moderns felt about how to understand religion in a world explained by science.

According to Ritschl, in the practice of science, we think about and organize the perceptions delivered to us by our senses, especially paying attention to their causes. But that kind of thinking does not occur in isolation; it is always accompanied and guided by feeling.[2] Ritschl argued that thinking results from paying attention to certain sensations, and attention is a matter of will; but then feeling determines the will insofar as feeling expresses the consciousness that something is worth knowing about. It is this feeling of worth that lies at the base of scientific knowledge and therefore imbues science with value.

There is still a distinction to be made, though, between science and religion, because not all values are the same. The kind of values associated with scientific thinking are "disinterested" values because they involve no moral ends. Religion, on the other hand, involves "independent" value judgments, which are "perceptions of moral ends or moral hindrances."[3]

It may seem, then, that since the values involved in science are disinterested, science is still able to claim an objectivity that religion cannot on Ritschl's account. But this is not the case, because Ritschl believed that the study of doctrine within the Christian religion did have objectivity for the Christian community.[4] That is to say, there are correct and incorrect articulations of Christian doctrine. Arguing against those who placed subjective experience at the foundation of theology, Ritschl said, "This is thoroughly modern; and is fitted seriously to compromise the objectivity of doctrine."[5] His aim as a theologian was to present what is universal about Christianity, and the basis for this was God's revelation in the Christian scriptures and the historical Christian community.

The proper identification of religion, then, is to be found in its "independent" value judgments and their identification of ends or purposes. For Christianity, the end or goal – or what might be called "the good" – is the most distinctive element of Ritschl's theology: the Kingdom of God. He defined it as follows:

The good in the Christian sense is the Kingdom of God, in other words the uninterrupted reciprocation of action springing from the motive of love – a Kingdom in which all are knit together in union with every one who can show the marks of a neighbour; further, it is that union of men in which all goods are appropriated in their proper subordination to the highest good.[6]

The Kingdom of God is the central doctrine for Ritschl, and all other doctrines are formed and defined in relation to it. Sin is shorn of the traditional doctrine of the Fall. Instead, it is described as that universal tendency of all humans for selfishness, which stands in opposition to the ideal of human unity that finds its fullest expression in the Kingdom of God. Salvation for Ritschl is not described with reference to the objective or juridical theories of atonement that had held sway since the time of Anselm, but is rather cashed out in a subjective theory in which God's forgiveness of sin allows our consciousness of guilt to be removed and thus enables us to fulfill our moral destiny in the Kingdom of God.[7] As such, Ritschl emphasizes reconciliation (which captures the original meaning of atonement: "at one-ment") over justification. Justification, he thinks, expresses only a passive determination for sinners – something is merely done to them. But reconciliation, on the other hand, expresses the fact that those who had been engaged in active opposition to God have been reunited with God, and they are able to actively participate in God's purposes, which is the Kingdom.[8]

It is the Kingdom of God that provides for Ritschl even the understanding of the nature of God. Ritschl had no use for abstract metaphysical definitions, and instead understood God from the effects on the world. And the doctrine of Christ rests not on theoretical speculation like that found in the doctrinal formulation of Chalcedon. That is really an attempt to be scientific in our understanding of Christ, and as such removes the person of Christ from the proper value judgments of religion which see him in relation to the end or purpose. Such theologians "would have us make confession of the Godhead of Christ in this particular formula, before ever His Godhead has been proved to us in His saving influence upon ourselves."[9] Such theologians are attempting to provide a Christology "from above". It is Ritschl's contention, in continuity with what we saw in Schleiermacher, that Christology must be conducted "from below".

2 HARNACK AND THE COMMANDMENT OF LOVE

Continuing in this vein was Ritschl's most prominent disciple, Adolf von Harnack. He was from a solidly confessional Lutheran family, who became increasingly uneasy with his attachment to Ritschl and Ritschlian theology. But Harnack always understood his work to be in service to the Church. It was just that he believed the Church and its external forms of religion had become distracted from the central message of Jesus.

Harnack's monumental work, *History of Dogma*, endeavored to expose the Hellenization of Christianity in the centuries after Christ. He contended that just like the earlier generations of Christians rejected Gnostic influences on Christian doctrine, so too we should reject the metaphysical speculations of the Church Fathers who introduced Greek concepts in their theologizing of Christ.

Especially troubling to Harnack was the two-nature formulation of Christology by Chalcedon, for it had lost all connection with the historical Jesus. The historical reconstruction of the life of Jesus was a necessary component to understanding Christianity correctly. He believed that we

HARNACK AND WWI

There is a curious incident about Harnack's support of Germany's justification for World War I – a move that led Barth to reject liberal theology as insufficiently committed to the gospel of Jesus Christ. After the war, Harnack remained engaged in government affairs, supporting the Weimar Republic and social reforms, and realizing his misguided support of German nationalism in WWI. He opposed the rising anti-Semitism in Germany, but did not live long enough to see the dissolution of the Weimar Republic and Hitler's rise to power. Some people wonder whether he would have supported Germany again in World War II, but it is difficult to believe that his penchant for German nationalism would have clouded his judgment again in this way.

cannot let theoretical dogmas replace our appreciation of Jesus himself and his message. Harnack wanted to clearly separate the original gospel *of* Jesus from the later gospel *about* Jesus.[10] In his most popular book, *What is Christianity?* he claimed that the gospel of Jesus could be organized around three dominant themes:

> Firstly, the kingdom of God and its coming.
> Secondly, God the Father and the infinite value of the human soul.
> Thirdly, the higher righteousness and the commandment of love.[11]

Harnack saw Jesus's message of the kingdom as both a future event when God will visibly rule the world, and as an inward event that was inaugurated at Jesus's preaching. The former, external aspect of the kingdom was taken over from the culture in which Jesus lived; the latter, internal aspect was an innovation in Jewish thinking and the real kernel of the message of the kingdom.[12]

The next central theme for Harnack was an emphasis on God as Father. Of course, that highlights in our relationship with God our role as children. This ought to give us confidence and peace that the God of the universe is on our side. Drawing from Jesus's comparison of us with the sparrows (Matthew 10:29), Harnack reflects,

> Jesus Christ calls to every poor soul; he calls to every one who bears a human face: You are children of the living God, and not only better than many sparrows but of more value than the whole world.[13]

Finally, the higher righteousness and commandment of love is the obvious outworking of the teachings of Jesus. Love is the root and motive of all that the Christian does. It is a love that is marked by humility as described in the Beatitudes of Matthew 5. It is there (and in the rest of the Sermon on the Mount) that Jesus described our ethical duty, which has tangible effects on how we treat others in our communities. "The love of one's neighbour is the only practical proof on earth of that love of God which is strong in humility."[14] It is to be expected, then, that those following Harnack would be drawn to what was called the Social Gospel.

3 RAUSCHENBUSCH AND THE SOCIAL GOSPEL

Walter Rauschenbusch (1861–1918) was the son of a German Lutheran pastor who became a missionary to the United States, where he converted to the German Baptist denomination. He was born in Rochester, New York, where his father had become a professor at Rochester Theological Seminary. After a few rebellious years as a teenager, he had a prodigal son conversion experience, returning to the pietistic roots of his family. After high school, he was sent to Germany to be educated and flourished there in a classical education of Greek, Hebrew, Latin, and French. He then returned to the US to enroll in his father's seminary in Rochester.

The seminary was conservative, but Walter was most attracted to the more "liberal" professors, not being able to accept the narrow view of biblical interpretation and of substitutionary atonement espoused by most there. But whereas it might be expected of one on such a trajectory that he would gravitate toward an academic career, two summers as pastor to a struggling Baptist congregation in Louisville convinced him that he could best understand and spread the gospel in a vocation of pastoral ministry. He wrote in a letter to a friend,

It is now no longer my found hope to be a learned theologian and write big books. I want to be a pastor, powerful with men, preaching to them Christ as the man in whom their affections and energies can find the satisfaction for which mankind is groaning.[15]

In 1886 Rauschenbusch accepted a ministerial call to the Second German Baptist Church in a rough neighborhood of New York City. He came with the evangelistic desire to see the souls of his parish saved, but the social conditions in which he found himself drove him to a different understanding of the gospel.

At the end of the nineteenth century, a version of extreme capitalism was loose in America with very little regulation to control it. As a result, the poor German immigrant population where Rauschenbusch ministered was exploited. People lived in cramped tenement buildings where malnutrition, disease, and squalor were rampant. His pietistic friends urged him to focus on the spiritual needs of his parishioners rather than to embroil himself in the social politics of the modern city, but Rauschenbusch could not separate the two. In this sense, the trajectory of liberalism was again a response to the modern condition that had attempted to keep religion cordoned off in the realm of value or private opinion. The social gospel of Rauschenbusch was a clear extension of the Ritschl/Harnack trajectory of thinking on the Kingdom of God.

After living in New York City for eighteen months, Rauschenbusch began writing and speaking on the topic of social reform. He joined with two other pastors in the city, Leighton Williams and Nathaniel Schmidt, and for twenty years this "Brotherhood of the Kingdom," as the group came to be called, spoke and wrote on the theme that the gospel must transform not just individuals but society itself. Rauschenbusch was influenced by the British theologian, F.D. Maurice, whom Richard Niebuhr identified as the chief contemporary exemplar of the "Christ Transforming Culture" motif in his classic work *Christ and Culture*. This was not just socialism of the sort that was becoming popular as a political ideology. Rauschenbusch was under no delusion that a just social order in itself would bring about individuals who were just and selfless. Personal and social salvation must be linked. Some descendants of the Social Gospel movement may have given up on personal salvation, but Rauschenbusch was convinced that the Church of his day had largely ignored the social dimension of what Jesus had claimed he came to do.

EXCERPT FROM *CHRISTIANITY AND THE SOCIAL CRISIS*

In personal religion the first requirement is to repent and believe in the gospel ... Social religion, too, demands repentance and faith: repentance for our social sins; faith in the possibility of a new social order. As long as a man sees in our present society only a few inevitable abuses and recognizes no sin and evil deep-seated in the very constitution of the present order, he is still in a state of moral blindness and without conviction of sin ... Regeneration includes that a man must pass under the domination of the spirit of Christ, so that he will judge of life as Christ would judge of it. That means a revaluation of social values. Things that are now "exalted among men" must become "an abomination" to him because they are built on wrong and misery. Unless a man finds his judgment at least on some fundamental questions in opposition to the current ideas of the age, he is still a child of this world and has not "tasted the powers of the coming age." He will have to repent and believe if he wants to be a Christian in the full sense of the word.[16]

Rauschenbusch's first two major books were *Christianity and the Social Crisis* (1907) and *Christianizing the Social Order* (1912). In keeping with his calling, these were not heady, theological tomes written for professors, but rather popular expositions attempting to call the Church to its proper place within society.

Then in 1917 Rauschenbusch wrote *A Theology for the Social Gospel*. In it he attempted to work through more systematically the theological underpinning of his social gospel movement. Introducing his work he said,

The first three chapters are to show that an adequate intellectual basis for the social gospel, is necessary, feasible, desirable, and legitimate. The remainder of the book offers concrete suggestions how some of the most important sections of doctrinal theology may be expanded and readjusted to make room for the religious convictions summed up in "the social gospel."[17]

So the Kingdom of God becomes "humanity organized according to the will of God"[18] and sin occurs whenever we "set our profit and ambition above the welfare of our fellows and above the Kingdom of God which binds them together."[19] Salvation, then, concerns not merely our relationship to God, but also toward our fellow human beings. Put most radically, Rauschenbusch said, "Salvation is the voluntary socializing of the soul."[20] And regarding eschatology, he looked to purge non-Christian ideas from the traditional view of the future that had been propagated. Instead of dying and going to a far-off heaven that is completely distinct from the present order of things, Rauschenbusch sought to reclaim the millennial reign of Christ on earth as a desire for,

> a social order in which the worth and freedom of every least human being will be honoured and protected; in which the brotherhood of man will be expressed in the common possession of the economic resources of society; and in which the spiritual good of humanity will be set high above the private profit interests of all materialistic groups.[21]

This type of society will not come by some catastrophic or even miraculous event, but by development and progress. Such an achievement will require all of our constructive and educational resources, and we should not expect that it will have some final consummation. Rauschenbusch does not rule out life after death for individuals, but it would have to be a continued existence in a society of other people who are still engaged in productive work for the Kingdom.

4 BULTMANN, TILLICH, AND RETHINKING CHRISTIAN DOCTRINE

The line of liberal theology we have considered has its natural end in optimism about human progress. The scientific developments that emerged from the modern period were remarkable and positively influencing society. But then World War I dealt a tremendous blow to the expectation that humanity would solve the problems of the modern world. It was difficult to believe that the world was getting better and better when the "Great War" was responsible for the deaths of more than 15 million people. Then within two decades it was obvious that all the major powers of the world would be involved in another even larger world-wide conflict, which would claim the lives of more than 70 million people. Thus the framework of modernism unraveled for many theologians because its tenets could not be squared with the reality of the world situation.

As we saw in the previous chapter, the philosophy of existentialism became a new framework or backdrop for Christian theology in the work of Barth. Existentialism had Christian roots in Kierkegaard and the Russian novelist Fyodor Dostoyevski, but it had become primarily atheistic in its orientation in philosophical circles. Inspired by Barth, two German theologians worked to appropriate existentialism for liberal Protestant thought in the middle of the twentieth century, primarily through the concept of human choice. We are confronted with a challenge or offer of a faith-filled life; how will we choose? We'll see how this plays out briefly in the thought of Bultmann and Tillich.

Rudolf Bultmann was primarily a New Testament scholar in his professional life. Thinking Barth's approach to the Bible to be naïve, he pioneered a method of critical Bible study called "form criticism." The approach looks at the Bible not as a source of information about God or Jesus Christ, but as information about the communities which developed the documents in the first place. Shifting the focus from God to humans is characteristic of the existentialist approach to his theology. The issue for Bultmann is not what God is like or what Christ has done for us; rather, the Word (the logos) has been preached through Jesus Christ and confronts us with the choice of interpreting our own existence through him and his life and death, or through the world's categories. Redemption seems to become an opportunity to understand ourselves as people who identify with the crucified and risen Christ, and faith is that which illuminates this understanding of ourselves.[22] In the language of existentialism, sin becomes "inauthentic existence" and salvation "authentic existence."

Changing terminology is part of Bultmann's strategy to "demythologize" the content of the Gospel for contemporary ears. It is not that the biblical authors were wrong, but that theirs was a worldview drastically different from ours. For example, twentieth-century Christians can't believe that

Christ will swoop down from heaven and return to the earth the way the first-century Christians believed. But that doesn't mean that the kernel of the idea must be thrown out as well. Instead, there is a deeper meaning which can be preserved and given new meaning in contemporary terms.

> We must ask whether the eschatological preaching and the mythological sayings as a whole contain a still deeper meaning which is concealed under the cover of mythology. If that is so, let us abandon the mythological conceptions precisely because we want to retain their deeper meaning. This method of interpretation of the New Testament which tries to recover the deeper meaning behind the mythological conceptions I call *de-mythologizing* – an unsatisfactory word, to be sure. Its aim is not to eliminate the mythological statements but to interpret them.[23]

Bultmann's concern to translate theological concepts to contemporary ears resulted in his famous quip, "It is impossible to use electric light and the radio and to avail ourselves of modern medical and surgical discoveries and at the same time to believe in the New Testament world of spirits and miracles."[24]

His countryman, Paul Tillich, continued this concern. After leaving Germany for America under the Nazi threat in 1933, Tillich became something of a theological superstar. He was probably better known among the general populace than any theologian was during the twentieth century. This was the result of an intentional focus by him: "My whole theological work has been directed to the interpretation of religious symbols in such a way that the secular man – and we are all secular – can understand and be moved by them."[25]

Much like Friedrich Schleiermacher had done in the nineteenth century, Tillich sought to make theology persuasive to religious skeptics. As such, all of his theology had an apologetic bent, and he was concerned less to offer doctrines about God than he was to answer questions that arose from secular society. He was harshly critical of neo-orthodoxy's tendency to eschew apologetic concerns and merely throw the Christian message at people "like a stone" instead of attempting to answer the questions put to it by contemporary culture.[26]

Tillich's primary theological approach was called "correlation." He claimed that culture, through its philosophy and art, posed questions of

PAUL TILLICH FROM *THE COURAGE TO BE*

The anxiety of meaninglessness is anxiety about the loss of an ultimate concern, of a meaning which gives meaning to all meanings. This anxiety is aroused by the loss of a spiritual center, of an answer, however symbolic and indirect, to the question of the meaning of existence.

There are no valid arguments for the "existence" of God, but there are acts of courage in which we affirm the power of being, whether we know it or not. If we know it, we accept acceptance consciously. If we do not know it, we nevertheless accept it and participate in it. And in our acceptance of that which we do not know the power of being is manifest to us. Courage has revealing power, the courage to be is the key to being-itself.[27]

significant existential importance, and that it was theology's task to provide answers to these based on the revelation of God and in the language that contemporary culture can understand. Religion communicates through symbols, and these symbols must be explained and accommodated to culture. His major academic work, *Systematic Theology*, is divided into five parts. Each of these parts correlates some component of the Christian religious tradition as an answer to a deep-seated question that has emerged in culture. For example, contemporary humans have expressed their existential angst of finitude – the threat of non-being – by asking the question how we can withstand the destructive forces that threaten to disintegrate our lives. Theologians respond with the religious symbol of God as the Creator. Tillich unpacks this symbol to mean that God is Being itself, he is the ground of all being, and hence is our ultimate concern. All attempts to ground our lives on anything other than God result in inauthentic life and incompleteness. It is the Christian message that the historical person Jesus became the bearer of the New Being available in God, and so was symbolized as Christ. "It is the certainty of one's own victory over the death of existential estrangement which creates the certainty of the Resurrection of the Christ as event and symbol."[28]

The figurative reinterpretations and abstractions of central doctrines of the Christian faith by the liberal Protestant theologians in the twentieth century seem to be a significant departure from what had come before. More conservative and traditional Christians were quick to point out that such revisions seemed to throw out the baby with the bathwater. Perhaps most famous of these indictments was this one by Richard Niebuhr:

> In similar manner the idea of the coming kingdom was robbed of its dialectical element. It was all fulfillment of promise without judgment. It was thought to be growing out of the present so that no great crisis needed to intervene between the order of grace and the order of glory. In its one-sided view of progress which saw the growth of the wheat but not that of the tares, the gathering of the grain but not the burning of the chaff, this liberalism was indeed naively optimistic. A God without wrath brought men without sin into a kingdom without judgment through the ministrations of Christ without a cross.[29]

Of course, there were other strands of Christian thought developing as well. We turn to them in the next chapter.

SUMMARY OF MAIN POINTS

1 Ritschl emphasized the Kingdom of God as the goal or end of Christian doctrine and practice.
2 Harnack believed that Christian thought should turn from theoretical speculation about Jesus to an appreciation of the message of Jesus.
3 Rauschenbusch understood the Kingdom of God to be progressively enacted as Christians worked to organize society according to the will of God.
4 Bultmann and Tillich adopted the framework of existentialism and emphasized human experience over and above literal doctrines about God.

FOR FURTHER READING

Gary Dorrien, *The Making of American Liberal Theology: Idealism, Realism, and Modernity, 1900–1950* (Louisville: Westminster John Knox Press, 2003). An extensive survey of the time period in which liberal theology transitioned to America.

Adolf von Harnack, *What is Christianity?* Thomas Bailey Saunders (trans.) (Philadelphia: Fortress Press, 1986). A collection of public lectures Harnack gave in 1899–1900 to explain his understanding of the Gospel to a popular audience.

Walter Rauschenbusch, *Christianity and the Social Crisis* (London: MacMillan & Co., 1914). His popular exposition of the social gospel.

Albrecht Ritschl, *The Christian Doctrine of Justification and Reconciliation*, Mackintosh and Macaulay, eds. (Clifton, NJ: Reference Book Publishers, Inc., 1966). A long but readable book that gives systematic treatment to Ritschl's theology.

J.B. Stump, "Liberal Theology" in *The Routledge Companion to Modern Christian Thought*, Chad Meister and James Beilby, eds. (London: Routledge, 2013). An article that goes into more depth on several of the topics in this chapter.

28

Major theological traditions and developments in the twentieth century

QUESTIONS TO BE ADDRESSED IN THIS CHAPTER

1   What conservative theological developments occurred in the twentieth century?
2   What were the effects of the most significant religious event in Roman Catholicism in the twentieth century?
3   What is the status of Eastern Orthodoxy in relation to the other major Christian traditions in the twentieth century?
4   How does process theology understand God and creation different than classical theism?

In the previous chapter we examined some of the key voices in liberal theology in the nineteenth and twentieth centuries. In this chapter we continue in the twentieth century by examining some of the major theological traditions and developments that occurred in that century. We first focus on developments in the three central streams of Christianity – Protestantism, Roman Catholicism, and Eastern Orthodoxy – while the final section examines a recent theological development that reaches across each of the streams.

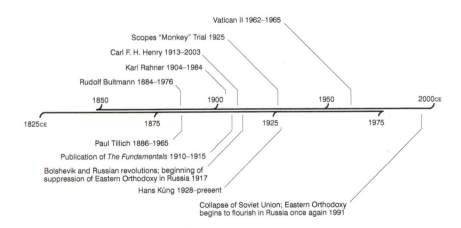

Timeline 28 Major theological traditions in the twentieth century

1 FUNDAMENTALISM AND EVANGELICALISM

The term "Evangelicalism" has not been used consistently across the ages. Literally, it comes from the Greek word for "good news" and is often confused with the similar term "evangelistic." On the continent in Europe today, Evangelicals are typically equated with Protestants, and in England they are often the less formal and liturgical brand of Protestants, like Baptists, as opposed to the Methodists and Anglicans. In America today, the Evangelical movement cuts across denominations and instead refers more specifically to the revivalistic attitude, which emphasizes personal conversion through the "born again" experience. Thus there are Evangelical Baptists, Methodists, and even Catholics in addition to the most rapidly growing demographic of Evangelicals – the non-denominational.

Toward the end of the twentieth century, Evangelicals became a political force in the United States and a major influence in the culture wars being fought there over social issues like abortion and rights of homosexuals. Twentieth-century Evangelicalism (or Neo-Evangelicalism, as the movement was called when it emerged mid-century) began, however, as an intellectual reaction to and engagement with both the more liberal strains of Christian thought and the more conservative Fundamentalism out of which it arose. The Evangelical movement, led by Carl F. H. Henry (1913–2003), emphasized the authority of Scripture and was wary of critical methods that undermined the historicity of biblical accounts or other traditional interpretations of Christian doctrines. Interestingly, Fundamentalism had a similar impulse at the beginning of the century.[1]

From 1910 to 1915 twelve volumes of some 90 essays by Bible teachers and pastors were collected by A. C. Dixon, the pastor of Moody Church in Chicago, and published under the title *The Fundamentals*. A southern California Christian businessman, Lyman Stewart, financed the effort and sent out free of charge more than three million volumes of the collection to Christian workers and students all over the English-speaking world.[2] The essays defended what they took to be the "fundamental" doctrines like the Virgin Birth of Christ, the deity of Christ, and the divine inspiration of Scripture against the onslaught of liberal theology. Ironically, their argument was that those who were giving up on the fundamentals were not being scientific enough. They argued that the best explanation of the data of Scripture when one took an unbiased and truly scientific look at the matter was that the doctrines were, in fact, as the Bible presented them to be. Despite the incredible volume of books that were distributed, they made relatively little impact on the scholarly world. There was an impact, however, on the mindset of a major portion of practicing Christians, who by 1920 had adopted the moniker "Fundamentalists" and saw themselves as combating the specious "scientific" conclusions of modernism by providing alternate scientific accounts that supported traditional Christian doctrines.

The relationship between fundamentalism and culture took a significant turn for the worse in 1925. The major news event of the summer was what has become known as the Scopes Monkey Trial. John Scopes was a high school teacher in Tennessee who agreed to teach Darwinian evolution in deliberate violation of a state law in Tennessee in order that the law could be subjected to review. His defense team aimed to show that the Fundamentalists supporting the law were ignorant yokels who knew nothing about science.[3] Even though Scopes was found guilty and fined $100 (though never had to pay due to a technicality), the defense achieved its goals, largely through the newspaper reports which set the uneducated Fundamentalists and their literal interpretation of Scripture against the modern force of science. This set up a culture war in which Fundamentalists embraced their identity in a sort of siege mentality against the "over-educated" and cultured forces which looked

ONE VIEW OF FUNDAMENTALISTS

H. L. Mencken, journalist reporting on the Scopes trial, characterizes Fundamentalists for the cultured elite on the east coast:

They are thick in the mean streets behind the gas-works. They are everywhere where learning is too heavy a burden for mortal minds to carry, even the vague, pathetic learning on tap in the little red schoolhouses. They march with the Klan, with the Christian Endeavor Society, with the Junior Order of United American Mechanics, with the Epworth League, with all the Rococo bands that poor and unhappy folk organize to bring some new light of purpose into their lives.[4]

down their noses at them. Fundamentalists increasingly withdrew from intellectual currents of society.

In 1947, a young theologian named Carl Henry published a book called *The Uneasy Conscience of Modern Fundamentalism*. It was a call for conservative "Bible-believing" Christians to reengage culture and demonstrate the rationality of their beliefs before they became completely irrelevant to society. In the preface he says,

> Unless we experience a rebirth of apostolic passion, Fundamentalism in two generations will be reduced either to a tolerated cult status or, in the event of Roman Catholic domination in the United States, become once again a despised and oppressed sect. The only live alternative, it appears to me, is a rediscovery of the revelational classics and the redemptive power of God, which shall lift our jaded culture to a level that gives significance again to human life... The hour is ripe now, if we seize it rightly, for a rediscovery of the Scriptures and of the meaning of the Incarnation for the human race.[5]

The result was that out of Fundamentalism emerged a new group known as Neo-Evangelicals. Their presence became felt both in popular culture through the charisma of the evangelist Billy Graham, and in academia through the rise of Evangelical seminaries like Fuller Theological Seminary, Asbury Theological Seminary, and Trinity Evangelical Divinity School. Also contributing to the climate of renewal, the Evangelical Theological Society formed in 1949 to promote serious scholarly engagement from an Evangelical perspective. Foundational to that perspective is the authority of the Bible and the Trinitarian doctrine of God.[6]

These two emphases on the Bible and the Trinity stem from Henry's work. First and foremost for him was the authority of the Bible. "Evangelical scholars are fully aware that the doctrine of the Bible controls all other doctrines of the Christian faith."[7] This is because in his view the Bible is the repository of God's propositional revelation to humanity. God has spoken – about himself and about what is necessary for humans to know concerning their salvation. The human authors of Scripture received divine inspiration to record God's words, thereby guaranteeing their truthfulness. Henry was influential in developing the Chicago Statement on Biblical Inerrancy in 1978 which became the closest thing Evangelicals have to a common creedal statement.

CHICAGO STATEMENT ON BIBLICAL INERRANCY, 1978

A Short Statement

1   God, who is Himself Truth and speaks truth only, has inspired Holy Scripture in order thereby to reveal Himself to lost mankind through Jesus Christ as Creator and Lord, Redeemer and Judge. Holy Scripture is God's witness to Himself.

2   Holy Scripture, being God's own Word, written by men prepared and superintended by His Spirit, is of infallible divine authority in all matters upon which it touches: it is to be believed, as God's instruction, in all that it affirms; obeyed, as God's command, in all that it requires; embraced, as God's pledge, in all that it promises.

3   The Holy Spirit, Scripture's divine Author, both authenticates it to us by His inward witness and opens our minds to understand its meaning.

4   Being wholly and verbally God-given, Scripture is without error or fault in all its teaching, no less in what it states about God's acts in creation, about the events of world history, and about its own literary origins under God, than in its witness to God's saving grace in individual lives.

5   The authority of Scripture is inescapably impaired if this total divine inerrancy is in any way limited or disregarded, or made relative to a view of truth contrary to the Bible's own; and such lapses bring serious loss to both the individual and the Church.

Because of the divine self-disclosure of God in the Bible, Evangelicals could shift the emphasis of Christian thought back to God. For Henry and the Evangelicals, the central message is that God is who the Bible says he is, namely transcendent and triune. If the liberal theologians had become abstruse in their existential characterizations of God, the Evangelicals would swing things the other way to a literal reading of the attributes of God. Furthermore, Henry emphasizes the need to understand and defend the rationality of the biblical positions.

> Divine revelation is the source of all truth, the truth of Christianity included; reason is the instrument for recognizing it; Scripture is its verifying principle; logical consistency is a negative test for truth and coherence a subordinate test. The task of Christian theology is to exhibit the content of biblical revelation as an orderly whole.[8]

Evangelicalism in America today is becoming increasingly diverse, partly due to the rise of non-denominational churches. Yet in at least a loose sense, Evangelicals are committed to the following:

1 Scripture as the ultimate authority.
2 The uniqueness of Christ and his achievement of redemption through death on the cross.
3 The need for personal conversion, or being "born again."
4 The importance of personal witness to others in evangelism.

In contrast to the decentralized nature of Protestant Evangelicalism, Roman Catholicism has continued its centralized and hierarchical structure. However, during the twentieth century we see new developments in Catholicism, both within its own teachings and with its relationships to those outside its tradition.

2 ROMAN CATHOLICISM

By just about any assessment, the Second Ecumenical Council of the Vatican, also called Vatican II, was the most significant event of the twentieth century for Roman Catholics. Vatican II, the twenty-first major council of the Roman Catholic Church, opened in 1962 and continued for several years, closing in 1965. It focused primarily on Church doctrine

Figure 28.1 A photo view of St Peter's Basilica, at Vatican City © Michał Ludwiczak/iStock

and practice and its relation to other religions, and its influence went far beyond the Catholic Church. Over a period of four years it created four constitutions, nine decrees, and three declarations.

With Pope John XXIII residing and over 2,500 participants, including leading Catholic theologians such as Karl Rahner and Hans Küng in attendance, a number of central themes emerged from Vatican II. While no new dogmas were created, those espousing reform were in the majority, and so there were significant developments which came out of the council.

One of the changes that emerged in Vatican II had to do with the mass. Prior to this time, the mass was always held in Latin. The Council opened the door to vernacular masses, however, and soon the mass was commonly being translated from Latin into local languages. This was revolutionary indeed, for now the common person could actually understand what was being said in the mass!

Another development had to do with Scripture.[9] The Dogmatic Constitution on Divine Revelation (Dei Verbum) produced at Vatican II had its own drama. The first draft of the document reflected a very conservative theological position. Pope John XXIII, unhappy with this, intervened and promoted instead the development of a new draft which was assigned to a different commission, consisting of both conservatives and progressives. The final document was based on this more progressive edition. It included the important point that revelation is primarily God's manifestation of himself – not simply doctrines expressed propositionally (one is reminded here of Barth's neo-orthodoxy). Furthermore, the Bible was described as the ultimate source of truth, to some extent perhaps even in contrast to the Bible and tradition as being equal partners of authority – the latter being a position the Protestant Reformers were so opposed to.[10]

A third development that emerged from Vatican II was ecumenism. There were a number of facets to this, including that Christ can be found outside the Catholic Church and an affirmation of a religious freedom of conscience.[11] It also included the notion that there is truth found in non-Christian religions (notably Hinduism, Buddhism, Judaism, and Islam), a turnabout from the previous Catholic renunciation of all non-Catholic traditions. Declaration *Nostra Aetate* included the following statement – a shock to many Catholic traditionalists at the time:

> The Church ... has this exhortation for her sons: prudently and lovingly, through dialogue and collaboration with the followers of other religions, and in witness of Christian faith and life, acknowledge, preserve, and promote the spiritual and moral goods found among these men, as well as the values in their society and culture.[12]

Also, for the first time in history, the Catholic Church recognized the Eastern Orthodox Church and Protestants as being true Christians, although they were still "separated brothers."[13] They were now recognized as a real part of the Christian kin, even if they were estranged relatives who would hopefully be brought back to the official family. Many saw these changes in the Catholic Church as revolutionary, and while Vatican II did reaffirm earlier councils, such as Trent (1545–1563) and Vatican I (1869–1870), it clearly reflected a new openness to ideas in the modern world.

One theologian whose work was especially influential to Vatican II and to a broader interpretation of Catholic doctrine and dogma was Karl Rahner (1904–1984). Rahner was a German, Catholic theologian who is widely considered to be one of the most important theologians of the twentieth century. In the twentieth century he was as influential in Catholicism as Barth was in Protestantism. His vast works have been collected into a twenty volume set entitled *Theological Investigations*. During his theological training he became especially interested in Ignatian spirituality, Thomistic theology, the transcendental philosophy of Immanuel Kant, the continental phenomenology of Martin Heidegger, and the neo-orthodoxy of Karl Barth – five influences that had a major impact on his own thought and practice.

Rahner's theological works are terse and dense, and often subject to controversies of interpretation. A primary emphasis of his scholarship was the attempt to merge the best thought of intellectual history with the best thought of the current day, and his broad theological and philosophical education provided him the intellectual tools necessary for bridging Catholic doctrine with the neo-scholastic theology of earlier generations. One of his major contributions to Catholic thought is his position known as the "supernatural existential." On this view, the grace of God is universally manifest throughout creation, and all human beings, regardless of race, religion, or location, have within their nature the created capacity to receive God's self-revelation; this is a fundamental element of human existence.

Following this train of thought, Rahner maintained a wideness in God's grace and mercy and developed the notion of the "anonymous Christian." This is an inclusivist view in which all people can be saved through Christ even if they have never heard about Christ or the gospel.

> Anonymous Christianity means that a person lives in the grace of God and attains salvation outside of explicitly constituted Christianity … . Let us say, a Buddhist monk … who, because he follows his conscience, attains salvation and lives in the grace of God; of him I must say that he is an anonymous Christian; if not, I would have to presuppose that there is a genuine path to salvation that really attains that goal, but that simply has nothing to do with Jesus Christ. But I cannot do that. And so, if I hold if everyone depends upon Jesus Christ for salvation, and if at the same time I hold that many live in the world who have not expressly recognized Jesus Christ, then there remains in my opinion nothing else but to take up this postulate of an anonymous Christianity.[14]

This position appears to run contrary to earlier Catholic teaching in which "it is altogether necessary to salvation for every human creature to be subject to the [Pope]."[15] However, while this papal bull (a charter issued by the Pope) continues to be affirmed by the Catholic Church, it is now widely reinterpreted through the lenses of Rahner's "anonymous Christian" theology. Rahner's work continues to be studied and applied not only in the Catholic Church, but in Protestant theology and even among those of non-Christian religious traditions.

Another influential Catholic of the twentieth century was the Swiss theologian, Hans Küng (1928–). He was appointed professor of theology at the University in Tübingen, Germany, and in 1962 he was appointed an official theologian by Pope John XXIII at the Second Vatican Council. He was a controversial theologian – calling for reform in the Church, questioning Church dogma, and attempting to unify Catholicism with other Christian denominations – and he had a major influence on the Second Vatican Council, even serving as an expert theological advisor to Council members.

Küng's doctoral dissertation focused on Barth's view of justification and its relationship to Roman Catholic views of the subject. Through this work Küng attempted to bring together Catholics and Protestants by demonstrating that Protestant neo-orthodoxy (à la Barth) and Roman Catholics really were saying the same thing in terms of justification, and that the differences were simply terminological ones.[16] He also argued for internal reform in the Roman Catholic Church and his criticisms, most notably of papal infallibility, eventually led to his being censored by the Vatican and his being banned from teaching as a Catholic theologian.

3 EASTERN ORTHODOXY

After the fall of Constantinople to the Islamic Ottoman Empire in 1453, the primary leaders of the Eastern Orthodox Church and its influence moved to Russia, in particular to Moscow. (Remember that Eastern Orthodoxy arose as a distinct stream of Christianity after the eleventh century schism between Eastern and Western Christendom; see Chapter 13). Orthodoxy thrived in Russia and what eventually became the Russian Orthodox Church, or the Orthodox Christian Church of Russia, flourished until the Russian Revolution of 1917 (which involved both the Bolshevik revolution and the Russian civil war). Once under communist

Figure 28.2 Cathedral of Christ the Saviour in Moscow, Russia. Copyright Fabio Lavarone/iStock

rule, the Church was suppressed, persecuted, and secularized. With the displacement of communism in Russia and Eastern Europe in the early 1990s, however, Orthodoxy began to flourish once again. Today there are approximately 225 million Eastern Orthodox Christians scattered throughout the world, primarily located in the former Byzantine Empire (Greece, Turkey, and nearby countries) and in Russia.[17]

The Orthodox Church, as with the Roman Catholic Church, claims to be the One Holy, Catholic and Apostolic Church. The former is a communion of churches that recognizes and is recognized by, not the Pope in Rome (as with Catholics), but the Patriarch of Constantinople (Istanbul, Turkey) – the highest ranking bishop who has a position as "first among equals."[18] This communion comprises fifteen separate autocephalous (self-governing) churches – each of which recognizes the others as being "canonical." Timothy "Kallistos" Ware describes the Eastern Orthodox Church this way:

Timothy Ware (1934–) – now known as the Most Reverend Metropolitan Kallistos (Ware) of Diokleia, a titular metropolitan of the Ecumenical Patriarchate in Great Britain – is one of the most well-known Eastern Orthodox academics of the twentieth (and now twenty-first) century and a bishop of the Church. Two of his most important works are *The Orthodox Church* and *The Orthodox Way*.

The Orthodox Church is … a family of self-governing churches. It is held together, not by a centralizing organization, not by a single prelate wielding absolute power over the whole body, but by the double bond of unity in the faith and communion in the sacraments. Each church, while independent, is in full agreement with the rest on all matters of doctrine, and between them all there is full sacramental communion.[19]

The beliefs of Eastern Orthodoxy have been constant through the centuries and include, among many, the following central ones:

- That there are three Divine Persons in God, and that the Persons are distinct yet equal (The Trinity doctrine).
- That the Eucharist is the center of worship in which believers partake mystically of Christ's body and blood.
- That salvation is a uniting of the human and the divine to overcome human mortality, with the goal of Christian life being to participate in the deified humanity of Jesus Christ.
- That the Holy Scriptures and Holy Tradition are of equal value and importance and that they complete each other.
- That there are seven sacraments: Baptism, Chrismation (Confirmation), Communion (Eucharist), Holy Orders, Penance, Anointing of the Sick, and Marriage.
- That the Seven Ecumenical Councils are to be affirmed: Nicea (325), Constantinople (381), Ephesus (431), Chalcedon (451), Constantinople II (553), Constantinople III (680), and Nicea II (787).
- That Mary, the mother of Jesus, is Theotokos, which means "God-bearer" or "the Mother of God."

While most of these beliefs are basically affirmed by Protestants and Catholics (although in some cases understood a bit differently), two are distinctive of Orthodoxy, namely their understandings of sin and salvation. For Protestants and Catholics, sin is generally understood in legal or forensic terms. Human beings sinned against God, breaking his perfect law, and so they need to be punished. By God's grace, however, they are justified through faith in Christ and so can be saved. For the Eastern Orthodox, salvation is not a matter of divine legal pardoning. Rather, it is establishing once again the proper relationship between human beings and God as it was in the Garden of Eden before the Fall. It is to participate in the deified humanity of Jesus Christ (this is sometimes referred to as "theosis" or "deification") – a gradual process by which Christians become more and more like Christ. Other differences between the Orthodox and the other two streams of Christianity include the doctrine of the Trinity and the role of icons in worship (as noted back in Chapter 13).

Figure 28.3 Holy Trinity © State Tretyakov

Along with its core beliefs, the central practices in the Orthodox Church have been stable as well. The Church sees the local congregation as the realization of the Body of Christ in that locale, and so takes the services extremely seriously. The liturgy, the seven sacraments noted above, worship, and the veneration of icons are deep spiritual practices laden with theological significance in the Orthodox tradition.

While a separation still exists between the Roman Catholic Church and Eastern Orthodoxy, important attempts at reconciliation have been renewed in recent decades. In 1964, for example, the Second Vatican Council issued the following statement:

> The Catholic Church holds in high esteem the institutions of the Eastern Churches, their liturgical rites, ecclesiastical traditions, and Christian way of life. For, distinguished as they are by their venerable antiquity, they are bright with that tradition which was handed down from the Apostles through the Fathers, and which forms part of the divinely revealed and undivided heritage of the universal Church.[20]

Eastern Orthodoxy itself is in many ways taking an active role in the pursuit of global ecumenism – with both Catholics and Protestants. For example, virtually all Orthodox churches have now joined the World Council of Churches. In fact, it appears that for the first time in Christian history there is a developing emphasis on dialogue, unity, and beliefs that unite the three major streams of the faith rather than on what divides them.

4 PROCESS THEOLOGY

We saw in Chapter 26 that in the twentieth century Barth and his Neo-orthodox followers attempted to bring the central, historic Christian doctrines back into theology (albeit in a manner acceptable to modern ears) rather than integrate modernist ideas of science and higher criticism into theology as the liberals did. In that same century Fundamentalism, Evangelicalism, Roman Catholicism, and Eastern Orthodoxy also sought to affirm or reaffirm orthodox doctrines – sometimes even at the expense of rejecting the science and critical studies of the day. But another group of thinkers sought to merge the findings of contemporary science with Christian thought, and to meld science and theology into a new philosophical system of process.

Process theology is a school of thought based on the philosophical work of Alfred North Whitehead (1861–1947) and further developed by Charles Hartshorne (1897–2000), John B. Cobb (1925–), and others. Rooted in evolutionary thought and relativity theory, process theology holds that God's existence and God's creation are not static but dynamic and in constant evolution. Reality is made up of active processes, not stable substances as traditionally held in Greek philosophy and traditional Christian theology. Other central tenets of process theology are these:

- *Dipolar theism* – God has both a changing aspect and an unchanging aspect; God is not static being, but divine becoming.
- *Panentheism* – (from the Greek terms *pan*, meaning "all," *en*, meaning "in," and *theos*, meaning "God"); the view that God contains the world but is not identical with it; God is in the world and the world is in God.
- *Directed process* – the universe is constituted by process and change, which are effected through the free will of self-determining agents – God, human beings, and other free creatures.

Process thinkers maintain that many of the historic attributes of God, which they believe are derived from ancient pagan Greek philosophy rather than scripture, cannot be rendered plausible because of intractable philosophical and theological difficulties. Consider, for example, the attribute of omnipotence, about which Charles Hartshorne makes the following point:

> The idea of omnipotence in the sense to be criticized came about as follows: to be God, that is, worthy of worship, God must in power excel all others (and be open to criticism by none). The highest conceivable form of power must be the divine power. So far so good. Next question: what is the highest conceivable form of power? This question was scarcely put seriously at all, the answer was felt to be so obvious: it must be the power to determine every detail of what happens in the world. Not, notice, to significantly influence the happenings; no, rather to strictly determine, decide, their every detail. Hence it is that people still today ask, when catastrophe

strikes, Why did God do this to me? What mysterious divine reason could there be? Why me? I charge [orthodox] theologians with responsibility for this improper and really absurd question.[21]

Process theologians reassess and reconstruct this and many other of the divine attributes. God is not omnipotent but limited in ability – God has persuasive rather than coercive power. God is not immutable but changes as God interacts with the evolving universe; God grows in experiencing new joys, in acquiring new knowledge of real events, and in experiencing the values created over time by free agents in the world. And similarly with other divine attributes. Nevertheless, the abstract aspects of God, such as God's wisdom, goodness, beneficence, and so on are eternally stable.

Although process theology has waned somewhat in recent decades, it continues in theological influence in Christian and Jewish thought, and advances in biology and physics continue to be utilized by these theologians to bolster their process views. We suspect that as science evolves, this neoclassical theology (as Hartshorne calls it) will continue to be a major player in theological discussions. Furthermore, an important movement has emerged recently in Protestant theology, which draws heavily on process thought and is called "open theism" or "the openness of God."

Open theism is the view that God is omniscient and omnipotent, but 1) God lacks knowledge of certain future events (such as future free human actions) because they do not yet exist and so cannot possibly be known, even by an omniscient being; and 2) God's power is not determinative with respect to human will but is persuasive – God values the free will of human beings and the relationship God has with them which entails such non-coercive freedom. Open theists are criticized by orthodox theologians for rejecting certain traditional doctrines, and they are criticized by process theologians for retaining too many traditional doctrines. Nevertheless, the openness of God movement is noteworthy and still growing among Evangelicals. Some of the more influential open theists include William Hasker (1935–), Clark Pinnock (1937–2010), John Sanders (1956–), and Gregory Boyd (1957–).

As we have seen throughout the pages of this book, theology is not static; it is a dynamic activity that, ideally, utilizes the best ideas and insights from all of the relevant fields of study as it attempts to understand

God and the ways of God in the world. It is not always practiced in an ideal manner, of course (no discipline is), but from its origins up through the twentieth century, practitioners of Christian theology have never ceased to engage with the leading thinkers and disciplines of the day. This continues to be so. In the next chapter, we conclude the book by examining some of the most recent developments in Christian thought, and we envisage where things may be headed as theology moves into the future.

SUMMARY OF MAIN POINTS

1   Evangelicalism grew out of Fundamentalism and holds to conservative interpretations of the Bible and traditional Christian doctrine.

2   The Second Vatican Council was the twenty-first ecumenical council of the Roman Catholic Church and reflected the Church's readiness to acknowledge the developments of the modern world.

3   By the end of the twentieth century Eastern Orthodoxy, while continuing to affirm its central historic beliefs, entered into ecumenical discussions with Catholicism and Protestantism.

4   Process theology holds that God's existence and creation are not static substances but dynamic and evolutionary processes.

FOR FURTHER READING

Walter M. Abbott, ed. *The Documents of Vatican II* (Piscataway, NJ: America Press, 1966). All sixteen documents of Vatican II are translated and comments are offered by both Catholics and non-Catholics.

John B. Cobb and David Ray Griffin, *Process Theology: An Introductory Exposition* (Philadelphia: Westminster Press, 1976). A solid introduction to process theology by two leaders of the movement.

Stanley J. Grenz and Roger E. Olson, *20th Century Theology: God and the World in a Transitional Age* (Downers Grove, IL: InterVarsity Press, 1992). A critical assessment of the theologies and theologians of the twentieth century.

Harriet Harris, *Fundamentalism and Evangelicals* (Oxford: Oxford University Press, 1998). An insightful analysis of the historical relationship between American Evangelicalism and Fundamentalism.

Charles Hartshorne, *Omnipotence and Other Theological Mistakes* (Albany: State University of New York, 1984). An accessible and important work challenging orthodox understandings of the attributes of God.

Mark Noll, *American Evangelical Christianity: An Introduction* (Oxford: Blackwell, 2000). An accessible overview of the Evangelical movement in America by a leading contemporary church historian.

Timothy (Kallistos) Ware, *The Orthodox Church* (Baltimore, MD: Penguin Books, 1963). A clear presentation of the history, beliefs, and practices of the Eastern Orthodox by one of its leading members.

29

Recent and emerging themes

QUESTIONS TO BE ADDRESSED IN THIS CHAPTER

1   What are several recent theologies that seek liberation from various forms of injustice and subjugation?
2   Christianity is growing most rapidly in what part of the world, and within which stream?
3   What broad and sweeping shifts in thinking over the last several decades, with respect to methodology and values, have influenced culture at large, including Christian culture?
4   How are some recent theologians grappling with religious diversity and the many non-Christian religious adherents that now comprise our communities and cultures?
5   What are the central goals of environmental theology?
6   What is astrotheology and what sorts of issues are those engaged in this field of study focused on?

1 LIBERATION, BLACK, AND FEMINIST THEOLOGIES

As can be seen in the last several chapters, theological reflection took a significant turn inward from about the seventeenth century onward toward human beings and human experiences. This subjective turn, as we can call it, entered into Christian theology and for all intents and purposes has never really left. Indeed, in some ways it seems to be a growing phenomenon. We see this reflected in a variety of ways, from liberation and black theology to feminism to specific cultural theological developments. We will look at several forms this turn has taken, beginning with liberation theology.

Liberation theology emerged in South America in the 1960s as a response, primarily by Catholic priests who were working with the poor and underprivileged, to their situation. According to these priests, Catholic theology as historically developed was inadequate to address such social ills. Several theologians soon took up the issue, including the Peruvian theologian and Dominican priest Gustavo Gutiérrez (1928–). Born and raised in Lima, Peru, Gutiérrez has spent much of his life living with and working with the poor in Lima. He and other theologians and priests and bishops began to believe that an emphasis on orthopraxy (right practice) is more important that orthodoxy (right beliefs), and that Christian thought should be rooted in Christian experience. For centuries Catholic theology had flourished in Latin America, but its abstract theological formulations seemed to do little to help those in real need, and this point was becoming increasingly obvious in the late twentieth century to liberation thinkers. These new theologians emphasized liberation in this life over and above salvation in the next and claimed that no one needed liberation more than the poor and oppressed of Latin America.

At the heart of liberation thought is the view that theology should be a matter for current situations rather than a set of abstract principles disconnected from real life. Theology should be for today, for here and now, for this particular situation, for this people group of suffering people. Salvation in liberation theology, then, becomes a matter of political liberation – even involving social revolution if necessary.

> It is becoming more evident that the Latin American peoples will not emerge from their present status except by means of a profound transformation, a social revolution, which will qualitatively change the conditions in which they now live. The oppressed sectors within each country are becoming aware slowly, it is true, of their class interests and of the painful road which must be followed to accomplish the breakup of the status quo.[1]

Liberation theology in the late twentieth century became entangled with Marxism and communism, and Rome eventually spoke out against this, even including it on the current Vatican webpage:

> The warning of Paul VI remains fully valid today: Marxism as it is actually lived out poses many distinct aspects and questions for Christians to reflect upon and act on. However, it would be "illusory and dangerous to ignore the intimate bond which radically unites them, and to accept elements of the Marxist analysis without

recognizing its connections with the ideology, or to enter into the practice of class-struggle and of its Marxist interpretation while failing to see the kind of totalitarian society to which this process slowly leads".[2]

After the fall of communism in the 1990s, enthusiasm for a Marxist liberation theology waned significantly. But there are signs of its resurgence in Central and South America.

Beyond this possible rebirth of liberation theology, there are other ways it continues to be relevant to contemporary and emerging Christian thought, most notably as a response to the oppression of different people groups. One such development is black theology.

Black theology, which emerged out of the civil rights movement in the United States, is a theology based in the liberation of the marginalized and oppressed, most notably blacks in American and South African contexts. Theologian Dwight Hopkins offers the following description:

> Black theology is a self-reflexive discipline questioning the intellectual consistency and practical accountability of African American people to the faith they seek to believe in and practice. ... it presupposes the reality of black people in churches and community organizations involving themselves in advancing the particular affirming encounter between African Americans and God and reconstructing individual and systematic brokenness and woundedness. Black theology arises out of this ongoing dynamic and challenges people of faith to pause and think critically about whether what they are believing in and witnessing to is what they profess as their ultimate hope and final vision for all of humanity. Specifically, black theology investigates notions of racial and cultural identity in relation to faith.[3]

James H. Cone, generally considered to be the father of black liberation theology, argues that Jesus' central message was liberation of the poor – the materially poor – and that identifying with Jesus and his cause is to also identify with oppressed minorities, which in North America means especially the identification with blacks. Since Cone's initial developments, many other theologians of black liberation have emerged and have taken black liberation theology in a number of unique and surprising directions.[4]

A very different form of oppression has had to do with women, and another important development in Christian thought is feminist theology. Throughout this book we have attempted to include many of the female voices that have been influential in the history of Christian thought. These voices are often marginalized today, as they often were in Church history. While women in Christian history have often been treated as second-class citizens, if not completely suppressed, in recent decades much work by feminists and others has been undertaken to remedy this problem and to provide an honest assessment of the influence woman have actually had in Christian history.

This marginalization and suppression has taken many forms, including the roles that women have been "allowed" to hold. For example, in the Catholic and Orthodox Churches, women have never officially been allowed to be priests, bishops, archbishops, or cardinals; even today they are disallowed from such positions of authority over men in the Church. Nor, until recently, have women ever been recognized as official theologians from whom the Church (Catholic or Orthodox) has sought theological council or direction.[5] Women have held the highest authority positions in various Protestant denominations, but there, too, this is the exception rather than the rule.

Why has this happened? There are many reasons, including the patriarchal societies from which Christianity emerged and flourished. Judaism certainly maintained a patriarchal structure. For example, the Book of Ecclesiasticus (also referred to as The Wisdom of Sirach), composed in Hebrew in the second or third century BCE and included in Roman Catholic, Greek, and Slavonic Bibles as a Deuterocanonical book, includes a number of misogynistic passages. One such passage reads: "It is a disgrace to be the father of an undisciplined son, and the birth of a daughter is a loss" (22:3). Another passage reads: "Any iniquity is small compared to a woman's iniquity" (25:19). Still another reads: "Better is the wickedness of a man than a woman who does good; it is woman who brings shame and disgrace" (42:14). Many of the ancient Greek philosophers, including no less a figure than Aristotle, considered women to be defective males (sadly, Thomas Aquinas agreed). But Christian theologians themselves have often been at the root of the cause. For example, a number of theologians of antiquity have been quick to interpret various passages in the Bible in misogynistic ways. Consider the words of Tertullian regarding women and the passages in the book of Genesis referring to Adam and Eve:

> Do you not know that you are Eve? The judgment of God upon this sex lives on in this age; therefore, necessarily the guilt should live on also. You are the gateway of the devil; you are the one who unseals the curse of that tree, and you are the first one to turn your back on the divine law; you are the one who persuaded him whom the devil was not capable of corrupting; you easily destroyed the image of God, Adam. Because of what you deserve, that is, death, even the Son of God had to die.[6]

Sadly, Tertullian was not the only Church Father to use theology as a tool to diminish and oppress women.[7]

In the nineteenth and early twentieth centuries women began campaigning for their rights – rights both within the Church and without the Church – and challenging what they perceived to be inferior treatment of women in Church and society. This movement, which occurred in the

The following are leading feminist theologians in the Christian tradition who, at the writing of this book, hold the titles listed: *Sarah Coakley* is Norris-Hulse Professor of Divinity and Fellow of Murray Edwards College, University of Cambridge; *Harriet Harris* is University Chaplain at the University of Edinburgh and formerly University Lecturer in Theology at the University of Oxford; *Sallie McFague* is E. Rhodes and Leona B. Carpenter Professor of Theology Emerita, Vanderbilt University and Distinguished Theologian in Residence, Vancouver School of Theology; *Rosemary Radford Ruether* is the Carpenter Emerita Professor of Feminist Theology at Pacific School of Religion and the Georgia Harkness Emerita Professor of Applied Theology at Garrett Evangelical Theological Seminary; *Janet Soskice* is University Reader in Philosophical Theology, University of Cambridge.

United States and the United Kingdom, is known as first-wave feminism and ushered in reforms in the workplace, higher education, and the right for women to vote.[8] Since that time different streams of feminism have evolved, but for our purposes we will focus on Christian feminism.

There are many important themes in Christian feminist theology; the following are four central ones: rethinking God-language, challenging the maleness of Christ, re-conceptualizing sin and salvation, and advancing the role of women in the Church.[9] Regarding God-language, Christian feminists generally hold that the portrayal of God as a masculine being has had deleterious effects on the way women are perceived and understood. The male pronouns that are used of God continuously in the Bible and in theological discourse should be countered with female pronouns as well, argue many feminists. Rosemary Radford Ruether (1936–), for example, proposes using the expression God/ess as a proper designation for the deity.[10] Such a move is not strictly an innovative phenomenon, for Julian of Norwich, back in the fifteenth century, proposed understanding God as both father and mother. Another move feminists have made to challenge the male God-language of the Bible is to develop new ways of imagining the divine in symbolic terms. Sallie McFague (1933–) proposes new models of God that are not gender-specific, such as "God the friend."[11]

Second, while the incarnation is at the very core of Christian thought, most Christian feminists are not comfortable with orthodox, Chalcedonian Christology. One reason for this is that with Christ as an incarnate *male*, men can be understood to be more like Christ, or closer to Christ. Maleness, in other words, provides an adequate image of God (as reflected in the incarnate Christ) whereas femaleness does not. In fact, this is one of the arguments presented by Catholics and Orthodox for limiting the priesthood to men. Feminists have responded in various ways to this. For one, they argue that gender, or specifically one's sex, is accidental to a person, not essential to her or his identity. Jesus' maleness, then, is simply a historical contingency.

A third issue that is a special concern to many women in Evangelical, Roman Catholic, and Eastern Orthodox contexts is the role of women in Church leadership. While liberal and mainline Protestant Churches commonly ordain women and offer them the highest places of leadership,[12] in many conservative Churches they are permitted leadership roles only in those cases where they are not leading men. For example, in many non-denominational Protestant Churches women cannot be pastors, elders, or deacons. The Catholic and Orthodox Churches also prohibit women from entering any clerical positions. Feminists affirm the Egalitarian view that all human persons are equal in worth and moral and spiritual status, and many argue that the Complementarian view (that men and women have different and non-overlapping roles and responsibilities in the church) is unbiblical and morally and socially unwarranted. One important Egalitarian movement within Evangelicalism is spearheaded by Christians for Biblical Equality. These Evangelical Egalitarians affirm that a proper interpretation of the Bible teaches the fundamental equality of women and men of all ethnic groups and economic classes.[13]

Feminist theologians, then, suggest fresh answers to old questions, but they also advocate reassessing many of the questions and issues themselves. While all feminist theologians are agreed that traditional, orthodox Christian theology is patriarchal and has generally ignored and suppressed women, they are not agreed on whether feminists should remain within the tradition and work on reform or break free from the Christian tradition altogether.

2 GLOBAL CHRISTIANITY AND PENTECOSTALISM

Christianity began as a Middle Eastern religion, located in a small region between the Jordan River and the Mediterranean Sea – an area called Palestine. Since its inception some two thousand years ago, it has spread across the globe, reaching all stripes of ethnic groups, races, and traditions. For the last half-millennium or so, however, the face of Christianity has been one dominated by white, European (and European-derived) peoples and cultures. But this is all changing in the twenty-first century. As religious historian Philip Jenkins contends,

> Christianity should enjoy a worldwide boom in [this] new century, but the vast majority of believers will be neither white nor European, nor Euro-American. ... Soon, the phrase "a White Christian" may sound like a curious oxymoron, as mildly surprising as "a Swedish Buddhist."[14]

In the early centuries of the Common Era, Christianity spread quickly to regions beyond the Middle East, including Africa. But with the Islamic conquest in the late seventh century, Africa quickly lost its prominence within Christianity. Over the last few centuries, however, this has begun to change, and Christianity is beginning to flourish there once again. If Jenkins is right, by the year 2050 Sub-Saharan Africa will become the heartland of Christianity. Furthermore, six countries will each have at least 100 million Christians: Brazil, Mexico, the Philippines, Nigeria, Zaire, and the United States.[15] In just a few decades only one Christian in five will be non-Latino and white; the key center of the Christian religion will have shifted to the Southern Hemisphere.

Jenkins makes the point that as Christianity becomes more globalized, asserting "what Christians believe" or what "modern Christians accept" is going to be problematic, for these phrases often mean only what a shrinking remnant of Western Christians believe.

> If demographic change just meant that Christianity would continue to be practiced in more or less its present form, but by people of a different ethnic background, that would of itself be a fact of some historical moment. But the changes of the coming decades promise to be much more sweeping than that. The types of Christianity that have thrived most successfully in the global South have been very different from what many Europeans and North Americans consider mainstream. These models have been far more enthusiastic, much more centrally concerned with the immediate workings of the supernatural, through prophecy, visions, ecstatic utterances, and healing. In fact, they have differed so widely from the cooler Northern norms as to arouse suspicion that these enthusiastic Africans (for instance) are essentially reviving the pagan practices of traditional society.[16]

The acceptance of what are called the "charismatic gifts" or "gifts of the Holy Spirit" is now an international phenomenon, most especially among Pentecostals.

Pentecostalism is a Christian renewal movement in both the Protestant and Roman Catholic traditions that emphasizes personal experience of God and the baptism of the Holy Spirit, manifested primarily through speaking in tongues.[17] It is a formidable force in contemporary Christianity and is currently spreading like wildfire in the global South, including Latin America, Africa, and Asia, where it is reshaping not only the

Figure 29.1 This image captures a large Pentecostal gathering in Argentina. Some of the main Pentecostal denominations are the Assemblies of God, the Pentecostal Church of God, the International Church of the Foursquare Gospel, and the Open Bible Standard Churches. Oneness Pentecostalism, also known as Apostolic Pentecostalism, is a group of Pentecostal denominations which all affirm the theological doctrine of Oneness – that God is one person, not three, who exists as Father, Son, and Holy Spirit

theological landscape but the political, social and economic landscapes as well. It is estimated that there are currently 500 million Pentecostal and charismatic Christians worldwide and that the growth rate is about 20 million per year.[18]

As we have seen throughout Christian history, oftentimes Christian experience influences Christian thought. This is perhaps nowhere more evident than in Pentecostalism. A common testimony among Pentecostals and other charismatics is that of an encounter with God, many times one that was uninvited or even one that contradicted the individual's personal theological views. Consider, for example, the story of Jack Deere, formerly a professor of Old Testament at Dallas Theological Seminary. To be a faculty member of this seminary requires adherence to the theological position called cessationism – the view that the charismatic gifts were for an earlier apostolic period in the Church of the first century and that they ceased soon afterward. Prof. Deere held this position until he was, as he describes it, surprised by the voice of God. In two books he chronicles his own theological shift away from cessationism to full acceptance of the "supernatural" gifts for today, including healing, prophecy, speaking in tongues, and miracles. In a significant way his religious experiences guided his theological understanding. Some years after his theological shift, he said this:

> Looking back on that time, I realize now that so much of the Bible actually seemed unreal to me. I had relegated many experiences in the Bible to the distant, unrepeatable past. It had become for me primarily a book of doctrines and abstract truths about God.[19]

But now, he notes, he sees theology with new eyes; he hears the biblical stories with new ears.[20] Deere is a trained scholar, and so attempts to explain his views biblically and theologically. But he is the exception rather than the norm among Pentecostals and charismatics. For the most part, the latter tend to be more experiential and less systematically theological as they live out their faith.

There is a new global Christianity emerging. Its unifying themes are yet to be determined, but it seems that what plays center stage has less to do with doctrine (as in earlier periods of Christian history) and more to do with personal experience and social concerns as reflected in particular indigenous cultural forms.

3 POSTMODERNITY

"Postmodernism" became a buzzword in the last couple of decades of the twentieth century. It is a slippery term that is thrown around in a variety of contexts. Often it appears as an expressive word without much explanation, probably because there is no clear and concise definition that could be agreed upon. That fact itself gives some insight into its meaning. Obviously, postmodernism has something to do with what comes after modernity. But beyond this it is difficult to pin down because the term appears in disciplines from philosophy and theology, to literature, media studies, and even to politics and architecture.[21] Instead of a definition, then, we might better approach an understanding of postmodernism by characterizing it as a series of shifts – shifts in emphasis, or in methodology, or in values. Some of these shifts would be from:

- Absolutes to Relativity
- Objectivity to Subjectivity
- Meaning to Interpretation
- Unity to Diversity
- Reason to Emotion
- Argument to Narrative
- Parts to Wholes
- Knowledge to Power

In keeping with the spirit of postmodernism, none of these shifts is absolute and all would need to be extensively qualified depending on the context. The story of how these shifts came about is too complex to tell in this short space.[22] Suffice it to say that they are reactions to long-held assumptions of modernity which came to be questioned largely because of the philosophies of Friedrich Nietzsche, Martin Heidegger, Michel Foucault, Jacques Derrida, Richard Rorty, and others. For our purposes in this section, we will briefly discuss several attitudes toward postmodernism. Consider these two claims:

1   Tradition-mediated thinking is anti-rational.
2   There is no escaping tradition-mediated thinking.

The first of these is one of the precepts upon which Modernism was founded. Tradition and the authority accorded it were looked upon suspiciously. Modern thinkers wanted to clear away the confused beliefs of their culture which had been passed down through traditions and rebuild their belief structures relying only upon the universal reason which was available to all human beings. Confining one's thinking to tradition was not to enter into the life of reason.

The second claim is the insight that arose in the twentieth century with the demise of positivism and with the new emphasis on the role of language. If thinking occurs only through language and language is disseminated only through culture, then cultural tradition plays an essential role in thinking. Inspiration for this can be traced back to Immanuel Kant and his claim that our thinking must conform to certain categories (see Chapter 23). But whereas for Kant these categories were hard-wired in all rational minds, the claim in the twentieth century is that the categories of thinking are provided by one's culture or community, and hence they vary among people. Furthermore, there is no stepping outside of these culturally defined modes of thinking.

We can note different attitudes toward postmodernism, then, according to their adoption or rejection of these two claims. There is certainly a continuum of options here depending on the strength with which the claims are adopted or rejected, but we'll note three main positions around which theological perspectives on postmodernism tend to cluster.

1   Full-orbed postmodernity accepts both of these claims. Thus thought is self-undermining and we are led into meaninglessness, or nihilism. Like any other subject on this view, talk of God is just a language game in which different communities compete in the hopes that their discourse will prevail. God as a being that transcends our existence and reality becomes an incoherent concept, and theology becomes a/theology. In this vein the controversial Anglican priest Don Cupitt defends a doctrine he calls non-realism. According to it we construct rather than discover truth, and truth is just the current consensus in a given community. On his view, religion can continue to flourish so long as we transform dogma into practical spiritual "truths" which guide us through life. This position is fully postmodern, but it is a postmodernity which is really the culmination of modernity.

2   A second attitude toward postmodernism asserts that there is a universal rationality that transcends traditions, and so they deny the second claim. Essentially, they accept the basic framework of modernism, though typically today it is a modified version in which the quest for absolute certainty is abandoned. Postmodernism should be resisted on this view because it undermines reason with its self-referentially incoherent claims. This attitude is typically found among the more traditional and conservative branches of theology today which trace their lineage from Evangelicalism and its emphasis on propositional claims that are true independent of any frame of reference or cultural tradition. "Truths that God has revealed are true in virtue of their correspondence with an extralinguistic realm..."[23] Knowing these truths is complicated by worldviews that predispose

us to accept certain claims, but ultimately we should be able to reason with people until they accept the truth. That this doesn't happen all the time is explained by the Fall and its effects on our cognitive faculties.[24]

3   Finally, there is a third approach to postmodernism, which affirms the second of the claims, but denies the first. These theologians agree that our thinking occurs in and through traditions. But rather than allowing this to pull them into nihilism and non-realism, they argue that rationality itself is embedded within these traditions. As such, rationality becomes relative to traditions and contexts, but truth does not have to become relative on this view. In many ways this approach reaches back before modernity to the method advocated by Augustine and Anselm: faith seeking understanding (see Chapter 14). These are postmodern theologians in a different sense than the first category because they have rejected modernity as a tradition that culminates in nihilism. Their theology aims to overcome that nihilism by rejecting modernity and its supposed objective standards which created the crisis for theology in the Modern period. John Milbank notes that with the end of modernity, "there also ends the predicament of modern theology. It no longer has to measure up to accepted standards of scientific truth or normative rationality."[25] Instead, Christian theology is weighed against its own standards.

We next explore three new theological movements that we believe will have tremendous influence on the future of theological discourse as well as practical import for Christian faith and practice in the emerging global community.

4 COMPARATIVE THEOLOGY

As we have noted in various places in this book, theologians have not infrequently gleaned insights, and on occasion even taken direction from, philosophical and cultural ideas that were foreign to the Christian tradition itself. Most of the early Christian apologists and theologians in the East and the West were highly influenced by Greek philosophical thinking. In fact, they believed that by utilizing Greek philosophy they were employing the best thinking of the day. So they co-opted it to assist them in crafting theological doctrines such as the Incarnation and Trinity.

Augustine, too, was influenced by the metaphysics and epistemology of Plato and the Neoplatonists. This shaped his understanding of God as a source of truth and goodness and his notion of the immateriality of the soul, to list just two ways in which Greek thought influenced his thinking about Christian faith. Thomas Aquinas is also significant in this regard. He utilized the philosophy of Aristotle and the writings of Islamic philosophical theologians as he crafted various doctrines of Christian faith. Indeed, Christianity would be unrecognizable today without the influences of Greek ideas. Furthermore, as contemporary theological and historical scholarship has demonstrated, an understanding of Christianity devoid of the influence of the Judaism of Jesus' day would be quite deficient and distorted. Examples of the influential role of ideas external to Christian theology and identity could easily be multiplied throughout its history. To ignore such influences in the history of Christian thought would be rather myopic.

It is not only in the annals of religious history that external influences can be seen to have an impact on Christian thought. In fact, with the proliferation of religious pluralism and the widespread influence of globalization, perhaps today even more than in times past pressures from the outside are playing a major role in shaping theological discourse and development. From our perspective, this is not necessarily a problem for Christian theology, but sometimes a plus. Comparative theology explores these influences and developments, but it also contributes to them.

One of the leaders in the field of comparative theology is Keith Ward, Regius Professor of Divinity Emeritus at the University of Oxford. Primarily through his five volume work on the subject, Professor Ward presents a systematic Christian theology from a global perspective while also engaging in comparative analysis of major topics among five world religions: Hinduism, Buddhism, Judaism, Christianity, and Islam.[26] Ward describes comparative theology as being "an intellectual discipline which inquires into ideas of the ultimate value and goal of human life, as they have been perceived and expressed in a variety of religious traditions." And, he continues, unlike religious studies, it is "primarily concerned with the meaning, truth, and rationality of religious beliefs, rather than with the psychological, sociological, or historical elements of religious life and institutions."[27]

There are several reasons why we believe that comparative theology is an important new field in the discipline of theology. First, truth and insight lie beyond the confines of any particular tradition of human thought. In Christianity, as we have already demonstrated, much has been culled from other traditions and cultures. The same is true across the spectrum of faiths. It is beneficial to know this about one's own religious tradition, not only for broad educational purposes, but also to recognize that one's own particular institution or denomination or religious group is only a fraction of the tradition as a whole.

Second, in doing or studying comparative theology, one can expand her or his own understanding of what it means to be a religious individual. It can also expand one's understanding of the nature of transcendent goods and values. For example, the Buddhist notion of detachment from greed and selfish desire has been highly influential in the lives of many Christians (including author and Trappist monk Thomas Merton), just as the Christian notion of selfless care for the underprivileged has impacted the lives of many Hindus (including many of those who renounced the caste system in India). It can be very dangerous to disallow dissenting viewpoints and to coerce assent to tradition, in theology no less than in politics or other social domains. As it turns out, the self-appointed custodians of a particular tradition tend to be those who are unfamiliar with the pensive disputes within the tradition itself and with the fact that their own (generally) very narrow viewpoint of the faith is just that.

Third, as the world becomes more pluralistic and globalized, it will be increasingly more important to be familiar with religious others. It will simply not do to view Islam as a religion of terror, for example, as, sadly, some Americans regard the religion. As Islam is one of the fastest (if not *the* fastest) growing religions in the world, it will continue to be more relevant to understand what it is that the vast majority of Muslims believe about God, fellow human beings, and the world. It will simply not do to view Judaism as a religion of works as opposed to grace, as many Christians do. Even a cursory study of Judaism and the history of Jewish thought will quickly controvert such a perverted view of that faith. And on and on. If we are going to take religious others seriously, as we would hope they would do for us and our own tradition, then we must strive for real interreligious understanding – giving other viewpoints a charitable read as we would expect they would do for us.

All of this is part and parcel of the practice of comparative theology.

5 ENVIRONMENTAL THEOLOGY

It is believed by many today that a global environmental crisis looms. There are many causes of the problem, but included are human-created environmental despoliation, massive destruction of habitats of many kinds, titanic and unsustainable uses of fuels, massive over-logging, mining, and more. It is our view that global warming is very likely occurring, that it is at least partly due to human causes, and that without serious, coordinated global efforts, the consequences for many, especially the poor and future generations, may be grim. Only a first-class conspiracy theorist would deny the findings of the United Nations Intergovernmental Panel on Climate Change, and the abundant, clear consensus of climate scientists about the facts of global warming. As a recent NASA report indicates:

> Multiple studies published in peer-reviewed scientific journals show that 97 percent or more of actively publishing climate scientists agree: Climate-warming trends over the past century are very likely due to human activities. In addition, most of the leading scientific organizations worldwide have issued public statements endorsing this position.[28]

Climate warming is creating a crisis of its own, including ice melting at rapid speeds at the Earth's poles, sea levels rising at alarming rates, and damaging ecosystem changes.

Fortunately we have moved beyond the days when Lynn White and his famous 1967 essay, "The Historical Roots of our Ecological Crisis" – accusing historical Christianity for virtually all our modern ecological problems – were widely influential. Christianity is not, nor has been, the primary problem. And many Christian theologians are now taking environmental and ecological crises seriously as they reflect on the nature of God and divine action, and our own moral, religious, and political responsibilities with regard to the planet. Indeed, many now hold the view that the religious life cannot be divorced from such concerns and that the well-being of the environment and all life, rather than economic growth, should be a broad organizing principle for public and political discourse. It is encouraging that there is an ascendency of a theology of Christian ecological stewardship (as one can see in the writings

In a recent encyclical on climate change, Pope Francis writes that the majority of us in the West live comfortable lives,

> far removed from the poor, with little direct contact with their problems...This lack of physical contact and encounter, encouraged at times by the disintegration of our cities, can lead to a numbing of conscience and to tendentious analyses which neglect parts of reality...Today, however, we have to realize that a true ecological approach always becomes a social approach; it must integrate questions of justice in debates on the environment, so as to hear both the cry of the earth and the cry of the poor (§49).

of Holmes Rolston III, Gary Comstock, Calvin DeWitt, and others). Nevertheless, the various environmental and ecological threats demand further, focused attention from theologians. This is a central goal of environmental theology. If we are to take seriously the biblical mandate of Genesis 1 to "fill the earth and subdue it" in a manner that fosters the sustainable flourishing of all variety of living things, we believe the significance of the work of environmental theologians will only increase over time.

6 ASTROTHEOLOGY

As these words are being penned, there are organized, global efforts to collect and share astronomical data about the universe within and beyond our own solar system. Thousands of exoplanets (planets beyond our solar system) have already been discovered, with many of them apparently existing in the "Goldilocks" zone of their stars – meaning that they are orbiting at just the right distance where liquid water could exist on the planets' surfaces and thus could have habitable conditions for life. Many professional astronomers and other scientists now believe that it is only a matter of time (and perhaps not too far into the distant future) before alien life forms will be discovered. This doesn't mean that

Figure 29.2 Space telescopes being utilized to monitor radio signals that may be coming from space, possibly sent by extraterrestrial intelligences

conscious life will likely be discovered, though that would certainly be an exciting development. Rather, the discovery of evidence that some form of living organisms is flourishing on planets or other celestial bodies other than Earth seems to be inevitable.

What would such a discovery mean theologically? Three thoughts come to mind. First, for some, an interpretation of the early chapters of the book of Genesis would need to change. The idea that God created the heavens and the earth such that the earth was the only planet populated with living things (which is not actually stated in the text) would turn out to be false. The creative hand of God would be much more expansive than such an interpretation would allow.

Second, the theological significance of planet Earth, with respect to the rest of the universe, would need to be rethought. Many theologians view Earth, and the attending life on it, as unique in the universe – a special divine creation that makes our planet incredibly exceptional in the vast expanse of the cosmos. Discovering life – any form of life – would call this "Earthian" exceptionalism into question.

Relatedly, a third point is that discovery of *conscious intelligent* life on another planet in the universe would elicit an earth-shattering theological rethinking about the specialness of *Homo sapiens* and our place in the universe. The Copernican Revolution (the acceptance of heliocentrism over geocentrism as proposed by Nicolaus Copernicus) was a revolution in human thought and indeed in Christian thought. For most of those before Copernicus, Earth was the center of the universe – both astronomically and theologically. For many Christians, this view was, as noted above, rooted in a particular interpretation of the Bible. After Copernicus, Earth has been seen to be one small planet in the Milky Way galaxy, a spiral galaxy that measures about 100,000 light years across and is thought to contain between 200 and 400 billion stars, which is itself within a vast universe that includes billions and billions of other galaxies – each of which contains billions of stars and planets. Our Solar System is located about 25,000 light years to the galactic center of our galaxy and about 25,000 light years away from the rim – a seemingly insignificant planet in a seemingly insignificant location in a seemingly insignificant galaxy. For many, we have become rather small and inconsequential.

Discovery of conscious intelligent life elsewhere would potentially do even more to promote such a low view of Earth and humanity. However, while it would certainly require some reimagining of what it means to be a special creation of God, it need not foster a low view of humanity – or any forms of life. In fact, we might see the work of God as even more vast, creative, complex, and beautiful than before such a discovery. Such a discovery would be, in our view, an example of the principle of plenitude that "a universe containing every possible variety of creature, from the highest to the lowest, is a richer and better universe than would be one consisting solely of the highest kind of being."[29] Nonetheless, it would undoubtedly create the need for titanic theological revisionings of central theological doctrines, including original sin, atonement, and the eschatological notions of a new heaven and a new earth (with the attending images of the cosmic Christ).

These are the kinds of issues that are explored in the new and advancing discipline of astrotheology, one which involves interactions between theologians and particular fields within the sciences, including cosmology, astrobiology, astrophysics, and those involved in SETI (the search for extraterrestrial intelligence).

SUMMARY OF MAIN POINTS

1   Several theologies that seek to liberate people from various forms of political, social, economic, and other forms of subjugation emerged in the latter part of the twentieth century and continue to play an important role in culture, including liberation theology (which seeks to liberate the poor), black theology (which seeks to liberate people of color), and feminist theology (which seeks to liberate women).

2   Pentecostal forms of Christianity are growing rapidly, especially in the Southern Hemisphere, so much so that within decades it is likely that only one Christian in five will be non-Latino and white.

3   A series of shifts in thinking occurred in recent decades from a modernist approach to truth and knowledge to a postmodern one, including a shift from objective to subjective thinking, and from absolute values and truths to relative ones.

4   Comparative theology is a recent field in theology that, in an open and dialectical manner, explores the values and goals of human beings as they are expressed in the major world religions – seeking ultimate meaning and purpose in the process.

5   A theology of Christian ecological stewardship is developing that focuses on our moral, religious, and political responsibilities with regard to the planet and the various environmental and ecological threats that it faces.

6   Astrotheology is a recent branch of theology that focuses on theological issues about the cosmos, notably whether the discovery of life beyond Earth would have theological import and what it might mean with respect to such doctrines as the Incarnation and the afterlife.

CONCLUSION

Histories need to be rewritten with each new generation, incorporating new insights and reflecting the values and norms that have evolved over time. Doing so does not have to become a revisionist practice so long as attention is paid to factual detail, although there is no doubt that the present colors our understanding of the past.

How will the people, events, and ideas be understood differently by future generations of theologians and historians of theology? What new unifying themes will they detect and describe in the development of Christian thought? While we have glimpses of where some themes may be going, and we have emphasized some of them in this chapter, all of this remains to be seen. Clearly, though, they will still be grappling with the ageless questions with which we began: What is God like? Who is Jesus and what is his significance? How do we overcome evil and oppression? We are confident that the rich answers of the Christian tradition will continue to be relevant and will speak to the times and places that Christians find themselves, wherever they may be across our globe or beyond.

FOR FURTHER READING

Wendell Berry, *The Gift of Good Land: Further Essays Cultural and Agricultural* (Berkley, Counterpoint Press, 2009). A leading voice of the bioregional movement which emphasizes fidelity to local contexts as a fundamental element of human fruition and environmental wholeness.

James H. Cone, *Black Theology and Black Power* (Maryknoll, NY: Orbis Books, 1997). Original edition published by Harper & Rowe, 1969. The first systematic presentation of black theology.

Calvin DeWitt, *Earth-wise: A Biblical Response to Environmental Issues* (Grand Rapids, CRC Publications, 1994). An insightful work on environmental issues by a leading Evangelical Christian.

Gustavo Gutiérrez, *A Theology of Liberation: History, Politics and Salvation* (Maryknoll, NY: Orbis, 1973). The classic work of liberation theology.

Gavin Hyman, *Predicament of Postmodern Theology* (Louisville, KY: Westminster John Knox Press, 2001). Compares leading approaches to postmodern theology.

Philip Jenkins, *The Next Christendom: The Coming of Global Christianity* (Oxford: Oxford University Press, 2002). A well-researched work on contemporary global Christianity and its possible transformations in the coming years.

Chad Meister and James Beilby, *The Routledge Companion to Modern Christian Thought* (London and New York: Routledge, 2013). Includes 72 fresh essays by leading thinkers of modern Christian thought, from the Enlightenment to the twentieth century and beyond.

Myron B. Penner, *Christianity and the Postmodern Turn: Six Views* (Grand Rapids, MI: Brazos Press, 2005). An inviting introduction to postmodernism through the interaction of six Christian thinkers with each other's positions.

Janet Soskice, *The Kindness of God: Metaphor, Gender, and Religious Language* (Oxford: Oxford University Press, 2007). A leading feminist scholar examines biblical imagery and the central teachings of Christian theology.

Keith Ward, *Religion and Revelation* (Oxford: Oxford University Press, 1994); *Religion and Creation* (Oxford: Oxford University Press, 1996); *Religion and Human Nature* (Oxford: Oxford University Press, 1998); *Religion and Community* (Oxford: Oxford University Press, 2000); *Religion and Human Fulfillment* (Norwich, UK: SCM Press, 2008). A brilliant example of comparative theology, in five volumes, from one of its founding visionaries.

Natalie K. Watson, *Feminist Theology* (Grand Rapids, Eerdmans, 2003). A concise, clear, and insightful introduction to feminist theology.

David Wilkinson, *Alone in the Universe? The X Files, Aliens, and God* (Crowborough, UK: Monarch Publications, 1997). A theologian/astronomer affirms the compatibility of Christianity and the search for extraterrestrial intelligence.

Glossary

Anabaptists
From the Greek terms *ana* (which means "again, twice") and *baptidzein* (which means "to baptize") and so means "re-baptize"; refers to the group of Protestant Christians originating in the sixteenth century Radical Reformation who baptized only adults (baptizing adults though they had been baptized as infants) and rejected the state Church.

Anglican Church
A global fellowship of Churches based on the teachings of the Church of England which recognizes the Archbishop of Canterbury as their leader and symbolic head.

Apocrypha
From the Greek term which means "hidden"; refers to collections of books accepted in the Roman Catholic and Orthodox traditions as part of the canon, but considered noncanonical by Protestants.

Apollinarianism
An early Church heresy, based on the teachings of Apollinaris, which affirmed that in the Incarnation the man Jesus received a new divine soul (the Logos) which displaced his human soul.

apologist
From the Greek term apologia (which means "a defense"); refers to one who offers a defense or justification of belief in God and Christianity.

Arianism
An early Christological heresy with widespread influence, based on the teachings of Arius, in which Jesus Christ is viewed as the supreme creature of God's creation, but not a member of the Godhead as the Orthodox believed.

Arminianism
Generally refers to the Protestant beliefs, originating with Jacob Arminius in the late sixteenth century, which affirm human free will and rejects the Calvinist view of predestination.

Atonement
From an old English word which literally means "at-one-ment;" while there are different theories of the Atonement, the term broadly refers to the saving work of Jesus Christ on the cross which brings reconciliation between God and human beings.

baptism
A Christian ritual utilizing water which symbolizes death to sin and resurrection with Christ; some denominations understand baptism as a sacrament and entrance into the Christian community.

Book of Common Prayer
The official prayer book of the Anglican Church.

bull
A decree or charter issued by a pope.

Byzantium
A village on the shores of the Bosphorus which was chosen in 330CE by the Emperor Constantine as the site of a new imperial capital, Constantinople. "Byzantine" referred to both the state and the culture of the Eastern Roman Empire in the Middle Ages.

Calvinism
Generally refers to the Protestant beliefs, originating with John Calvin in the sixteenth century, which include the doctrines spelled out in TULIP (*see* TULIP).

canon
From the Greek term *kanon* (which means "measuring rod" or "rule"); the body of writings officially accepted by the Christian Church as the rule of faith – the Holy Scriptures.

Cappadocian fathers
From the area of Cappadocia in ancient Asia Minor (modern Turkey), refers primarily to three theologians: Basil of Caesarea, Gregory Nazianzus, and Gregory of Nyssa; they were influential in the development of Christian theology, most especially the Trinity.

catechumen
From the Latin *catechumenus;* refers to one receiving instruction in the doctrines of Christianity.

catholic
A term which is used to refer to the universality of the Christian Church.

Catholicism
See Roman Catholicism.

Chalcedon, Council of
Traditionally understood by Roman Catholics and Eastern Orthodox to have been the Fourth Ecumenical Council which was held in Chalcedon (near modern Istanbul, Turkey) in 451 and established the divinity formulation of Jesus Christ as one person with two natures.

Christology
The study of the person and nature of Jesus Christ.

Congregationalism
Denominational structure in which each congregation is self-governing.

Council of Chalcedon
See Chalcedon, Council of.

Council of Trent
See Trent, Council of.

crusades
From the Latin term *crux* (which means "cross"; the Crusaders wore a cross on their garments); military expeditions during the eleventh through the thirteenth centuries in which Christians attempted to recapture Jerusalem (the Holy Land) from Islamic control.

Dark Ages
Refers to a period of alleged cultural decline in European history from about the time of the fall of Rome in the fifth century to the eleventh century.

Dead Sea Scrolls
A large collection of texts discovered between 1947 and 1956 in caves near the Dead Sea.

deism
Popularly, a view which affirms God as creator of the world but rejects any further divine involvement or interference in the world; when coined in the seventeenth century the term referred to those who believe in God on the grounds of reason, but reject the divinity of Christ and Christian revelation.

diet
In the Holy Roman Empire, a formal assembly.

Docetism
From the Greek term *dokein* (which means "to seem or appear"); an early Christological heresy in which Jesus was held to be an immaterial spirit who only appeared to be a human being.

Dort, Synod of
A National Synod or council that was held in Dordrecht (a city in the Netherlands) by the Reformed Church from 1618–1619 in order to deal with a controversy which arose on account of Arminianism.

double predestination
A view of predestination, developed by John Calvin, in which God predestines some people for salvation and others for damnation.

Eastern Orthodoxy
The stream of the Christian Church which separated from Roman Catholicism in 1054 and which developed from the earlier Greek-speaking traditions of the Eastern half of the Roman Empire (Byzantine Empire).

ecumenical council
From the Greek term *oikoumenikos* (which means "universal"); assemblies of bishops from various locations which were convened by the pope and accepted by the Church as authoritative (distinguished from a synod).

Edict of Milan
A declaration by emperors Constantine I and Licinius in 313CE which sanctioned religious toleration in the Roman Empire.

election
From the Latin term *eligere* (which means "to choose"); the doctrine that God chooses certain individuals for salvation without reference to their faith or works.

encyclical
A papal letter addressed to the Church bishops or to the hierarchy of a country.

Enlightenment
Refers to the scientific and philosophical thought of eighteenth-century Europe which emphasized reason over tradition and authority with respect to religious questions and issues.

eschatology
The branch of theology concerned with the final events in world history.

Essenes
An ascetic Jewish sect which flourished from the second century BCE to the first century CE; they lived communally in preparation for the messiah.

Eucharist

From the Greek term *eucharistia* (which means "thankfulness" or "gratitude"); the sacrament of Holy Communion in which bread and wine are consumed in remembrance of Jesus (*see also* Mass).

Evangelical

A member of any Christian denomination who affirms a personal conversion to Christ, the divine inspiration of the Bible, and the importance of preaching in contrast to ritual.

existentialism

A movement that began in the nineteenth century, originating with Søren Kierkegaard, which emphasizes individual human existence and involves free choice, anxiety, and despair.

Fall

The event which introduced sin into the human race – traditionally ascribed to Adam and Eve disobeying God in the Garden of Eden; this entailed a spiritual fall from a harmonious relationship with God.

filioque

A Latin expression literally meaning "and from the Son"; added to the Nicene Creed by Western bishops in Rome so that it reads that the Holy Spirit "proceeds from the Father and the Son"; this was rejected by the Eastern Orthodox Church, and the dispute ultimately led to the Great Schism in 1054 between the Eastern and Western Churches.

Franciscans

Members of the Catholic religious order, founded by Francis of Assisi (1182–1226), who follow the rule of St. Francis, most notably living a life of poverty.

Gnosticism

From the Greek term *gnosis* (which means "knowledge"); a diverse group of religious believers who flourished in the second through the fourth centuries and affirmed that they could escape this evil, material world and be saved through secret knowledge.

Gospel
From the old English term *godspell* (which means "good news"); refers to the good news of salvation as taught and proclaimed by Jesus and the apostles.

Gospels
Any of the first four books of the New Testament (Matthew, Mark, Luke, and John) – each of which proclaims the "good news" of salvation through Christ.

grace
God's unmerited favor given to human beings in order that they can be redeemed and sanctified.

Great Awakening
A series of religious revivals in colonial America which began in the 1730s.

Hellenism
The culture and influence of the Greeks in the ancient world.

heresy
From the Greek term *hairesis* (which means "a choosing; faction"); in church history the word was used by the church fathers to refer to doctrines which were not universal or orthodox.

hermit
From the Greek *eremia* (which means "desert"); a person who goes to a solitary place (such as the desert) for purposes of spiritual growth and a concentrated relationship with God.

Holy Spirit
The third person of the Trinity.

homo-ousias
A Greek term which means "of the same substance"; this term was applied to the nature of Christ with reference to God at the Council of Nicea.

hypostasis

A Greek term which in the ancient Christian Church denoted "complete individual existence"; the term was at the heart of the Chalcedonian Christological discussion.

hypostatic union

A phrase used in the early Church to denote the presence of two natures in Jesus Christ: human and divine.

icon

From the Greek term *eikon* (which means "image"); pictures of God, Christ, and the saints which are venerated by those in the Eastern Orthodox Church.

immanence

From the Latin *in manere* (which means "to dwell in; remain"); refers to God's indwelling and participating in the universe.

Incarnation

From the medieval Latin term *incarnare* (which means "to make flesh"); the Christian doctrine of the Incarnation is that the eternal Son of God (Second Person of the Trinity) took on human flesh, becoming truly human while remaining truly God.

indulgence

The remission, granted by the Catholic Church and based on the merits of Christ and the saints, of part or all of the temporal and purgatorial punishments due for sins.

infralapsarianism

From the Latin phrase *infra lapsum* (which means "after the Fall"); a Calvinist doctrine in which God's decrees of election and reprobation logically came after God's decree of the Fall (compare with supralapsarianism).

inspiration

The view that the Spirit of God moves individuals to write or speak the words of God; this is most notably applied to the Bible, but many early Christian theologians believed that God inspired many of the works that were not included in the biblical canon.

irresistible grace
A Calvinist doctrine in which the saving grace of God is effective in bringing those God chooses to salvation – even against their own fallen will.

justification
The doctrine regarding the act whereby God makes an individual just or righteous.

limited atonement
The Calvinist doctrine according to which Christ died only for the elect.

logos
A Greek term which means "word" or "discourse" or "rational principle"; the opening verse of the Gospel of John includes this term and applies it to Christ.

Magisterial Reformation
An element of the Protestant Reformation in which the reform movements were supported by magistrates or ruling authorities; Martin Luther and John Calvin were Magisterial Reformers.

martyr
A person who dies for her or his religious faith, often rather than renouncing that faith. It is derived from the Greek *martos* which means "witness."

Mass
The Roman Catholic or Anglo-Catholic name for the celebration of the Eucharist, derived from the Latin expression *ite, missa est,* the concluding words of the rite which mean, "Go; it's the dismissal" (*see also* "Eucharist").

Mennonites
An Anabaptist group named after Menno Simons (1496–1561); they are known today primarily for their commitment to nonviolence.

messiah
From a Hebrew term which means the "Anointed One" – God's deliverer; translated into Greek as "Christ."

Methodism
A Protestant revival movement the roots of which are traced back to John and Charles Wesley, and George Whitefield; it is known primarily for its Arminian theology, mission work, and stress on personal holiness.

monergism
The theological position, often associated with Calvinism, that God brings about the salvation of an individual without the cooperation or will of that individual (compare with synergism).

Montanism
A movement founded by Montanus in the second century CE which rejected the Church and which manifested ecstatic prophecies, affirmed a modalistic view of the Trinity, and maintained that Montanist prophecies superseded those of the apostles; it was considered a heresy by the orthodox.

Moravians
A group of Protestant pietists from Moravia who followed Count Zinzendorf (1700–1760).

mysticism
A form of religious experience which places emphasis on direct awareness of, and sometimes personal union with, God; one classical Christian mystic is Teresa of Ávila (1515–1582).

natural theology
A branch of theology in which it is maintained that the existence of God can be demonstrated through the use of reason unaided by special revelation (e.g. the design argument).

Neo-orthodoxy
A movement which arose within Protestantism in the early twentieth century which opposes liberalism and which sought to recover certain traditional Christian doctrines which had been rejected by liberals, including the Trinity and a Chalcedonian view of Christ.

Neoplatonism

A philosophical system rooted in Platonism and developed in the third century by Plotinus and his successors; includes mystical Christian and Jewish elements and emphasizes "the One" as the ultimate source from which all existence emanates.

New Testament

The second part of the Bible (the Christian addition to the Old Testament or Hebrew Bible) containing twenty-seven books.

Nicene Creed

The document that is based on the creed formulated at the Council of Nicea in 325 but which was formalized at the Council of Constantinople in 381 (sometimes called the Niceno-Constantinople Creed); it defined the nature of Christ as homo-ousious (which means "of the same substance") with God.

Old Testament

The first part of the Bible and the Christian name for the Hebrew Bible (as included with the New Testament).

original sin

The sin of Adam and Eve which affected all future human beings; the act which ushered in the sinful nature of human beings.

orthodox

From the Greek terms *orthos* (which means "right") and *doxa* (which means "belief"); adherence to traditional or standard doctrines of the Church (contrasted with "heretical").

Orthodoxy

See Eastern Orthodoxy.

ousia

A Greek word which means "substance" or "essence" and refers to the nature of a thing.

parousia

A Greek expression literally meaning "being present"; refers to the Second Coming of Jesus Christ.

Patripassianism
From the Latin *pater* (which means "father") and *passus* (which means "having suffered"); the idea that the suffering of Christ on the cross was equally experienced by the Father.

patristic
A descriptive term for the early church fathers or their writings.

Pelagianism
The view, originating with Pelagius (*c*. 354–*c*. 420), that grace is not necessary for salvation and that through their own efforts people can live without sin.

penance
A discipline imposed on an individual by a priest for sins confessed.

Pentecost
From the Greek term *pentekonta* (which means "fifty"); Jewish holiday held fifty days after Passover and now celebrated by Christians commemorating the coming of the Holy Spirit.

Pentecostalism
A twentieth century Evangelical movement distinctive for its teachings on the necessity of the manifestation of the Holy Spirit in the lives of believers in emulation of the apostles at Pentecost (including speaking in tongues).

Pietism
A Protestant reform movement that began in the seventeenth century which emphasized the need for personal holiness.

pope
The title given to the Bishop of Rome who is the head of the Roman Catholic Church and understood to be the successor of the Apostle Peter.

predestination
The doctrine that God has preordained the salvation of the elect.

prevenient grace
From the Latin term *praevenire* (which means "to come before"); this is God's grace which precedes and enables human decision for salvation.

Protestantism
The stream of the Christian Church that originated with the "protests" against some of the practices and doctrines of the Catholic Church in the sixteenth century.

purgatory
According to Roman Catholic theology, a place or condition for Christians who, after death, need to have their souls purified from sins committed while on earth before entering into heaven.

rationalism
An approach to knowledge that relies on reason rather than experience and authority; in religious contexts, it is often contrasted with revelation as the source of knowledge about God and the world.

Reformation
A sixteenth-century movement which began in Europe with objections to certain Roman Catholic doctrines and resulted in the formation of Protestant Churches.

reprobation
The part of the Calvinist doctrine of double predestination in which God predestines some people for eternal damnation.

resurrection
An individual's being fully brought back to life after death; the same body is involved in the process. The resurrection of Jesus is central to traditional Christian belief.

Roman Catholicism
The denomination of the Christian Church that traces its origin and authority to the Apostle Peter as the first pope; its ecclesiastical authority has been located in Rome for most of its history.

Sabbath
In Jewish thought, the last day of the week which commemorates God's resting from the act of creation by worship and rest.

sacrament
A ritual recognized by the Church that is an outward sign of the inward administration of God's grace.

sanctification
From the Latin term *sanctus* (which means "holy"), the transformation of people into the likeness of Christ which follows conversion.

Schleitheim Confession
The most important Anabaptist doctrinal statement, adopted by the Swiss Brethren in 1527, which distinguishes their beliefs from other Christian Churches.

Scholasticism
In the Middle Ages, the university educational system which emphasized rational philosophical and theological speculation and disputation primarily involving the Latin authorities and Aristotle.

sin
Rebellion or offense against God typically characterized by a violation of religious or moral law.

sola fide
The Latin phrase adopted by the Protestant Reformers about the doctrine of justification which means "faith alone."

sola gratia
The Latin phrase adopted by the Protestant Reformers about the doctrine of salvation which means "grace alone."

sola scriptura
The Latin phrase adopted by the Protestant Reformers about supreme authority in matters of faith and practice which means "the scriptures alone."

soteriology
The branch of theology which is concerned with the doctrine of salvation.

supralapsarianism
From the Latin phrase *supra lapsum* (which means "prior to the Fall"); a Calvinist doctrine in which God's decrees of election and

reprobation logically came before God's decree of the Fall (compare with infralapsarianism).

synergism
The theological position that God works with an individual's free will in bringing about his or her salvation (compare with monergism).

synod
A local or special church council formally convened to discuss a religious matter (distinguished from an ecumenical council).

synoptic
From the Greek *synoptikos* (which means "seen together"); refers to the New Testament Gospels of Matthew, Mark, and Luke because of their similarities in structure and content.

theism
The belief in the existence of a God or gods.

theosis
A characteristically Eastern Orthodox conception of the process in which one becomes united with God.

theotokos
A Greek word which literally means "God bearer"; applied to Mary by Orthodox Christians because she gave birth to the Son of God.

Thirty-nine Articles
The doctrinal positions of the Church of England (Anglican Church), established in 1563.

Thomism
The tradition of thought, rooted in the work of Thomas Aquinas, which dominated the scholastic period and has continued to our own day primarily among Roman Catholic thinkers.

transcendence
From the Latin *transcendere* (which means "to climb or go beyond"); refers to God's existence beyond or apart from the physical universe.

transubstantiation
The Roman Catholic doctrine that during the celebration of the Eucharist the bread and wine turn into the actual body and blood of Christ.

Trent, Council of
An official response to the Protestant Reformation which lasted from 1545–1563 and instituted reforms within Roman Catholicism.

Trinity
The Christian doctrine that within the nature of the one God there are three co-equal and eternal persons: Father, Son, and Holy Spirit.

TULIP
An acronym for the five distinctive doctrines associated with Calvinism: Total depravity, Unconditional election, Limited atonement, Irresistible grace, and Perseverance of the saints.

Vatican II
A council of the Roman Catholic Church, from 1962–1965, which recognized the need for updating some of the teachings and practices of the Church for the modern world.

Westminster Confession
A confession of faith produced by a group of Presbyterian theologians assembled by English Parliament from 1643–1647.

Notes

INTRODUCTION

1 The Latin for "before Christ" is *ante Christum*, but it is the English phrase and its abbreviation that became standard.
2 Of course giving a precise line of demarcation between science and non-science is notoriously difficult. And there are traditions which treat theology as a science – it was called the "Queen of the Sciences" during the Middle Ages. Our point here is not to resolve such issues, but merely to draw attention to the fact that theologians attempt to give explanations.
3 Gregory Nazianzen, Oration 27, in Frederick W. Norris, ed., *Faith Gives Fullness to Reasoning: The Five Theological Orations of Gregory of Nazianzen*, Lionel Wickham and Frederick Williams, trans. (Leiden: E. J. Brill, 1991), 218.

1 THE PRE-HISTORY OF CHRISTIAN THOUGHT

1 "God said to Abraham, 'As for you, you shall keep my covenant, you and your offspring after you throughout their generations. This is my covenant, which you shall keep, between me and you and your offspring after you: Every male among you shall be circumcised. You shall circumcise the flesh of your foreskins, and it shall be a sign of the covenant between me and you'" (Genesis 17:9–11).
2 Of course the Islamic tradition finds its origins in Abraham as well as through his other son Ishmael, born to Hagar.
3 There is some ambiguity in the use of the terms Hebrew, Jewish, and Israelite. We follow the scholarly consensus in beginning to use the term Jewish for the people resettled in Judah around the time of the prophet Ezra, circa 458BCE.
4 Everett Ferguson, *Backgrounds of Early Christianity* (Grand Rapids, MI: Eerdmans, 1987), 319.
5 Michael Grant, *The Classical Greeks* (London: Phoenix Press, 1989), xiii, xi.
6 "On Who is Heir of Divine Things," XLII, *Philo Judaeus*, Vol. II, C.D. Yonge, trans. (London: Bohn, 1854), 134.

7 One story was that the golden head of an ass was found there; another was that a kidnapped man was being held captive there and being fattened up so the Jews could eat him. The first century historian Josephus discusses such legends in his *Against Apion* and thoroughly discredits their authenticity.

8 This point is made by Robert M. Grant, *Gods and the One God* (Philadelphia, PA: Westminster Press, 1986), 61.

9 Cicero, "On Behalf of Flaccus," XXVIII in *The Orations of Marcus Tullius Cicero*, Vol. 2, C.D. Yonge, trans. (London: G. Bell and Sons, 1913–21).

10 One of our best sources of information on this period is the Jewish historian Josephus.

11 Antipas ultimately got into trouble, though, not long after he had John the Baptist beheaded at the request of his niece and her mother Herodias (whom he had married). The story is found in Mark 9:14-29 (n.b., "King Herod" in this passage is actually Antipas, who took the name "Herod" as a title, like subsequent Roman emperors took the name "Caesar" after Julius Caesar). Herodias kept pushing her husband to seek greater titles from Rome; but Antipas didn't have the political savvy of his father with the powers in Rome, and he was deposed in 39CE.

2 JESUS OF NAZARETH

1 Of course what counts as orthodox is a matter of contention. The question of orthodoxy and heterodoxy will be discussed more thoroughly in Chapter 7.

2 This point is made by Luke Timothy Johnson, *The Real Jesus* (San Francisco, CA: HarperSanFrancisco, 1996), 141. Further in this vein he says, "The most destructive effect of the Jesus Seminar and recent Historical Jesus books has been the perpetuation of the notion that history somehow determines faith, and that for faith to be correct, the historical accounts that gave rise to it have to be verifiable" (141).

3 Richard A. Burridge, *What are the Gospels? A Comparison with Graeco-Roman Biography* (Grand Rapids, MI, MI: Eerdmans, 2004), shows that the four gospels of the New Testament fit squarely within the tradition of biography in the ancient world.

4 Robert W. Funk, Roy W. Hoover, and the Jesus Seminar, trans. and eds, *The Five Gospels: The Search for the Authentic Words of Jesus* (New York: Macmillan Publishing Company, 1993).

5 *The Five Gospels*, 36.

6 Ibid., 357.

7 Ibid., 5.

8 Ibid., 25.

9 San Francisco, CA: HarperSanFrancisco, 1996.

10 On these points, see especially Chapters 1, "The Good News and the Nightly News" and 4, "The Limitations of History."

11 See, for example, E.P. Sanders, *The Historical Figure of Jesus* (London: Penguin Books, 1993) and N.T. Wright, *The Challenge of Jesus* (Downer's Grove, IL: Intervarsity Press, 1999).

12 Keith Ward, *Re-Thinking Christianity* (Oxford: Oneworld, 2007), 4.

13 Again, the words of Keith Ward aptly summarize the situation: "The foundation of Christianity in the person of Jesus is clear – Jesus was seen as

the source of the new life of liberation from sin and unity with God through the Spirit that the first Christians experienced. What is not clear, however, is exactly what Jesus himself taught and how he taught it" (ibid., 22).

14 See, for example, Bruce Chilton and Craig Evans, eds., *Authenticating the Activities of Jesus* (Leiden: Brill, 1999); N.T. Wright, *Jesus and the Victory of God* (Minneapolis, MN: Fortress Press, 1997); Robert Funk, ed., *The Acts of Jesus: What Did Jesus Really Do? The Search for the Authentic Deeds of Jesus* (San Francisco, CA: HarperCollins, 1998); and Paul Fredriksen, *Jesus of Nazareth, King of the Jews: A Jewish Life and the Emergence of Christianity* (New York: Alfred Knopf, 1999).

15 Sanders, *The Historical Figure of Jesus*, 280.

16 *The Challenge of Jesus*, Chapter 2, "The Challenge of the Kingdom" 34–53. On this point see also Dallas Willard's *Divine Conspiracy* (San Francisco, CA: HarperSanFrancisco, 1998).

17 N.T. Wright, *The Original Jesus* (Grand Rapids, MI: Eerdmans, 1996), 48–49.

18 N.T. Wright counts at least 17 different messiah movements in the first and second centuries.

19 For example, E.P. Sanders, *The Historical Figure of Jesus*, 242; and Geza Vermes, *Jesus the Jew* (New York: Macmillan, 1974), 140.

20 This point is made by Michael Grant, *Jesus: An Historian's Review of the Gospels* (New York: Charles Scribner's Sons, 1977), 102.

21 *The Historical Figure of Jesus*, 248.

3 THE APOSTLE PAUL: HIS THOUGHT AND CONTEXT

1 Louis Boyer, *The Spirituality of the New Testament and the Fathers* (London: Burns & Oates, 1963), 60.

2 Paul Barnett works out these calculations in *The Birth of Christianity: The First Twenty Years* (Grand Rapids, MI: Eerdmans, 2005), 23–26. Of course there are others who disagree with the dating of these events.

3 E.P. Sanders, *Paul and Palestinian Judaism* (Philadelphia, PA: Fortress Press, 1977).

4 N.T. Wright, *What Saint Paul Really Said* (Grand Rapids, MI: Eerdmans, 1997), 28.

5 For example, in 1 Corinthians 7, Paul seems to cite Jesus's teaching on divorce, but then goes on to give his own interpretation; in 1 Corinthians 9:14, Paul notes that Jesus "commanded" that missionaries should receive financial backing for their work in missions, but Paul goes on to say that he has not done this himself.

6 See, for example, Karen Armstrong, *The First Christian: Saint Paul's Impact on Christianity* (London: Pan, 1983) or even more extremely, Hyam Maccoby, *The Mythmaker: Paul and the Invention of Christianity* (New York: Harper & Row, 1986).

7 Ivor J. Davidson, *The Birth of the Church* (Grand Rapids, MI: Baker Books, 2004), 60–61.

8 Apparently, Princeton theologian Geerhardus Johannes Vos coined the phrase "already not yet." See his *The Pauline Eschatology* (Phillipsburg, NJ: P&R Publishing, 1979).

9 Alister McGrath, *Iustitia Dei: A History of the Christian Doctrine of Justification*, 3rd edition (Cambridge: Cambridge University Press, 2005), 1–5.
10 N.T. Wright, *What Saint Paul Really Said*, 116.
11 It should be noted that the NIV translation uses "sinful nature" for the Greek word *sarx* which should be translated literally as "flesh." A good discussion of this is Dallas Willard's "St. Paul's Psychology of Redemption" which is Chapter 7 of his *Spirit of the Disciplines* (San Francisco, CA: Harper, 1988).
12 Sanders, 554.

4 THE BREAK FROM JUDAISM

1 This is suggested by F.F. Bruce, *New Testament History* (New York: Doubleday, 1971), 282.
2 "So then, about eating food sacrificed to idols: We know that an idol is nothing at all in the world and that there is no God but one. ... But not everyone knows this. Some people are still so accustomed to idols that when they eat such food they think of it as having been sacrificed to an idol, and since their conscience is weak, it is defiled. But food does not bring us near to God; we are no worse if we do not eat, and no better if we do. Be careful, however, that the exercise of your freedom does not become a stumbling block to the weak. ... Therefore if what I eat causes my brother to fall into sin, I will never eat meat again, so that I will not cause him to fall" (1 Cor. 8:4–13, NIV). It is also significant to note in this regard that even after the controversy over circumcision, Paul would have Timothy circumcised in order not to offend some Jews (cf. Acts 16:3).
3 Some have interpreted Paul's visit to the "pillars" in Jerusalem recounted in Galatians 2 as the same event called the "Council of Jerusalem" in Acts 15. This seems unlikely unless one of the writers got the details of the visit significantly wrong. The Acts version seems to be a public forum with James the brother of Jesus presiding, while Paul's visit in Galatians 2 was a private meeting. Furthermore, the decisions reached in the two accounts are very different and require considerable gerrymandering to synchronize them – though it is not out of the realm of possibility that they are different accounts of the same event. For a thorough discussion of the options, see Nicholas Taylor, *Paul, Antioch and Jerusalem* (Sheffield: Sheffield Academic Press, 1992).
4 For more on this issue see John Knox, *Chapters in a Life of Paul*, revised edition, (Macon, GA: Mercer University Press, 2005).
5 Eusebius, *Ecclesiastical History*, II.xxv.
6 Kirsopp Lake, ed., *Apostolic Fathers* (Cambridge, MA: Loeb Classical Library, 1912).
7 Quoted in Bruce, 383. It should be noted, though, that the first-century historian Josephus, whose chronicle is something of a defense of the Roman Empire, claimed that Titus did not want the temple destroyed because it would be a nice prize for them to keep and display (*The Jewish War*, XI.241).
8 Hippolytus, *Expository Treatise Against the Jews*, §7; in Alexander Roberts and James Donaldson, eds., *The Ante-Nicene Fathers* (Peabody, MA: Hendrickson, 1994, reprinted from 1886 edition), Vol. 5, 220. Hereafter citations to this series will be ANF.

9 Eusebius, *Ecclesiastical History*, III.v; p. 203.
10 James Dunn, *The Parting of the Ways* (London: SCM Press, 1991), 232.
11 Bruce, 280.

5 PERSECUTION OF CHRISTIANS

1 See Simeon Guterman, *Religious Toleration and Persecution in Ancient Rome* (Westport, CT: Greenwood Press, 1971).
2 Tertullian, *Apology*, §40, ANF03, 48.
3 Pliny the Younger, *Epistles*, XCVIII.
4 Rodney Stark, *The Rise of Christianity* (Princeton, NJ: Princeton University Press, 1996), 97.
5 Ibid., 98–99.
6 "You shall not murder a child by abortion, nor kill them when already born." *Didache*, Chapter 2.
7 Robin Lane Fox, *Pagans and Christians* (New York: Kopf, 1987), 354.
8 *Apology* XXXIX, ANF03, 46.
9 *Exhortation to Martyrdom*, XXVIII in *Origen: Selected Writings*, Rowan A. Greer, ed. (New York: Paulist Press, 1988), 60.
10 "Letter to the Romans" §6, in *The Apostolic Fathers*, J.B. Lightfoot, ed. (Peabody, MA: Hendrickson Publishers, 1989), 561.
11 *Against Heresies*, Book III, Chapter XVIII, §5, ANF01, 447.
12 *Ecclesiastical History*, §5.1.20, J.E.L. Oulton, ed. (Cambridge, MA: Harvard University Press, 1932), 415.
13 Ibid., §5.1.41, p. 427.
14 *Martyrdom of Perpetua and Felicitas*, §5.2, in Anne Fremantle, *A Treasury of Early Christianity* (New York: Viking Press, 1953), 216–217.
15 Cyprian, "On the Glory of Martyrdom," §2, ANF05, 579.
16 "On the Unity of the Church," §6, ANF05, 423.
17 *Epistle LXXII*, §21 (Oxford edition, Epistle LXXIII), ANF05, 384.
18 Jaroslav Pelikan, *The Emergence of the Catholic Tradition* (Chicago, IL: University of Chicago Press, 1971), 123.
19 Tertullian, *Ad Scapula*, §5.1, ANF03, 107.
20 W.H.C. Frend, *Martyrdom and Persecution in the Early Church* (New York: New York University Press, 1967), 221.

6 SPIRITUALITY AND ASCETICISM

1 Eusebius, *The Life of Constantine*, Book I, Chapter 28, in Philip Schaff, ed., *Nicene and Post-Nicene Fathers*, Series 2, Vol. I (Peabody, MA: Hendrickson, 1994, reprinted from 1886 edition), 490. Hereafter citations to this series will be NPNF.
2 Cassian, *Conferences*, §1.7, in Owen Chadwick, *Western Asceticism* (Philadelphia, PA: Westminster Press, 1958), 198.
3 Prominent historian of spirituality, Louis Bouyer, is especially clear on this point. See his *Spirituality of the New Testament and the Fathers* (New York: The Seabury Press, 1982), 315.

4 J. Heinrich Arnold, *Discipleship* (Farmington, PA: The Plough Publishing House, 1994), v.
5 Evagrius, *Praktikos*, §15, translated by Luke Dysinger (public domain).
6 Ibid., §29.
7 Laura Swan, *The Forgotten Desert Mothers* (New York: Paulist Press), 43.
8 Ibid., 54.
9 Athanasius, *On the Incarnation*, §54 in *Christology of the Later Fathers*, Edward R. Hardy, ed. (Philadelphia, PA: The Westminster Press, 1954), 107. The passage could be translated literally, "He was humanized that we might be divinized."
10 St. Gregory, "On the Soul and the Resurrection," in *Ascetical Works* (Washington, DC: The Catholic University of America Press, 1967), 239.
11 St. Gregory, "On What it Means to Call Oneself a Christian," in *Ascetical Works* (Washington, DC: The Catholic University of America Press, 1967), 87.
12 Sebastian Brock in Introduction to Ephraem, *Hymns on Paradise* (Crestwood, NY: St. Vladimir's Seminary Press, 1990), 39.
13 Ephraem, *Hymns on Paradise*, 46.
14 "On the Soul and the Resurrection," in *Ascetical Works*, 210.
15 Letter 234, §1, NPNF2–8, 274.
16 Roberta Bondi, "Christianity and Cultural Diversity," in *Christian Spirituality*, Bernard McGinn, ed. (New York: Crossroad, 1986), 158.
17 Ivor Davidson, *A Public Faith* (Grand Rapids, MI: Monarch Books, 2005), 146.

7 THE CHRISTIAN APOLOGISTS

1 Justin Martyr, *The Second Apology*, ANF1, Chapter 12, 192.
2 Justin Martyr, *First Apology*, ANF1, Chapter II, 163.
3 For more on Justin Martyr, see Leslie William Barnard, *Justin Martyr, His Life and Thought* (Cambridge: Cambridge University Press, 1967).
4 Karen L. King, for example, argues that the Gnostic concept is an artificial entity derived from the early Christian apologists in their attempt to demarcate and demonize the other (those who disagreed with them) from their own "orthodox" views. For more on this theme, see her book *What is Gnosticism* (Cambridge, MA: The Belknap Press of Harvard University Press, 2003).
5 The details of the story can be found in James M. Robinson, ed., *The Nag Hammadi Library* (San Francisco, CA: HarperSanFrancisco, 1988), 22–26.
6 Tertullian, *Against the Valentinians*, ANF3, Part II, Chapter 4, 505.
7 For more on Gnostic teaching, see Robert M. Grant, *Gnosticism and Early Christianity*, 2nd edition (New York: Columbia University Press, 1966) and the more recent work by Kurt Rudolph entitled *Gnosis: The Nature and History of Gnosticism*, R. McL. Wilson, trans. (San Francisco, CA: Harper & Rowe, 1987). See also Elaine Pagels, *The Gnostic Gospels* (New York: Vintage Books, 1979). For a concise and readable description, including Gnostic history, sources, and developments, see "Gnosticism" by Kurt Rudolph, in *The Anchor Bible Dictionary* (New York: Doubleday, 1992), Vol. 2, 1033–1040.

8 Bart Ehrman sets the Ebionites and the Marcionites at polar ends of the theological spectrum in his book, *Lost Christianities: The Battles for Scripture and the Faiths We Never Knew* (Oxford: Oxford University Press, 2003), 95–112.

9 Most scholars now believe that Tertullian merely conjectured that the founder was a man named Ebion. The Hebrew word *ebyon* means "the poor," and it is very likely the case that the Ebionites were adhering to a life of poverty.

10 For more on early Jewish Christianity, see H.-J. Schoeps, *Jewish Christianity: Factional Disputes in the Church*, Douglas Hare, trans. (Philadelphia, PA: Fortress Press, 1969).

8 THE EARLY CHURCH COUNCILS

1 Eusebius, *Life of Constantine*, Book III, Chapter 8, NPNF2-01, 522.

2 Here "begotten" refers to the familial relationship between the Father and Son, and does not imply that there was a point in time prior to the Son's coming into existence.

3 Eusebius of Casesarea, "Letter to the Church of Caesarea" §4, NPNF2-04, 75. Almost certainly it was not Constantine himself who came up with this formulation. Most historians speculate that it was probably Ossius (alternative spelling: Hosius) of Córdoba who suggested the term.

4 Justo L. González, *A History of Christian Thought* (Nashville, TN: Abingdon, 1987), Vol. 1, 268–271.

5 See *Discourses Against the Arians*, Discourse III, Chapter XXVI, §30–35, in NPNF2-04, 410f., and *On the Incarnation of the Word*, NPNF2-04, 31f.

6 *Theotokos* is the transliteration of the Greek word for "God-bearer." Its significance is discussed later in the chapter.

7 *Prosopon* and *hypostasis* are technical, transliterated Greek words that mean complete, individual existences. A specific person would be an example of a *prosopon* or *hypostasis*.

8 Translated by and quoted in J.N.D. Kelly, *Early Christian Doctrines*, revised edition (San Francisco, CA: HarperSanFrancisco, 1978), 339–340.

9 Ibid., p. 342.

10 *On the Divinity of the Son and Holy Spirit*, V. Quoted in William Placher, *A History of Christian Theology* (Philadelphia, PA: Westminster Press, 1983), 68.

11 *The Great Catechism*, XI, in NPNF2-05, 144.

12 Quoted in Jaroslav Pelikan, *The Emergence of the Catholic Tradition (100–600)* (Chicago, IL: University of Chicago Press, 1971), 239.

13 Ibid., 240.

14 The evidence is not conclusive on this point, but Pelikan seems to support this interpretation. Ibid., 241–242.

9 TRINITARIAN DEBATE

1 For a comprehensive discussion of Roman religious practices, see Valerie M. Warrior, *Roman Religion* (Cambridge: Cambridge University Press, 2006).

2 The situation may be more complicated than this for the Jews. A case could be made that at least the early Jews did in fact believe the world to be populated by gods other than their God, Yahweh. But certainly they believed Yahweh to be the one God above all other gods and the only one deserving of worship.

3 This is the New Revised Standard Version. Some variants of the ancient manuscripts bring out the identification of Father and Son even more explicitly: " ... has given us understanding so that we may know the true God."

4 Thomas Oden, *The Living God* (San Francisco, CA: HarperCollins, 1987), 184.

5 §7 in Cyril C. Richardson, ed. and trans., *Early Christian Fathers* (Philadelphia, PA: Westminster Press, 1953), 174.

6 See Olson and Hall, *The Trinity* (Grand Rapids, MI, Eerdmans, 2002), 22, for a description of these.

7 Justin Martyr, *First Apology*, Chap. 6; ANF01, 164.

8 Letter CXXV, NPNF2-08, 195.

9 Paul Tillich goes so far as to say that, "when the Greek thinkers produced a confession or creed, it may seem like abstract philosophy to us, but to them it was the mystical intuition of essences, of powers of being ... seemingly abstract philosophical concepts could become mystical confessions" in *A History of Christian Thought* (New York: Harper & Row, 1968), 68.

10 Jaroslav Pelikan, *The Emergence of the Catholic Tradition* (Chicago, IL: University of Chicago Press, 1971), 178.

11 *Against Praxeas*, Chapter I, ANF03, 597.

12 Ibid., Chapter II, ANF03, 598.

13 Augustine argues against the suggestion that the Trinity is to be understood on a familial model like Father, Mother (Holy Spirit), Son (Jesus) in his *On the Holy Trinity*, XII.5 (NPNF1-03, 156f). Methodius (died *c.* 311) was attributed with the position that Adam and Eve and their children were representative of Father, Spirit, and Son. It is certainly plausible to think that the heavily patriarchal society in which the Church was institutionalized removed this option from orthodox believers.

14 *The Emergence of the Catholic Tradition (100–600)*, 212.

15 Basil the Great, Letter 38.3, NPNF2-08, 137.

16 Gregory Nazianzus says the unity of humanity is "only conceivable in thought; and the individuals are parted from one another very far indeed, both by time and by dispositions and by power" (Oration 31,15, NPNF2-07, 322).

17 J.N.D. Kelly, *Early Christian Doctrines* (San Francisco, CA: HarperSanFrancisco, 1978), 268.

18 Letter 38, 4, NPNF2-08, 139.

19 Quoted in Ivor Davidson, *A Public Faith* (Grand Rapids, MI: Baker, 2005), 97.

20 Ronald J. Feenstra, "The Trinity" in *Routledge Companion to Philosophy of Religion*, Chad Meister and Paul Copan, eds. (London: Routledge, 2007), 538.

21 *On the Holy Trinity*, V.10, NPNF1-03, 92.

10 FORMATION OF THE NEW TESTAMENT CANON

1 For a discussion of the Islamic view of divine revelation, see Abdullah Saeed, *Islamic Thought: An Introduction* (London: Routledge, 2006), 15–18.

2 The Protestant version of the Bible includes sixty-six books. The official Roman Catholic edition which follows the Latin Vulgate includes additional books, and the Greek Orthodox edition which follows the Greek Septuagint includes several more. These additional books are often referred to as the Apocrypha by Protestants and while they will be noted briefly later in the chapter they will not be discussed in detail as they belong to the Old Testament.

3 The one exception to this in the New Testament might be the book of Revelation, which purports to be an account of what was directly revealed to John by an angel sent from Jesus Christ.

4 The first person to use the word "canon" in this sense was Athanasius. Cf. F.F. Bruce, *The Canon of Scripture* (Downers Grove, IL: InterVarsity Press, 1988), 77.

5 See Chapter 2 for more discussion of Paul's letters.

6 There is debate about whether the orthodox canon developed as a result of Marcion's canon or whether Marcion's canon developed in response to a canon which the orthodox were already accepting and using.

7 The ten books are Galatians, 1 and 2 Corinthians, Romans, 1 and 2 Thessalonians, Ephesians, Colossians, Philippians, and Philemon. For a helpful and concise treatment of Marcion and his teaching, see F.F. Bruce, *The Canon of Scripture*, 134–144 and Bart D. Ehrman, *Lost Christianities: The Battles for Scripture and the Faiths We Never Knew* (Oxford: Oxford University Press, 2003), 103–112.

8 This practice is indicated in I Thessalonians 5:27 and I Timothy 4:13.

9 Luke 10:7 is referenced in I Timothy 5:18; also, Paul's writings in 2 Peter 3:16 are mentioned as Scripture.

10 Eusebius, *Ecclesiastical History* 8.2, Loeb edition, Kirsopp Lake, trans. (Cambridge, MA: Harvard University Press,1926), 2:257–59.

11 The emperor's letter is preserved in Eusebius's *Life of Constantine*, 4.36.

12 For lists of early New Testament collections, see Lee Martin McDonald and James A, Sanders, eds., *The Canon Debate* (Peabody, MA: Hendrickson Publishers, 2002), Appendix D. See also Bruce M. Metzger and Bart D. Ehrman, *The Text of the New Testament: Its Transmission, Corruption, and Restoration*, 4th edition (Oxford: Oxford University Press, 2005), 52–134. For more on this and related topics, see also Norman L. Geisler and William E. Nix, *A General Introduction to the Bible* (Chicago, IL: Moody Press, 1986), which covers the topics of inspiration, canonization, transmission, and translation of the Bible from a conservative perspective.

13 Technically, Matthew and Mark are not included either, but this is almost certainly because the fragment is torn at the very location where they would be listed.

14 The complete Muratorian Fragment can be found on pages 305–307 in Bruce M. Metzger, *The Canon of the New Testament* (Oxford: Clarendon Press, 1987).

15 I Clement 63.2, as quoted in F.F. Bruce, *The Canon of Scripture* (Downers Grove, IL: InterVarsity Press, 1988), 266.

16 As quoted in Bruce Metzger, *The Canon of the New Testament* (Oxford: Clarendon Press, 1987), 197.

17 For example, one of the first recorded acts of the martyrs is a book entitled *The Martyrdom of Polycarp* which details the martyrdom of this church father by the Romans in the second century. This early writing includes the phrase "the catholic rule (i.e. canon) of the Church."

18 For more on this see Bruce Metzger, *The Canon of the New Testament*, 251–253, and F.F. Bruce, *The Canon of Scripture*, 260–261. It was also the case that the canon was in a sense determining orthodoxy, for the various theological and ecclesiological doctrines which later developed were themselves rooted in the canonical writings. For a concise and helpful summary of some of the issues involved in this discussion, see Roger E. Olson, *The Mosaic of Christian Belief: Twenty Centuries of Unity and Diversity* (Leicester: Apollos, 2002), Chapter 2, "Sources and Norms of Christian Belief," 49–69.

19 Augustine, *On Christian Doctrine*, Book II, Chapter 8 (12), NPNF1–2, 538.

20 For more information on the criteria for canonization, see Bruce M. Metzger, *The Canon of the New Testament*, 251–254, and F.F. Bruce, *The Canon of Scripture*, 255–269.

21 We are following here those biblical scholars who make a distinction between the apocryphal and pseudepigraphal writings – the latter being those works which were rejected by the majority of church fathers as being canonical (the word "pseudepigrapha" literally means "false writings"). This can be confusing, for another way the term "pseudepigrapha" is often used is in reference to pseudonymous writings, or writings written under a false name.

22 The Apocrypha (also called the deuterocanonical books) included in Catholic and Orthodox versions of the Bible are the following: Tobit, Judith, Additions to Esther, Wisdom, Ecclesiasticus, (also called Sirach or Ben Sira), Baruch, Additions to Daniel, (Song of the Three Children, Story of Susanna, and Bel and the Dragon), 1 Maccabees, and 2 Maccabees. While Protestants acknowledge their literary, historical, and spiritual significance, most do not view them as authoritative Scripture as Roman Catholics and the Orthodox do.

23 For an extensive list and description of New Testament apocrypha, see Bart Ehrman, *Lost Scriptures: Books that Did Not Make It into the New Testament* (Oxford: Oxford University Press, 2003).

24 For example, Robert Funk, founder of the Jesus Seminar, suggests creating several new New Testaments – including one shorter and one longer. See his "The Once and Future New Testament" in Lee Martin McDonald and James A. Sanders, eds., *The Canon Debate* (Peabody, MA: Hendrickson, 2002), 541–557.

25 Bruce Metzger notes this point in ibid., 271.

26 *The Canon of the New Testament*, 271.

11 AUGUSTINE

1 Augustine, *Confessions*, R.S. Pine-Coffin, trans. (New York: Penguin Books, 1961), Book III, Chapter iv, 59.
2 This point anticipates by over 1,000 years the very similar one made by Descartes which launched the Modern period of philosophy, namely, the one certainty – even if we're deceived about everything else – is that we are sure of our own existence because of our mental activity we recognize as our own: I think, therefore I am. See Chapter 24.
3 See Plotinus, *Enneads*, H. Armstrong, trans. (Cambridge, MA: Harvard University Press, 1966), I.8, 279–317.
4 Augustine wrote an entire book on free will in which he offers his free will theodicy. See his *On the Free Choice of the Will*, Thomas Williams, trans. (Cambridge: Hackett, 1993).
5 Augustine, *Confessions*, Book XII, Chapters xii and xvi, 148, 150.
6 Ibid., Book VIII, Chapter xii, 177.
7 Ibid., 178.
8 For a helpful, concise summary of the Donatist controversy and Augustine's evolving response to it, see John M. Rist, *Augustine: Ancient Thought Baptized* (Cambridge: Cambridge University Press, 1994), 239–245. See also David F. Wright "The Donatists in North Africa" in Tim Dowley, ed., *The Eerdmans Handbook to the History of Christianity* (Berkhamsted: Lion Publishing, 1977), 202–203.
9 See Augustine's tract, "On Baptism, Against the Donatists" in *The Anti-Donatist Writings*, in *The Nicene and Post Nicene Fathers*, Philip Schaff, ed. (Peabody, MA: Hendrickson, 1994), Vol. 4, 411–514.
10 This is the view of Justo L. González. See his *A History of Christian Thought*, (Nashville, TN: Abingdon Press, 1987), Vol. II, 29–30.
11 There is debate about Augustine's view of free will. It is noteworthy that in his book, *Retractions*, which he wrote toward the end of his career and in which he retracted all of his earlier teachings with which he disagreed, he never retracted his view of free will as presented and defended in his earlier works.
12 Augustine, *The Spirit and the Letter*, Chapters 4–5. NPNF1–5, 84
13 Augustine, *Confessions*, NPNF1–1, 45.

12 MONASTICISM OF THE EARLY MIDDLE AGES

1 Rom 10:20, quoting Isa. 65:1, John Leith, ed., *Creeds of the Churches*, 3rd edition (Louisville, KY: John Knox Press, 1982), 38.
2 St. Gregory, *Dialogues*, II, introduction, Henry James Coleridge, ed. (London: Burns and Oates, 1874), 55.
3 Benedict, *The Rule of St. Benedict in English* (Collegeville, MN: The Liturgical Press, 1982), prologue 35–41.
4 Ibid., 43.1–2.
5 Ibid., 64.1.
6 Ibid., 73.6.
7 Ibid., 73.8.

8   St. Gregory, *Dialogues,* II.33.
9   Justo L. González, *A History of Christian Thought* (Nashville, TN: Abingdon, 1987), Vol. II, 70.
10 *Bede's Ecclesiastical History of England,* A.M. Sellar, trans. (London: George Bell and Sons, 1907), 2.1.
11 The *Life of Benedict* is packaged now as Book II of his *Dialogues.*
12 Some interesting commentary on Gregory's approach to theology: "With Gregory, dogma and spirituality are one; faith and the life of faith are part of the same experience; he never separates the practice of virtue from contemplation, nor the latter from the mysteries which are its object." Jean Leclercq, François Vandenbroucke, and Louis Bouyer, *The Spirituality of the Middle Ages* (New York: Seabury Press, 1968), 6.
13 Leclercq, *et al.,* 24.
14 Recall from Chapter 7 that those who had lapsed in their faith in the face of persecution had to undergo penance to be received back into good standing.
15 Augustine said, "After the resurrection, there will be some of the dead to whom, after they have endured the pains proper to the spirits of the dead, mercy shall be accorded, and acquittal from the punishment of the eternal fire" in *City of God,* XXI, xxiv; NPNF1-02, 470.
16 St. Gregory, *Dialogues,* IV.39; Coleridge, 275–276.
17 Bede, *Ecclesiastical History,* 5.12.
18 Epistle LXXVI, To Mellitus, NPNF2–13, 85.
19 Alister McGrath, *Historical Theology* (Oxford: Blackwell Publishing, 1998), 97.
20 Thomas O'Loughlin, *Celtic Theology* (London: Continuum, 2000), 55–56.
21 Ibid., 56.
22 *Penitential of Finnian,* §1–2 in *The Irish Penitentials,* Ludwig Bieler, ed. (Dublin: The Dublin Institute for Advanced Studies, 1963), 75.
23 Ibid., §37–38, 89.
24 Ibid., §29, 85.

13 EASTERN CHRISTIANITY SPLITS FROM THE WEST

1   Timothy Ware says the time of the incident was in the afternoon (*The Orthodox Church* (London: Penguin, 1993), 43), and Stephen Tomkins identifies the time as three o'clock in the afternoon in *A Short History of Christianity* (Grand Rapids, MI: Eerdmans, 2005), 99; but much more rigorously documented from the original sources is the account given by Richard Mayne in "East and West in 1054" in *Cambridge Historical Journal* 11(2):133–148 (1954) in which the eight o'clock hour is named. Regardless, not much hinges on the specific time for our purposes.
2   Gibbon says in *The History of the Fall and Decline of the Roman Empire,* Chapter LX, "The rising majesty of Rome could no longer brook the insolence of a rebel; and Michael Cerularius was excommunicated in the heart of Constantinople by the pope's legates ... the Greeks have never recanted their errors; the popes have never repealed their sentence; and from this thunderbolt we may date the consummation of the schism" (J.B. Bury, ed., (New York: Fred De Fau & Company, 1907), vol. X, 323).

3 Jaroslav Pelikan, *The Spirit of Eastern Christendom* (Chicago, IL: University of Chicago Press, 1974), 161.
4 Aeneas of Paris, quoted in Pelikan, *op. cit.*, 164.
5 *Documents of the Christian Church*, 2nd edition, Henry Bettenson, ed. (Oxford: Oxford University Press, 1967), 100.
6 Ibid., 26.
7 Peter Damian (1007–1072), *Against the Error of the Greeks on the Procession of the Holy Spirit*, quoted in Pelikan, 195.
8 Justo L. González, *A History of Christian Thought II: Augustine to the Eve of Reformation*, revised edition (Nashville, TN: Abingdon Press, 1987), 200. The argument was also made that depicting the divine nature constituted an attempt to circumscribe or delimit that which is infinite.
9 These three treatises collected in *On Holy Images*, Mary H. Allies, trans. (London: Thomas Baker, 1898).
10 Ibid., 15–16.
11 "Definition of the Second Council of Nicea" in *Documents of the Christian Church*, 94.
12 John Meyendorff, *Byzantine Theology*, 2nd edition (New York: Fordham University Press, 1979), 51.
13 There are different accounts of how this council came about and decisions were made. See J.M. Hussey, *The Orthodox Church in the Byzantine Empire* (Oxford: Clarendon, 1986) for a discussion of the situation.
14 *On Holy Images*, 39.
15 *The Philokalia* (four volumes), compiled by St. Nikodimos of the Holy Mountain and St. Makarios of Corinth, G.E.H. Palmer, Philip Sherrard, and Kallistos Ware, eds and trans. (London: Faber and Faber, 1979–1995).
16 Gregory Palamas, *Topics of Natural and Theological Science and on the Moral and Ascetic Life*, in *The Philokalia*, vol. 4, 380.
17 Symeon the New Theologian, *On Faith*, in *The Philokalia*, vol. 4, 18.

14 ANSELM, ABELARD, AND BERNARD

1 In the preface to his *Monologium* he states, "I have not been able to find that I have made in [this book] any statement which is inconsistent with the writings of the Catholic Fathers, or especially with those of St. Augustine" (Sidney Norton Deane, trans. (Chicago, IL: Open Court, 1926)), 35.
2 The longer passage is, "For I do not seek to understand that I may believe, but I believe in order to understand. For this also I believe, – that unless I believed, I should not understand." *Proslogium,* Chapter 1; ibid., 6.
3 *Lectures or Tractates on the Gospel According to St. John*, Tractate XXIX, 6; NPNF1-07, 184.
4 A similar point is made by Étienne Gilson in his *Reason and Revelation in the Middle Ages* (New York: Charles Scribner's Sons, 1938), 32.
5 There are strong affinities in this approach with a contemporary movement called "Reformed Epistemology" or "Reformed Apologetics." Advocates of these positions are not actively trying to convince those outside the faith that they are wrong. Like Anselm's approach, Reformed Apologetics is oriented defensively. They aim to show that their beliefs are rational and that they

are within their epistemic rights to believe as they do. The leading Reformed Epistemologist at the end of the twentieth century was Alvin Plantinga.

6   Étienne Gilson, *The Spirit of Medieval Philosophy* (Notre Dame, IN: University of Notre Dame Press, 1991), 34–35.

7   For a contemporary discussion of the argument, see Graham Oppy, "The Ontological Argument" in Paul Copan and Chad Meister, eds., *Philosophy of Religion: Classic and Contemporary Issues* (Oxford: Blackwell, 2007).

8   *Why God Became Man*, preface; Deane, translation *op. cit.* 175.

9   Gregory of Nyssa, *The Great Catechism*, Chapter XXIV; NPNF2-05, 152.

10 *Why God Became Man*, I.XIX; Deane, translation *op. cit.* 221.

11 *Exposition of the Epistle to the Romans* Book II, 2–3, in Eugene R. Fairweather, ed., *A Scholastic Miscellany: Anselm to Ockham* (Philadelphia, PA: Westminster Press, 1956), 283.

12 Ibid., II, 3; Fairweather, 284.

13 *Sic et Non*, prologue; W.J. Lewis, trans., Internet Medieval Source Book (http://www.fordham.edu/halsall/source/Abelard-SicetNon-Prologue.html) accessed 13 August, 2008.

14 Bernard of Clairvaux, *Epistles* 190.7.17, quoted in Jaroslav Pelikan, *The Growth of Medieval Theology (600–1300)* (Chicago, IL: University of Chicago Press, 1978), 129.

15 Abelard, *Exposition of the Epistle to the Romans* II, 3; Fairweather, 284.

16 "Selections from the Condemnation of 1277," in Gyula Klima, ed., *Medieval Philosophy: Essential Readings with Commentary* (Oxford: Blackwell, 2007), Chapter 22.

17 Bernard of Clairvaux, *Epistles* 190.8.20, cited in Pelikan, 138.

15 ISLAM AND JUDAISM IN THE MIDDLE AGES

1   For more on this, see Michael Cook, *Muhammad* (Oxford: Oxford University Press, 1983).

2   Actually, the distinction goes back at least to the earlier Muslim philosopher Al-Farabi and perhaps even to Boethius or Plotinus. But Avicenna develops the idea which was then borrowed from Thomas Aquinas.

3   The argument as stated is a modification of that provided by Norman Geisler and Win Corduan in *Philosophy of Religion*, 2nd edition (Grand Rapids, MI: Baker Books, 1988), 157. For a full exposition of Avicenna's argument from contingency, see M.E. Mamura, "Avicenna's Proof from Contingency for God's Existence in the Metaphysics of *al Shifa*," *Medieval Studies* (1980) 42: 337–52.

4   Averroës, *In Libros de Anima*, III, t.c. 14, Venice, 1574, vol. 6, fol. 159v, as quoted in Armand A. Maurer, *Medieval Philosophy*, revised edition (Ontario, Toronto: Pontifical Institute of Mediaeval Philosophy, 1982), 100.

5   For more on this subject, see Sayyed Misbah Deen, *Science Under Islam: Rise, Decline, and Revival* (UK: Lulu Enterprises, 2007), Chapter 2. It should be noted that this book is controversial among contemporary Islamic scholars. See also Ehsan Masood, *Science and Islam: A History* (London: Icon Books, 2009).

6 Moses Maimonides, *The Guide for the Perplexed*, 2nd ed. (New York: Dover, 1956), 2.
7 This point is noted in William Lane Craig, *The Cosmological Argument from Plato to Leibniz* (Eugene, OR: Wipf and Stock, 2001), 152.
8 While he never mentions the Kabbalah, it is possible that the Dominican friar Meister Eckhart (*c.* 1260–*c.* 1328) was influenced by Kabbalistic teachings, for he does seem to affirm an emanation view of an undifferentiated God; God thus resembling in some sense Ein Sof and the *sefirot*.
9 Peter the Venerable, as quoted in Pelikan, *The Growth of Medieval Theology* (Chicago, IL: University of Chicago PRess, 1978), 242.
10 Ibid.

16 WOMEN AND THEOLOGY IN THE MIDDLE AGES

1 Hildegard of Bingen, *Scivias*, Declaration/Prologue; Columba Hart and Jane Bishop, trans. (New York: Paulist Press, 1990), 59.
2 By analysis of her descriptions of her visions, Charles Singer famously diagnosed Hildegard with scintillating scotoma in his 1917 essay, "Scientific Views and Visions of Saint Hildegard." Reprinted in Singer, *From Magic to Science: Essays on the Scientific Twilight* (New York: Dover, 1958), 232.
3 Hildegard claimed in a letter to Guibert of Gembloux, "What I do not see, I do not know, for I am not educated but I have simply been taught how to read. And what I write is what I see and hear in the vision. I compose no other words than those I hear, and I set them forth in unpolished Latin just as I hear them in the vision, for I am not taught in this vision to write as philosophers do." Quoted in Barbara Newman, "Hildegard of Bingen: Visions and Validation." *Church History* 54 (1985), 165.
4 See John Van Engen, "Abbess: 'Mother and Teacher'", in *Voice of the Living Light: Hildegard of Bingen and Her World*, Barbara Newman, ed. (Berkeley, CA: University of California Press), 47.
5 Speaking of God's work in creation, Hildegard says, "For if the Lord were empty of His own vitality [viridity], what then would have been His deeds?" (*Scivias* II.2.1, Hart and Bishop, 161). Regarding the Incarnation, "The same Word lighted upon Israel when the Only-Begotten of God came into the high fecundity [viridity] of the Virgin" (*Scivias* I.4.32, Hart and Bishop, 129).
6 There are other confirmed English female authors before Julian, including those writing short romance novels, but their writings are not in English.
7 Julian of Norwich, *Revelations of Divine Love*, Elizabeth Spearing, trans. (New York: Penguin Books, 1998), the long text, #6, page 49.
8 *Revelations*, the long text, #86, page 179.
9 Ibid., Chapter 58, 138.
10 For one interesting feminist work on Julian, see Grace Jantzen, *Julian of Norwich: Mystic and Theologian* (Eugene, OR: Wipf and Stock, 2000). It should also be noted that there is an Order of Julian of Norwich within the contemporary Episcopal Church which was founded in 1982. It follows the three historical, sacred vows of monastic life: *poverty* (to resist the temptation of money), *chastity* (to resist the temptation of sex), and *obedience* (to resist the temptation of power). It also adds a fourth vow of prayer.

11 *Dialogue*, §47; in Amy Oden, ed., *In Her Words: Women's Writings in the History of Christian Thought* (Nashville, TN: Abingdon, 1994), 199.
12 Ibid., §11; Oden, 191.
13 Ibid., §134; Oden, 203.
14 "To Three Italian Cardinals" in Katharina M. Wilson, ed., *Medieval Women Writers* (Athens, GA: University of Georgia Press, 1984), 259.
15 St. Teresa of Ávila, *Interior Castle*, E. Allison Peers, trans. and ed. (New York: Image Books, Doubleday, 1989), 28.
16 *Interior Castle*, 31.
17 She was so honored in September, 1970 by Pope Paul VI (one week before Catherine). In 1997, Theresa of Lisieux was the third woman to be given the title.

17 THOMAS AQUINAS

1 G.K. Chesterton tells this anecdote and makes this point in Chapter 4 of his *Saint Thomas Aquinas* (New York: Doubleday, 1956).
2 *Summa Theologica*, I,12,12. All translations of the *Summa Theologica* are taken from the Benziger Brothers translation.
3 This discussion draws heavily on the very perspicuous commentary of G.K. Chesterton, 137–142.
4 Unfortunately, though, it is the way it is typically explained in the secondary literature. Such an explanation is reading Aquinas through modern eyes rather than medieval ones.
5 Even in the Second Way, that of efficient causes, Aquinas is not arguing in the temporal, mechanistic way. See F.C. Copleston, *Aquinas: An Introduction to the Life and Work of the Great Medieval Thinker* (New York: Penguin, 1955), 121–124.
6 *Summa Theologica*, I.44.1.
7 This understanding of God's relationship to existence renders Anselm's ontological argument ineffectual. See Chapter 14.
8 Ibid., I.8.1.
9 *Summa Contra Gentiles*, I.4.3.
10 *Summa Theologica.*, I.12.12–13.
11 *Summa Gentiles*, I.2.4.
12 *Summa Theologica*, I.1.8.
13 Ibid.(Part I of Second Part, Q85, A2).
14 *Commentary on De Trinitate*, II.3, in *The Trinity and the The Unicity of the Intellect*, Rose Emmanuella Brennan, trans. (London: B. Herder Book Co., 1946), 59.
15 *Summa Theologica* (Part I of the Second Part, Q83, A1).
16 Ibid., I.12.1.

18 PREPARATION FOR REFORM

1 One of the lasting contributions of Eckhart is that he was the first serious thinker who employed the vernacular German (which would later become so formative for theology) in the service of theology.

2 Meister Eckhart, "The Holiness of Being," in Matthew Fox, ed., *Breakthrough: Meister Eckhart's Creation Spirituality in New Translation* (New York: Image Books, 1980), 85.

3 Meister Eckhart, "God Must Give Himself," in Raymond B. Blakney, ed., *Meister Eckhart* (New York: Harper Torchboooks, 1941), 185.

4 In this vein Oliver Davies says about Eckhart, "Any proposition extracted from his work must be seen in the context of his entire thinking if we are not to mistake expressive, imagistic language for the discourse of scientific reflection" (*Meister Eckhart: Mystical Theologian* (London: SPCK, 1991), 196).

5 "God Must Give Himself," Blakney, 185. Furthermore, this is consistent with the Apostle Paul's claim that "In him we live and move and have our being" (Acts 17:28).

6 Eckhart, *In Johannem*, I, 43; quoted in Jeanne Ancelet-Hustache, *Master Eckhart and the Rhineland Mystics*, Hild Graef, trans. (New York: Harper Torchbooks, 1957), 59. Steven Ozment notes in this regard, "In the final analysis, Eckhart begrudged all reality beyond the eternal birth; for him, man was meant to be in God, not to live as a creature in the world" (*The Age of Reform: 1250–1550* (New Haven, CT: Yale University Press, 1980), 132).

7 Eckhart, "The Love of God," in Raymond B. Blakney, ed., *Meister Eckhart* (New York: Harper Torchboooks, 1941), 127.

8 Ibid.

9 "The Defense," I, in Raymond B. Blakney, ed., *Meister Eckhart* (New York: Harper Torchboooks, 1941), 259.

10 A complementary point can be made too that realism and rationalism played a role in scientific revolution. See particularly the work of Alexandre Koyré for this perspective.

11 William of Ockham, *Dialogus*, 3.1.2.20, in Arthur Stephen McGrade and John Kilcullen, eds., *A Letter to the Friars Minor and Other Writings* (Cambridge: Cambridge University Press, 1995), 172.

12 This point is developed in Phillip H. Stump, *Reforms of the Council of Constance* (Leiden: E.J. Brill, 1994), 6.

13 For an extended discussion of Wycliffe's view of the Eucharist, see Stephen Penn, "Wyclif and the Sacraments," in Ian Levy, ed., *A Companion to John Wyclif* (Boston, MA: Brill, 2006), 241–292.

14 Gordon Leff develops the realist underpinnings of Wyclif's doctrine of the Bible in "Wyclif and Hus: A Doctrinal Comparison" in Anthony Kenny, ed., *Wyclif in His Times* (Oxford: Clarendon Press, 1986).

15 From Wyclif, *De Ecclesia*, quoted in G.H.W. Parker, *The Morning Star: Wycliffe and the Dawn of the Reformation* (Grand Rapids, MI: Eerdmans, 1965), 37.

19 MARTIN LUTHER

1 Martin Luther, *First Principles of the Reformation or The Ninety-Five Theses and the Three Primary Works of Dr. Martin Luther*, Henry Wace, ed. and trans. (London: John Murray, 1883), 6.

2 Recorded in Roland H. Bainton, *Here I Stand: A Life of Martin Luther* (Nashville, TN: Abingdon Press, 1978), 144.

3 Ibid., 145.

4   Wace, 7.
5   Aquinas, *Summa Theologica*, Supplement to Part III, Q25.
6   Thesis 27, in Wace, 8.
7   Hans J. Hillerbrand, *The Reformation: A Narrative History Related by Contemporary Observers and Participants* (Grand Rapids, MI: Baker, 1987), 42–43.
8   Ibid., 44–45.
9   Wace, 11.
10   On this point, see Alister McGrath's *Iustitia Dei: A History of the Christian Doctrine of Justification*, 3rd edition (Cambridge: Cambridge University Press, 2005).
11   From Luther's "Preface to the Complete Edition of Luther's Latin Writings" sometimes called the "Autobiographical Fragment," in John Dillenberger, ed., *Martin Luther: Selections from his Writings* (New York: Doubleday, 1961), 10–11.
12   Ibid., 11.
13   From Luther's Sermon, "Two Kinds of Righteousness" in Dillenberger, 87–88.
14   Luther, *Disputation Against Scholastic Theology*, in Timothy F. Lull, ed., *Martin Luther's Theological Writings* (Minneapolis, MN: Fortress, 1989), 13–14.
15   Erasmus, *On the Freedom of the Will,* in E. Gordon Rupp and P. Watson, eds., *Luther and Erasmus: Free Will and Salvation* (Philadelphia, PA: Westminster, 1969), 90.
16   Luther, *Bondage of the Will*, Rupp and Watson, 102.
17   Erasmus, *Paraclesis*, in Carter Lindberg, ed., *The European Reformations Sourcebook* (Oxford: Blackwell, 2000), 48.
18   Ibid., 140.
19   Jaroslav Pelikan notes that all heirs of the Reformation "are agreed on this doctrine as the foundation of the entire Reformation, in fact, the chief doctrine of Christianity and the chief point of difference separating Protestantism from Roman Catholicism," in *Reformation of Church and Dogma (1300–1700)* (Chicago, IL: University of Chicago Press, 1984), 139.
20   From Luther's commentary on Psalm 130. Quoted in Bernhard Lohse, *Martin Luther's Theology* (Minneapolis, MN: Fortress, 1999), 258.
21   Luther, "Freedom of a Christian," in Dillenberger, 66.
22   Luther, "Preface to the Epistle of St. Paul to the Romans," in Dillenberger, 23.
23   Luther, *Commentary on The Epistle to the Romans*, Theodore Mueller, trans. (Grand Rapids, MI: Zondervan Publishing House, 1954), 99.
24   In support of this caricature, this excerpt from a letter to Philip Melancthon is given: "God does not save people who are only fictitious sinners. Be a sinner and sin boldly." The passage continues, though, with the charge to "believe and rejoice in Christ even more boldly. For he is victorious over sin, death, and the world." Letter no. 99 (1521), translated by Erika Flores. Public Domain.
25   From Luther's "Preface to the Epistle of St. Paul to the Romans," in Dillenberger, 23–24.
26   In his "Freedom of a Christian" Luther says, "Man, however, needs none of these things for his righteousness and salvation. Therefore he should be guided in all his works by this thought and contemplate this one thing alone, that he may serve and benefit others in all that he does, considering nothing except the need and the advantage of his neighbor." Dillenberger, 73.

20 THE REFORMED TRADITION

1 David B. Barrett, George T. Kurian, and Todd M. Johnson, eds., *World Christian Encyclopedia* (Oxford: Oxford University Press, 2001), 18.

2 Nestorius was the Archbishop of Constantinople in the fifth century who was accused by the Alexandrians (Cyril in particular) of making Christ into two distinct people because he emphasized so strongly the separation of the two natures. See Chapter 8 for discussion.

3 For example, Zwingli said, "When I was younger, I gave myself overmuch to human teaching, like others of my day, and when about seven or eight years ago I undertook to devote myself entirely to the Scriptures I was always prevented by philosophy and theology. But eventually I came to the point where, led by the Word and Spirit of God I saw the need to set aside all these things and to learn the doctrine of God direct from his own Word" ("Of the Clarity and Certainty of the Word of God," in *Zwingli and Bullinger*, G.W. Bromily, ed. (Philadelphia, PA: Westminster, 1953), 90–91.

4 Zwingli, "On the Providence of God," in *On Providence and Other Essays*, Samuel Macauley Jackson and William John Hinke, eds. (Durham, NC: Labyrinth Press, 1983), 150.

5 Ibid., 157–158.

6 Ibid., 181–182.

7 Ibid., 187.

8 Aquinas's understanding of predestination and foreknowledge is rather complex. He notes, for example, in his *Summa Theologica*, Question 23, Article 2, that "Predestination is not anything in the predestined; but only in the person who predestines [i.e. God]." He wants to ensure that God is the one credited for determining who is predestined and who is not, while at the same time allowing for human responsibility.

9 The death penalty may not have been used often, but most famously in 1553 the Spanish humanist Michael Servetus was burned at the stake in Geneva for advocating a non-Trinitarian theology.

10 Calvin, *Institutes of the Christian Religion*, 3.23.7; Henry Beveridge, trans. (Grand Rapids, MI: Eerdmans, 1975), II:232.

11 *Institutes*, 1.16.1; ibid., I:172.

12 *Institutes*, 1.16.8; ibid., I:179.

13 *Institutes*, 3.23.8; ibid., II:232–233.

14 *Institutes*, 3.21.5; ibid., II:206.

15 On this issue Calvin says, "We should speculate soberly and with great moderation, cautiously guarding against allowing either our mind or our tongue to go a step beyond the confines of God's word ... never to attempt to search after God anywhere but in his sacred word, and never to speak or think of him farther than we have it for our guide." *Institutes*, 1.13.21; ibid., I:128–129.

16 We should note, however, that Catholics face a similar issue when they wonder whether they have committed mortal sin that has not been forgiven.

17 *Institutes*, 3.2.7; ibid., I:475.

18 "If we are in communion with Christ, we have proof sufficiently clear and strong that we are written in the Book of Life." *Institutes*, 3.24.5; ibid., II:244.

19 *Institutes*, 3.24.7; ibid., II:247.

20 *Institutes*, 3.24.6; ibid., II:246.
21 Arminius, *Examination of Dr. Perkins's Pamphlet on Predestination*, in James Nichols and William Nichols, eds. and trans., *Works of James Arminius* (Grand Rapids, MI: Baker Book House, 1991), 3:470.
22 Carl Bangs, *Arminius* (Nashville, TN: Abingdon, 1971), 195.
23 For the original text in Dutch, Latin, and English see "The Five Arminian Articles," in Philip Schaff, *The Creeds of Christendom*, 6th edition (Grand Rapids, MI: Baker Books, 1996), III:545–549.

21 PROTESTING AGAINST THE PROTESTANTS

1 Roman Catechism, Ad parochos, De bapt., 2, 2, 5. The Catechism on baptism can be retrieved online at http://www.vatican.va/archive/catechism/ccc_toc.htm.
2 Didache, Chapter 7, "Concerning Baptism," in Bart Ehrman, ed., *The Apostolic Fathers I* and *II* (Cambridge: Harvard University Press, 2003), 429. The Philip Schaff translation can be retrieved online at http://www.catholicplanet.com/ebooks/didache.htm.
3 *On Baptism,* 18.5, ANF3, 678.
4 Cyprian says the following: "But in respect of the case of the infants, which you say ought not to be baptized within the second or third day after their birth, and that the law of ancient circumcision should be regarded, so that you think that one who is just born should not be baptized and sanctified within the eighth day, we all thought very differently in our council. For in this course which you thought was to be taken, no one agreed; but we all rather judge that the mercy and grace of God is not to be refused to any one born of man. ... And therefore, dearest brother, this was our opinion in council, that by us no one ought to be hindered from baptism and from the grace of God, who is merciful and kind and loving to all. Which, since it is to be observed and maintained in respect of all, we think is to be even more observed in respect of infants and newly-born persons, who on this very account deserve more from our help and from the divine mercy, that immediately, on the very beginning of their birth, lamenting and weeping, they do nothing else but entreat. We bid you, dearest brother, ever heartily farewell." Epistle 58, ANF5, 354.
5 For a concise summary of this event, see William R. Estep, *The Anabaptist Story: An Introduction to Sixteenth Century Anabaptism*, 3rd edition (Grand Rapids, MI: Eerdmans, 1996), 9–28.
6 Balthasar Hubmaier, "On the Christian Baptism of Believers," presented in a letter of June 10, 1525, to the Zurich council, and republished in *Balthasar Hubmaier: Theologian of Anabaptism*, H. Wayne Pipkin and John H. Yoder, trans. and eds (Scottdale, PA: Herald Press, 1989), 117–118.
7 Balthasar writes, "And finally, we now see here most clearly what sort of gross error has been introduced and brought into Christianity by those who deny human freedom of the will and say that this freedom is an empty and idle concept, without substance. By this our God is shamed and blasphemed, likened to a tyrant who would condemn and punish humans for something they could do nothing about. ... By denying free will, much cause is given to evil people to lay all of their sin on God, saying, "It must be God's will

that I be an adulterer and run after harlots. Well, God's will be done! After all, who can thwart the will of God? If it was not God's will, I would not sin. When God wills it, I will stop sinning! ... All of this is the work of an evil, sly, and blasphemous devil! I do not see how a more harmful Satan could arise among Christians to hinder righteousness and godliness on earth. For through this falsehood the greatest part of the holy scriptures are thrown out and made powerless. May the almighty, good and merciful God help us against this gross error and crush it by the breath of his mouth through Jesus Christ our Lord." "Concerning Free Will," in *Quellen zur Geschichte der Täufer IX: Balthasar Hubmaier Schriften*, ed. Westin/Bergsten (Gütersloh: Verlaghaus Gerd Mohn, 1962), as quoted in *Early Anabaptist Spirituality*, edited and translated by Daniel Liechty (New York, Paulist Press, 1994), 37–38.

8 Menno Simons, "True Christian Faith," in *The Complete Writings of Menno Simons*, Leonard Verduin, trans., and John Christian Wenger, ed. (Scottdale, PA: Herald Press, 1956), 399.

9 Ibid., "Why I Do Not Cease Teaching and Writing," 300.

10 As quoted in Estep, *The Anabaptist Story*, 92.

11 This historical event of Anabaptist martyrology can be found in the work of Thieleman J. van Bracht, translated as *Martyrs Mirror* (Scottdale, PA: Herald Press, 1950), 741–742. A longer version of the story is described in *Mennonite Life* 45, no. 3 (1990:18–23).

12 Menno Simons, *The Complete Writings of Menno Simons*, 13.

22 REFORMATION CONTINUES

1 She was so dubbed by John Foxe in his *Book of Martyrs* (1571).

2 Various editions of the Book of Common Prayer can be found online at http://justus.anglican.org/resources/bcp/bcp.htm.

3 The word "Anglican" comes from a medieval Latin term which means "English."

4 See John H. Leith, ed., *Creeds of the Churches*, 3rd edition (Louisville, KY: John Knox Press, 1982), 266–281. The 1801 American edition of the Articles can be accessed online at http://anglicansonline.org/basics/thirty-nine_articles.html.

5 The main branch of the Anglican Church in the United States today is the Episcopal Church.

6 Four main groups were represented at the Assembly: Episcopalians, Presbyterians, Congregationalists, and Erastians. For more on this Assembly, see Benjamin B. Warfield, *The Works of Benjamin B. Warfield – Volume 6: Westminster Assembly and Its Work* (Grand Rapids, MI: Baker Book House, 2003).

7 There is another view of Baptist history, called "Baptist perpetuity" or "Baptist succession," in which certain Baptist historians and theologians have argued that there is an ongoing and unbroken link from the days of Christ and the apostles to the Baptist Church of today (sometimes called "Landmarkism"). They maintain that these earlier Baptists were called by other names (such as the Waldenisians, Dontatists, Montanists, Albigenses, and so on), but that

nevertheless affirmed central Baptist doctrines. Those defending this view also maintain that since Baptists existed from the time of Christ, long before the origin of the Roman Catholic Church, they should not be considered a part of the Protestant Reformation. For one example of a scholar defending the Baptist perpetuity view, see John T. Christian, *A History of the Baptists* (Texarkana, TX: Bogard Press, 1926). This complete work can be found online at http://www.reformedreader.org/history/christian/ahob1/ahobp.htm.

8   For a helpful overview of some of these issues, see Michael Mullett, *The Catholic Reformation* (New York: Routledge, 1999).
9   As quoted in William C. Placher, *A History of Christian Theology* (Louisville, KY: Westminster John Knox Press, 1983), 203.
10   "Decrees of the Council of Trent," *Creeds of the Churches*, 3rd edition, John H. Leith, ed. (Louisville, KY: John Knox Press, 1982), Chapter IV, 411.
11   The term "deuterocanonical" comes from the Greek and means "belonging to the second canon." These books were contrasted with the protocanonical books of the Hebrew Bible – the books which are in the Hebrew Bible and the Protestant Old Testament.
12   Perhaps its most famous case of the Roman Inquisition involved Galileo Galilei in the seventeenth century.

23 THE CHALLENGE OF MODERNISM

1   E.A. Burtt, *The Metaphysical Foundations of Modern Science* (Atlantic Highlands, NJ: Humanities Press, 1992), 17.
2   For a defense of religion as the ultimate cause of the war see Carl J. Friedrich, "The Religious Motive Reaffirmed," in Theodore K. Rabb, ed., *The Thirty Years War: Problems of Motive, Extent, and Effect* (Boston: D.C. Heath and Company, 1964).
3   Meic Pearse, *The Age of Reason* (Grand Rapids, MI: Baker Books, 2006), 163.
4   Georges Pagès, "The War as a Dividing Point Between Medieval and Modern Times," in Rabb, 24.
5   Interestingly, some attempted to save the theory by postulating a perfect crystalline sphere which encircled the moon and remained undetectable by Galileo's telescope.
6   Speaking of the inspiration of Scripture by the Holy Ghost, Galileo says, "The intention of the Holy Ghost is to teach us how one goes to heaven, not how heaven goes." He attributes this saying to Cardinal Baronius (1538–1607) who had probably visited Galileo in 1598 before the controversies over the geography of the universe became so heated later on. The quotation is from Galileo's "Letter to the Grand Duchess Christina," in Stillman Drake, ed., *Discoveries and Opinions of Galileo* (Garden City, NY: Doubleday, 1957), 186.
7   Quoted in Michael Buckley, *At the Origins of Modern Atheism* (New Haven, CT: Yale University Press, 1987), 71.
8   Quoted in Giorgio de Santillana, *The Crime of Galileo* (Chicago, IL: University of Chicago Press, 1967), 312.
9   Descartes, *Meditations*, Donald Cress, trans. (Indianapolis, IN: Hackett, 1993), 1.

10 "I think, therefore I am" does not appear in the *Meditations* in that formulation. It comes from an earlier work called *Discourse on Method*.

11 Descartes, *Meditations*, ibid., 19.

12 The now classic documentation of this story is found in Michael Buckley, *At the Origins of Modern Atheism* (New Haven, CT: Yale University Press, 1987).

13 James M. Byrne, *Religion and the Enlightenment: From Descartes to Kant* (Louisville, KY: Westminister John Knox, 1997), 103.

14 Benjamin Whichcote, *Moral and Religious Aphorisms* (London: J. Payne, 1753), Aphorism 76, 13–14.

15 Matthew Tindal, *Christianity as Old as the Creation* in William Placher, ed., *Readings in the History of Christian Theology, Volume 2* (Louisville, KY: Westminster John Knox, 1988), 88.

16 This is the suggestion of Charles Taylor in his *A Secular Age* (Cambridge, MA: Harvard University Press, 2007), 225.

24 PIETISM AND REVIVALISM

1 *Idea Studiosi Theologiae* (*The Idea of a Student of Theology*) (1712) in August Hermann Francke, *Werke in Auswahl*, Edhard Peschke, ed. (Witten-Ruhr: Luther, 1970), 172, as translated by Jaroslav Pelikan in his *The Christian Tradition* (Chicago, IL: The University of Chicago Press, 1989), Vol. 5, 54.

2 John Wesley, "A Plain Account of Christian Perfection," in *The Works of John Wesley*, ed. Thomas Jackson, vol. 11 (Franklin, TN: Providence House, 1994 (1872)), 366–346. It can be found online at http://www.ccel.org/ccel/wesley/perfection/files/perfection.html.

3 A number of historians believe this was a meeting of Moravians.

4 *The Journal of John Wesley*, May 24, 1739.

5 The term "Wesleyan Quadrilateral" was first coined by Albert C. Outler in 1964 in a collection of Wesley's he edited. For an excellent presentation of what Wesley meant by these four elements of theological method, see Don Thorsen, *The Wesleyan Quadrilateral: Scripture, Tradition, Reason and Experience as a Model of Evangelical Theology* (Lexington, KY: Emeth Press, 2005).

6 Wesley understood prevenient grace in Arminian terms, namely that it is the grace of God that comes before (the Latin word *praevenire* means "to come before") one's choice to receive Christ in faith, and it helps one to freely respond to the work of God in one's life. This is in contrast to the Calvinistic view in which prevenient grace *causes* one to receive Christ in faith (i.e. the irresistible grace of TULIP).

7 John Wesley, Sermon 128, "Free Grace," in *The Works of John Wesley*, 3rd edition (Baker Book House reprint (1998) of the 1872 edition by the Wesleyan Methodist Book Room, London), Volume 7, 378. This sermon can be found online at Christian Classics Ethereal Library, http://www.ccel.org/ccel/wesley/sermons.viii.ii.html. The sermon was preached at Bristol in the year 1740.

8 See, for example, Earle E. Cairns, *Christianity Through the Centuries*, 3rd edition (Grand Rapids, MI: Zondervan, 1996), 384.

9 Jonathan Edwards, *The Works of the Jonathan Edwards*, Edward Hickman, ed. (Carlisle, PA: Banner of Truth Trust, 1974), Vol. 1, xiii.

10   Jonathan Edwards, "Sinners in the Hands of an Angry God," *The Works of Jonathan Edwards*. This famous sermon can be found online at http://www. ccel.org/ccel/edwards/sermons.sinners.html.

11   Jonathan Edwards, "God's Sovereignty in the Salvation of Men," in Sermon IV of *Seventeen Occasional Sermons*, in *The Works of Jonathan Edwards*, (Carlisle, PA: The Banner of Truth Trust, Reprinted 1995), Vol. 2, 849–854. It can be found online at Christian Classics Ethereal Library, http://www. ccel.org/ccel/edwards/sermons.gssm.html.

12   In his work *On the Freedom of the Will*, Edwards argued for determinism, both on the basis of the logical incoherence of a will determining itself (it must be determined by its strongest motive or desire) and on the basis of a fallen human will that is morally incapable of following and obeying Christ. He didn't address the apparent problem of whether God's will itself is determined, and what the ramifications of this might entail.

13   Jonathan Edwards, "A Faithful Narrative of the Surprising Work of God," in *The Works of the Jonathan Edwards* Vol. 1, 348.

14   Some historians refer to this as the First Great Awakening, for several others were to follow later.

25 ROMANTICISM'S RESPONSE TO ENLIGHTENMENT THEOLOGY

1   The Scottish Skeptic David Hume (1711–1776) had previously made the same point about miracles in his *Enquiry Concerning Human Understanding* (published 1748). Lessing was, no doubt, familiar with Hume's work. Curiously, Lessing at first compares historical testimony to that of first-hand experience: "Miracles, which I see with my own eyes, and which I have the opportunity to verify for myself, are one thing; miracles, of which I know only from history that others say they have seen them and verified them, are another" (*Lessing's Theological Writings* (Stanford, CA: Stanford University Press, 1957), 51). But of course even first-hand experience is still experience and not in the same category as rational demonstration. Later in the essay, Lessing's comparison is explicitly between historical truths and rational truths. See G.E. Michalson, "Lessing, Kierkegaard, and the 'Ugly Ditch': A Reexamination," *The Journal of Religion,* 59:324–334 (1979).

2   *Lessing's Theological Writings*, 53.

3   Ibid., 55.

4   *Lessing's Theological Writings*, 42–43.

5   Lessing, *Nathan the Wise*, Patrick Maxwell, trans. (New York: Bloch Publishing Company, 1917), 252.

6   Schleiermacher, *The Life of Schleiermacher, as Unfolded in His Autobiography and Letters*, Frederica Rowan, trans. (London: Smith, Elder and Co., 1860), I.46–67.

7   Ibid., 50.

8   Jonathan Hill, *The History of Christian Thought* (Downers Grove, IL: IVP, 2003), 232.

9   Schleiermacher, *On Religion*, Richard Crouter, trans. (Cambridge: Cambridge University Press, 1998), 22–23.

10 Similarly, in the feeling of dependence on some other object which has affected my consciousness, there is always some counter-influence that I have on that object, even if it is only the renunciation of acting on it.

11 Schleiermacher says, "But neither an absolute feeling of dependence, i.e. without any feeling of freedom in relation to the co-determinant, nor an absolute feeling of freedom, i.e. without any feeling of dependence in relation to the co-determinant, is to be found in this whole realm ... It is the same in the case of Nature: towards all the forces of Nature – even, we may say towards the heavenly bodies – we ourselves do, in the same sense in which they influence us, exercise a counter-influence, however minute. So that our whole self-consciousness in relation to the World or its individual parts remains enclosed within these limits" (*The Christian Faith*, H.R. Mackintosh and J.S. Stewart, eds. (Edinburgh: T&T Clark, 1999), 15).

12 *The Christian Faith*, 17.

13 *On Religion*, 49.

14 *The Christian Faith*, 55–56.

15 "Everything is related to the redemption accomplished by Jesus of Nazareth," ibid., 52.

16 Ibid., 144.

17 Schleiermacher uses a masonry metaphor, calling the Trinity the "coping-stone" of Christian theology. Ibid., 739.

18 Ibid., 394.

19 Ibid., 367.

26 NEO-ORTHODOXY

1 Søren Kierkegaard, *Journals and Papers*, vol. VI, trans. Howard V. Hong and Edna H. Hong (Bloomington, IN: Indiana University Press, 1978), 70–71.

2 For more on Kierkegaard's notion of truth as subjectivity, see his *Concluding Unscientific Postscript*, Alastair Hannay, ed. (Cambridge: Cambridge University Press, 2009), 159–251.

3 Written under the pseudonym of John Climacus, in Kierkegaard's *The Sickness Unto Death* he makes the point that only Christian faith can save one from utter despair.

4 Stanley J. Grenz and Roger E. Olson make the point about Barth's shift toward the demolition of liberal theology after this discovery in their *20th Century Theology: God and the World in a Transitional Age* (Downers Grove, IL: 1992), 66–67. For more on this, see Karl Barth, *God, Gospel, and Grace*, trans. James S. McNab, *Scottish Journal of Theology Occasional Papers No. 8* (Edinburgh: Oliver and Boyd, 1959).

5 For more on these events, see Victoria Barnett, *For the Soul of the People: Protestant Protest Against Hitler* (New York: Oxford University Press, 1992). Bonhoeffer's books and letters, including his letters from prison, were highly influential during this time.

6 For more on this intriguing situation, see Renate Kobler, *In the Shadow of Karl Barth: Charlotte Von Kirschbaum* (Louisville, KY: Westminster John Knox Press, 1989).

7 For an interesting work on von Kirschbaum and Barth, see Suzanne Selinger, *Charlotte von Kirschbaum and Karl Barth: A Study in Biography and the History of Theology* (University Park, PA: Penn State University Press, 1998).

8 Karl Barth, "Protestant Theology in the Nineteenth Century," in his *The Humanity of God* (Atlanta, GA: John Knox Press, 1978), 14.

9 It is important to note that in his earlier writings, including his work on Romans, he introduced certain Neo-orthodox themes that he later disagreed with, including radically differentiating the historical and non-historical and pressing paradox to the extreme. In fact, he never liked the term "Neo-orthodox," and sought to distinguish himself from Neo-orthodox representatives such as Rudolf Bultmann and Emil Brunner.

10 It is no accident that in contrast to Schleiermacher, who placed his discussion of the Trinity at the very end of his book, *Christian Faith*, Barth places the Trinity at the very beginning of *Church Dogmatics*.

11 Karl Barth, *Evangelical Theology: An Introduction* (Grand Rapids, MI: Eerdmans, 1992), 18.

12 See, for example, Luke 9:35.

13 For example, Ephesians 1:4 states, "just as he chose [elected] us *in Christ* before the foundation of the world." This phrase, "in Christ," used often in Paul's Epistles.

14 Karl Barth, *Church Dogmatics*, Volume II.2, *The Doctrine of God*, G.W. Bromiley and T.F. Torrance, eds (Edinburgh: T. & T. Clark, 1957), 162–163.

15 Barth was invited to Rome by the Vatican and had personal conversations with Pope Paul VI.

16 Daniel W. Hardy, "Karl Barth," in *The Modern Theologians: An Introduction to Christian Theology Since 1918*, 3rd edition, David F. Ford with Rachel Muers, eds (Oxford: Blackwell, 2005), 39.

17 Sadly, he died two days before the formal ceremony.

18 Brunner and Barth disagreed about the role of natural theology, the former arguing that a common ground could be found between believers and others through natural theology – enough at least to point to the gospel.

19 H. Richard Niebuhr, *The Kingdom of God in America* (New York: Harper and Row, 1937/1959), 193.

20 It is also worth noting that Barth's influence is strongly seen in the contemporary work of the Anabaptist theologian John Howard Yoder.

27 LIBERAL PROTESTANTISM

1 James Orr, *The Ritschlian Theology and the Evangelical Faith* (New York: Thomas Whittaker, n.d.), 1.

2 Ritschl, *The Christian Doctrine of Justification and Reconciliation* (Clifton, NJ: Reference Book Publishers, 1966), 204.

3 Ibid., 205.

4 Though, of course, we should note that the situation is more complex when we consider the objectivity of the Christian community as a whole. Ritschl was not concerned with interfaith dialogue in this sense and perhaps not sufficiently attuned to its implications for claims of objectivity.

5 Ritschl, *A Critical History of the Christian Doctrine of Justification and Reconciliation* (Edinburgh: Edmonston and Douglas, 1872), 567.

6　Ritschl, *The Christian Doctrine of Justification and Reconciliation*, 334–335.
7　Ibid., 79.
8　Ibid., 78.
9　Ibid., 399.
10　This is the classic formula of nineteenth century liberal theology according to Paul Tillich, *Perspectives on 19th and 20th Century Protestant Theology* (New York: Harper & Row, 1967), 223.
11　Adolf von Harnack, *What is Christianity?* Thomas Baily Saunders, trans. (Philadelphia: Fortress Press, 1986), 51.
12　Ibid., 55–56.
13　Ibid., 67.
14　Ibid., 73.
15　Quoted in Gary Dorrien, *The Making of American Liberal Theology: Idealism, Realism, and Modernity, 1900–1950* (Louisville: Westminster John Knox, 2003), 78–79.
16　Walter Rauschenbusch, *Christianity and the Social Crisis* (London: Macmillan & Co, 1914), 349.
17　Rauschenbusch, *A Theology for the Social Gospel* (Nashville: Abingdon, 1987), 1.
18　Ibid., 142.
19　Ibid., 48.
20　Ibid., 99.
21　Ibid., 224.
22　See Bultmann's *Kerygma and Myth: A Theological Debate*, H. W., Bartsch, ed. (London: SPCK, 1972), 41–42.
23　Bultmann, *Jesus Christ and Mythology* (New York: Charles Scribner's Sons, 1958), 18.
24　Bultmann, *Kerygma and Myth*, 5.
25　Tillich said this during a seminar course at the University of California, Santa Barbara, in the spring of 1963. The conversations between Tillich, the students, and other professors were recorded and their transcripts edited into the book *Ultimate Concern: Tillich in Dialogue*, D. Mackenzie Brown, ed. (New York: Harper & Row, 1965). The quotation comes from pages 88–89.
26　Tillich claimed that Neo-orthodox theologians believed that the attempt to find common ground between those in the Church and those outside would destroy the uniqueness of the Christian message. If this is correct, Tillich reasoned, then there could be no answer to the questions implied in the situation of secular man, and "The message must be thrown at those in the situation – thrown like a stone." This method might be effective in some situations, but "it does not fulfil [sic.] the aim of the theological function of the church." *Systematic Theology*, Vol. I (New York: Harper & Row, 1967), 7.
27　Tillich, *The Courage to Be* (New Haven, CT: Yale University Press, 1952), 47, 181.
28　Tillich, *Systematic Theology*, Vol. II, 155.
29　H. Richard Niebuhr, *The Kingdom of God in America* (New York: Harper & Row, 1937), 193.

28 MAJOR THEOLOGICAL TRADITIONS AND DEVELOPMENTS IN THE TWENTIETH CENTURY

1 For more on the relationship between American Evangelicalism and Fundamentalism, see Harriet Harris, *Fundamentalism and Evangelicals* (Oxford: Oxford University Press, 1998).

2 George Marsden, *Fundamentalism and American Culture* (Oxford: Oxford University Press, 1980), 119.

3 The climax of the trial occurred when Clarence Darrow, the head of the defense, brought staunch anti-evolutionist William Jennings Bryan (three-time presidential candidate and Secretary of State under President Woodrow Wilson) to the stand and interrogated him about his literal interpretation of the Bible and his ignorance of modern science. Darrow said later, "I made up my mind to show the country what an ignoramus he was and I succeeded" (Edward J. Larson, *Summer for the Gods* (New York: Basic Books, 1997), 190).

4 Quoted in Marsden, *Fundamentalism and American Culture*, 188.

5 Carl F. H. Henry, *The Uneasy Conscience of Modern Fundamentalism* (Grand Rapids: Eerdmans, 2003), xv–xvi.

6 The current doctrinal statement of the Evangelical Theological Society reads, "The Bible alone, and the Bible in its entirety, is the Word of God written and is therefore inerrant in the autographs. God is a Trinity, Father, Son, and Holy Spirit, each an uncreated person, one in essence, equal in power and glory."

7 Carl F. H. Henry, *Frontiers in Modern Theology: A Critique of Current Theological Trends* (Chicago: Moody Press, 1966), 138.

8 Carl F. H. Henry, *God, Reason, Authority* (Waco, TX: Word Books, 1976), I:215.

9 R. A. F. Mackenzie, in reference to the Dogmatic Constitutions of Vatican II, notes that "Important as the Constitution on the Church is generally agreed to be, it is equaled in stature by the Constitution on Divine Revelation; the two are the most fundamental documents produced by the Second Vatican Council." *The Documents of Vatican II*, edited by Walter M. Abbott (Piscataway, NJ: America Press, 1966), 107.

10 For more on this theme, see the "Dogmatic Constitution on Divine Revelation" (Dei Verbum), in *The Documents of Vatican II*, especially 118–121.

11 This affirmation basically amounted to a rejection of Pope Pius IX's *Syllabus of Errors*.

12 "Declaration on the Relationship of the Church to Non-Christian Religions" (Nostra Aetate), in *The Documents of Vatican II*, 662–63.

13 The "Decree on Ecumenism" (Unitatis Redintegratio), *The Documents of Vatican II*, 349, states the following: "Catholics must joyfully acknowledge and esteem the truly Christian endowments from our common heritage which are to be found among our separated brethren. It is right and salutary to recognize the riches of Christ and virtuous works in the lives of others who are bearing witness to Christ .... Whatever is truly Christian never conflicts

with the genuine interests of the faith; indeed, it can always result in a more ample realization of the very mystery of Christ and the Church."

14 Karl Rahner, *Karl Rahner in Dialogue: Conversations and Interviews 1965–1982* (New York: Crossroad, 1986), 135.

15 The 1302 papal bull, issued by Pope Boniface VIII, entitled *Unam Sanctam*.

16 This work was published in English as *Justification: The Doctrine of Karl Barth and a Catholic Reflection*.

17 There is also a growing number of Eastern Orthodox adherents in the United States.

18 It is the Patriarch who convenes major Orthodox conferences, after consultation with the leaders of the other Orthodox churches.

19 Timothy Ware, *The Orthodox Church* (Baltimore, MD: Penguin Books, 1963), 15.

20 Decree on the Eastern Catholic Churches, *The Documents of Vatican II*, 373

21 Charles Hartshorne, *Omnipotence and Other Theological Mistakes* (Albany, NY: SUNY Press, 1984), 10–11.

29 RECENT AND EMERGING THEMES

1 Gustavo Gutiérrez, *A Theology of Liberation: History, Politics and Salvation* (Maryknoll, NY: Orbis, 1973), 88.

2 Vatican webpage, "*Instruction on Certain Aspects of the "Theology of Liberation"*", VII.7, http://www.vatican.va/roman_curia/congregations/ cfaith/documents/rc_con_cfaith_doc_19840806_theology-liberation_ en.html.

3 Dwight N. Hopkins, "Black Theology of Liberation," in David Ford, ed. with Rachel Muers, *The Modern Theologians*, third edition (Oxford: Blackwell, 2005), 451.

4 For a helpful introduction to and overview of black liberation theologies, see Dwight N. Hopkins, *Introducing Black Theology of Liberation* (MaryKnoll, NY: Orbis Books, 1999).

5 In 2004, for the first time in Catholic Church history, female theologians were appointed to the Vatican's International Theological Commission. In the Orthodox Church, they are still not permitted such positions.

6 Tertullian, *De Cultu Feminarum*, section I.I, part 2 (trans. C.W. Marx).

7 For more on this issue, see Beverly Clack, *Misogyny in the Western Philosophical Tradition* (New York: Routledge, 1999), Part II: The Church Fathers.

8 For an overview of the various waves of feminism, see Anne M. Clifford, *Introducing Feminist Theology* (Maryknoll, NY: Orbis, 2004).

9 For a helpful and concise presentation of a number of key themes in Christian feminism, see Natalie K. Watson, *Feminist Theology* (Grand Rapids, MI: Eerdmans, 2003), Chapter 2.

10 See her classic work, *Sexism and God-Talk: Toward a Feminist Theology* (Ypsilanti, MI: Beacon Press, 1993).

11 See her *Metaphorical Theology: Models of God in Religious Language* (Philadelphia: Fortress Press, 1982).

12 Eighty-four denominations now ordain women.

13 See information about the organization and movement, along with articles and further references, at the following website: http://www. cbeinternational.org/.

14 Philip Jenkins, *The Next Christendom: The Coming of Global Christianity* (Oxford: Oxford University Press, 2002), 2–3.

15 Ibid., 89–92.

16 Ibid., 107. See also 2–14.

17 For more on the development of Pentecostalism, see Donald W. Dayton, *Theological Roots of Pentecostalism* (Peabody, MA: Hendrickson, 1991).

18 For more on Pentecostal and charismatic growth, see David B. Barrett and George T. Kurian, eds., *World Christian Encyclopedia: A Comparative Survey of Churches and Religions in the Modern World*, second edition (Oxford: Oxford University Press, 2001). See also the essay entitled "The New Face of Global Christianity: The Emergence of 'Progressive Pentecostalism,'" *Pew Forum on Religion and Public Life* online at http://pewforum.org/events/index.php?EventID=101.

19 Jack Deere, *Surprised by the Voice of God* (Grand Rapids, MI: Zondervan, 1996), 19.

20 Deere's other book that also details his experiences is *Surprised by the Power of the Spirit* (Grand Rapids, MI: Zondervan, 1993).

21 *The Routledge Companion to Postmodernism*, second edition, Stuart Sim, ed. (London: Routledge, 2005) has chapters related to a variety of contexts in which postmodernism has had an influence.

22 Stanley Grenz attempted to make this story accessible in his *A Primer on Postmodernism* (Grand Rapids: Eerdmans, 1996). A collection of articles by various people that displays more of the diversity of approaches toward postmodernism is Merold Westphal's *Postmodern Philosophy and Christian Thought* (Bloomington, IN: Indiana University Press, 1999).

23 R. Scott Smith, "Christian Postmodernism and the Linguistic Turn" in Myron B. Penner, ed., *Christianity and the Postmodern Turn: Six Views* (Grand Rapids, MI: Brazos, 2005), 65.

24 This is called the "noetic effects of sin" by Alvin Plantinga and developed at some length in his Reformed Epistemology. See especially, *Warranted Christian Belief* (Oxford: Oxford University Press, 2000).

25 John Milbank, "Postmodern Critical Augustinianism: A Short *Summa* in Forty-Two Responses to Unasked Questions" in Graham Ward, ed., *The Postmodern God: A Theological Reader* (Oxford: Blackwell, 1997), 265.

26 The five volume series (four from OUP and the fifth from SCM Press) are *Religion and Revelation; Religion and Creation; Religion and Human Nature; Religion and Community,* and *Religion and Human Fulfillment.*

27 Keith Ward, "Theology as a Comparative Discipline," in *By Faith and Reason: The Essential Keith Ward*, eds., Wm. Curtis Holtzen and Roberto Sirvent (London: Darton, Longman, and Todd, 2012), 263.

28 http://climate.nasa.gov/scientific-consensus/.

29 This definition is from John Hick, who borrowed the phrase "principle of plenitude" from Arthur Lovejoy's *The Great Chain and Being* and applied it to Augustine's solution to the problem of evil. Found in John Hick, *Evil and the God of Love* (New York: Harper & Rowe, 1966), 260.

Index